A FORCE FOR NATURE

A Force for Nature

NANCY RUSSELL'S FIGHT TO SAVE
THE COLUMBIA RIVER GORGE

Bowen Blair

Oregon State University Press   Corvallis

Cataloging-in-publication data is available from the Library of Congress.

ISBN 978-0-87071-218-0 (paperback); ISBN 978-0-87071-219-7 (hardcover);
ISBN 978-0-87071-220-3 (ebook)

♾This paper meets the requirements of ANSI/NISO Z39.48-1992
(Permanence of Paper).

Oregon State University
OSU Press

Oregon State University Press
121 The Valley Library
Corvallis OR 97331-4501
541-737-3166 • fax 541-737-3170
www.osupress.oregonstate.edu

To three generations of strong women:
Joan, Jennifer, and Louise

Contents

Illustrations

COLOR PLATES
(following page 132)

Prologue
Dinner at The Shire, July 31, 1979

Bruce Russell was puzzled by John Yeon's call. As a Merrill Lynch broker, he was often called by potential clients, many of whom—like Yeon, an internationally known architect—were prominent citizens. But he sensed that the dinner invitation to The Shire, Yeon's property in the Columbia River Gorge, was extended to Russell as a courtesy. He believed it really was intended for his wife Nancy, whose love of Gorge history and wildflowers was becoming well known. After accepting the invitation, both Russells were surprised when Yeon postponed the dinner, without explanation, and days later postponed again.

Late in the afternoon on the last day of July 1979, Yeon finally collected the Russells at their home in southwest Portland and drove north. Crossing the Columbia River at Vancouver, Washington, they followed an upriver breeze toward the Gorge. The breeze lifted spray from the crests of waves as their car followed the river route of Lewis and Clark's 1805–1806 expedition and the path of emigrants three decades later who often described the rapids-laden Gorge as the most perilous part of their two-thousand-mile journey.[1] The trip was familiar to the Russells, who had researched and explored the Corps of Discovery and the Oregon Trail over the last two summers.

As the only sea-level passage through a mountain range in the western United States, the Columbia River Gorge transitions from temperate rainforest to high desert in an eighty-five-mile stretch and from valley floor to five-thousand-foot-high mountains in a few thousand yards. Nearly a thousand wildflower species thrive in the Gorge, and sixteen exist nowhere else in the world. This botanical laboratory attracted early plant collectors—from England's Thomas Nuttall in 1811, who retraced the Corps of Discovery route, to Scotland's David Douglas in 1825, who scoured the Gorge for plant species unknown in Europe. A century and a half later, the landscape attracted Nancy Russell, who put together a Portland Garden Club presentation on wildflowers and the explorers and collectors evoked by their eponymous names: *Lewisia* (Meriwether Lewis), *Clarkia* (William Clark), *Nuttallii*

1

(Thomas Nuttall), and *Douglasia* (David Douglas).[2] Her popular presentation—its insights and the knowledge and passion of the speaker—had drawn
Yeon's attention.

Half an hour from home, the Russells, with Yeon at the wheel, passed the
mill towns of Camas and Washougal. Camas was named for the lily whose
bulb had sustained the Gorge's Native residents for thousands of years, but
the town was better known in 1979 for its century-old paper mill, a sprawling
structure that spewed smoke from tall twin chimneys, infusing the area with
a distinct sulfuric odor. "The smell of money," according to locals, for the
plant employed several hundred workers, considerably fewer—due to auto-
mation—than the twenty-three hundred jobs that had existed four decades
earlier.[3]

After crossing Gibbons Creek, the Columbia Gorge unfolded before
the travelers. Steigerwald Lake's vast meadows, browned by the summer
sun, flowed into the gray-green Columbia. Across the river, in Oregon, rose
the precipices of Crown Point, tinted a honey hue by the western sun and
shrouded by the dark green boughs of the fir David Douglas first encountered just downstream in 1825.[4] The sandstone walls and green-tiled roof of
Vista House, an observatory completed in 1918 to honor Oregon pioneers,
adorned Crown Point.

Continuing east and gaining elevation, Yeon and the Russells drove
through the forests and farms of Mount Pleasant and Mount Zion, high above
the Columbia. They stopped on the narrow shoulder of the two-lane Evergreen Highway, which clung to vertical cliffs called Gibraltar by early settlers
and later named Cape Horn after the ferocious winds at South America's
stormy tip. Ignoring the traffic whizzing past, the Russells and Yeon enjoyed
the view, leaning on the waist-high rock wall that separated them from a
sheer seven-hundred-foot drop to the river. Below, Phoca Rock jutted just
offshore, and 848-foot-high Beacon Rock, the plug of an ancient volcano,
rose a few miles ahead—both named by Lewis and Clark. The white slash
of Bridal Veil Falls across the Columbia and The Shire's mile of shoreline
in the mid-distance were framed by a cloudless sky, the broad river, and the
palisades of the "Grand Canyon of the Columbia."[5] Above this panorama
towered Mount Hood, the 11,244-foot-high snow-covered volcano named
Wy'east by the Gorge's earliest inhabitants.[6]

Yeon had bought the farmstead that he shaped into The Shire in 1965,
but his history in the Columbia River Gorge ran deep. His father, Ontario-
born French Canadian John B. Yeon, started as a dollar-a-day teenage laborer

in Ohio's rugged timber camps before moving to Oregon in 1865. He bought and sold timberland, becoming a millionaire, and late in his career over-saw—for a dollar a year—the building of the Columbia River Highway, the first paved highway in the Pacific Northwest. Young John had delighted in visiting road crews with his father on the "King of Roads" and had carried the tail of the flag at Vista House's 1916 dedication when he was five.[7]

The Historic Columbia River Highway, as it is now called, exemplifies the rift between Oregon and Washington over the Gorge. Sam Hill, former Great Northern Railway executive, peripatetic world traveler, philanthropist, and booster of the Good Roads movement, first proposed the highway for the Washington side of the river, an easier route because of its gentler terrain. In 1913, after Washington's governor and legislature proved disinterested, Hill turned to Oregon, bringing its governor and legislators by special rail car to Maryhill—his mansion in the eastern Gorge—to show them experimental roads built by engineer and landscape architect Samuel Lancaster. The high-way was opened between Troutdale and Hood River by 1916, and within twenty years nineteen state parks had been established on the Oregon side of the Gorge; Washington had one.[8]

The division between the states is rooted in geography and blossoms in politics. In the western Gorge, Oregon's cliffs are dark and precipitous, with an unsurpassed collection of year-round waterfalls. The land is mostly owned by the federal government, part of the Mount Hood National Forest, which was created to secure the primary drinking water supply for the City of Portland, less than fifteen miles distant. The Gorge's south-facing slopes on the Washington side are sunnier, more developable and, therefore, mostly in private ownership. These private lands are across from Oregon's public lands and Oregonians' views, and 150 miles away from Washington's population and economic center in Seattle.

After crossing Cape Horn, Yeon and the Russells descended to the valley floor. Slowing, Yeon turned into a drive concealed by tall weeds and bushes and stopped before The Shire's dark red metal gate, which he described as "intentionally obscure," its padlock encased in a metal cylinder to protect it from "sharp-shooting trespassers."[9] He unlocked the gate, and they entered The Shire.

They drove down a narrow rock and dirt lane, enveloped in a hardwood forest interspersed with meadows to the right and left. After a quarter mile, a large hay meadow emerged to the west, and a startling panorama of Oregon cliffs and 620-foot-high Multnomah Falls appeared to the south. Yeon parked under a handsome Oregon ash that grew at the base of a grass berm he had sculpted into an amphitheater, curling around and above the westernmost of The Shire's three bays, and—to preserve the element of surprise—blocking visitors' views of the river. He customarily received guests under the tree, which served as a foyer for The Shire, where he allowed no above-ground structures. Yeon opened the door of a dark maintenance shed built deep into the berm and guided the Russells through a clutter of mowers, tools, and gasoline cans. He slid away the far wall to reveal a hidden bunker that contained a small kitchen, a bathroom, and a living room decorated with furniture and lamps he had designed, Asian paintings and screens, antique green-blue Chinese porcelain bowls, and a couch that converted into a bed.

Yeon then led the Russells west over the narrow, seventy-five-acre property, walking on four-foot-wide mowed trails that wound between meadows and woods. Crossing a stream that spilled from a beaver-dammed pond, they paused at the property's end where the river flowed around pilings that once had supported a nineteenth-century logging railway, their cavities now used by purple martins. Here and there, small openings in the canopy—carefully excised by Yeon—framed Multnomah Falls, much as landscape painter Albert Bierstadt had framed it a century before.

By 1979, Yeon had been fighting for the Columbia River Gorge for almost fifty years, calling it "the most noble unprotected landscape in the United States." When he was in his twenties, he had written two reports for the Pacific Northwest Regional Planning Commission's Columbia Gorge Committee, which he chaired. The 1935 report proposed an interstate park for the western Gorge and land acquisition by the National Park Service. Its recommendations were not implemented. In 1937, Yeon's committee issued its second report regarding Bonneville Dam, a hydroelectric facility being constructed in the western Gorge and part of President Franklin Roosevelt's effort to pull the Northwest out of the Depression. The project would hire thousands of workers, among other benefits, and Yeon's committee offered proposals to mitigate its impact on the Gorge's scenic, natural, and recreational resources. Years later, Yeon dismissed the 1937 report, saying it "has been as forgotten as if it disappeared in a Black Hole." But those reports revealed the Gorge's vulnerability and the threats against it. And a proposal in the 1937 report averted—at least momentarily—the industrialization of the western Gorge.[10]

John Yeon's purpose that summer evening in 1979 was to court Nancy Russell and recruit her to the battle. He was an intensely private man who was driven by beauty. Both purist and prophet, his comments—while often caustic—were persuasive, pointed, and memorable. He was approaching seventy and sensed what he would soon acknowledge: "I have no constituency. . . . I am too old to run with the ball. I am a lousy public speaker; my own worst advocate."[11] He believed Russell had the passion and talent to take up the cause.

Returning to the top of the berm, the party settled on blankets arranged on The Shire's broad lawn—rare Astoria bent grass, chosen by Yeon for its color, durability, and soft texture.[12] The Columbia and The Shire's unobstructed views were now fully unveiled. A crescent moon ascended above Multnomah Falls, the Columbia lapped against the ribbon of rocks and pebbles below, and alpenglow flushed the Oregon cliffs. Over a simple dinner served on a seventeenth-century traveling table made for Emperor Kangxi, Yeon explained the existential threat confronting the Columbia Gorge.

A fifteen-minute drive from the Gorge's entrance, the Interstate 205 highway and bridge would be completed in three years, and the strong winds and winter ice that had long protected the western Gorge would no longer deter homeowners who wanted million-dollar views, river frontage, and a quick commute to Portland. Soon, some of the most spectacular highlands in the lower Gorge—Mount Pleasant, Mount Zion, Cape Horn, and the undeveloped shoreline extending upriver to Beacon Rock—would be a short drive from the city. All of those landmarks were in unzoned Skamania County, whose western border was three miles from the Gorge's entrance.

Yeon recounted for the Russells how land prices in Skamania County were rising as the bridge neared completion, how the population of Clark County was spilling eastward into the Gorge, and how Skamania County's leadership showed no interest in controlling development. Worse yet, at the entrance to the Gorge—on a sliver of land in Washington's Clark County, less than a dozen miles from the planned I-205 bridge—was Steigerwald Lake, one of the most historic, scenic, and visible properties in the western Gorge. Although the lake had been partially drained in the 1960s, only a small portion had been developed, but Steigerwald was minutes away from the bridge and had been zoned for heavy industry. Its abundant wildlife, resplendent vistas, and thousand acres of marshes were poised to be replaced by factories, sewage treatment facilities, and parking lots.

As the Russells listened to Yeon, Nancy felt herself an unlikely recruit for his campaign. While she knew the Columbia River Gorge and cared deeply about it, she had never been an activist nor had she raised money for a cause.

To her knowledge, she had never met a politician. But she was focused, determined, and competitive, and she had acquired the organizational, diplomatic, and leadership skills required of a forty-seven-year-old mother. Her four children were now enrolled in school, freeing her time, and the lectures she gave at the Portland Garden Club had created a following.

Years later, Russell described that evening as "magical," a night that "changed my life."[13] Yeon had planned every detail. He had postponed dinner twice so clouds would not block the rays of the setting sun from coloring the Oregon cliffs, the moon would rise over Multnomah Falls at the proper hour, the crystalline air would not be blurred by haze, and a cooling breeze would not chill. As Russell later mused, Yeon had decided that "it was going to be a perfect evening or not at all."[14] She left The Shire that night inspired and determined, somehow, to assist in the effort to protect the Gorge.

But there were limits to what John Yeon could control and threats were materializing sooner, and closer, than expected. The Port of Camas-Washougal, roused from dormancy by the prospect of federal development funds, was seeking to industrialize Steigerwald Lake. And a former army colonel, now part-time developer, was preparing his land for Skamania County's largest development in twenty years, directly across from Multnomah Falls and adjacent to The Shire.

Chapter 1
The Source, 1932–1949

"Revolution Feared," the *Oregonian* warned on January 11, 1932, the day Nancy Neighbor was born in Portland. Thousands of unemployed men had jammed into the National Mall in Washington, DC, demanding that the federal government create more jobs. The situation throughout the nation was dire, especially in Oregon, where the timber-led economy had been souring for years. Having decimated New England's woods in the nineteenth century and more recently stripped bare the Upper Midwest, the timber industry in 1928 was hemmed in by the Pacific Ocean, yet it produced more lumber than the market could absorb—and at half the profit—than eight years earlier. "For every $3 paid" timber workers in 1929, the *Oregonian* reported, "$1 was paid" two years later.[1]

The supply of wood, wool, wheat, pears, and apples that had been barged for decades from the interior through the Columbia River Gorge to Portland—turning the city into the sixth busiest port in the nation—was evaporating. While selling apples for pennies on New York City Street corners became a symbol of hard times, orchardists in Washington State were paying thirty cents a box to get rid of their crop. In the Gorge, Bartlett pears were sold in Hood River at a loss of more than four dollars a ton; income from apples was down by half.[2] The Depression would buffet nations, states, and families, including Nancy Neighbor's family, but it would also forge personalities and passions and help determine the future of the Gorge.

Although Nancy's maternal grandfather, William Lee Bishop, represented the third generation of physicians in the family, its wealth came primarily from timber. In 1891, Walter Young, Nancy's maternal great-grandfather, founded W. D. Young Lumber Company in Bay City, Michigan, where he was considered "a man of wealth, affluence and standing" and his home was "one of the show places of Bay City." Young owned the world's largest floor-paneling plant and several sawmills and other plants, almost all dependent on hardwood maple trees from northern Michigan. By 1908, enough maple remained in those forests for fifteen years of operations. Looking to diversify his investments—and perhaps scout timberland in the Pacific Northwest—Young traveled to Dundee, a small town in the Willamette Valley southwest of Portland.[3]

The Red Hills of Dundee, between the Cascade and Coast Ranges, are known for their volcanic soils, a fertile mix of clay and iron that bestows a distinct color and bountiful crops. Walter Young bought a farm in the hills and soon amassed over eight hundred acres. While he never lived in Dundee, four years later his daughter Fanny and her husband, William Lee Bishop, a country doctor, left Billings, Montana, with their daughters Mary Ann and Elizabeth and settled on the farm that Young soon gave to Fanny. Dr. Bishop was reportedly brilliant, a dreamer, a gadfly, a poor businessman, and a challenging personality with a quick temper. For the remainder of his life he practiced medicine sporadically, which his wife attributed to his inability to get along with nurses and other colleagues.[4]

The Bishops found the land overgrown and its two cottages and farmhouse in a dilapidated condition, but the hand-hewn timbers of the main house were strong and the soils were productive. They started to reclaim the farm, planting wheat and apples and raising cattle and pigs. When the United States entered World War I, however, their farmhands enlisted in the armed forces and no replacements could be found. So they sold the livestock, and in the fall of 1918 moved to Portland. A decade later, as the Upper Midwest's timber supply closed out and the Depression closed in, Walter Young lost almost his entire fortune, over $11 million in 2021 dollars.[5]

Nancy's paternal grandfather, Robert Neighbor, fared no better during the Depression. He also moved to Portland in 1918, as a salesman for E. C. Atkins and Company, which manufactured large saws used by timber mills. The next year, while visiting two new sawmills in central Oregon, he came across an obscure alpine lake populated by eastern brook trout. An avid fisherman, he was captivated by Elk Lake, located at five thousand feet in the Cascade Range and a two-day drive from Portland. To get to the lake, Neighbor followed the Columbia River Highway into the Gorge, through the Cascades, then paralleled the mountains south to the lumber-mill City of Bend before navigating a winding, dirt road for several more hours.

In 1923, Neighbor took a ninety-nine-year US Forest Service lease on a lot and paid a local man $500 to build the only cabin on the lake. But as his Elk Lake footprint expanded, Oregon's timber economy contracted. Mills overproduced and started closing, and the industry tumbled first into recession and then depression. When Neighbor, now the successful manager of

E. C. Atkins's Pacific Coast division, was asked to take a wage cut, he refused and quit his job. At a time when four of every five lumber mills in the region had closed, this proud and prosperous man—who once chaired the board of Waverley, Portland's most prestigious country club—did not work again until he was close to destitute, eventually accepting employment as a low-wage laborer in Portland's Kaiser shipyards during the war. Neighbor's son Bob had helped him at Elk Lake, peeling pine logs from nearby woods for the cabin's walls and hauling stones for the fireplace. By the mid-1920s, Bob was attending the University of Oregon in Eugene but had to quit when the university began charging in-state students their first tuition—thirty-six dollars for the upcoming fall semester.[6]

At about the same time, Mary Ann Bishop was earning straight As as a freshman at the University of Washington. When her father pulled her out of school in 1923, disapproving of a suitor who had followed her to Seattle from Portland, she accompanied her aunt on a tour of Europe and never returned to college. He had thwarted his daughter's intentions, and perhaps she then took an opportunity to thwart his. She soon met and fell in love with Bob Neighbor, who was poor and whose prospects were as bleak as the times. He and Mary Ann married on October 25, 1929, a portentous date, as the stock market had crashed the day before and Black Tuesday arrived four days later.

The Neighbors made an attractive, if unlikely, couple. Bob was a tall, gregarious man who loved to fish and was happiest when casting a fly and drinking with friends at Elk Lake or along the Deschutes River in central Oregon. Mary Ann, born to wealth in Bay City, was petite and "prim and proper."[7] She seemed content keeping house and raising their children— Bobby, born in late 1930, Nancy just over a year later, and Betsy seven years later, in 1939. Her shy disposition, which tended toward anxiety, may have resulted from a series of illnesses she experienced as a young girl, when she had nearly died of rheumatic fever at the Dundee farm.

Mary Ann's anxieties would soon rise. As the Depression worsened, at least one-third of Portland workers lost their jobs. Bob worked occasionally, selling bonds and insurance, but people weren't buying much insurance as future risk seemed less daunting than the present. With two young children, the Neighbors struggled to pay rent, and the family moved at least eleven times between 1932 and 1937, looking for cheaper housing or staying with Bob's or Mary Ann's parents when they could not find or afford a place to live. Finally, in the spring of 1935, "without a nickel to rub together," according to their daughter Betsy, and with neither set of parents able or willing to lend them money, the young couple sought refuge at the family farm in the Red Hills of Dundee, where jobs might be scarce but food could be grown and rent was free.[8]

Neither Bob nor Mary Ann was suited for farm life. Bob once built a chicken coop that collapsed for the lack of an essential element—nails. Mary Ann was reduced to baking biscuits to sell for a few dollars, sewing her children's clothes, and planting fruit trees.[9] When not attending to children or chores, she swept and scrubbed the farmhouse, over and over again, until it gleamed.

Dundee, however, was utopia for the children. The farmhouse sat high on a hill, facing east, and Bobby and Nancy awoke to the sun rising above Mount Hood's distant, snow-covered flank. The farm's fields descended to the Willamette River, while apple orchards and oak stands behind the house blanketed foothills that rose to form the Coast Range, which separated the valley from the Pacific Ocean. When spring arrived and their mother was busy indoors, the siblings roamed across meadows glittering with pale yellow and lavender wildflowers and through orchards bursting with pink blossoms. They raced through wheat fields in the autumn and splashed across crystal clear creeks where crawdads waved rust-flecked pincers in the current. In the summer, after waiting for July's heat to melt the fifteen to twenty feet of winter snow that typically fell in the mountains, the children drove with their parents to Elk Lake, a trip that launched a tradition Nancy would observe each summer, with her own children, for the rest of her life.

The drive was shorter than Bob's father had experienced sixteen years earlier. With the completion of a high bridge over the Crooked River in 1927 and a shortcut connecting Mount Hood to the town of Maupin in 1929, the 230-mile route had been reduced by a quarter. But central Oregon's roads were still dirt or gravel, and the last section from Bend to Elk Lake constituted "two ruts of pumice stone dust." The trip took sixteen hours. The Neighbors competed for right of way with Basque herders driving sheep to mountain grass and logging trucks careening around blind corners, often carrying a single enormous yellow-bellied pine log to a sawmill. Fifty years later, Bob recalled the time when the radiator cap blew off and drenched Mary Ann in hot, rusty water: "I am afraid the words she used in describing all my family would not be fit to print," he said. But the family drove on "under a full Eastern Oregon moon which lit up the Cascade Mountain range all the way from Mt. Hood to Mt. Bachelor and was so beautiful we had forgotten this unfortunate experience."[10]

After arriving at Elk Lake Lodge — a few half-log, half-canvas cabins and a small building with an office, dining room, and store — the family unpacked the car and rowed for ten minutes across the lake to their cabin. The next day, Nancy and Bobby woke early, excited and freezing. Even in July, night temperatures at the lake dipped into the thirties, and the cabin's only sources of heat were a fireplace and a wood stove. The six-hundred-square-foot, two-bedroom cabin had no running water, electricity, or plumbing, and food was kept in a nearby stream. But it was outdoor adventure that attracted the children and their father, and in the mornings, before the stove could warm the cabin, they rushed outside into the cool, pine-scented mountain air.

Years after Nancy's father had peeled logs and carried fireplace stones for her grandfather, a few other cabins had been built — including one next door owned by the Russell family from Portland — but little else had changed. As a teenager, Nancy organized hikes through miles of alpine meadows that had been transformed into a burnt-orange, lavender, and yellow mosaic of paintbrush, lupine, and balsamroot, and onto the slopes of Mount Bachelor, Broken Top, and South Sister, whose peaks towered above Elk Lake. She often capped the daylong hikes with a bracing, three-mile swim to the end of the lake and back. But it wasn't just the setting that forged lifelong impressions, it was also the intimacy of three generations living closely during difficult times. During the day, her grandmother planted Indian paintbrush around the cabin and fed cookies and pancakes to grandchildren as they sat on rocks in the lake while their grandfather, often a quarrelsome man when away from Elk Lake, demonstrated the patience necessary to catch a skittish trout. After the sun set, three generations of Neighbors would hold impromptu concerts around a bonfire or, if the weather was foul, the cabin's fireplace.[11] Nancy's favorite songs, from musicals like *Paint your Wagon*, *Oklahoma*, and *South Pacific*, burst with energy and romance and crackled with Wild West adventures of discovering gold and love or desire at Bali Hai. Her singing voice, it was widely agreed, was more enthusiastic than musical, which seemed to inspire rather than deter her.

The Neighbor family returned to Elk Lake each summer, experiencing the "sting of the sun and cool of the shade," and the "smell of the woods, the crushing of pine needles." The lake offered a sense of constancy for the itinerant family as they moved at least four times over the next three years. After leaving the Dundee farm for Portland in 1936, their travels included a year-long stint with Nancy's maternal grandparents, then they rented a small house a short walk away. With the Depression easing, Bob found occasional work as a salesman, and in 1938 a friend at City Insurance Agency hired him. When Nancy's sister Betsy was born a year later, the family crossed the Willamette River to a home in the West Hills, a heavily wooded part of the Tualatin Mountains whose neighborhoods—high above Portland's business district and riverfront industrial area—were popular with young families. Bob stayed with City Insurance for three years and settled his family for the first time in a decade. Years later, Nancy would describe her childhood as "fabulous" and remember her West Hills neighborhood as "absolutely wonderful, [with] every kind of person" and "varied houses of mixed importance."[12]

In 1939 the Neighbors squeezed into a small, nondescript house at the corner of Southwest Fern Street and Montgomery Drive. A neighborhood grocery run by the Strohecker family was around the corner, a park with a tennis court and backboard was nearby, and Mary Ann's parents' modest Victorian home was just blocks away. When not in school, Nancy was outdoors, mostly in trees—climbing as high as the branches could support her—where she and a friend would call down to startle pedestrians. Like "elves in the forest," Nancy and her circle of neighborhood girls walked everywhere together or "plodded in the rain," roller skated, and during the occasional silver thaw ice skated on deserted streets. "We loved our walks noticing trees, plants and flowers, the rain, snow, sunlight, clouds," Susi Seley, a longtime friend, remembered. "Walking, instead of riding in a car, allowed us to see nature and feel it as well."[13]

Nancy and her mother were opposites. Nancy was a "tomboy" by her own admission, while Mary Ann was increasingly frail and uncomfortable outside the house. Her health deteriorated and her anxieties mounted as the family's fortunes ebbed and flowed, mostly ebbed. She had once been an accomplished tennis player, pushed to a city title in 1920 as her father shouted instructions from the bleachers, but now she rarely left the house and declined invitations from longtime—and more affluent—friends. She even refused requests from Nancy, who loved to chase and hit balls on the tennis court but stopped asking her mother to join her. "Mother is a housewife to the core," Nancy wrote in a yearbook article in 1949, "and I often wonder how she stands it." Nancy's brother Bobby later remembered that his mother used her energies and her confinement to scrub their home "within an inch of its soul, continuously." She worried constantly, and her reaction to adversity resembled Portland's winter storms, low depressions that stacked dark clouds over the city for weeks.[14]

Nancy rarely worried. Only one friend remembered Nancy being upset when young, when she cried at the unfairness of being born a girl without her brother's freedoms. Betsy recalled Nancy's annoyance at being teased by classmates for wearing the same clothes for four years—clothes that swallowed her whole one year and pinched another—but that blew over like a summer squall. Nancy's personality matched her father's. Despite frequent moves and sporadic employment, Bob maintained a breezy, affable disposition that focused "on the Sunny Side of the Street," a song that was one of Nancy's favorites. He also made regular trips to the Deschutes River, where he and a close group of fishing friends consumed cutthroat trout and Cutty Sark. Mary Ann and Bob were devoted to their children, and holidays were celebrated with multigenerational dinners. All in all, it was a "terribly conventional family and it was very satisfying and very simple," according to Nancy. "What more can you ask?"[15]

Some might have asked for a thin financial cushion. The Neighbors "lived very close to the bone," Nancy said, but "we never knew we were poor." She remembered that "there sure wasn't any loose change, you didn't think about using a pay phone, you didn't think about spending a nickel on a candy bar. There just wasn't any spare change. . . . The Great Depression was a very real thing for a lot of people." Reminiscing decades later about her joy at receiving a birthday gift of an old bicycle from the Salvation Army that her father had "wonderfully painted . . . a beautiful battleship gray," Nancy explained that "it never made any difference to little kids whether they were playing with some old, reconditioned wreck of a wagon or some big shiny new thing—they didn't care." And Nancy really didn't care. Bobby emphasized that "money was never inherently important" to his sister. Because of the Depression, and later during World War II, children living in the West Hills before television were "not exposed to the outside world very much." Living in the relative economic diversity of the West Hills also made being less affluent easier, or at least less conspicuous.[16]

Bob's age and poor eyesight exempted him from service, and the family was accustomed to the austerity the war imposed. Most things were inexpensive in any case, a trend that continued through World War II, when rationing was in place. Nancy delighted in scrap drives for the war effort, and a photograph in the June 16, 1942, *Oregonian* shows ten-year-old Nancy and two friends posing with "a huge ball of cut stocking strips" they had been "industriously collecting," presumably for parachutes and powder bags.[17] A head taller than her friends, she is wearing a simple embroidered dress, has her hair pulled straight back, and is gazing directly at the camera with a crooked smile.

Nancy was bigger, stronger, and more athletic than her brother Bobby, who was eighteen months older. Both were "stubborn as hell," Bobby remembered, although Nancy was more competitive and liked to be in charge. Their mother once forced the two children—at ages seven and eight—to model sailor uniforms in a local Junior League fashion show. When the spotlight illuminated the pair, Nancy ordered her brother to open his coat. He refused, she escalated, and they started brawling on stage. Mary Ann sunk lower and lower in her chair until order was restored by her sister Elizabeth. The siblings shared a bedroom, and each morning, Bobby remembered, "the first thing we would do . . . is we would hit the other, and then mother would come up and paddle our behinds with a hairbrush." By her own admission, Nancy was "very competitive and loved reading," and she excelled at Ainsworth, the neighborhood elementary school, where she skipped an early grade and landed in Bobby's class, stoking the sibling rivalry. "Nancy always wanted to be the best," her sister Betsy summed up, "and she was."[18]

In the fall of their graduation from Ainsworth in 1945, Bobby entered Lincoln High School, but Nancy chose another path. "By the time I was out of grade school, or even in grade school," she later said, "I knew the importance, if I was going to get anywhere, of getting straight As, because my parents didn't have much of a cushion." The Catlin-Hillside School—a progressive girls school established in 1911 that educated many of the children from Portland's elite families—was an ideal launchpad for her. The school wanted students from "various economic backgrounds" who were "chosen for their promise in qualities of character, intelligence, responsibility, and purpose." Mary Ann had graduated from Catlin in more prosperous times and was eager for Nancy to attend, but Bob believed that private school was "a terrible waste of money." So, at age thirteen, Nancy requested and completed the scholarship application herself. In June, she learned that she would receive a half-year, $175 scholarship for the upcoming fall term, support that would continue throughout her four years at the school.[19]

Catlin could be intimidating, according to Kate Mills, who was a year behind Nancy in school, and some of the students were "fancy people." There was a dress code, and students stood when teachers or the principal entered the room. But Catlin also "encouraged girls to be in charge" and "gave you confidence." Nancy already knew several students who lived in her neighborhood, and she was successful in both sports and academics. "I loved being a good student," Nancy later said, and "always had this drive toward writing and reading and being number one in the class." She was "continually at the top of every class she took," Susi Seley said, and "was also the top player in all our sports." Kate Mills's first impression of Nancy was "terrifying," she said. "I can still see her coming at me" on the basketball court, "her face all red, determined that I wasn't going to shoot a basket."[20]

Nancy excelled at basketball, skating, and skiing, but she dominated at tennis, a sport that suited both her talents and her family's finances. As a young girl, Nancy walked to Strohecker's Park every summer day to spend hours hitting tennis balls against the backboard. Her parents did not encourage her, "feeling that it was a little bit unfeminine . . . to spend too much time doing sports," Nancy remembered, and there was "no money spent on things like lessons, or trips to a tennis camp." Nevertheless, Nancy developed into a champion player, relying on her strength and coordination, an unorthodox amalgam of front-facing slices, slashing volleys, and choppy serves and an unerring accuracy and consistency that resulted from her battles with Strohecker's backboard, where an errant shot would bounce down a wooded ravine, requiring a long search and a steep trudge back.[21]

While Nancy thrived on the tennis courts and in classrooms, her father seemed to break out of his cycle of fitful employment. After three years at City Insurance, Bob started his own general insurance company in 1941 when a fishing friend gave him the insurance account for Tidewater Barge Lines, a company that employed over a hundred people.[22] Optimistic over the prospects of R. W. Neighbor and Company, he and Mary Ann bought a larger house higher in the West Hills, with a sweeping view up the Willamette Valley.

Disaster soon struck, however, as Mary Ann suffered the first of several heart attacks. Always frail and anxious and now afflicted with a failing heart and narcolepsy—a disease closely linked to depression—she began a steady decline.[23] Bob struggled to attract clients, and with Mary Ann's medical bills mounting and income falling, the family was forced to sell the house. Mary Ann's father had recently passed away, and once again, the family crowded into Fanny Bishop's cramped Victorian down the hill—this time with three children and a nearly incapacitated Mary Ann—while Bob's business foundered. The family would continue to drift, moving at least four times in three years, staying for periods in a friend's farmhouse on the outskirts of Portland and on a farm in Hillsboro.

But Nancy did not drift. She liked living with her grandmother, who she remembered as "very motherly, very sweet, and refined, and interested in beautiful things and had beautiful taste." She continued at Catlin, thanks to her scholarship and the family's small contributions, and her progress must have been reassuring to them. She was on the honor roll every year, taking particular interest in classes on the Romantic poets—Blake, Wordsworth, Coleridge, Byron, Shelley, and Keats. Her *joie de vivre* and positive outlook, reflected in the caption under her senior yearbook picture—"Born with the gift of laughter"—gave her a large circle of close friends.[24]

By the time she was seventeen and graduating from Catlin, those who knew her best tended to describe her the same way: intelligent and independent; confident and competitive; tough and tenacious, yet always smiling; direct, driven, social, and stubborn. Most agreed—her siblings especially—that it was Nancy's determination that set her apart. Her sister Betsy recalled looking out the bedroom window early one "very muddy, rainy, horrid November day" during the eighteen months the family stayed in a friend's farmhouse. There was teenage Nancy coaxing a calf into the barn, a long rope around its neck. The calf pulled one way, Nancy the other, and soon she was being dragged face down across the barnyard, skimming across a sea of mud and manure, a foul coffee-colored wake roiling behind her. After ten minutes, which seemed like an hour to Betsy and probably longer to her sister, Nancy hoisted herself up, led the exhausted calf to the barn, released the rope, cleaned up, and went to school.[25]

When high school finished for the year, the Neighbors continued their pilgrimages to Elk Lake. Soon after Nancy's graduation, a group of boys, including Bruce Russell, decided to climb the 10,358-foot South Sister, nine miles away. They reconnoitered at four in the morning to begin the difficult hike, which gains almost five thousand feet in five and a half miles. Bruce's friends were dressed in full mountaineer gear—boots, ice axes, crampons, packs, and ropes—and he groused at the "glacial" pace they set. When the group finally summited, they were surprised—and not a little embarrassed— to see Nancy, "who had slept to a normal hour and ambled up the mountain in her cotton shirt and tennis shoes" by herself.[26] Later that afternoon, after skipping down from the summit, Nancy swam for a mile, across Elk Lake and back.

Her gambol down the South Sister and plunge into Elk Lake revealed another trait: her lifelong passion for wilderness that would later shape a legendary American landscape. In time, the Columbia River Gorge would provide the beauty and physical connection to nature that Nancy craved as a teenager. The Gorge offered an astonishing history of Native people, explorers, and settlers; a diverse landscape, with cultivated fields and wilderness, open savannahs flush with wildflowers, and basalt canyons overflowing with waterfalls; and challenging politics too. The landscape would stir Nancy's emotions, her intellect, and her competitive nature.

The Columbia Gorge is a place of complexity and unreconciled conflict—conceived by fire and flood, alluring in beauty and profit, cherished and exploited. Formed millions of years ago by the continent's largest lava flows, which cooled into basalt layers up to five thousand feet deep, and by tectonic plates clashing underneath the coastline of present-day Washington State, the Gorge drains water from a quarter million square miles of seven states and a province: Washington, Oregon, Idaho, Montana, Wyoming, Nevada, Utah and British Columbia. It is one of the few places in North America where a major river cleaves a mountain range at sea level.

Eighteen thousand years ago, Ice Age glaciers advanced and retreated as the climate cooled and warmed, causing a two-thousand-foot-high ice dam in contemporary southwest Montana to breech, reform, then breech again. This pattern, which repeated scores of times over three millennia, discharged the planet's largest floods toward the Pacific Ocean and through what became the Columbia Gorge. Enormous "slurries of mud"—water, ice, rock, and sediment—carried huge iceberg-encased boulders at speeds approaching sixty miles per hour, obliterating everything in their path.[27]

When the Missoula Floods squeezed through the narrow walls of the Gorge, their energy intensified, forcing the Columbia's tributaries to flow backward. The Deschutes at the eastern edge of the Gorge, one of Oregon's largest rivers, reversed course for fifty miles. The floods transformed the V-shaped Gorge into a broader and steeper U shape, scoured away vegetation, and sheared off dozens of creeks in midair, creating hanging valleys and the largest year-round collection of waterfalls in North America.[28]

Visitors to the Gorge today usually flow in the opposite direction, from the west, leaving the Portland-Vancouver metropolitan area behind them. They cross the Sandy River in Oregon or Gibbons Creek in Washington, pass marshes and ponds brimming with waterfowl before climbing to Crown Point on the south and Cape Horn on the north—twin sentinels, once submerged by the Missoula Floods—that rise hundreds of feet above the river. At Crown Point, John Yeon wrote, "the Gorge dramatically appears with a suddenness similar to the first sight of Yosemite from the entrance tunnel." From this vantage, visitors can look downriver a mile and a half to the Steigerwald Lake floodplains on the north shore and pastures perched on cliffs at Mount Zion and Mount Pleasant, a sublime landscape framed by the Columbia and an extinct volcano, the four-thousand-foot-high Silver Star Mountain. Upstream, past riverside farms and woodlots, are Beacon Rock and Phoca Rock, a giant flood-borne erratic near Cape Horn that was named by explorer William Clark, presumably for the harbor seals (*Phoca vitulina*) he and other members of the Corps of Discovery encountered there in 1805.[29]

The view from Cape Horn across the river is similar in scale to the view from Oregon's Crown Point, but subtly different. Upstream from the confluence of the Sandy and Columbia Rivers, Douglas-firs dominate and the steep cliffs are often cast in shade. The south bank is dramatic, as waterfalls spring from creekbeds and crash hundreds of feet into plunge pools or evaporate in midair before reuniting as tumbling cataracts near the valley floor. In winter, waterfalls form sparkling veils of gust-driven ice across broad cliff faces. Beyond the waterfall corridor the Gorge unfolds, panel by panel, below Mount Hood.

East of Cape Horn, past Beacon Rock, the basalt cliffs of Table Mountain and Greenleaf Peak are linked by the Red Bluffs escarpment and rise thirty-four hundred feet from the north bank of the Columbia. Botanist David Douglas first recorded summitting Greenleaf Peak in September 1825. Finding few fall plants and forced to overnight on the mountain, he and a companion roasted a bald eagle for dinner and rested their feet the next day while "fishing and shooting seals, which were sporting in vast numbers in the rapid where the salmon are particularly abundant." The talus slopes at the base of these mountains evince the cliffs that sloughed off and temporarily blocked the river, triggered by the Missoula Floods and more recent earthquakes. Native people tell how the Great Spirit built a land bridge at this place to unite his sons Wy'east (south of the river) and Klickitat (north), who were separated by the Columbia. But the sons quarreled over the beautiful Loo-wit, hurling fire and boulders at each other, and the Great Spirit destroyed the bridge and turned Wy'east, Klickitat, and Loo-wit into stone—Mount Hood, Mount Adams, and Mount St. Helens. The boulders scattered downriver like tears and created the four-and-a-half-mile stretch of Cascade Rapids, from which the mountain range eventually took its name.[30]

The walls of the Gorge narrow and steepen as the Columbia divides the Cascades farther east. The winter sun—when it penetrates the stratum of clouds often massed on the windward, Pacific side of the range—does not shine on the valley floor for long, blocked by 5,010-foot-high Mount Defiance on the south bank. At the river's edge, the shifting talus slopes of nearby Shellrock Mountain frustrated generations of road builders who labored to connect Portland to the interior. Remnants of their efforts in the form of a dry-stone masonry wagon road built in 1876 are still visible. Upriver and above the tree line, alpine meadows sweep across south-facing Dog Mountain, where spring displays of lupine, balsamroot, and Indian paintbrush are so spectacular that they can be seen from the river three thousand feet below.

The flora in the Gorge, which fascinated botanists and naturalists like David Douglas, Thomas Nuttall, and John Muir, is the result of an unusual blend of marine environment in the west and desert in the east, separated by the thin crest of the Cascade Range. The climate develops over the Pacific Ocean, more than seventy miles away, as water vapor forms and is carried east by prevailing winds. The Cascade Range forces the winds higher, and water is released as the moisture-laden air ascends and cools. Average rainfall at Cascade Locks—a sea-level town in the Gorge on the west flank of the Cascades—measures close to ninety inches a year.[31] Thirty miles away, at the western entrance to the Gorge, the average is forty-nine inches, while the eastern entrance, some fifty miles distant, averages twelve.

The unique topography and climate also affect wind patterns. In the summer, heat builds in eastern Oregon and Washington, while the marine environment at the coast remains cool and moist. The resulting pressure gradient—high pressure in the west and low in the east—builds winds from the west, which accelerate as they are compressed by the four-thousand-foot-high walls of the Gorge. In winter, the process reverses, as Canadian fronts flow into the interior, plunging temperatures and building cold air behind the Cascades while the coast remains moderate and the pressure gradient flips. Cold air pours through the Gorge as low pressure attracts high. Savage storms with horizontal rain, snow, and ice pellets—driven by strong east winds amplified by the wind tunnel—often lay down thick sheets of ice in the lower Gorge.

East of the Cascades, the changes wrought by the driving winds, disparate rainfall, and diverse topography are startling. The dense Douglas-fir and western hemlock forests west of the mountains yield to open stands of ponderosa pine and Oregon white oak. Larch Mountain salamanders, lace leaf ferns, and phantom orchids give way to rattlesnakes, desert parsleys, and wildflowers with illustrative names—grass widows, yellow bells, and smooth prairie stars—that appear early in the spring, weeks before their westside counterparts. Nowhere in the world but in the open meadows of the eastern Gorge can you find the lyrically named poet's shooting star, an exquisite wildflower with a sleek, rocketlike shape that flows from a dusky stamen and dazzling yellow corolla cone to brilliant pink and lavender petal fins. Sharp-eyed observers notice that the evergreens in this part of the Gorge are flagged to the east, their fresh branches bent leeward by late-spring west winds. In the lower Gorge, their counterparts are flagged the opposite direction, their windward branches snapped off by the fierce winter gales that roar out of the east.

Eighty-five miles long and averaging three miles from rim to rim, the cliffs that line the Columbia River Gorge rise from sea level to almost a mile in elevation, embracing rain forest and desert and providing sea-level habitat for sea lions, osprey, and salmon and high-elevation habitat for mountain lions, peregrine falcons, and pikas. The mile-wide Columbia River presents an effective migration barrier, and the Gorge hosts the northernmost range of some species and the southernmost of others, including almost a thousand species of wildflowers, sixteen of which are found nowhere else in the world.[32]

The cascading tributaries that surge out of deep canyons—the White Salmon, Hood River, and, as Woody Guthrie wrote in "Roll on Columbia," the Klickitat, too—are exposed, no longer camouflaged or softened by the rainforest canopy downstream. Synclines and anticlines fold toward the Columbia, and a massive basalt arch curves several hundred feet above Catherine Creek, a few miles east of the White Salmon River. Talus slopes are laced with rock walls, cairns, and pits built hundreds of years ago by the Gorge's earliest residents. Mount Hood is fully revealed here, as is the top of Mount Adams, rising 12,280 feet thirty miles to the north. Farther east, a series of grassy hills laced with springs and prehistoric trails—the Columbia Hills—ripple almost three thousand feet above the north bank of the river. Fleeting spring rains transform their slopes into jade-green hummocks, save for bright yellow swaths at the summit where the world's only population of Dalles Mountain buttercup grows, its blossoms forced low by the wind.

Upstream from the Columbia Hills, the land is parched, its moisture wrung out by the sun and wind. Rain, which seldom falls, instantly evaporates. Plants flaunt formidable names—bitterroot, poison oak, prickly pear cactus, dense-spike primrose—and impressive defenses. Views seem infinite, guided on both banks by massive colonnades of columnar basalt scoured by the Missoula Floods. Thousands of years ago, the Missoula Floods destroyed anything, and anyone, in their path. Centuries ago, Native people painstakingly painted and carved pictographs and petroglyphs on smooth rock faces. Today, their descendants still build wooden fishing scaffolds that cling to rock walls above the Columbia.

Prior to 1850, some of the world's largest fish runs—estimated at 10 to 16 million salmon a year—migrated up the Columbia through the Gorge, the largest Chinooks over four feet long and more than a hundred pounds. The people who lived along the river called it Nch'i-Wána, the Sahaptin word for Great River; they called themselves People of the Salmon for the fish that served as a bedrock of their lives, providing nutrition, spiritual sustenance, and trade goods. They lived in villages sited near the best fishing places, usually at the mouths of tributaries or along major rapids where fish would converge and pause—making them easier to catch—before renewing their upstream journey.[33]

One of North America's premier Native fisheries was an eleven-mile stretch of river upstream from The Dalles, which included the Long Narrows—a hundred-foot-wide, several-mile-long reach that Natives described as the river "turning on its side"—and, farther upstream, Celilo Falls, an extraordinary series of basalt islands, cascades, chutes, and falls, including Horseshoe Falls, over twenty feet high during autumn's low water. Fishing Celilo was a death-defying choreography, where fishermen in the midst of the maelstrom struggled to see, hear, and stand. Blinded by sunlight and wind-driven sheets of spray and deafened by the river's roar, they balanced on slippery-as-ice platforms that glistened from a patina of cold water and fish slime acquired over decades. When fishermen snared a salmon, they fought to hoist their catch—writhing in a four-to-five-foot-wide dipnet attached to a twenty-foot pole—out of the fast current. A slip could lead to drowning unless thick ropes, wrapped around a fisherman's waist and anchored to the scaffolds, held. Boys, not much larger than the biggest fish, dashed across narrow footbridges to help secure caught salmon. Beginning in the early 1930s, the fishermen loaded the boys and the salmon into improbably small cable cars and, swaying high above the river, pulled themselves to shore.[34]

Located on a major transportation corridor between the coast and the interior, where hot summer temperatures and desert winds dried salmon into an easily exchanged commodity, the eastern Gorge became one of the continent's preeminent trade centers. River People exchanged salmon—dried as jerky or pounded with berries and the meat of other game animals into pemmican—with coastal tribes for shells, skins, and furs. Later generations traded fish with Great Plains tribes for "horses, buffalo robes, feather headdresses and pipestone" and later yet with Europeans for blankets, metal, ironware, buttons, and glass beads. On the Corps of Discovery's downriver voyage in the fall of 1805, William Clark estimated a single stock of dried fish in an eastern Gorge village at ten thousand pounds. Celilo Village—built near the falls on the Columbia's south bank—is considered by many to be North America's oldest continuously occupied site.[35]

Estimating the Native population prior to 1805, whether at Celilo or throughout the Gorge, is challenging, as written records did not exist, multiple languages and dialects were spoken, and populations would swell and recede by season and food availability. European diseases decimated Native people well before the Corps of Discovery's arrival. Two generations earlier, perhaps seventeen thousand Native people lived in the Gorge, before smallpox, malaria, influenza, and other diseases, carried to the New World by Spanish conquistadors and shipwrecked sailors, made their way to Gorge communities. By 1806, Lewis and Clark estimated the Gorge's population to be less than eight thousand. Native people had no immunity to European diseases, and their cultural practices—comforting sick family members, purifying through sweat lodges, and fleeing villages when the disaster struck—often spread disease. Experts estimate that within a century of contact with Europeans, 80 percent of the Northwest Coast population died from European diseases: the death rate in the Gorge, a vital trade route where large dugout canoes carried diseases as efficiently as they carried trade goods, probably exceeded 90 percent.[36]

In May 1792, twenty years after the first smallpox epidemics reached the Northwest Coast, American Capt. Robert Gray confirmed that the muddy water he had noticed flowing from shore weeks earlier was the "Great River of the West," which he named after his ship *Columbia Rediviva*. Months later, Lt. William Broughton—corroborating Gray's discovery—sailed upriver to present-day Steigerwald Lake and declared the territory for Britain. In 1805, Meriwether Lewis and William Clark and the Corps of Discovery navigated the rapids in the eastern Gorge—"this agitated gut, swelling, boiling & whirling in every direction." They spent thirty-seven days in the Gorge, mostly on their return voyage in the spring of 1806. John Jacob Astor's North West Company and voyageurs working for the Hudson's Bay Company canoed supplies and furs through the Gorge several years later, and missionaries Marcus and Narcissa Whitman traveled the Columbia in 1836 without incident—save an attack by fleas and wind delays—before being killed in 1847 by Cayuse warriors who believed Dr. Whitman had intentionally infected them with smallpox. From 1843 to 1855—until the Barlow Road over Mount Hood became popular—perhaps twenty-two thousand Oregon Trail emigrants made their way down the Gorge rapids.[37]

Gold was struck in eastern Oregon in the early 1860s, and steamboats carried miners and their supplies upriver while treasure flowed down. Dozens of sternwheelers and sidewheelers navigated the Gorge during the era of steamboats, using portage railroads to bypass the Cascade Rapids, the Long Narrows, and Celilo Falls. Passenger receipts for a single ship, not counting lucrative freight charges, could exceed $10,000 in a day. Each steamship required roughly four cords of wood an hour to feed its boilers, and riverfront forests were reduced to cordwood stacks piled at intervals along the banks. Just west of Celilo, three hundred men reportedly worked in cordwood camps, and an accomplished woodsman could cut two cords a day, earning two dollars for himself and thirty minutes of fuel for the *Relief*, the *Idaho*, or the *Inland Empire*.[38]

When Oregon Railway & Navigation Company rails linked Portland to the interior through the Gorge in 1883, the interior's natural wealth—"gold, grass and grain"—could be moved even more economically. Railcars and steamboats carried gold, cattle, sheep, and tons of soft white wheat from Columbia Basin fields downriver to Portland and Pacific markets. By 1890, a full grain ship left Portland for foreign markets each week, on average. In 1896, a three-thousand-foot canal bypassed the Cascade Rapids, and twenty years later an eight-and-a-half mile-long canal was blasted through ancient lava flows to skirt Celilo Falls.[39]

Fishwheels arrived in 1879. The river-powered contraptions resembled Ferris wheels that scooped up salmon in their spinning baskets for transport to nearby canneries, where Chinese workers—who had also helped build the railways—sliced the fish apart for canning. The best workers were able to clean seventeen hundred fish a day. One fishwheel caught sixty thousand pounds of salmon in eight hours. At least seventy-nine fishwheels operated in the Gorge, and by the time they were banned in Oregon in 1926 and in Washington eight years later, the Columbia's salmon runs were racing toward extinction.[40]

Cities—their residents drawn by fishing, farming, logging, and transportation—were also established in the Gorge. City leaders sought river frontage, flat land, and tributary confluences, often building on land where Native villages had once flourished. The largest city in the Gorge, The Dalles, was a major port and agricultural center built on a wide scenic bend in the river below the Long Narrows. Its four newspapers advertised the services of a dozen attorneys, several doctors and dentists, and "The Largest And Finest Hotel In Oregon," the Umatilla House, a three-story structure with 126 bedrooms and a dining room and bar that could entertain 450 customers.[41]

In 1895, twenty river miles downstream from The Dalles, the City of Hood River was established where its namesake tributary flowed into the Columbia. Logging employed more than a thousand men in the Hood River Valley in 1908, and commercial fishing thrived. It was Hood River's apples, however, that brought the city international acclaim, winning the grand prize at the St. Louis World's Fair in 1904 and leading to the shipment of thousands of boxes of apples to European markets the next year. Several miles farther downstream, the rain-soaked town of Cascade Locks rose above the canal and locks that bypassed the Cascade Rapids—Lewis and Clark's "Great Shute." In 1893, George Stevenson bought land the federal government had donated under the 1850 General Land Grant Act across the river from Cascade Locks—parcels that became the foundation for the town of Stevenson, Washington. Across from Hood River, the City of White Salmon was incorporated in 1907 on land acquired from Klickitats in 1852, a few years before they and other Gorge tribes were removed to reservations.[42]

If the rate of change in the century inaugurated by Lewis and Clark seemed rapid, the twentieth century's pace was precipitous. "The canoe, the horse, the river boat, the stagecoach, even the railroads, impinged lightly on the Oregon landscape," summarized writer Terence O'Donnell, "whereas the impact of the automobile was major." The first automobile arrived in Oregon in 1899, and its successors required roads—along with promoters, financiers, designers, builders, and, above all, dreamers. Sam Hill was such a dreamer. A wealthy industrialist who had worked for the Great Northern Railway, he recognized the benefits that roads provided a developing society, but he was no mere roads enthusiast. "Good roads are more than my hobby," he declared, "they are my religion." And, according to Hill biographer John E. Tuhy, the Columbia River Highway was his Holy Grail.[43]

A road through the Gorge was considered impossible. "You can't survey a road along the Columbia River," a future Washington highway commissioner warned Hill, "let alone build one." But Hill was smart, stubborn, and rich. In 1906, he lured Sam Lancaster, a "brilliant engineer with the soul of a poet," away from the federal government where Lancaster was "preach[ing] the gospel of good roads." He whisked Lancaster off to the First International

Road Congress in Paris in October 1908, and they toured Europe by automobile, examining two-thousand-year-old Roman roads as well as Switzerland's renowned Axenstrasse. Hill then commissioned Lancaster to construct a series of experimental roads at Maryhill, Hill's seven-thousand-acre estate in the eastern Gorge, where he was building a Beaux Arts mansion that included a dining room for two hundred and fifty guests and ramps so cars could enter the building, deposit passengers in the reception hall, and exit the opposite side. Using convict labor and designing much of his equipment, Lancaster built seven types of roads over ten miles, including a set of winding loops that scaled the Columbia Hills from river edge to Maryhill, eight hundred feet above the river.[44]

When Washington governor Marion Hay proved indifferent to Hill's entreaties to build his highway on the north bank's more hospitable terrain, Hill lobbied the State of Oregon. In February 1913, he brought its entire legislature to Maryhill by special railcar—entertainment, food, and drink provided. But it took more than the legislature's support to create Oregon's first paved highway; Portland's leading businessmen also had to back the effort. Before long, those enterprising men had envisioned a trifecta: a new link to eastern Oregon's "gold, grass and grain"; a tourist bonanza for Portland; and a boost to civic pride, especially in the competition to become the Northwest's preeminent metropolis, as Seattle had recently pulled ahead in population and was favored with a road from Tacoma to Mount Rainier National Park.[45]

Oregon lumberman Simon Benson donated $10,000 to construct an experimental road over Shellrock Mountain, the historic barrier to overland travel in the Gorge, and backed a $75,000 Hood River bond measure to support the highway project, which was largely funded by the counties. He later bought all of the bonds. Millionaire John B. Yeon served as Multnomah County roadmaster for a dollar a year and worked long days supervising the road crews that built the highway in two years.

One challenge faced by Lancaster and Yeon was capping the highway's grade at 5 percent to lower the costs of hauling freight, as grades on prior Gorge roads—mostly built for wagons—could be as steep as 20 percent. Lancaster also ordained that curves have a minimum radius of a hundred feet for drivers' safety. These requirements demanded custom engineering solutions, except the goal wasn't merely to pass through the Gorge but, as Lancaster later wrote, "to find the beauty spots, or those points where the most beautiful things along the line might be seen in the best advantage, and if possible to locate the road in such a way as to reach them." Lancaster further pledged that "none of this wild beauty should be marred where it could be prevented" and "not one tree was felled, not one fern crushed, unnecessarily."[46]

The Columbia River Highway was dedicated at Crown Point before ten thousand celebrating spectators on June 7, 1916. At the White House, President Woodrow Wilson pressed a button that unfurled an American flag before the Gorge crowd. "The people of the Oregon Country have constructed perhaps the greatest highway, in the most magnificent setting in the world," a New York newspaper editorialized. "They have pierced the mountains through with cloistered tunnels and carried the road around sheer precipices on buttressed walls, being careful to keep the natural beauty all about them."[47]

To harmonize its discordant goals of accessing and preserving the Gorge's beauty, the highway employed twenty-four bridges, seven viaducts, four tunnels, and three sets of hairpin loops.[48] In the western Gorge, Lancaster used his Maryhill loops experience to build two and a half miles of roadway over a distance of one and a half miles, designing the highway to parallel itself five times while dropping six hundred vertical feet within one forty-acre tract. At Crown Point, Yeon suggested that Lancaster encircle the basalt outcropping instead of routing the highway behind it, so they hung a viaduct for the road and outer sidewalk from sheer cliffs seven hundred feet above the river, achieving an illusion that the highway was "standing on air." In 1918, Yeon built Vista House at Crown Point, a five-story, domed observatory faced by sandstone and topped with matte-glazed green tiles and a copper crown. It was "akin to ornamental structures in old-world parks and gardens," Yeon's son later observed, "the pavilions, follies, 'eye catchers' erected to enhance a view or terminate a vista. Here, where the garden is vast indeed and hardly in need of an artificial focal point, a similar role is nevertheless performed. The views which encompass the Vista House are more famous than the views from it."[49]

In the eastern Gorge at Mitchell Point west of Hood River, the highway builders carved the Tunnel of Many Vistas, four hundred feet long with a ten-degree curve, considered the "first important highway tunnel built in the United States."[50] Modeled after a tunnel at Lake Lucerne, Switzerland, that Lancaster and Hill had visited years earlier, the tunnel included five floor-to-ceiling, sixteen-foot-wide windows overlooking the Columbia. Two additional tunnels, spanning almost five hundred feet, were bored between Hood River and the town of Mosier, seven miles away. The Mosier Twin Tunnels included two eight-by-ten-foot windows separated by an open-air interlude, complete with a walkway carved into the face of the cliff. A few miles farther east, at Rowena Crest, two sets of horseshoe curves, overlaid in an almost perfect figure eight, wound seven hundred feet down the mountain to The Dalles.

When Sam Hill promoted the highway, he claimed that "we will cash in, year after year, on our crop of scenic beauty, without depleting it in any way." Thousands of middle-class families proved him right, touring in Model Ts and camping out like "Thoreau at 29 cents a gallon." But tourists wanted bathrooms, campgrounds, automobile repair garages, restaurants, and hotels, and Hill's crop soon showed signs of blight. A ninety-six-lot subdivision named Thor's Heights was platted above and behind Vista House five months before the highway was dedicated in June 1916, and prosperous Portlanders built lavish second homes in conspicuous places. Merchant and future governor Julius Meier built Menucha, a mansion with sweeping views and a cliff-edge pool on Chanticleer Point, just west of Vista House; his cousin Edward Ehrman imported Italian stone to construct an eleven-thousand-square-foot summer retreat nearby.[51]

Others had grander ideas yet, including Columbia Highlands, a proposal for golf links and polo grounds on top of Angel's Rest, a fifteen-hundred-foot-high bluff, and a lodge a thousand feet higher on nearby Devil's Rest. Access would be provided by the "highest elevator in the world," powered by an enormous plant using energy from Wahkeena Falls, one of the Gorge's best-known waterfalls. In 1915, another entrepreneur proposed "a massive hotel to wrap around Crown Point," reached by a gondola suspended by cable from Rooster Rock, a large basalt obelisk on the Columbia River. The hotel would include a "giant pipe organ and chimes [that] would broadcast concerts through the Gorge for miles."[52]

Many Portlanders were alarmed. Simon Benson, who was already concerned about the proliferation of "hot dog stands and . . . chicken shacks" in the Gorge, bought almost a thousand acres along the river, three hundred acres of which—including Multnomah and Wahkeena Falls—he donated to Portland, whose city limits were more than twenty miles away. Other land donations included eleven acres from George Shepperd at Shepperd Dell, two acres from Osmon Royal at Crown Point, and land near Bridal Veil Falls from Charles Coopey. But private gifts could not match the scale of development generated by the highway, and its benefactors turned to public entities to protect their dream. Oregon State Parks, created five years after the highway was dedicated, received the gifts of land made to Portland; a century later, the names of state parks attest to the generosity of those early donors—Benson, Dabney, Shepperd, Coopey, Yeon, and others.[53]

The business community recognized, however, that even the state's ability to preserve the Gorge landscape was limited. In 1907, the Portland Chamber of Commerce lobbied for national park designation for Mount Hood and seven surrounding townships—252 square miles in all, including much of the western Gorge in Oregon.[54] By 1916, the proposal had gained traction after the Chamber allied with the Progressive Business Men's Club, but there was opposition, especially from the US Forest Service.

The US Forest Service, established in 1905 within the Department of Agriculture, was responsible for sixty-three million acres of forest reserves previously managed by the Department of the Interior. The first chief of the agency was a territorial and sharp-elbowed friend of Theodore Roosevelt's, Gifford Pinchot, who chafed at creating national parks out of forest reserves, especially if they were not managed by the Forest Service. He believed the reserves should be managed conservatively, for the benefit of all people but ultimately for practical—and profitable—purposes, and he opposed the growing interest in national parks. He considered a separate federal parks agency "no more needed than two tails to a cat."[55]

Despite Pinchot's opposition, by late 1915 agreement was close to establishing the National Park Service within the Interior Department. On December 24, still hoping to block the creation of a rival agency and also acceding to the wishes of Portland's business community, the Forest Service withdrew from development 13,873 acres of land on the Oregon side of the Columbia Gorge, considering them "more valuable for their scenic beauty, and for public recreation and camping grounds, [than] for agriculture." The *Oregonian* celebrated the new classification—apparently the first such withdrawal in the nation—as a "Christmas present" and enthusiastically but inaccurately proclaimed that the "Forest on Highway is National Park."[56]

The order created the Columbia Gorge Park Division of the Oregon National Forest, but the *Oregonian*'s continuing confusion over the next half year is understandable. The National Park Service had not yet been created, and existing national parks and monuments were managed by a hodgepodge of agencies, including the Departments of War, Interior, and Agriculture. While the newly classified lands generally did not reach the Columbia River or even its narrow valley floor, the designation kept the uplands largely free from timber harvesting and development, including the Columbia High-lands project with its polo fields, golf links, and elevator. The Forest Service declined a similar designation for a four-mile stretch of national forest on the north bank later named for Gifford Pinchot.[57]

Despite its intentions, the Forest Service order did not stop efforts to create a national park. Former Oregon governor Oswald West huddled with the US senator for Oregon, George Chamberlain, in February 1916 and proposed a national park for most of Mount Hood and the Oregon side of the lower Gorge—including the fourteen thousand acres recently set aside by the Forest Service—which the senator agreed to introduce to Congress. On August 25, President Woodrow Wilson created the National Park Service, and a week later Secretary of the Interior Franklin Lane announced support for Chamberlain's "Mount Hood National Parks" bill, conditioned on Park Service management of the new park. That same day, Stephen Mather, director of the Park Service, was escorted through the Gorge by a group led by John B. Yeon and Sam Lancaster. When Mather toured the Gorge again in November, he "discuss[ed] with Portland businessmen the subject of the future of the Columbia Gorge."[58]

By fall, however, opposition to the proposed national park had grown, led by the Forest Service and local residents. Wasco County residents and the Hood River Commercial Club supported local sheepmen, who worried that the Park Service might restrict summer grazing on Mount Hood. The Forest Service was "not enthusiastic over the Mt. Hood National Park project," the *Oregonian* reported, having "sympathy with the sheepmen" and preferring to build more roads, including a loop road connecting the Columbia River Highway with Mount Hood.[59]

Nineteen sixteen was a portentous year for the Gorge. The Columbia River Highway was dedicated and established a pattern that would play out, time and again, over the next sixty years: new access to the Gorge spawned development, which threatened the resources that had initially attracted the access. Development, in turn, promoted efforts—primarily in Portland—to protect the Gorge; but comprehensive protection proved elusive. Although the national park proposal died in 1916 and became increasingly unrealistic as more land in the Gorge was developed, the National Park Service continued to advocate for a landscape that, sixty-four years later, it still considered "a nationally significant resource that warrants protection."[60] Its efforts would be thwarted by Forest Service opposition and Washington State's indifference, an attitude that later shifted to outright hostility.

Perhaps the earliest disagreement between the two states over the Gorge involved Beacon Rock. Called Che-che-op-tin by Natives and named Beacon Rock by William Clark, the rock bordered Wahclellah, a large village that the Corps of Discovery visited in 1805. The expedition first noticed the ocean's tidal influence here, eighteen months after leaving St. Louis and one hundred and forty river miles from the Pacific.[61]

Almost a century later, in November 1904, the *Oregonian* announced under a full-page photograph of Beacon Rock that Portland banker Charles Ladd had bought this "picturesque point" for reasons "not known." Also not known was that Ladd had purchased only a one-third interest. The remaining interests were bought by Henry Biddle—an eminent Portlander and descendant of the editor of the Lewis and Clark journals—and by Columbia Contract Company, which had recently incorporated to "buy and sell stone . . . [and] to develop quarries," among other purposes. A few months earlier, Columbia Contract had agreed to supply two hundred and forty thousand tons of rock to the Army Corps of Engineers for a jetty at the mouth of the Columbia, but its main quarry along the Columbia had subsequently been condemned by the Portland and Seattle Railway Company for a right of way. Columbia Contract needed a new source of rock to meet its obligations.[62]

In 1906, Beacon Rock's new owners—reluctantly, they said—bored holes in the landmark to accommodate one hundred and twenty tons of explosive powder. They planned to reduce the rock to rubble with "the biggest blast ever set off on the Pacific Coast," according to the *Oregonian*. A public furor erupted instead. Ladd protested that he had bought Beacon Rock to keep it from being quarried and had only changed his mind after being persuaded by the Corps that its high-quality stone was needed for the jetty. Others saw a ploy to increase the value of the right of way between Beacon Rock and the river as the railroad contemplated another condemnation.[63]

Biddle reasoned that excavating 3 million tons of rock would be "hardly noticeable," as it constituted just 5 percent of the monument, but another owner said that the entire monolith would be demolished. Biddle also complained that "a great deal of the wealth of Portland is due to the destruction of the primeval forests around Portland, and no cry has been raised." Ladd emphasized the inevitability of the landmark's destruction: "If the progress of the Northwest demands it, it must be taken down." The *Oregonian* echoed this point in a prescient editorial: "When sentiment and commercialism go to war the former is very apt to suffer defeat . . . [Beacon] Rock will in a few years cease to be a monument to the grandeur and prodigality of Nature and will enter bodily into the works of man as dictated his pride, his need and his ambition."[64]

But if the landowners and editors believed that Beacon Rock's destruction was inevitable, the public did not. Ladd and Biddle were called "plutocrats," and probably worse, and hiking, labor, literary, and other organizations passed resolutions to protect the monument. "Clergymen, leading citizens, women, teachers and all classes in Portland and throughout the state were horrified at the proposed destruction of such a majestic landmark," the *Oregonian* reported. "From every corner of the state came determined protest." Even the State of Washington joined in, seeking an injunction to prevent its nearby lands from being damaged by the blast.[65] Beacon Rock's owners believed that James Hill initiated the state's injunction to save him time and expense as he raced his nemesis E. H. Harriman to complete a rail line through the Gorge. The rival owners used litigation and sticks of dynamite lobbed at each other's work crews to gain advantage.[66]

In July 1906, a Skamania County jury ruled in favor of the railway's condemnation, awarding Beacon Rock's landowners $5,000, not the $100,000 to $500,000 they demanded. Nine years later, Ladd and Columbia Contract sold their interests to Biddle for a dollar, subject to deed restrictions that required the landmark not be "unnecessarily injured or damaged," except as necessary to build a trail to the summit.[67]

In the end, Ladd and Biddle are credited with saving Beacon Rock. Biddle was public-spirited and loved the Gorge. He financed and led significant archeological expeditions at Wishram and Miller Island and studied the Gorge's flora. He preserved much of Hamilton Mountain and would build a public trail to the top of Beacon Rock. Some believe that Ladd and Biddle were simply playing a bad hand, that they had always intended to protect Beacon Rock and—once the railroad considered condemning a right of way—were maximizing the land's value and their revenue. But this does not explain their purchase of Beacon Rock just months after the Columbia Contract Company had contracted to supply rock for the Columbia jetty. Nor does it account for their secret partnership—nor that Ladd was a stockholder in Columbia Contract and Biddle would become one.[68]

The outcry over Beacon Rock was the first widespread public protest over a Gorge landmark. As with subsequent Gorge protection efforts, legends would grow, saviors would become villains, villains would become saviors, and profits and pride would tempt even the most devoted. One constant though, through most of the twentieth century, was Oregon's consistent interest in protecting the Gorge and Washington's disinterest.

In 1918, Henry Biddle fulfilled his dream of building a public trail to the top of Beacon Rock, employing fifty-two hairpin turns and twenty-two wooden bridges over almost a mile to encircle the monolith. He lived another ten years, time enough to enjoy the trail's universal popularity, to deplore those who defaced it—picking wildflowers, rolling stones, and scratching names into its surface—and to wonder: "When will the uncivilized element of our population be educated to the point that it will be content to enjoy beauty without trying to destroy it?" After Biddle's death, his children sought to secure their father's dream and offered to donate Beacon Rock in the early 1930s to the State of Washington as a park. Governor Roland Hartley, a conservative, contrarian Republican who ran against government "waste and extravagance," accused Biddle's heirs of attempting a tax scam and refused the offer. His resistance did not deter Sam Boardman, who oversaw Oregon's state parks. Why not make Beacon Rock an Oregon state park, he wondered. "Why should we let just the width of a river destroy a scenic asset woven into a recreational garland belonging to both states. How should we stand by and see the death of a relative, though a bit distant."[69]

After reaching an agreement with Portland attorney Erskine Wood, a Biddle heir, to donate Beacon Rock to the State of Oregon, Boardman contacted the press. The *Oregonian* offered full-throated support, though acknowledging that "so far as we know no state in the union now owns a park in another state. It is a gift unprecedented." As Boardman had to have known, newspapers and citizens in Washington reacted to Oregon's audacity.[70] By 1933, Clarence Martin, a Democrat, replaced Governor Hartley and within two years Beacon Rock and part of nearby Hamilton Mountain, 263 acres in total, had been donated to Washington subject to deed restrictions that required the land be used "as a perpetual natural park" and "for no other purposes." Furthermore, no "unsightly buildings" would be permitted.[71] Washington had acquired its first park in the Columbia Gorge. Oregon had nineteen.

As the Wood family was trying to donate Beacon Rock, John Yeon was turning his attention to roads in the Gorge, an interest he had acquired as a young boy. By 1931, the number of cars in Oregon had exploded. They were also faster and larger, which forced the state to institute driving tests. These cars also put pressure on the narrow lanes and copious curves of the highway built by Yeon's father. That spring the *Oregonian* reported that "leading citizens" from The Dalles and Hood River had approached the Oregon Highway Commission to request that the historic highway be "widened and straightened into a super-highway." The highway's curves and attractions were a "menace to tourists," read one headline. Yeon was now twenty and quick to defend his beliefs—especially when they concerned the Columbia

Gorge and roads—and his voice was amplified by his family's wealth and connections.[72]

For several years he battled the Oregon Highway Commission, in particular its chairman Leslie Scott, on the alignment of the new highway. Scott dismissed Yeon's call for a gradual, curving highway that would preserve Gorge landmarks, enhance views, and still provide fast and safe transit. "Our people cannot live on scenery," said Scott, who was a generation older than Yeon. "[They] must have industry; will starve otherwise." Yeon responded with an eloquent defense of the economic benefits of tourism and a tart suggestion that, instead of locating a statue honoring Scott's father, Harvey, in Portland's Mount Tabor Park, "the stacking yard of the Hawley paper mill in Oregon City [would be] more consistent with your attitude."[73]

The highway through the Gorge was not the only project on which Yeon and Scott would clash. When a dance hall was proposed for Chapman Point on the north Oregon Coast, threatening the principal viewshed from Ecola State Park—the state's first coastal sanctuary, established in 1932—Yeon borrowed against an insurance policy and bought the oceanfront property. By then he had been appointed to the first Oregon State Parks Commission, whose charge was to advise the highway commission. The parks commission prioritized Chapman Point for purchase, but Scott opposed parks as much as he did curved roads. Spending "fifteen thousand dollars on that park," Scott said, "is like dumping it in the ocean." Yeon hoped to outlast Scott and convey the land to a suitable agency, but it would be a long wait. He would spend sixty years restoring the property: buying lots in an 1890s subdivision, vacating phantom roads, stabilizing sand dunes, and building fences to thwart trespassers.[74]

While sparring over Chapman Point, Yeon continued to battle Scott over the new Gorge highway. When the parks and highway commissions met jointly in June 1933, the highway commission announced that "Oregon's new state parks commission will have nothing to say as to highway alignment as far as the present state highway commission is concerned." Lest any ambiguity remain, one participant was happy to clarify: "'We,' heatedly declared Chairman Scott, 'are not going to build kinky roads—and that's final!'" In addition to serving on the parks commission, Yeon chaired the Columbia Gorge Committee of the Pacific Northwest Regional Planning Commission, a Roosevelt-inspired agency, and in August 1934 wrote a committee report attacking highway department policies that precluded "every vital consideration, except the attainment of a fast route." The report recommended a four-lane, river-level highway that preserved and revealed as much of the Gorge's beauty as a modern highway could. It called for limited access and the acquisition of significant rights of way, without which "roadside parasites, of every description, and their advertisements, will crowd along the road to capitalize on the public investment, mar the highway scenery and reduce the value of the route to the commonwealth constructing it." The highway commission had a different vision. "The people are howling for roads," Chairman Scott said, "and we haven't even enough money for roads." [75]

Yeon finally went over Scott's head, and with maps, photographs, surveys, and drawings flew to Washington, DC, to meet with Thomas MacDonald, the chief of the Bureau of Public Roads, who oversaw the nation's highway system. "With fear and trembling," Yeon entered MacDonald's immense office where the chief sat at a huge desk, "like Mussolini's." McDonald proved to be quite genial, however, and was intrigued by Yeon's presentation. He agreed to send his head landscape architect, Wilbur Simonson—who had designed the Mount Vernon Memorial Highway—to review the project. In June 1935 Simonson visited the Gorge and met with both the Columbia Gorge Committee and the Oregon Highway Commission, which soon capitulated—probably less from an aesthetic epiphany than from a practical assessment of how defiance might disfavor future federal funding. The three-mile "straight gash" that would have left an "angry scar" through the bottomlands below Crown Point was replaced by Yeon's "very gradual curve," which protected the scenery and views for future motorists. [76]

That year, an even more challenging issue faced the Gorge. The nation was stuck in the Depression, and the year before Governor Meier declared that Oregon was "dead broke." When President Franklin Roosevelt had campaigned in Portland in September 1932, he told voters that his goal was to employ as many people as quickly as possible. The Columbia River system held over 40 percent of the nation's hydroelectric potential, and building a dam and locks at Bonneville—just three miles downstream from Cascade Locks—could employ thousands of workers. Ignoring skeptics' concerns that the region could not generate the industry or river traffic to justify the dam's estimated $36 million cost—which would more than double by its completion—Roosevelt moved ahead with the plan and within a year the first of five thousand workers were clearing land for a work camp. While there were still skeptics of what some labeled the "Dam of Doubt," a dam at Bonneville was popular in Oregon and in Washington, too, especially after Roosevelt authorized Grand Coulee Dam four hundred and fifty miles upriver. [77]

Although John Yeon did not publicly oppose Bonneville Dam, he understood its potential consequences for the Gorge. The same month that Wilbur Simonson visited the Gorge, in June 1935, Yeon wrote a confidential report for his Columbia Gorge Committee proposing an interstate park— state parks on both sides of the Gorge—and extensive land acquisition by the National Park Service. Describing the Gorge as "a region of wild and magnificent scenery without parallel either in category or quality in all the varied landscapes of America," the report identified 159 tracts for Park Service acquisition in five areas of the western Gorge: Cape Horn, Beacon Rock, and the Little White Salmon River Canyon in Washington and Crown Point and Latourell Falls in Oregon. Yeon admired the National Park Service. Using a national platform provided by the magazine *American Forests*, he would soon recommend that an Olympic National Park be created out of seven hundred thousand acres of the Olympic National Forest, and his committee now proposed that the Park Service hold Gorge lands until they could be transferred to another agency.[78]

In 1937, Yeon's Columbia Gorge Committee published another report that identified the likely effect that Bonneville Dam would have on the Gorge landscape. The hundred-page report acknowledged that recent development and the economic potential of the Gorge had "preclude[d] its inclusion in the national park system" but reiterated the Gorge's national significance, "without parallel either in category or quality in all the varied landscapes of America." The committee again recommended an interstate park and emphasized that Bonneville Dam had precipitated a "crisis" in the Gorge that, if not addressed, would have "disastrous consequences."[79]

The report's eight detailed recommendations ranged from zoning to land acquisition to design standards for public works, but "the crucial factor in shaping the destiny of the Columbia Gorge" was the "power rate policy for Bonneville." The rate charged for electricity by the Bonneville Power Administration, which Congress created in 1937, was politically explosive and would almost single-handedly determine the future of the Gorge. The Portland Chamber of Commerce wanted graduated rates—lower for local companies, higher for those more distant from the dam—while the region's more remote cities, including Seattle, wanted a flat rate that provided no advantage for proximity. A graduated rate, where price increased with distance, would encourage industry to locate in the Gorge where rates were lowest, while a flat rate would not benefit a Cascade Locks factory over one built in Tacoma.[80]

John Yeon, never one to equivocate, foretold the inevitable consequences of a graduated rate:

> Factories strewn along the shore, for example, across from Multnomah Falls would irreparably damage the fine natural environment for the second highest waterfall in America. Factories near the basins of McCord Creek, Horsetail or Latourell Falls would rob them of their wild and picturesque settings. Factories near the base of Beacon Rock would cause this great monolith to loom above a spoliated foreground. The views from its summit would be over slag heaps and iron roofs, and all the miscellaneous jumble required by heavy chemical or metallurgical processing plants.
>
> Wherever industrialization occurred along the shores of the river, the trees would be cleared, the white sand beaches would disappear under pilings and wharves, and over a scraped and graded landscape would appear the factory mass and its satellite dumping yards and sheds, and its monotonous rows of working men's houses.[81]

It was not just belching factories and the infrastructure for thousands of workers that Yeon envisioned. "Large signs," he predicted, "would project their glaring messages in paint by day and in lights by night down the corridor of the Gorge." And with industry would inevitably come "noxious and growth-destroying fumes," that would subject the Gorge's "verdant slopes . . . to the withering gases as they rose vertically and prevailing winds through the Gorge would carry their effects over wide areas horizontally."[82]

Although Yeon would depreciate the value of his reports almost a half century later, he had sounded the clarion and solved what his committee believed was the "crucial factor": ensuring that Bonneville Dam did not set a graduated rate for its electricity. Seven months after the report was completed, President Roosevelt signed the Bonneville Project Act, creating a "postage stamp" rate that established a uniform cost for the dam's electricity, no matter how far it traveled. The Bonneville Power Administration sold its initial megawatts of power the following year, and one of its first customers was Cascade Locks which used the electricity to run the town's merry-go-round.[83]

As the nation entered World War II and war-related industry located in Portland to exploit Bonneville's inexpensive electricity, the Dam of Doubt critics were soon proven wrong. Shipbuilding and aluminum industries, which demanded enormous amounts of electricity, were attracted by Bonneville's

cheap power. The Kaiser shipyards would employ ninety-four thousand workers—including Nancy Neighbor's grandfather—and could build a Liberty
ship in two weeks. In 1944, a single aluminum plant used more of the dam's
electricity than did the entire City of Portland.[84]

Chapter 2
The Confluence, 1946–1979

When World War II ended in September 1945, President Harry Truman said winning the war would have been "impossible" without the Columbia River's hydroelectric dams, and Woody Guthrie celebrated the dams that made Washington and Oregon "factories hum / making chrome and making manganese and light aluminum."[1] The aluminum plants and other industries powered by the Columbia's currents propelled Portland into an era of unprecedented prosperity, which had favorable implications for many of the city's citizens, including the Neighbor family. But it would also raise new threats. The Columbia Gorge was bound to Portland, and as the city grew pressure on the Gorge increased. Its roads had to accommodate more cars, its vistas more visitors, its forests more clear-cuts, and its farms and fields more houses. Like most teenagers in Portland, thirteen-year-old Nancy Neighbor was not attuned to the relationship between her city and the landscape around it when she graduated from Ainsworth School in 1945, or four years later, after graduating from Catlin Gabel with high grades in history and low grades in typing. Instead, she focused on college.

Her best friends planned to go east, and Nancy wanted to attend Smith College in Massachusetts where a great aunt had been educated. But her brother Bobby was also heading to college, and their parents told Nancy that tuition and travel expenses for two children were beyond their means.[2] While unhappy that Bobby's education was favored over hers, Nancy did not linger over her disappointment and decided to attend a presentation by Scripps College, a women's liberal arts school in Claremont, California. She was drawn to photographs of the beautiful campus and the strong academics, and she reasoned that a scholarship would be easier to win at a school where there was less competition from New England students and none from boys. She also knew that travel to Southern California would not be costly. Just months after hearing her parents' disappointing news, Nancy won an acceptance letter from Scripps, a scholarship, a student loan, and an on-campus waitressing position. Fanny Bishop bought her granddaughter a train ticket, and Nancy and a Scripps-bound friend boarded the Southern Pacific Cascade for the twenty-hour trip to the Bay Area, where the girls transferred to the Lark and arrived in Los Angeles thirteen hours later.

The college was founded by Ellen Browning Scripps, a businesswoman, suffragist, and philanthropist, and its motto—*Incipit vita nova* or "Here begins a new life"—was prescient for a seventeen-year-old who had never traveled farther than Elk Lake. Nancy had never seen a palm tree—which she found "unbelievably exciting"—a cactus, an orange tree, or "pepper trees with those pink berries." She called attending Scripps a "fairy tale."[3]

The architecture was mostly Spanish Colonial Revival,[4] a Southern California style that borrowed heavily from Mediterranean countries and the region's Spanish mission heritage. Buildings were graced with arches, and breezy loggias formed inner courtyards, their walls lightly colored and thickly plastered. Roofs of rounded pan tiles, in soft spectrums of red and orange clay, matched terra cotta pots and basket-weave brick pavers below. Decorative ironwork railings and trim on heavy wooden doors provided contrast and detail, as did cast stone columns and copper downspouts, burnished moss green. Students enjoyed private bedrooms and balconies overlooking interior gardens, where fountains splashed against mosaics of hand-colored tiles.

The profusion of trees and flowering plants—selected by the college's gardeners to bloom during the school year—and Scripps's formal and informal gardens captivated Nancy. Long *allées* of tulip, olive, and ornamental orange trees with boxwood hedges framed views of the San Gabriel Mountains. Sycamores, coast live oaks, purple orchid trees, pomegranates, peppers, silk floss, butterfly orchid trees, a kumquat tree, and a carob, "large and squat . . . powerful in its massive trunk and branching structure," grew on campus.[5] Wisteria, hibiscus, camellias, azaleas, and exotic bird of paradise plants flourished, and the fragrance of blooming orange trees, lemon-scented gum trees, jasmine, honeysuckle, oleander, and flowering quince infused the air. Scenes from Shakespeare had been carved in bas relief at Sycamore Court, and a garden wall displayed *The Flower Vendors*, a multipaneled mural by Alfredo Ramos Martinez depicting indigenous women with brightly colored flowers overflowing their arms and baskets and, seemingly, the mural itself.

The setting—plantings, architecture, and artwork—shaped Scripps's culture, as did formal candlelight dinners and afternoon teas on the Olive Court terrace. The campus was different from anything Nancy had experienced, and she was determined "to make her best effort and not let opportunities go to waste." She even enjoyed waitressing, despite the long hours, and was soon promoted to head waitress and given the responsibility of recruiting and training other waitresses and organizing the dining rooms. She studied late into the night and excelled in a course load weighted toward the humanities. Romantic poets were once again a favorite.[6]

By her senior year, Nancy had blossomed. The sun had lightened her dark hair, and she was physically strong from playing tennis and spending weekends at the beach, where she swam for miles in the warm Pacific, or in the mountains, where she led hikes deep into the San Gabriels. When not immersed in her studies or working in the dining halls, she was outdoors, where the more studious aspects of her disposition were edged aside by a gregarious nature and a ready-to-laugh personality. She had scores of friends, including boys from nearby colleges. One boy who Nancy was "crazy about," according to an old friend, was the son of an MGM Goldwyn Girl, but when he pressed for a more intimate relationship, Nancy refused, feeling "immature . . . way out of my comfort level," and the relationship ended.[7]

At graduation in 1953, Nancy received high marks for leadership and character. "Nancy has made the best adjustment, and has been the best organized and accomplished . . . of any girl that I have yet seen here in Scripps," the head of residence remarked.[8] The college had reinforced and polished many of the qualities that Nancy had possessed when she first arrived: a love of beauty, a natural enthusiasm, and the drive and discipline necessary to succeed. More than anything, though, Nancy left Scripps with a preternatural confidence in her own abilities.

Paying back her college loan was her first priority, and she got in touch with a Scripps alumna whose husband owned the Camelback Inn in Scottsdale, Arizona, to arrange employment for herself and a friend in the fall. Nancy would teach tennis and swimming at the resort, while Susi Seley would be a dining room hostess and arrange social events for guests' children. After a few months working as an assistant librarian at Reed College while living in her parents' new West Hills home—Bob's company was finally prospering—Nancy and Susi drove south.

September and October at the Camelback Inn were luxurious, hot, and dry. Weeks of entertaining and teaching children slid by for the two friends, enlivened by early morning hikes up Camelback Mountain, scorpions in their shoes, and a rattlesnake "lounging on our doorstep." The routine ended abruptly one November evening when Nancy joined Susi, who was overseeing the resort's formal dining room. At one table, a toddler was screaming and throwing food while her parents ignored her. Nancy marched through the dining room and quietly but firmly informed the parents that this was "unacceptable behavior." She plucked the startled child from the table and swooped out of the room, leaving the stunned parents staring at the empty high chair and its scattered detritus, as though a hawk had glided down from the McDowell Mountains and snatched a protesting piglet from its peccary pack. Nancy was fired the next day.

According to her sister Betsy, Nancy "thought she was right . . . knew she was right, and had confidence in her decision." The owner—or perhaps his wife—gave Nancy and Susi $100 apiece before they drove to Portland, where Nancy found a job as a receptionist for an RCA distributor and resumed her assistant librarian responsibilities at Reed. Years later, she acknowledged that her actions at Camelback were due to her "youth and incompetence" and that getting fired was "a shock [and] quite a comeuppance."[9]

Greater comeuppance came a year later when Nancy announced her engagement to Bill Brown, by all accounts a charming, good-looking Yale graduate whom she had met at Camelback. Wedding invitations were mailed, and everyone was thrilled for Nancy, including Mary Wall, an inquisitive and astute family friend who was fiercely protective of the young people in her life. When Mrs. Wall's Yale friends said they didn't know Bill, she called the Yale registrar, who had no record of his attendance. She unearthed the phone number for Bill's mother—who lived somewhere in the South—and that conversation did not go well. Mrs. Wall then called Mary Ann Neighbor and insisted that she talk with Mrs. Brown directly. Nancy soon learned, with her wedding just days away, that she was engaged to a "total fraud." Bill had never attended Yale; furthermore, he had a daughter from a previous marriage. Nancy didn't want pity, which just made her feel worse. She canceled the wedding, sent out notices, and went back to work.[10]

A few months later, work—and Mary Wall—once more led Nancy away from Portland. Mrs. Wall's daughter Caroline, about to join her family at their St. Croix estate in the Virgin Islands, asked to bring along her close friend Betsy Neighbor. Cane Garden, a former sugar cane plantation, sat on a hill overlooking the Caribbean. The front lawn swept down to the estate's mile of beachfront, and ruins of former plantation buildings littered the 265-acre grounds. Lincoln High School insisted that the two girls be tutored during their semester-long absence, and Mrs. Wall asked if Nancy would accept this responsibility and also serve as secretary for her husband, Howard Wall, who imported rum and exported wood products. Nancy didn't hesitate.

After tutoring her charges in the morning—including Caroline's fifth-grade brother, Macy—and assisting Mr. Wall in the afternoon, Nancy spent her evenings dancing to the rhythm of steel drums at one of St. Croix's little nightclubs. "Nancy was very, very popular," recalled Hunty Wall, Caroline's sister, "and there were more eligible young men than there were women." When the Walls went back to Portland, Nancy chose to stay for several more months, living at Cane Garden and working for the manager of a new hotel.[11]

Returning to Oregon that summer of 1956, she spent time with Bruce Russell. Almost nine years older than twenty-four-year-old Nancy, Bruce was intelligent and creative, a wiry, handsome man with craggy features and a wry sense of humor. He loved the outdoors—riding horses, clearing brush, building post and rail fences—as much as he enjoyed prowling the Oregon Historical Society's stacks for a pioneer diary or studying military campaigns and the frontier West. Bruce "surround[ed] himself with art and engage[d] in artistic endeavors constantly," his son Aubrey recalled, "often with many over-lapping projects involving oil and watercolor paintings, story writing, callig-raphy, drawing, crafts and photography." Four of Bruce's great-grandparents had come over the Oregon Trail in 1852, and his family's wealth originated from a settler who had been wounded in an Indian attack. An arrow had pierced his back, and it took almost eight years to work its way through his body. In gratitude for years of nursing and rehabilitation provided by Bruce's ancestors, the settler had left a bequest in 1881 that became the family's pro-prietary stake in Olds, Wortman & King, a Portland department store.[12]

Bruce quoted—extemporaneously and frequently—passages by Oliver Wendall Holmes, Shakespeare, cowboy poets, and others to buttress opinions that were unvarnished and entertaining. He was as comfortable in the frayed jeans, worn cowboy boots, and the tattered flannel shirts he wore to cut trees and repair gates at his parents' property in Portland's West Hills as he was in the seersucker suits, narrow ties, and brightly banded straw hats he wore to his job at Merrill Lynch, where his financial strategies attracted clients and grew portfolios.

The couple shared a passion for beauty, nature, the landscapes and history of the American West, and almost any strenuous activity, including hiking, tennis, and dancing. Both were curious, enjoyed hard work, and drew pleasure from tangible accomplishments. Neither liked to waste time or money. Bruce's family motto, "Honesty–Industry–Frugality," and one of his favorite quotes, "Pleasure is not an end to itself, but the byproduct of doing a hard job well," resonated with Nancy.[13]

The couple had their first date in a second-hand Old Town wood canoe with a canvas batwing sail during a summer squall at Elk Lake. In *Old Time Memories of Elk Lake*, which Bruce later wrote for their children, he recounted standing on shore "when Nancy chanced along. I promptly suggested a little sail, she was game and we got the canoe and took off. It was a big wind, a real blow, coming from the north right down the South Sister . . . [and] the sailboats on the lake were tipping way over and just flying along. . . . As soon as the wind hit our sail we took off like a scalded rabbit!" The gale subsided as quickly as it arose, forcing Bruce to "laboriously" sail back over two-thirds of the lake, against the wind. "But however much I revealed my inadequacies as a sailor tacking our way home," he wrote, "I can't imagine, company considered, that I was in much of a hurry."[14] Nancy and Bruce courted over the summer and fall, and in November she headed back to Cane Garden for six months to resume her tutoring and secretarial work.

Bruce's weekly correspondence with Nancy was light and humorous, brimming with details about his Merrill Lynch strategies and his work at Westwinds, the property his parents had named for the Pacific breezes that crossed the Coast Range and brushed against the Tualatin Mountains that form Portland's West Hills. He wrote about the changing seasons, politics, the sculpture and painting classes he was taking, Broadway plays he saw, books he was reading, and research he was doing. The letters were always affectionate: "*I miss you.* Bought a new pair of heavy work shoes the other day and found myself thinking as I put them on for the first time: wonder how many times I'll put these on to go hiking with Nancy. Hope it'll be many . . . and not too long from now." He disclosed having recently read Boswell's *In Search of a Wife* and described himself as a "fireside-and-book-man" who was leading such a quiet life that he was considering relearning French. And he reminded Nancy what she was missing, "down there in your insect-infested outpost," by celebrating the blooming of crocuses at Westwinds, enclosing the season's first Johnny Jump Up, or simply describing a sunset and sunrise: "Tonight, it was particularly beautiful with a great diagonal slash of red across the sky above a delicate gradation of blues down to the foothills and into the dark valley. In the morning [Mt.] Jefferson peeps above the southern hills. . . . Mt. Hood stands in dark silhouette against the blazing orange sky . . . and St. Helens stands cold and aloof in the sparse light to the north."[15]

In early April, Nancy invited Bruce to visit her, and he agreed immediately: "A nice day yesterday and last night a bright quarter moon. When it's full I'll be with you!" He arrived in St. Croix on Sunday morning, April 14.

Nancy Russell on her
wedding day in St.
Croix. Russell archives.

Six days later, he and Nancy were engaged. On April 25, Nancy sent a letter
to her parents and Betsy announcing their engagement and explaining that
the wedding would be in three days. "Bruce & I are going to be married this
coming Saturday," Nancy began the seven-page letter.

> I do want for you to be happy with us & not feel neglected or left out.
> You are most certainly the most important people in my life (next
> to Bruce) and I love you all so much, even if I am poor at showing
> it at times, and the last thing I want to do is to hurt you or make you
> feel that you as parents are missing something by not giving me a
> large wedding with trimmings. We had talked about the large wedding
> only in a vague way, but you, Mother, have said yourself that small
> weddings are nicer, and *this* is a small wedding.

They would be married at St. Paul's, an early nineteenth-century Angli-can church in Frederiksted. Nancy had already talked with the minister and procured a wedding license—for forty cents—from a local judge. Although Episcopal tradition called for the bride to be given away, "I felt that as long as father could not be here I would prefer to have no one," Nancy wrote, "and the minister said that was alright." Ever frugal, Nancy wore her white sundress, and Bruce borrowed Howard Wall's pants. The Walls served as wit-nesses. "Oh yes," Nancy beamed in the letter's last line, "I will have a bouquet of white oleander & white plumeria."[16]

Woven through the whirlwind, romantic week in the Caribbean were bands of pragmaticism. Nancy's view of relationships had matured since her broken engagement two years earlier and had evolved even during her nine-month courtship with Bruce. "I had other romances," she said,

> and got through the super romantic stage to thinking about something a little more permanent than great roman[ce]. It was a gradual thing that worked out very, very well because we really liked each other—we loved each other—but we really liked each other and got along tremendously well. Our families knew each other and . . . it's awfully easy to have that kind of marriage where everybody knows who everybody is and everyone gets along with everybody. It misses a lot of the surprises that make life exciting but I'm sure it also avoids a lot of the tar pits people fall into when they marry someone they don't know very well or don't know their family.[17]

Back in Portland, the newlyweds moved into a one-bedroom basement apartment a quick walk from Westwinds, where Bruce had been born thirty-seven years earlier. He lived there with his mother, Helen Wortman Russell; his father, Allan, had died almost a decade before. Nine months later, Nancy gave birth to Sally; twenty months after Sally, Wendy was born. Soon after, Bruce's mother bought a house nearby, and Bruce, Nancy, and their children moved to Westwinds.

Bruce's parents had bought Westwinds in 1919. The one-story, modest house was modeled after Cloud Cap Inn on Mount Hood, where Allan Russell loved to hike.[18] Although less than three miles from downtown Port-land, Westwinds had an orchard and patches of tall Douglas-fir whose heavy boughs caught storm-driven gusts, causing their crowns to bow high above the property. The pastures at Westwinds grew knee-high grass in the spring and sloped down to the south and west, creating views of coastal peaks and the valley floor a thousand feet below.

The Russells settled into a routine. Bruce arrived at his Merrill Lynch desk by six-thirty in the morning, in time for the opening of the New York Stock Exchange on the West Coast, and returned home soon after the market's one o'clock close. After hugging his daughters and playing catch or pushing them on a tree swing or go-carts he had built, he repaired fences, mended gates, pruned trees, caught moles, and chopped wood. He bought a flock of sheep—as much for the ambience as for weed management—and later ordered, from Switzerland, sheep bells whose timbre he particularly enjoyed. Inspired in equal parts by self-reliance and frugality, Bruce also built furniture and managed much of the carpentry, plumbing, and remodeling around the house, taking pleasure in doing a hard job well.

Nancy was "occupied all the time, every single day." She looked after the sheep and their German shepherd, cleaned house, cooked, washed dishes, mowed Westwinds' large lawn, planted and watered the gardens, and oversaw household finances. Bruce, who wanted dinner served promptly at six each evening, also required some looking after. More than anything, though, she immersed herself in motherhood. "I adored having a child," she later said. "I couldn't even believe the bond."

> There isn't anything more demanding, more important, anything that is harder work, that exists. And to keep it interesting for yourself so that you are taking children on trips and inviting friends over. I think being a mother and doing it in a way that keeps everybody sane and happy and having fun is a tremendous challenge and worth doing too.[19]

In the laundry room, Nancy hung a print of Edgar Degas's *Women Ironing*, which portrays two working-class women, one leaning hard on an iron over a rumpled shirt, the other upright, stretching, hand supporting her head and yawning broadly from exhaustion. Nancy found ways to alleviate much of the drudgery, however, inviting other young mothers to the house, where they watched their toddlers chase the lambs across the lawn and sway on the swing Bruce had dangled from the limb of a pin oak tree planted by his parents before the war.

As a teenager, Nancy had been frustrated at the unfairness of being a girl, and she "terribly" wanted to have a son, according to friends. In late April 1963—five years after Sally was born—Nancy gave birth to Hardy Christian

Nancy Russell with her son Hardy. Russell archives.

Russell, named for Bruce's grandfather, Hardy Christian Wortman, a child of Oregon Trail immigrants who may have earned his name when his mother delivered him, alone, in a log cabin along the banks of the Willamette River. Having a son was "the icing on the cake," according to his Aunt Betsy. With wavy blond hair, pink cheeks, bright blue eyes, and an engaging disposition, he was Nancy's "golden boy." In a photograph taken the following spring, Nancy carries Hardy in a backpack. A broad smile illuminates her face as she turns toward her son, whose mouth, open in laughter, nudges his chubby cheeks against his eyes while his left hand rests on his mother's shoulder.[20]

In February 1965, two months before his second birthday, Hardy came down with a fever, and Nancy took him to see the family's pediatrician, Lendon "Dunny" Smith. In addition to practicing medicine, Smith acted, appeared regularly in the *Oregonian*'s society pages, and hosted *Call the Doctor* on Portland's NBC affiliate, where he dispensed medical advice. After giving Hardy a "cursory glance," the doctor sent them home. The boy's fever spiked the next day, and when Smith finally returned Nancy's increasingly panicked calls, he told her: "You're strong, you can weather this one, he's just got the flu. Just put him in a cold bath before he goes to bed." Nancy begged Smith to admit Hardy to the hospital, but to no avail. She tried to sooth her son, but when she placed him in a cold bath he started convulsing. Nancy and Bruce rushed him to the hospital, where he died that evening.[21]

Nancy was inconsolable and became deeply depressed. "The world disappeared for her," Sally remembered, recalling her mother sobbing uncontrollably, months later, during routine chores or when a waitress asked the family, "where's your cute little boy?" She "couldn't shake" Hardy's death and talked about nothing else. Bruce compared Nancy's anguish to the protagonist in *Giselle*, who collapsed in spasms of grief and died of a broken heart. He arranged for friends to stay with her while he was at work and worried for his daughters. She eventually saw a therapist, although she spent the first four sessions crying.[22]

Nancy's depression challenged her family. The upbeat, cheerful mother and wife whom they relied on to be resilient and in charge had vanished, but the couple "wanted to keep our family going," according to Nancy, and "we went through the motions of family life." She rarely discussed Hardy's death: not with her mother, who had her own experience with depression; not with her sister Betsy, with whom she shared a close relationship; and not with her immediate family. Nancy "shut down emotionally when Hardy died," Sally remembered, and the subject of his death would remain "simply untouchable, something that you never, ever, ever talked about."[23]

After Hardy's death, Dunny Smith's career, at least as a showman, continued to thrive. He wrote several books and appeared frequently on television, hosting a daily spot on ABC from 1966 to 1969—*The Children's Doctor*—and logging dozens of appearances on *The Tonight Show* with Johnny Carson, *The Mike Douglas Show*, and the *New Hollywood Squares*. His medical philosophy included an almost messianic faith in megavitamin doses and homeopathic remedies and an aversion to modern drugs and vaccines. He was twice placed under probation by the Oregon Board of Medical Examiners between 1970 and 1975 for wrongfully prescribing medication and finally surrendered his medical license in 1987 under pressure over unethical practices.[24]

Nancy emerged from her depression a year after Hardy's death. One friend credited her therapist with helping to "unplug the grief." Passage of time helped, along with her antipathy to being pitied, and playing tennis gave her something to look forward to, providing the hard exercise that had always been her "medicine" and forcing her to concentrate on something other than Hardy. She also set incremental goals for herself, including securing employment as executive secretary for Oregon's World Affairs Council. More than anything, though, she recognized that "we had two other children, and responsibilities." And she was pregnant again. Alison was born in June 1966, followed by the Russells' last child, Aubrey, two years later. "We had a boy," Nancy recounted years later, "and that was the end of having children."[25]

Once again, she immersed herself in her children. "We didn't have a big social life," Nancy recalled, "but there were always kids over here playing hide and seek, olly olly oxen free." Bruce "loved being in a child's world," according to Aubrey. When home, he painted, sang, told stories, and played chess with his children. He built toys and tree forts, a zip line from the top of the barn to the ground, and plywood wagons with rudimentary steering wheels that they would race down the driveway. Although neither Nancy nor Bruce was a particularly firm disciplinarian, their children were not allowed to sleep late or spend their days idly, adhering to Bruce's admonition from *King Lear* that "nothing will come of nothing."[26]

Music from a record player filled their home: musicals from Nancy's childhood, "the Boston Pops, Herb Alpert, folk music, classical piano and symphonies," Aubrey remembered.[27] She could enliven a dull day by dancing to an early Beatles hit, to her children's horror and delight. The Russells' small black-and-white television was relegated to a closet, brought out on occasional weekends so the children could watch *Wild Kingdom* or *Wonderful World of Disney*. Nancy paid bills and oversaw expenses, collected S&H Green Stamps for redemption at the grocery, patched worn clothes, made curtains, canned Westwinds peaches, pears, and plums—much as her mother did in Dundee during the Depression—and fulfilled Bruce's family motto.

In many ways, Bruce set the pattern of the family's life, one that was consistent and centered on home. He worked at Merrill Lynch in the morning, played with his children in early afternoon and at bedtime—reading them to sleep or spinning stories about the Wild West—and did chores at Westwinds in the late afternoon. He disliked going out for dinner, so they rarely did. Nancy cooked dinners for six, at six, and by day's end, Bruce would be restored. After dinner he painted a landscape, researched frontier history, or wrote memoranda on topics ranging from the "meaning of art" to morality.[28]

By the end of her day, Nancy would be worn out. While she appreciated all that Bruce did for the family, she started to chafe at how responsibilities were not shared equally, especially the mundane, laborious tasks that filled her days. To introduce the children to new activities—and to make it more interesting for her—she took them swimming or to her tennis games in Portland's Rose Garden and Strohecker's Park, where they slid down hills on cardboard sheets and hit balls to their mother. As the children grew older, their outings stretched to historic landmarks such as the Willamette Stone, the origin point for land surveys in Oregon and Washington, and the Pittock Mansion, the home of an early *Oregonian* publisher, or the Rhododendron Test Garden, the Berry Botanical Garden, and the Japanese Garden.[29]

Soon their excursions moved farther afield to the farms, beaches, and roadside stands of Sauvie Island, where the Willamette River flows into the Columbia, and to the western Columbia Gorge. The children rolled down the dunes on Sand Island near Phoca Rock, raced along Rooster Rock's mud-flats across from Mount Pleasant and Mount Zion, swam where the Hood River joins the Columbia, and climbed four thousand feet to the top of Larch Mountain, high above Multnomah Falls. They walked trailside with their mother as she recited the histories and Latin names of wildflowers, including one of her favorites, *Penstemon barrettiae*, a Gorge endemic with serrated leaves and understated pink and purple flowers that thrives on thin-soiled cliffs and talus slopes. It is one of few botanical species named after a woman, Almeta Hodge Barrett, an Oregon pioneer and nurse who transplanted seeds from nearby cliffs to her Hood River garden.[30]

The family spent vacations at Elk Lake or on the eastern slope of Wyoming's Bighorn Mountains at Eaton's Ranch, founded in 1904 by three Eaton brothers. Year after year in late spring, the Russells returned to the same cabin, where they rode horses from sunup to sundown. Bruce loved Eaton's and prepared over the winter for the long days on horseback by mounting a saddle he rigged on ropes in their barn's hayloft. At the ranch, he galloped at full speed around a set of unimproved roads, called the "racetrack," and led the family through public lands and pine forests and over mountain passes. Nancy hiked, scouring the hillsides for wildflowers, and when she rode, she often belted out Cole Porter's "Don't Fence Me In":

> Oh, give me land, lots of land under starry skies above
> Don't fence me in
> Let me ride through the wide-open country that I love
> Don't fence me in
> . . .
> I want to ride to the ridge where the west commences
> And gaze at the moon till I lose my senses
> And I can't look at hobbles and I can't stand fences
> Don't fence me in.[31]

Nancy Russell with her children at Rooster Rock State Park in 1971. Russell archives.

In 1973, with all of her children in school, Nancy was free of the day-to-day obligations of child-raising. "Finally, after years of being a mother," she later remembered, "I was able to have some time to myself which I loved because I had compelling interests and was always sort of frustrated at being a mother. I loved being a mother . . . but still there are conflicts when you are raising children; you can't do everything you want to."[32] She joined organizations that combined her passion for the outdoors with her intellectual interests and that appealed to her social nature. She researched the Oregon Trail and studied native plants and wildflowers at the Portland Garden Club, mastering subjects that provided opportunities for leadership and drew her toward the Columbia Gorge. She also returned to the tennis court, with a vengeance.

In her youth, Nancy had excelled at tennis. Unable to afford lessons, her game had developed into a mishmash of choppy strokes and an unconventional, forward-charging style. She rushed to the net and pressured her opponent into making mistakes. She hit backhand volleys with her forehand, forcing her racquet up and over her head, from right to left, and contorting her upper body until it paralleled the court. She faced her opponent squarely, and her consistency and compulsion to chase down every shot more than compensated for her unconventional strokes.

Tennis professional Mike Metz later observed that Nancy "used her athleticism to correct a lousy stroke" and "was probably one of best woman athletes in the country." But it was her mind, he insisted, that won most games. On the court, her intensity allowed few smiles, little chatter, and few compliments for her opponent. Her friend Mary Bishop, a competitive player, once asked Nancy why she had to beat her so badly. "If I lose my focus, for even a minute," she responded, "I'm lost." She hated losing a single point and even tried to win warm-ups, where she drilled corner shots against bewildered opponents and analyzed and exploited their weaknesses, playing, Metz observed, for "the thrill of the kill [where] each point was war."[33]

Her game was a generation ahead of most of her competitors, according to Metz. She "played like a man [and] was willing to sweat, and be seen sweating" at a time when women "were not supposed to show that you tried that hard [or] cared that much." Nancy was aggressive at net when women played primarily from the baseline. Most women played upright, but Nancy attacked, face flushed, sweat pouring, knees bent, and eyes level before slamming a sharp, angled volley to finish the point. "Hit and go forward, hit and go forward" was her strategy, and it wore opponents down. According to Metz, Nancy not only played like a man, but she liked playing against men. For her, tennis was less camaraderie than competition.[34]

Nancy won the Portland City Championship for singles and doubles in 1964, the year before Hardy died. At the end of her year-long depression after his death, the sport helped her emerge from the darkness. By 1967, she had again won Portland's doubles title and was runner-up in singles. During the 1970s, with her children in school, she won the club championship at the West Hills Racquet Club for the entire decade, every year but one.[35]

Tennis fulfilled her need for hard exercise and competition, but she also needed intellectual stimulation. In 1973, drawn to pioneer accounts of the Oregon Trail—often written by women, many of whom had faced the harrowing passage through the Columbia Gorge—she volunteered at the Oregon Historical Society, working as a docent and giving tours and lectures. The Oregon Trail turned into a family project, and Nancy and Bruce soon discovered—after nights poring over pioneer journals and maps by their evening fire—that many of the so-called authoritative books on the Oregon Trail were wrong on key details. Motivated by curiosity as much as by correcting the record, they inspected the trail from Independence, Missouri, to Oregon City over a series of vacations from 1977 to 1979, their children often in tow.[36]

On the road, Bruce and Nancy corralled ranchers—whose furrowed faces resembled their dusty washboard roads—to guide them to isolated sections of the Oregon Trail. They documented wagon ruts four feet deep in sandstone near Guernsey, Wyoming; Douglas-fir, scarred where overlanders had used ropes to lower wagons down Laurel Hill on Mount Hood; and striking vistas like the Sweetwater River Valley, Devil's Gate, and South Pass, where the Russell children collected agates striped red and white, pink and blue-gray. One day, when Nancy and Bruce were exploring a secluded ranch in Wyoming, they were ordered off the property by "two tough and hostile gun-slinging cowpokes." They complied but were "determined to explore that part," Nancy said, "so now we're trying to locate the owners of the property and hopefully get back in, without getting shot at."[37]

They enjoyed their time together outdoors, often trekking miles over rough terrain. Bruce sometimes stopped to paint a memorial scene—such as where the trail climbed a Gorge hillside along the Deschutes River—while Nancy studied wildflowers, many named after, or by, early explorers whom Oregon Trail emigrants had admired: beargrass, with its plumes of creamy white flowers, large yellow mule ears, and the lavender and yellow blooms of Rocky Mountain irises. She learned about more than the Oregon Trail, including how the National Park Service had set high standards for protecting and interpreting national historic sites and national monuments. By 1980, Nancy and Bruce had created an Oregon Trail program for the state's public school curriculum, which Nancy presented to the legislature on Oregon's 122nd anniversary. Her daughter Sally later said that her mother's work—her exhaustive research, attention to detail, and "strong sense and understanding of this place, the people who touched it and the actual landscape"—was ideal training for an advocacy campaign.[38]

In 1973, Nancy joined three organizations, all of them dedicated to preserving Oregon flora: the Berry Botanical Garden, the Native Plant Society of Oregon, and the Portland Garden Club (PGC). While she participated in all three, it was the Garden Club that would especially reward her. The club had been founded in 1924 to address broader horticultural interests than the Portland Rose Society, whose mission was to "perpetuate . . . the glory of the rose." Four years later, the PGC joined the New York City–based Garden Club of America (GCA). Before long, it was one of the national organization's largest affiliates and one of only two to own a clubhouse, which was located on a half block of land in the West Hills donated by the Biddle-Wood family eight years after it donated Beacon Rock to the State of Washington.[39]

While the GCA was not founded as a traditional advocacy organization, it soon recognized that attaining its mission—"to aid in the protection
of native plants and birds," among other goals—would require the garden
gloves to come off. During the 1910s and 1920s, the GCA led a series
of successful campaigns: to conserve American wildflowers, particularly
along roadsides; to protect hollies, western pines, and mountain laurel
from indiscriminate holiday overharvesting; and to impose restrictions on
imported bulbs, a stance that earned the club the enmity of the American
Nurserymen lobby. In 1930, a delegation from the GCA's annual meeting
in Seattle traveled in private railcars to the redwood groves of Northern
California, where they witnessed thousand-year-old trees, two hundred
fifty feet tall and thirty feet in diameter, being cut down for railroad ties
and telephone poles. Incensed by the destruction and "horrified by 'hot
dog stands' and other tourist concessions invading the roads that rambled
through the trees," the GCA purchased a stand of redwoods, the 2,552-acre
Canoe Creek Grove. Within a half century, the national organization and
its affiliates had bought sixteen more groves, eventually protecting over five
thousand acres of redwood forests.[40]

Portland Garden Club membership was by invitation only, and the club
was thriving when Nancy was invited to join in 1973. With three hundred
members, twenty-seven standing committees—including eleven "Hort
groups"—met monthly. Horticulture was valued over flower arranging and
conservation was a PGC tradition. In the 1920s, the club had sponsored
legislation to protect wildflowers on state lands from sale and export, and in
the late 1940s the club had saved 160 acres of rare myrtle trees in southern
Oregon. Nancy began to organize wildflowers hikes in the Gorge for Garden
Club members. She also guided Native Plant Society hikes, where she met
experts like historian Ivan Donaldson. "I learned more about the historic
significance of the Gorge on that day," Nancy recalled about a hike with
Donaldson, "than I had in all the years before." Soon she was photographing
wildflowers in the Gorge and was encouraged to assemble a slide show.[41]

Her first presentation on Gorge wildflowers was to the Portland Garden
Club in January 1978. Images of flowers in bright orange, crimson, violet,
and yellow hues, framed by silvery escarpments and the blue Columbia
River, dropped from her carousel as Nancy wove through Gorge history,
emphasizing stories of early explorers and collectors and their relationship to
the plants that carried their names. To her surprise, the show proved "quite
popular,"[42] and she presented it before another fifteen or twenty groups by the

end of the year. Wallace Huntington, a leading Portland landscape architect, was impressed and invited a friend, John Yeon, to attend one of her lectures.

Forty-one years earlier, in 1937, Yeon's Columbia Gorge Committee had issued its last report. He had also completed an architectural commission that year for Aubrey Watzek, his friend and Oregon State Parks Commission colleague, which earned him international acclaim. Yeon had selected four acres in the West Hills for Watzek's home and had designed the residence, its interior, much of its furniture, and its landscaping and garden. He had employed minimalist, elegant lines, natural materials, and sensitivity to the house's surroundings, and as a result of this design many credited Yeon with founding the Northwest Regional style of architecture. The house remains Portland's only National Historic Landmark residence, and Yeon bought it thirty-seven years after it was built "to protect it from change."[43]

In the Gorge, implementation of Yeon's 1937 report calling for a postage stamp rate for Bonneville's electricity had discouraged factories from relocating to the area, although the Columbia's clean water and abundant energy provided ample inducement. Ranchers like Paul Martin were also attracted by clean water and the grass it produced, and in 1946 Martin moved with his wife, Verla, and daughter, Paula, to a fifteen-hundred-acre cattle ranch on the Sandy River Delta. Considered Oregon's portal to the Gorge, the Sandy River flowed north into the Columbia, and the two rivers formed the western and northern boundaries of Martin's ranch. Both rivers kept the marsh grass fresh and green, ideal for raising cattle, and sustained "great numbers of waterfowl of Different kinds," as Lewis and Clark had discovered in November 1805 when they named the Sandy the "Quicksand River."[44]

The same year the Martin family moved to the Sandy's east bank, Reynolds Metals Company opened a plant on the west bank. The plant poured chemical compounds into large pots through which electrical current was passed, creating temperatures near two thousand degrees Fahrenheit and reducing the mixture to aluminum. A byproduct of the process was the daily release of almost three thousand pounds of poisonous fluorine gas into the air.[45] John Yeon's prophecy of factories emitting "withering gases" carried through the Gorge was deadly accurate with respect to the Reynolds plant. The windows of the Martin house were soon etched by the emissions, as if by acid, and Paul Martin noticed his cattle behaving strangely. His family experienced dysentery, shortness of breath, and other symptoms diagnosed as liver disease from fluorine poisoning. Reynolds Metals denied responsibility, and the Martins sued the company eight times over seventeen years. Reynolds fought the Martins at every step and encouraged seven other major aluminum and chemical companies to join the fight, claiming that a $91,000 judgment in favor of the Martins for poisoning their land constituted a "staggering burden" that would "smother" the defense industry and weaken national security.[46]

Tired of Reynolds's obstinacy and in declining health, Paul Martin erected a billboard on his property in the early 1960s, adjacent to the new Columbia River Highway:

THIS RANCH IS CONTAMINATED
831 Cattle Killed in past six years
FLUORIDE POISON from REYNOLDS
METAL CO.
kills our cattle * * * endangers
human health
CONTROLS MUST BE ENFORCED
THIS STATEMENT PAID FOR BY
PAUL R. MARTIN

Reynolds sued for defamation. The litigation outlasted Paul Martin, who died in 1964, and the Martin family was eventually awarded $253,000 in damages. They settled with Reynolds in 1968 when the company purchased the ranch for an undisclosed amount. The same year that Paul Martin died, orchardists upriver in The Dalles sued Harvey Aluminum Company, contending that fumes from its Gorge plant had damaged millions of dollars of fruit crops, and forced the company to install fluoride control systems. Across the river from the Martin ranch, at the Washington entrance to the Gorge, plans to drain Steigerwald Lake and zone it for heavy industry were underway. Some even considered the Gorge—with its plentiful water, supposed seismic advantages, and existing power transmission infrastructure—attractive for a nuclear power plant.[47]

On October 15, 1946, the year that the Martins and Reynolds Metals moved next to each other, John Yeon appeared before the Oregon Roadside Council to berate Oregon's Highway Department. A decade after ceding to Yeon's proposal for gentle curves on the new highway, the agency had returned to its straight, cliff-hugging alignment farther up the Gorge. "Yeon Lashes Road Policy," roared *Oregonian* headlines the next day. An editor of the paper subsequently "made enough noise," Yeon said, to force the state to adopt his position and abandon a nearly completed bridge over Wahkeena Creek. One woman who would later serve on the board of the roadside council was likely in its audience that day. Born into a wealthy Portland family, Gertrude Glutsch Jensen ran her own real estate business, rented a hundred apartments on the side, and worked as a freelance reporter for the *Oregonian* and other newspapers. In 1951, she drove her sick mother, who always enjoyed seeing the Gorge, on a portion of the historic highway that had survived construction of the new highway. Near Wahkeena Falls, she noticed a logging operation along the road. Leaving her mother in the car, she approached a small shack, calling out its occupants. A man emerged, and, after interrogation, revealed that Multnomah County had just sold the land for delinquent taxes. One of the state's most scenic areas, having escaped a power plant four decades earlier and avoided a freeway incision at the base of its cliffs, was scheduled to be logged.[48]

Oregon's westside forests had been heavily harvested to meet the government's demand for timber during World War II, so such activity in the Wahkeena basin was not exceptional. Propaganda posters—with appeals like "Log Like Hell! The Woods Are Also a Front Line"—had emphasized that timber was needed for war material. Workers poured into the region to work for the Kaiser shipyards and other Bonneville-powered wartime industries, and Portland needed timber to build housing for its swelling population. To address the housing shortage, Edgar Kaiser built Vanport, "the largest wartime housing project in the United States and the second-largest city in Oregon," in just four months. The city of forty-two thousand people rose on Columbia River floodplains north of Portland, twenty miles downstream from the Gorge and its forests.[49]

After the war, demand for timber continued to surge as GIs returned to Portland and its suburbs, started families, and built homes and businesses. Chainsaws, a new invention, enabled loggers to cut fifteen times more trees than their predecessors had and helped establish record timber harvests. During the 1940s, 70 billion board feet of timber were cut in Oregon, more than twice that of the previous decade, and for the first time Oregon's harvests surpassed Washington's, whose economy was diversifying. In the 1950s, Oregon set another harvest record by cutting 87 billion board feet of timber, enough to build over 9 million houses.[50]

Whether or not Jensen was aware of the post-war trends buffeting the Northwest on the day she drove her mother to Wahkeena Falls, the clear-cuts made it obvious to her that the Gorge was under attack, and Gertrude Glutsch Jensen was not a woman to be trifled with. Intrepid and driven by the conviction that she was accomplishing the Lord's work, she did not seem to consider tact a virtue. Fond of attention, she was instantly recognizable by the flamboyant hats she favored—their rims overflowing with feathers, flowers, and fruits—and she had a habit of referring to herself in the third person, as in "the family asked Gertrude to give the benediction."[51]

After returning from Wahkeena Falls, Jensen alerted several organizations to the logging threat. The Portland Women's Forum created a Save the Gorge Committee and appointed Jensen chair. In a burst of enthusiasm, *Oregon Journal* editor Marshall Dana declared: "The women have taken over the job of saving the gorge [and] I predict that they will win it."[52] With research provided by the Portland Chamber of Commerce, Jensen discovered that the county had sold "thousands of acres" in the Gorge for delinquent taxes and that those trees could be logged. Within months, she appeared before the Oregon Highway Commission. With allies that included the Bureau of Land Management, the Oregon Roadside Council, and Marshall Dana, Jensen ordered the highway commission to protect Oregon's western Gorge and demanded that it exchange the threatened land—almost six thousand private acres between Crown Point and Wahkeena Falls—for public land outside the Gorge. The commission must work with the National Park Service, she continued, to implement John Yeon's 1937 report. When the highway commission proved uninterested, Jensen pronounced: "We're taking the whole issue directly to the Governor." And she did.[53]

In June 1952, Governor Douglas McKay assured Jensen that he would appoint a committee to explore land acquisition and exchanges in the Gorge, recommend policies on industrial and commercial development, and propose legislation to restrict land use. Eight months later and just weeks after McKay had resigned to become President Dwight Eisenhower's secretary of the interior, legislators representing Multnomah County introduced a bill, at the urging of the Chamber of Commerce, to create a Columbia River Gorge Commission with regulatory authority to protect the Oregon portion of the Gorge and $500,000 to buy timberlands. That bill did not pass, but a weaker bill creating an unfunded advisory commission did. Jensen did not know who gutted the Gorge bill—"If I ever find out, I'd like to take them by the scruff of the neck and give them a good shaking," she warned—but the evidence seemed unequivocal, as opposition was led by a senator whose district was far from the Gorge but critical to the timber industry.[54]

The new three-person Columbia River Gorge Commission met for the first time in September 1953, elected Jensen chair, and set tentative boundaries for its jurisdiction from the Sandy River to Hood River, later extended upriver past The Dalles to the Deschutes River. Jensen relished her new position. A picture taken in 1955 shows her standing before the Oregon Parks Commission, pointing at documents held in her left hand. Jensen is clad in black, and an ostrich plume juts from her hat. Three of the four men seated before her are looking down, avoiding her gaze and perhaps her wrath, while the fourth is hunched over, cradling his head with his left hand, under which he peeks out at Jensen. The men look nothing so much as offenders awaiting their sentences.[55]

Jensen crusaded against logging over the next sixteen years as chair of the Gorge commission. She battled the highway commission, threatening the commissioners' jobs and declaring herself "furious, disappointed and disgusted" at their unwillingness to protect the Gorge. Members of the highway commission complained about "her kicks and abuse," vowed to report her to the governor, and "suggested there may be no further time on their agenda" for Jensen or her commission. Despite bridges burned, and with considerable assistance from Dana and Yeon, Jensen achieved some notable successes, primarily the acquisition, mostly through land exchanges and donations, of three thousand acres in Oregon's western Gorge, including Chanticleer Point just west of Vista House.[56]

For her efforts, Jensen was ridiculed and, according to her grandson, almost run off the road several times. But when judged by what Jensen called "my guide and my bible"—John Yeon's 1937 report—her accomplishments are found wanting. Yeon's report viewed the western Gorge as an integral unit, Oregon and Washington together, but Jensen's attention was almost entirely on Oregon. And while Yeon's report emphasized the need for zoning to supplement land acquisition and combat sprawl and roadside development, Jensen—who once called the removal of trees for a power line "the worst thing to have ever happened in the gorge"—maintained a blinkered focus on logging. She seemed oblivious to the industrialization that killed Paul Martin and to the surge of suburbanization intruding on the nation's marshes, farms, and forests in the 1950s, leaving disconnected housing developments in its wake. Yeon recognized that "forests, cut or burned, can regenerate . . . but the creeping transformations of suburbia are irreversible." His report and efforts were strategic, comprehensive, and proactive, while Jensen's successes seemed scattershot.[57]

Ultimately, Gertrude Glutsch Jensen—christened by some as the Angel of the Gorge and the Crusader of the Columbia Gorge—was seduced by the attention she received and beguiled by the awards and accolades proffered by politicians in lieu of action. In public presentations, she often read, word for word, the generic text that accompanied her awards while thanking the men, "my good friends," who had bestowed them. Perhaps the most poignant episode came in 1969, at the end of her sixteen-year reign as chair of Oregon's Gorge commission, when Governor Tom McCall refused to reappoint her. McCall likely was retaliating for Jensen's opposition to a steel scrap mill planned two miles east of Cascade Locks, opposition that Jensen had ironically withdrawn months earlier contingent only on the plant meeting existing pollution regulations and providing cosmetic screening. McCall, who later would be recognized for his environmental leadership and for standing up to smokestack industries, asserted that he was instituting the two-term limit for good public policy, but he exempted others from that policy, as Jensen pointed out. She was wounded by the rebuff, but McCall flattered her with an "Oregon Conservationist" award that he created for the occasion. She later declared that "the Gorge is safe. Saved for all time."[58]

But the Gorge was not saved. Jensen's tenure on the Gorge commission had left it vulnerable. Even along the Historic Columbia River Highway, where Jensen had concentrated her attention, some of its best known and admired features had been destroyed. By 1954, when the last section of the new Columbia River Highway was completed, the tunnel at Oneonta Gorge and the Tunnel of Many Vistas at Mitchell Point had been abandoned. The Mosier Twin Tunnels had been discarded, filled with rubble, and conveyed to Hood River County and private landowners. By 1956, only two years after the new highway was completed, it was determined that an even wider, faster interstate highway was needed, and within a decade Mitchell Point had been blasted apart to accommodate it. The Tunnel of Many Vistas, one of the world's most famous engineering landmarks with arched, floor-to-ceiling windows overlooking the Columbia River, was obliterated, its ruins used to pave the interstate.[59]

Another federal project was completed in 1957, one with unprecedented consequences for the Columbia's anadromous fish and the people who relied on them. At ten o'clock on a rainy March morning, the Army Corps of Engineers gave the "down gates" command, and the river rose behind The Dalles Dam. Four and a half hours later, the Long Narrows, Celilo Falls, and thousands of Native cultural sites were gone, submerged under forty feet of water. Ten thousand spectators watched the Columbia transform that day, including many Native people who sang funeral songs, mourning the loss of a place and a way of life that had sustained them for millennia. Celilo chief Tommy Thompson chose not to witness the flooding. He died two years later, never having looked at the dam and never having accepted $3,750 in federal compensation for his destroyed fishing sites.[60]

Ten years later, the third iteration of a Columbia River Highway in fifty years—Interstate 80N—was completed through the Gorge. The interstate's route shadowed now-flooded Celilo Falls and paralleled the Evergreen Highway in Washington. The Evergreen was a state highway with unlimited access, a convenience that encouraged unlimited sprawl. In 1962, Skamania County, one of Washington's least populous counties with just over five thousand residents spread over 1,656 square miles, seized this convenience and approved its largest residential development yet.[61]

Developer C. H. Woodard located the million-dollar development, which he named Woodard Marina Estates, at Skamania Landing, a former Native campsite and later boat landing downriver from Beacon Rock and across the Columbia from Yeon Mountain. The sixty-one-acre subdivision was the only major development on the sixteen-mile, mostly pristine stretch of river between the Gorge's western entrance and Beacon Rock. Woodard proposed 120 residential lots, a marina, a restaurant, a private club, and a lake. Advertisements ran in the *Oregonian* with maps, bucolic drawings, and increasing urgency: "Only 15 River Lots Left!" The target market was Portland metro residents—ONLY 50 MINUTES FROM PORTLAND, one ad promised— who could afford a summer house or were willing to commute. Lots were sold and houses constructed.[62]

Woodard Marina Estates was just a ripple of what was to come. The Columbia Gorge had survived lava flows, floods, highways, factories, hydroelectric dams, and clear-cuts, but a wave of residential development now threatened to inundate its Washington bank. Twenty years earlier, Portland had anticipated this swell and had hired Robert Moses, known as "America's greatest road builder," to design a plan for the city's expansion. He had proposed more highways and a new bridge over the Columbia near Vancouver. By mid-1960, the bridge and connecting interstate had been pushed upriver to accommodate the area's sprawling population. A flood of development, fueled by a prosperous America and cheaper land, transportation, and construction, now flowed toward the Gorge's western entrance.[63]

As Woodard Marina Estates lots were selling in 1965, John Yeon turned fifty-five. His attention, however, was focused on another Skamania County property, located a few miles below the subdivision. This riverside property, seventy-eight-acres and a mile long, was being marketed for industry. Yeon was weary from his efforts to restore Chapman Point; for three decades he had added land to stabilize adjacent dunes, vacated century-old phantom streets that crisscrossed his property, and evicted trespassers who climbed his fences and uprooted the beach grass and spruce trees that he had planted. His conservation efforts had created a "deep cultural clash" in the community according to Yeon expert Randy Gragg. "Locals of modest means and a conservative bent versus a lumber scion they considered to be a wealthy interloper. Gossip targeted his homosexuality." While admiring his coastal property, the National Park Service and Oregon State Parks had declined to buy it. The state reasoned, according to Yeon, that "John Yeon won't do anything to spoil it, [so] why should we buy it?" Yeon lamented that "there were so many defeats, time after time, at Cannon Beach . . . that I thought I would throw in the sponge, really and buy land that I had long admired on the Columbia River opposite Multnomah Falls."[64]

As Yeon vacillated on selling Chapman Point he considered persuading an acquaintance, Nani Warren, to buy the Columbia River property. Warren had the means. Her grandfather had founded ESCO in Portland, a family-owned business that manufactured steel parts for mining, logging, and construction, and her husband Bob had started Cascade Corporation, an international company that manufactured construction equipment. Warren owned property in the western Gorge near Prindle Mountain, downstream and adjacent to the land that Yeon admired. Her grandfather had developed the property in 1918, prior to the completion of the Evergreen Highway, and over the years the family had created a compound with several houses and a large dock extending into the Columbia. Yeon thought Warren might protect the Columbia River property to save her view.[65]

But Warren was vacationing in Europe when Yeon called in 1965. Worried that the property would sell to a developer before she returned, Yeon bought it and set about restoring its blackberry-choked fields and beaver-dammed creeks. He planted "Elysium Grass seed to make Elysium Fields," and created what Gragg described as "an inverted English picturesque landscape in which nature instead of architecture has become the 'folly.'" He named the property The Shire, endorsing a friend's observation that his underground bunker, filled with Asian art, would suit a Tolkien hobbit quite well. But Yeon was not content saving just a mile of riverfront, and his vision for the western Gorge would soon collide with Nani Warren's philosophy.[66]

In 1965 Warren was forty-one. She had a conservative and straightforward worldview that was centered on family, faith, and free enterprise. Politically savvy and well connected, she advanced her philosophy through support of the Republican Party—organizing Portland precincts, fundraising for candidates, and donating substantial sums to the cause. Small in stature, she wore oversized glasses that accentuated a probing stare and an outsize personality. Retreat—except in its vacation home iteration—was a concept she neither espoused nor observed. When Oregon's Republican Governor Tom McCall decided not to reappoint Gertrude Glutsch Jensen to the Gorge commission in 1969, he chose Warren—a Gorge enthusiast and campaign supporter—to replace her.[67]

John Yeon believed that the two-state, six-county Gorge, with a federal presence that included two national forests, two hydroelectric dams, and an interstate highway, was too complicated to be protected by state and local governments alone. He compared the appointment of Warren, a fervent antifederal proponent, to putting a "faith healer . . . in charge of a municipal hospital."[68] Nonetheless, by force of personality and not a little bravado, she was named chair of the Oregon Gorge commission and immediately raised its profile by securing a good working relationship with the Washington Gorge commission, sharing staff and holding joint meetings. The year following her appointment, Warren arranged for Governor Tom McCall and Washington governor Dan Evans to attend a conference hosted by the two commissions.

Yeon also attended the October 1970 conference, calling it "deadly dull, vague and windy," and tendered its only specific proposal. When introducing his recommendation, he reviewed the "political accidents [that] have divided [the Gorge] lengthwise down the middle by a state line and crosswise by county borders." He accused the US Forest Service of "remain[ing] aloof from the twentieth century problems besetting the Gorge" and detailed the "imminent threats" facing "the most threatened and vulnerable of the great landscapes of America." He concluded that "the Gorge is on the endangered species list" and needed protection. His solution was to designate the Gorge a national recreation area (NRA).[69]

National recreation areas were recent creations. Composed mostly of federal lands, the congressionally designated areas are typically managed for recreational purposes by the National Park Service or the US Forest Service. They differ from national parks, where land is usually protected for its environmental or cultural significance, and from national forests, which are managed for multiple uses, including timber harvesting. The laws establishing an NRA tend to be more general than those for other protected units, giving considerable discretion to the managing agency. Importantly, NRA land is protected primarily through federal land purchase and ownership, not by regulation. Yeon noted that public agencies were responsible for "most of what has already been permanently preserved" in the Gorge. "What remains to be preserved, particularly the still predominately natural areas on the Washington side," he said, "requires the same kind of protection."[70]

At the end of the conference, a motion from the floor to endorse and promote a national recreation area in the Gorge received unanimous support. The *Oregonian* approved, as did Gertrude Glutsch Jensen. Yeon hoped that the Oregon and Washington Gorge commissions would press for a federal study—the first step in determining whether an NRA should be created—but they remained silent. His phone calls and letters went unanswered. "Finally, during a social confrontation with Nani Warren," he discovered that she "had no intention of doing anything." Her family's philosophy, Yeon would charge, was "private enterprise *uber alles*."[71]

Over the next decade, Yeon tried to circumvent Warren. After Oregon elected Democratic Governor Bob Straub in 1974 and President Jimmy Carter was elected two years later, Yeon asked the governor to request a federal government study of what Yeon called the "Columbia–Cascades NRA," which included the western Gorge and Mount Hood, adding considerable federal land but few private acres. He invited Straub and his staff to tour The Shire and suggested that they consult with environmental organizations. But Straub would serve just a single term, losing to Republican Victor Atiyeh in 1978, and Yeon's proposal died.[72]

With development pressure mounting on the western Gorge—construction on the Interstate 205 bridge began in 1977—Yeon became desperate. Knowing that Warren had already served two terms on the Oregon Gorge Commission—the limit, according to state policy—he applied for the position. Governor Atiyeh ignored the term limit and reappointed Warren, a valued political campaigner, donor, and fundraiser. He reminded commission appointees that state law required them to forfeit their position—and the governor to immediately replace them—if they missed two consecutive meetings and directed his clerks to record recent attendance. Warren had missed almost half of the Gorge commission meetings over the previous eighteen months, including three consecutive sets of meetings, but Atiyeh determined that the law would be "unfair to enforce," and Warren stayed on the commission.[73]

Warren had proven resilient and politically adroit, and Yeon was tired and frustrated. He believed that his proposal was sound but acknowledged that he possessed neither the skills nor the temperament to promote it effectively. "I am my own worst advocate, and I don't throw any weight at all," he confessed to a senior member of Governor Straub's staff. "With me the [NRA] idea hasn't gotten off the ground after quite a time, and after quite some effort." If he could not lead the effort to protect the Columbia Gorge, he thought he knew someone who could. He had attended Nancy Russell's Portland Garden Club lecture on wildflowers and had come away impressed. As he recalled almost three years later:

> Her lecture on wildflowers of the Columbia Gorge is the best on any botanical subject that I have ever heard; my personal and professional interests have exposed me to a lot of these. Nancy's lecture flows like a mountain stream—crystal clear and sparkling. It is interspliced with the history of early botanical explorations and illustrated with her own excellent color slides of the plants and their habitats. The lecture matches the delight of its subject.[74]

Yeon decided to invite Russell to The Shire. He called Bruce and made arrangements, and on the last day of July 1979, he picked up the Russells, crossed the Columbia River, and headed upriver. That evening "has the substance of a dream now," Nancy Russell remembered years later, "the intense, dedicated older man, the ancient Chinese table set on the broad sweep of lawn, the pink-hued cliffs and waterfalls in the fading light. John told me of all the failed efforts of forty-five years and that the Park Service was now interested in protection of the Gorge. His words struck responsive chords in his dinner guest. He had invited the right woman to dinner."[75]

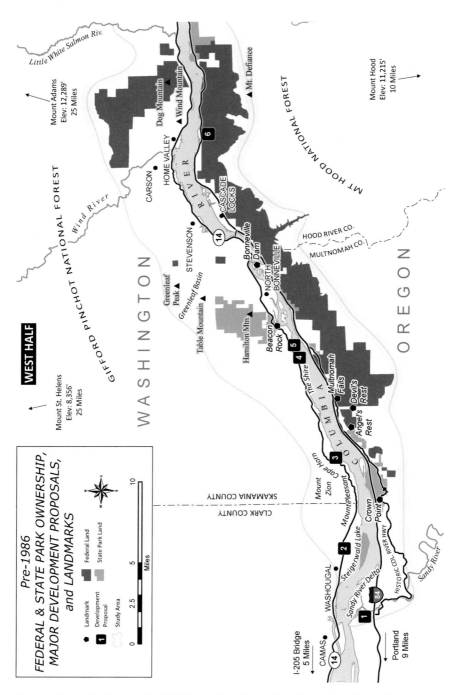

Western Columbia Gorge: Pre-1986 Federal and State Park Ownership, Major Development Proposals, and Landmarks. Map by Mike Schrankel.

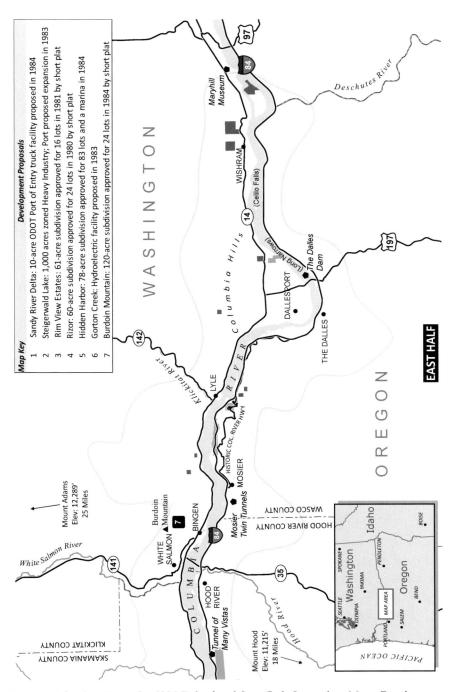

Map Key

Development Proposals

1 Sandy River Delta: 10-acre ODOT Port of Entry truck facility proposed in 1984
2 Steigerwald Lake: 1,000 acres zoned Heavy Industry; Port proposed expansion in 1983
3 Rim View Estates: 61-acre subdivision approved for 16 lots in 1981 by short plat
4 Rizor: 60-acre subdivision approved for 24 lots in 1980 by short plat
5 Hidden Harbor: 78-acre subdivision approved for 83 lots and a marina in 1984
6 Gorton Creek: Hydroelectric facility proposed in 1983
7 Burdoin Mountain: 120-acre subdivision approved for 24 lots in 1984 by short plat

Eastern Columbia Gorge: Pre-1986 Federal and State Park Ownership, Major Development Proposals, and Landmarks. Map by Mike Schrankel.

Chapter 3
Into the Maelstrom, 1979–1982

Yeon was hopeful. More than sixty years after his father had escorted National Park Service director Stephen Mather through the Gorge and Senator George Chamberlain's National Park bill had failed, the Park Service had returned its attention to the Gorge. President Jimmy Carter seemed conservation-minded, and his secretary of the interior, Cecil Andrus, had been born in Hood River and knew the area well. Yeon had particularly high hopes for Nancy Russell, who had impressed him over dinner at The Shire with her knowledge and passion for the Gorge. Days later, he gave her a box of background material, including his committee's two reports from the 1930s, and tutored her on efforts to protect the Gorge, its immediate threats, and its politics. While Russell's role would not be defined by the fall of 1979, she proved to be a quick study and a natural advocate, and she was starting to commit herself to Yeon's cause.

But was there enough time? Realtors from San Francisco, Seattle, and Spokane, knowing that the I-205 bridge would soon be completed, were pestering Yeon and his neighbors to sell their Gorge properties. Land prices near the bridge were starting to surge, and a local realtor estimated that a completed bridge would add $7,000 to $8,000 of value to every house east of Vancouver, Washington. Landowners were "sitting on gold mines," another realtor said. And the Port of Camas-Washougal had just released a draft environmental impact statement that proposed industrializing the wetlands at Steigerwald Lake, a thousand acres of vital habitat and beauty that, together with the unprotected farmlands of Mount Pleasant and Mount Zion, dominated the views from Crown Point and Vista House.[1]

The National Park Service's interest in the Gorge had been sparked by writer and photographer Chuck Williams. Williams had lived in California while studying to be an engineer, drifting from job to job, often sustaining himself by selling photographs and articles about national parks. He loved the Gorge, where his ancestors—including his grandmother, Kalliah, a Cascade Indian—had lived, and he moved there in the mid-1970s. Thirty-six years old, Williams was a politically shrewd, 1960s-era protester who armed himself with a typewriter, camera, and chains for locking himself to developers' front doors. His pale, moon-shaped face orbited a rotund body and flushed when he was angry or exorcised, which was often, as his temperament teetered between jovial and intense. His hair—thinning and often pulled into a ponytail—hung below his shoulders, and his beard was heavy and full. His friends called him "the last hippie environmentalist left on earth."[2]

Friends of the Earth hired Williams as its National Parks representative in 1975. Three years later, on behalf of the environmental advocacy organization, he urged the Park Service to assess whether the Gorge qualified as a national recreation area. An earlier Interior Urban Parks Study had supported an NRA designation for the western Gorge, he wrote National Park Service director William Whalen, and he proposed that the concept go further. A Columbia River Gorge National Recreation Area, he suggested, should encompass both rainforest and "cold desert" and stretch for eighty-five miles, from the Sandy River in the west to the Deschutes River in the east. He decried the "massive land rush . . . now begun in the Gorge with out-of-state speculators gobbling up land and sending prices and taxes sky-rocketing" and warned Whalen that unless the Gorge was designated a national recreation area within four years "we will just be fighting over the scraps." The next year, Williams urged Department of the Interior Assistant Secretary Robert Herbst to designate the Gorge and two other areas as national scenic areas, an invented classification that would protect those "sacred places that have almost gotten away: those landscapes that in their natural states could be among our most spectacular national parks, but which have been too developed to make traditional national parks practical."[3]

The Park Service released for public comment a draft study of alternatives for the Columbia River Gorge in November 1979. The purpose of the three-hundred-page study, finalized several months later, was to inform Congress on key aspects of the Gorge, including its significance, vulnerability, economy, and management alternatives. Detailed maps identified sensitive land and important scenic, natural, cultural, and recreational resources. The Gorge, the study concluded, was a "nationally significant resource that warrants protection." Current trends, it continued—especially residential pressure on unzoned Skamania County—"could irreversibly change the character of the Columbia River Gorge."[4]

The study laid out four alternatives for Congress to consider: continue existing policies, expand the role of the Columbia River Gorge commissions, establish a multigovernmental commission, or create a national recreation area in the western Gorge. The boundaries for three of the alternatives resembled Williams's eighty-five-mile-long recommendation, but the NRA option stopped west of Hood River, where most public lands in the Gorge ended. A fifth alternative, a bistate compact, was omitted from the final report, partly because it was considered "unlikely" that the two states could agree on Gorge management and, regardless, a bistate compact alone could not control federal activities. While avoiding a recommendation, the study concluded that the Gorge's "current health is tenuous, and its future is uncertain."[5]

John Yeon was gratified that the study recognized the national significance of the Gorge, as his own report had concluded four decades earlier. Near the beginning of the New Year, he took Nancy Russell, recently appointed conservation chair for the Portland Garden Club, to meet with him and Chuck Williams, who had formed the Columbia Gorge Coalition, a loose confederation of local groups that had independently fought isolated developments. The Coalition's president, Craig Collins, and Vera Dafoe, who a decade earlier had defeated plans for a tramway that would have run from Cascade Locks to the Benson Plateau four thousand feet above, also joined them.[6] Dafoe now served on Oregon's Gorge commission with Kate McCarthy, an orchardist from Hood River. Both women had been appointed by Governor Vic Atiyeh's predecessor, Bob Straub, and supported conservation.

At their meeting, the small group favored a combination of the study's alternatives: a Park Service-managed NRA for the western Gorge and management of the eastern Gorge by a regional commission. Williams wanted the eastern half protected immediately, along with the Columbia's seven major tributaries in the Gorge: the Sandy, Hood, Deschutes, Klickitat, White Salmon, Little White Salmon, and Wind Rivers. Yeon worried, however, that such a requirement would complicate support for the western Gorge, which was in the path of development overflowing the Portland-Vancouver metropolitan area. Economic development boosters and most Gorge residents preferred the study's "continuation of existing policies" alternative. The political leadership from five of the six Gorge counties also opposed additional protection; Multnomah County was the exception.[7]

At the state level, the two Gorge commissions were crafting a response to the Park Service study. Jeff Breckel, staff director for both commissions, was an even-handed, able administrator who tried, with mixed success, to guide the commissions toward nonpolitical, fact-based positions. At its December 1979 meeting, with Nani Warren away in Saudi Arabia, the Oregon commission approved a letter drafted by Breckel. "The problems of the Columbia River Gorge," he wrote, "are too massive and interrelated for resolution by individual commissions with only advisory powers. We have concluded that an effective management for the Gorge must be singular in nature. It should have authority and funding appropriate in scale to the national significance of the Gorge, and provide for the strongest possible protection."[8]

This circumspect support for federal management so irked Governor Atiyeh—who preferred state government to federal and chafed at the Park Service's perceived lack of deference to him—that his staff excluded the Gorge commission from state agency meetings called to respond to the study. He subsequently agreed with Washington governor Dixie Lee Ray—who had proclaimed that "anything that the private sector can do, the government can do worse"—to advocate a political palliative: an incremental increase in funding and authority for the advisory Gorge commissions. The governors executed a letter to this effect on joint Oregon-Washington letterhead, but Governor Atiyeh, presumably for political cover, felt obligated to consult his commission before releasing the letter. There was little risk, as Warren, back from Saudi Arabia and confident that she had three of the five votes needed to support the governors' decision, scheduled its approval for the commission's January meeting.[9]

Events did not unfold as planned. Although a Gorge snowstorm made attendance difficult at the January meeting, the governors' position encountered substantial public opposition. Russell, testifying as a citizen, supported a national scenic area (NSA) and challenged Warren directly: "It is largely to you that Oregonians have entrusted the welfare of their beloved Gorge, and it is you who will be remembered in the future as you succeed or fail in your task. How will you feel in 1990 if you look across the river and see a hodgepodge of poorly controlled land development?" John Yeon, reminiscent of his battles with Highway Commission Chair Leslie Scott decades earlier, attacked Warren for her "anti-government phobia" and described how in a private moment she had told Yeon that she was determined to "keep the Feds out of the Gorge." Furthermore, Yeon said, Warren "objected to parks," as "they brought noise and litter." An angry Warren asked Yeon not to personalize the discussion and then, with two proxies from absent commissioners giving her a majority, voted to approve the governors' decision.[10]

Craig Collins had been aware of Warren's plan to use proxies, however, and had alerted Rick Bauman, an Oregon state representative and one of the Coalition's board members. Collins also tipped off Portland media that "a dramatic showdown was likely." Bauman now stood up and read an attorney general's opinion that prohibited the use of proxies for state commission business. Warren was suddenly in the minority as the two remaining commissioners—Dafoe and McCarthy—supported the commission's December letter. Instead of demonstrating "unity between the two states [and] their capacity to adequately handle the complexities of Gorge management," Collins and Dafoe reminisced years later, the two governors had created "a public relations debacle that had been given wide media attention." When Breckel informed Atiyeh that the Oregon commission had voted down his position, the governor was forced to rip up the pre-signed letter. The Oregon governor and the chair of the Oregon commission then signed a weak letter with Governor Ray—on Washington commission letterhead—that advocated for the status quo and pledged to seek additional funding and authority for the two commissions.[11]

Weeks later, Nancy Russell drove to Salem with Barbara Bailey, a former geology major from The Dalles who loved the eastern Gorge and its monumental rock formations. Bailey had married into one of the area's cherry-growing families and had recently helped stop a zirconium plant from being built across the Columbia from The Dalles. She and other orchardists had worried that their crops would suffer if the plant was built, as had happened a decade earlier when Harvey Aluminum Company was forced to install pollution scrubbers. The two women had an appointment with Governor Atiyeh.

Russell showed Atiyeh slides and maps of landscapes across the Columbia from popular Oregon viewpoints in the Gorge and explained how their vulnerability would increase when the I-205 bridge was completed. She was direct: "I am a very practical woman. I don't believe in good fairies and I really don't think the State of Washington has ever demonstrated any intention of doing anything about those lands." Bailey recalled, years later with a smile, that she "didn't have to say anything," as Russell did all of the talking. Atiyeh responded with platitudes about his love for the Gorge, reiterated his promise to seek additional funding and authority for the Oregon Gorge commission, and assured them that they should trust him. Both women were so irritated by the conversation that they forgot where they had parked their car.[12]

A few days later, Russell stopped at Crown Point on her way back from the eastern Gorge. Since childhood her favorite moments had been spent outdoors, swimming in rivers and alpine lakes and leading wildflower hikes as she had done that morning. Russell connected physically, emotionally, and intellectually with western landscapes. Now, looking across the Columbia to the farms on Mount Pleasant and Mount Zion, a new feeling came over her, almost a compulsion. "Yes, there is a motivation to be involved in something larger than oneself, that pushes us on," she wrote a friend years later. "It is also true that when one has a compelling love for [a] great landscape, the idea of its destruction, its utter trashing, is so repellant that it is practically impossible not to become involved. I would have died rather than look across from Crown Point and see the gentle slopes of the upland farms turned into A-frames, Burger Kings, mobile homes, gravel pits, and the rest of the flotsam and jetsam of American culture."[13]

Meanwhile, Governor Atiyeh had launched an effort to scuttle federal legislation. Just days after meeting with Russell and Bailey, he asked for help from Sam Johnson, a timberman and political kingpin, who chaired the board of trustees at the Oregon Historical Society. Five days after Atiyeh's meeting with Russell and Bailey, Johnson delivered: he sent a letter to the governor on OHS letterhead "as president of the Oregon Historical Society," opposing federal involvement in the Gorge. He copied Oregon's congressional delegation. The letter stunned Russell. She had recently created an Oregon Trail program for OHS, whose board included the state's most influential and philanthropic citizens, the very people whose support was critical if the Gorge was to be protected. She had sought the society's endorsement of federal legislation but had been told that board approval was required and that the trustees would not meet soon. Yet here was Johnson's letter.[14]

Russell responded with a diplomatic letter to Johnson, copied to the congressional delegation and the Oregon Historical Society board and its executive director, Tom Vaughan. She explained her relationship to OHS, the historical significance of the Gorge, the inadequacies of advisory state commissions in the face of development, and the necessity for federal involvement. It would be assumed that Johnson spoke for the institution, she wrote, and not as an individual. She mentioned her pleasure at pouring punch for Mrs. Johnson at OHS's recent Christmas party, and she hoped that Sam Johnson would respond to her letter and allow her to take him to lunch. Then Russell raised hell. Enlisting Garden Club friends, several of whose husbands served on the OHS board, and John Yeon and his admirers, Russell orchestrated what Yeon described as an "explosion of protest." Within days, Johnson had received scores of phone calls and letters, most copying Governor Atiyeh, the delegation, and the OHS board and staff. In a follow-up letter to the governor, copied to the original recipients, he apologized for "mistakenly" writing as board chair and using OHS stationery.[15]

Either in pique or apathy, Governor Atiyeh rescinded even his modest promise to seek additional funding and authority for the commissions, which Governor Ray had similarly revoked. Within months, he had dismissed Dafoe and McCarthy from the commission. John Yeon was outraged, charging that Atiyeh would be responsible "for all the future misfortunes of the Gorge." For Russell, Johnson's response confirmed the benefits of a polite, fact-based, no-retreat approach and the importance of having vocal and high-profile allies. The only organization supporting federal management, however, was the Columbia Gorge Coalition, and Williams's group had not been able to raise enough money to be effective. He had recently stepped aside to write a coffee-table book—*Bridge of the Gods, Mountains of Fire: A Return to the Columbia Gorge*—that he believed would galvanize public pressure on Congress.[16]

By midsummer, the Columbia Gorge Coalition had exhausted its funds, and Russell volunteered to find someone to plan a fundraising event. After several unsuccessful attempts, she decided to tackle the task herself and persuaded John Yeon to host a picnic at The Shire—a significant accomplishment, as Yeon prized the retreat for its solitude and insisted that a "certain decorum" be observed there. Russell enlisted forty friends, most of them from the Portland Garden Club, to serve as the host committee. With Yeon and The Shire as main attractions, the $25-per-couple picnic attracted three hundred people and raised a record $3,500 for the Coalition. Even Sam Johnson sent Russell a check. "The day was perfect," a relieved John Yeon recounted. "The day before cloudy, the day after too hot. No wind. No mosquitoes. No one drowned. So many people saying 'what can I do?'—the big question still."[17]

Before Yeon's question could be answered, another emergency arose. In August, Nani Warren met with the board of the Seattle Garden Club to discuss the Gorge. Jean Stevenson, whose family owned the wetlands at Steigerwald Lake, had arranged the meeting and accompanied Warren.[18] The Stevenson family owned timber and development properties throughout Oregon and Washington and was the Gorge's largest private landowner, owning thousands of acres, including Steigerwald, which they were promoting for industrial development. The family patriarchs, brothers Wally and Bruce, were vehemently opposed to federal legislation, which they believed would devalue their holdings in the Gorge.

Two months earlier, Russell had hosted a successful two-day tour of the Gorge for Seattle Garden Club members, with stops to view The Shire, west-side waterfalls, eastside wildflowers, and Maryhill Museum. The group—which included Gretchen Hull, the new conservation representative for the

Nancy Russell and John Yeon at Crown Point in summer 1980. Russell archives.

western region of the Garden Club of America—had been enchanted, and Jean Stevenson's meeting with Nani Warren was likely called in response. As chair of the Oregon commission and a Skamania County landowner, Warren assured the Seattle Garden Club that she was familiar with most Gorge properties and that none were threatened. And, she implied, Russell and other Portland Garden Club women supported her position on how the Gorge should be managed. Russell knew that Warren's lobbying could undermine the Garden Club of America's endorsement of federal legislation, which she believed was essential. All club affiliates within a zone—and there were eleven of them in the four-state Zone XII—had to give their approval before GCA could support legislation protecting the Gorge. Opposition by Seattle or any regional affiliate would make that impossible.[19]

After a sleepless night, Russell wrote Gretchen Hull and proposed that she present her botany slide show to the Seattle chapter. In addition, she suggested, Portland Garden Club president Maggie Drake, who had helped host the summer fundraiser at The Shire, could contact her Seattle counterpart with accurate information. She advised that the granddaughter of Beacon Rock's benefactor—and Russell's predecessor as conservation chair for the Portland Garden Club—could dispute Warren's claims that the Gorge was not threatened and that there was widespread support for continued management by the advisory commissions. Hull followed Russell's advice, and the Seattle chapter soon endorsed federal protection for the Columbia Gorge.[20]

That victory came at a cost, in time and energy, and perhaps emotions as well. Russell, a Republican by affiliation, was naive about politics and was startled weeks later when she was assailed at a dinner party by Governor Atiyeh's "furious" campaign finance chairman, Blake Hering. Hering, a pillar of Portland's business community, had married one of Russell's closest childhood friends, and she had known him since high school. She recalled that he confronted her at a party, shouting that Nani Warren had "paid her dues," unlike Russell, by supporting Republican candidates. Russell had "no right" to challenge Warren's policies, he continued, or "God dammit" to tell another person or state what to do with their property.[21]

Russell received another blow in October, when John Yeon saw logging trucks emerging from his next-door neighbor's property. George Rizor, a member of the Camas Planning Commission, had bulldozed roads and logged his sixty-acre riverfront property, directly across from Multnomah Falls, to ready it for development. Like all of Skamania County, the property was unzoned, and Rizor circumvented the minimal state subdivision laws that required posting notices and holding hearings by conveying ten-acre tracts to family members who divided their tracts into four parcels apiece. This time-honored county practice, called short-platting, created a twenty-four-lot subdivision. And it occurred at Orchid Point, the midpoint in the near-pristine, sixteen-mile stretch of the Columbia between Steigerwald Lake's wetlands and Beacon Rock, bordering The Shire and just upriver from the Prindle compound owned by Nani Warren. The Shire, long touted by Russell and Yeon as an example of what the Gorge could be if federal legislation passed, now better exemplified what the Gorge had become—besieged.[22]

Given her lack of experience in politics, law, media, and land development, Russell was uncertain about where to turn. Fortunately, she had met someone at her summer fundraiser who was an expert at such things. Don Clark was Multnomah County's highest elected official, its chief executive officer, and a Democrat. He was energetic, curious, and bright. Early in his career, he had guarded inmates at San Quentin and had learned not to be intimidated, a trait that helped him manage prisoners and, later, politicians. He often took stands that were not in his political interests, the antithesis of a political caricature. Clark also cared for the environment, especially the Gorge. His grandfather had worked for John Yeon's father as a day laborer on the Historic Columbia River Highway. In 1964, as county sheriff, Clark wrote "fellow Gorge lover" and Governor Mark O. Hatfield, lamenting that modern highways lacked "beauty of line" and "grace" and urged him to restore, not replace, the historic highway's "artful retaining walls, guardrails and bridges." Later, as county commissioner, Clark had bucked political convention and opposed Interstate 205 and its bridge, fearing they would promote urban sprawl.[23]

In mid-October, just as the public was learning about George Rizor's development, Cecil Andrus flew to Portland to meet with Clark to build last-minute support for President Carter's reelection. Clark had read the Park Service study on the Gorge and was concerned that it had generated little momentum toward legislation. He assured Andrus that there was ample political support and asked him to make Gorge legislation a priority for the Carter administration's second term. Andrus promised that legislation would be introduced.[24] Ronald Reagan was elected president three weeks later.

Clark called Mark Hatfield, who had been elected to Congress in 1966 and in January would assume one of the government's most powerful positions, chair of the Senate Appropriations Committee, which determined where federal funds were spent. Hatfield would work across party lines if it benefitted Oregon, Clark believed, and he updated the senator on the Park Service study and Andrus's commitment and asked him to support federal legislation. Hatfield was interested but cautious. He had "taken a beating" on wilderness and other environmental issues, he told Clark, and he needed more support. "I will be your champion," Hatfield promised, "*if* you get me an army that's bipartisan, that is bistate and that's at both ends of the Gorge, and is broad-based. Then I will get out in front of that army. I will lead it and we will get you your federal legislation." Clark's next call was to Nancy Russell. He had asked Sally Anderson, one of his most experienced staff members, to determine who in the community could best generate momentum for the Park Service study. She had returned with a few names, and Nancy Russell topped the list. He met with Russell and made more calls.[25]

Two weeks after the election, he held a press conference at the Portland Garden Club, chosen for its nonpartisan reputation. He named a four-person steering committee — Nancy Russell, Craig Collins, and two Washington businessmen — to advocate for a Park Service–managed national scenic area for the entire Gorge. Russell and Clark called on both states' governors and congressional delegations to support federal legislation, citing the Rizor subdivision and threats posed by the I-205 bridge. "Ours may be the generation that lost this heritage," Clark warned, "and failed in our responsibility to safeguard its unique

Portland Garden Club press conference, November 18, 1980. Don Clark with PGC president Maggie Drake (left) and Nancy Russell. FOCG archives.

character." Conservation and civic representatives, from the American Institute of Landscape Architects to the Sierra Club, attended the press conference in solidarity, as did several businessmen and politicians, including Weyerhaeuser president Bob Wilson and former Oregon governor Tom McCall.[26]

The press conference generated editorials—favorable in Oregon, less so in Washington—from the *Oregonian*, the *Oregon Journal*, the Vancouver *Columbian*, and Portland's KATU-TV. The *Skamania County Pioneer* decried outsiders and "flatlanders" who supported the "federal takeover" and suggested that they address "their own . . . trash problems before using their 'expertise' out here." The call for federal legislation must have seemed quixotic to most observers, though, as the president-elect, the governors of Washington and Oregon, and all but one of the six Gorge counties opposed it. For almost seven decades, moreover, legislation to protect the Columbia Gorge had never reached the congressional committee level, despite more favorable political conditions. "It's the worst time in my lifetime for proposing anything," said John Yeon. "The Gorge will go down the drain unless some miracle happens."[27]

While political conditions were terrible for their purposes, the timing was favorable for Russell and Clark to begin their work together. Clark was eyeing a run for governor, and while his support for the cause was motivated by passion more than politics, protecting the Gorge was popular in Oregon's vote-heavy metropolitan areas. At the same time, Russell was looking for new challenges and experiences. Experts had assured her that passing legislation would take two years, and she told herself that she could work on behalf of the Gorge and still be home to serve dinner by six.[28]

Their first forays "braved the lions in their den," as one reporter described it. They met with county commissioners in the five counties that objected to legislation and with residents, one hundred in The Dalles and fifty in Hood River. Their audiences were mostly hostile, but Clark was a seasoned politician and Russell had confidence in her knowledge of the Gorge and its vulnerabilities. They were on a mission, but they tempered their zeal with logic, explaining the problems facing the Gorge, citing the Park Service study, and reporting how the Rizor subdivision had laid bare Skamania County's indifference. Clark identified "creeping incrementalism" as a central problem, especially in the western Gorge, where the drip, drip, drip of new houses caused by the I-205 bridge threatened to wash away the landscape's national significance.[29]

In February 1981, three months after their first press conference, Russell and Clark held a second one, also at the Portland Garden Club. They announced a new organization, Friends of the Columbia Gorge, and released a report that emphasized the significance of the Gorge and the absence of a solution that was equal to the threats it faced. All of the existing management approaches had weaknesses, the report pointed out. Traditional bistate compacts, for instance, had failed at Lake Tahoe and would fail in the Gorge, and designation as a national park or recreation area was problematic in a place where the vast majority of land was privately owned. Russell had drafted the report with two Portland attorneys—Gail Achterman, a natural resources and public lands expert, and Borden Beck, a business lawyer who was respected by Governor Atiyeh. Both worked pro bono at Russell's request.

A new approach was needed, the report concluded. A Columbia River Gorge National Scenic Area managed by the National Park Service would be the nation's first. It would include the entire Gorge, west and east of the Cascades and on both sides of the river. Industrial and most commercial development would be restricted to existing towns, where it was most appropriate and least harmful, and those towns would be exempt from the legislation's regulations. A regional commission, with local, state, and federal representatives, would create a unified management plan for the scenic area, funded and guided by the Park Service.[30]

On trips through the Gorge to build support for their proposal, Russell and Clark emphasized that the solution had to be as big as the problem. They argued that federal legislation was the only viable solution for the Gorge, which had over fifty jurisdictions with land use authority. A county could not be expected to zone land in ways that protected views from another state. Some exceptional lands should be acquired for parks, but—as John Yeon had long argued—it was unreasonable to expect the counties or states to buy the land. And imagine the benefits, Russell said, of a park at Cape Horn that replicated Crown Point, a pair of portals that would appeal to millions of Gorge visitors and preserve an extraordinary landscape for generations. Only the federal government had the authority and the resources to protect the Gorge.[31]

Russell and Clark developed a close working relationship. "He was, as always, up front," Russell said, describing Clark's reaction to local officials' scorn, whether it was a Skamania County commissioner telling him to "keep his nose on [his] side of the river" or the manager of the Port of Klickitat asking, "Who the hell does Don Clark think he is?" Russell remembered that Clark "said what he knew was right and, for that, he was shot at." Clark's view of Russell was that she was "unlike anyone else" he had worked with. She was polished, gracious, and refined yet "brutally honest" and willing to "slug it out with opponents," and she had a "backbone of steel—nobody could back her down."[32]

Russell had demonstrated her ability to "slug it out with opponents" early on when she and Clark visited Congressman Denny Smith, a conservative Republican who represented much of rural and coastal Oregon. As the only Democrat in the room, Clark had kept quiet. "Nancy talked to him, and he began giving her the old party line of free enterprise and the federal government interfering with private land rights," Clark recalled years later, his face beaming. "And boy! Nancy lit into him! And she said, didn't he know that he was in the party of Teddy Roosevelt, the finest conservationist that ever lived, and just ate him up one side and down the other. . . . I was mightily impressed."[33]

They relied on each other. Clark knew politics and how to build public support around an issue, while Russell knew the Columbia Gorge. In February, Clark turned the leadership of the steering committee over to Russell, and she bore down. She focused on building Friends of the Columbia Gorge and raising public awareness of the forces allied against the Gorge. Clark gave her space to work in Multnomah County offices and directed Sally Anderson, who had managed several library and school board campaigns, to serve informally as her chief of staff. He also instructed county attorneys and planners to scour Washington subdivision and shoreline development laws, which he then used to hammer Skamania County on Rizor's application. In a series of letters to the Skamania County commission chair and planning director, Clark accused the county of "serious legal error" and charged that it was opening itself up to "financial liability" for disregarding state laws that required an environmental impact statement and public hearings.[34]

Following Senator Hatfield's admonition, Russell and Anderson chose a board of directors based on geographic diversity, one that represented both states and all six Gorge counties. Russell was elected chair of the board in March. To gain credibility for the new organization, she called friends of friends to fill out her sponsors list, which soon included six former and future governors and scores of political, civic, and business leaders. She relied, once again, on her network of tennis and Garden Club friends to increase membership in the Friends of the Gorge, person by person. She cajoled all of her acquaintances, and their friends, to pay the ten dollar membership fee, twenty-five dollars for a family, and handwrote thank you letters to all of them, asking them to get in touch with Congress. By the end of 1981, Friends of the Columbia Gorge had almost six hundred members.[35]

Nonprofit membership organizations generally rely on dues, donors, and foundations to offset their costs, and costs were particularly high for the Friends. It now had three staff—executive director Carol Kirchner, Russell's daughter Sally who managed the Portland office and volunteers, and a Seattle coordinator—and the organization had to operate in two states and in Washington, DC. Board members usually fundraise, but the Friends board was chosen for political reasons and had no experience raising money.

Portland's business community members agreed to help, much as their forebears had helped protect the Gorge more than a half-century earlier. Several were married to Garden Club members, but most were outdoorsmen who enjoyed hiking or fishing in the Gorge, as did their employees. Brot Bishop, whose family owned Pendleton Woolen Mills, led the effort. He and Bob Wilson—Weyerhaeuser's board chair and an early supporter whose wife Bobbie had grown up in Hood River—were joined by a half dozen others, including: Don Frisbee, chair of Pacific Power and Light; Lou Perry, president of Standard Insurance and chair of the Oregon Economic Council; and Charles Luce, who had once lived in Vancouver and was the former chair and CEO of Consolidated Edison, one of the nation's largest utilities. These men solicited their contacts on Russell's behalf and gave the new organization needed credibility. At Russell's request, they were not shy about exerting their political power and influence. Pendleton's mill in the western Gorge, for example, was the largest employer in Washougal. Pacific Power and Light was a principal employer in southwest Washington. And Weyerhaeuser was a major employer and landowner throughout Washington.[36]

Russell's knowledge and love for the Gorge was infectious, and she became an accomplished fundraiser. She committed herself to the cause—days, nights, and financially—and she was persistent. She asked everyone for money—friends, acquaintances, and strangers—and ended few conversations, whether at a cocktail party or waiting in line at Strohecker's grocery store, without requesting support. She knew that her constant requests grated on some and worried that friends would hide when they saw her, but she persisted. Rejections could annoy her, but they did not discourage her. "She wanted everybody to enjoy those flowers and the viewpoints," Friends board member Kate Mills recalled. "She wanted to share all of that."[37]

Russell took prospective supporters on tours of the Gorge in her well-worn Volvo wagon. Her targets included donors, reporters, politicians, and civic leaders: people like Eric Pryne, a *Seattle Times* reporter who wrote several articles that influenced public opinion; Seattle City attorney Doug Jewett, who would advise the Friends on Washington politics; and King County executive Randy Revelle, for whom she baked a carrot cake and—probably not fulfilling John Yeon's desire for decorum—grilled hot dogs on a hibachi at The Shire. Russell led her prospects up near-vertical trails to view waterfalls, petrified stumps, wildflowers, or century-old Chinese bake ovens. She took less fit prospects on gentle walks through fields of balsamroot, lupine, and paintbrush. For those not capable of walking, she introduced them to the Gorge on the historic highway or on back roads seldom traveled by the public. She drove almost everyone to Vista House, where she could point across the Columbia and imagine a dystopian future without federal legislation: Rizor's twenty-four houses blighting the view from Multnomah Falls, century farms on Mount Pleasant and Mount Zion converted to narrow view lots glutted with mansions and three-car garages, and an industrialized Steigerwald Lake. Sometimes she took people to The Shire or the fields above Cape Horn, where over picnic lunches she had prepared that morning she described a future blessed with federal legislation—an overlook at Cape Horn rivaling Crown Point and Steigerwald's wetlands intact and populated with wildlife. She also drove potential supporters—captive audiences, really—to the Gorge's eastern reaches, where they could walk the abandoned section of the historic highway between Hood River and Mosier, see Oregon Trail ruts worn into the hills west of the Deschutes River, visit Sam Hill's Maryhill, and gaze at the calm waters that had submerged Celilo Falls. Russell told them what could be achieved with their support and what would certainly happen without it. Only the strongest agnostic could spend a day with her and deny her appeals.[38]

Russell soon supplemented her Volvo trips with group tours in microphone-equipped buses. Civic organizations from the Oregon League of Women Voters to the American Institute of Architects signed up for her excursions. She gained expertise in tour minutiae: the distance between public bathrooms, which roads were too steep or too narrow for forty-foot buses, which overlooks were best for a crowd, and how much time septuagenarians needed to disembark. She asked each rider to join the Friends and write their congressman.

If people spent time in the Gorge, she reasoned, then they would learn to love and protect it. The first summer picnic she hosted for Friends of the Columbia Gorge was at The Shire in August 1981. Over a hundred people, including Gertrude Glutsch Jensen, showed up, despite gray, gloomy weather and a threatening sky. She had asked friends to bring food, knowing that if they had a responsibility then they were more likely to come. The summer picnics proved so popular that Russell added a winter picnic in 1982, solicited free food and beer, and attracted four hundred paying guests. She started a Hiking Weekend, when Friends sponsored dozens of hikes led by Russell and volunteers she had recruited. Hikers were always asked to join the Friends and write their congressmen.[39]

She could not lure everyone to the Gorge, so she raised $10,000 from three foundations to make a twenty-five-minute multimedia slide production that brought the Gorge to them. With Russell's and Yeon's assistance, Craig Collins supervised a team of experts—including twenty-two photographers, two painters, eleven musicians, and two narrators—to produce *The Columbia River Gorge: Who Is Watching?* Using an original musical score, historic and contemporary photographs, and quotes from Oregon pioneer diaries that Russell had uncovered at the Oregon Historical Society, the show traced the history of the Gorge from its earliest Native inhabitants through the Lewis and Clark Expedition, the Oregon Trail, the building of the historic highway and the Bonneville and The Dalles Dams, to the threats posed by the I-205 bridge and the proposed industrialization of Steigerwald Lake. The program acknowledged the debt owed to the "Class of 1915"—Sam Lancaster, John B. Yeon, and Sam Hill—"that generation whose idea of development included

conservation." The show concluded: "For better or worse, we are the custo-
dians now" and inquired "How will we exercise our stewardship?" The final
image was of an iconic petroglyph in the eastern Gorge whose broad face and
piercing eyes—each formed by six concentric circles—stared at viewers while
the narrator intoned: "Now, She Who Keeps On Watching . . . watches us."[40]

Russell took the show on the road. After daylong tours in the Gorge, she
cooked dinner for her family and washed the dishes before heading out for
evening presentations, hauling 156 slides in two cassette trays, an audiovisual
unit, two projectors, a dissolve unit, a stacker, a speaker, a screen, and assorted
power cords and plugs. She set up a speakers' bureau and trained others to
show *Who Is Watching?* but remained its primary and most popular presenter,
running through projector bulbs—advertised to last a year—in weeks.

Russell presented to thousands of people in 1981 and 1982, driving her
Volvo over ten thousand miles for performances in 1982 alone. Her audiences
ranged from conservation organizations to garden clubs and college students,
business and civic groups such as the Kiwanis, the Oregon Hotel and Motel
Association, and the Mt. Hood Rock Club. She gave special attention to
chapters of national conservation organizations, knowing that local members
influenced their organizations' national policies, which could sway Congress.
In a letter thanking National Audubon Society vice president Brock Evans for
his work on behalf of the Gorge, she asked him to "keep in touch regarding
the endorsement of the National Audubon" and reminded him that "I spoke
to the Willapa Hills Audubon (Longview) this week. It was a very large crowd.
Next week I'll be in Seattle to speak to the Seattle Audubon. It's a lot of work;
my heart is in it." When Evans wrote that he needed her to keep working
hard, she replied, "I'll turn that around to say that we need you—it is really
the environmental organizations that make the difference."[41]

While she looked for engagements that furthered the Friends' mission,
Russell spoke to any group that could muster an audience. After running the
show, she often implored her audience:

> I see all of you in the Gorge, skiing, surfing, picnicking, driving. It's
> you who own some of the Gorge. Don't say she'll do it. [Or] let George
> do it. You are George and if you want future generations to enjoy this
> place as ours has, you had better get out of your chair and write to your
> senators and representatives and demand that they solve the problem
> we are discussing here today.[42]

And then, of course, she asked them to join Friends of the Columbia Gorge.

The Friends had a thousand members by the end of 1982,[43] nearly double its 1981 totals and surpassing the membership of most Northwest-based conservation organizations. And Russell knew them. Some were friends or friends of friends, and she had met others at picnics, during Hiking Weekend, on tours and at presentations, or while waiting in line at the grocery store. She wrote thank you letters—in sharp, clear cursive strokes—to those who renewed their membership. Her letters to Washington members were particularly grateful. While Oregon's delegation was more powerful, Congress would not steamroll Washington on a bistate issue, and as Senator Hatfield had recognized, success meant creating a constituency in both states.

To that end—or at least to give a more favorable impression of geographic diversity than existed—the Friends board would elect two Vancouver businessmen, David Cannard and Mitch Bower, to serve as cochair and treasurer. Cannard was well known in southwest Washington, where he had a thriving insurance agency, and he possessed the enthusiasm of a successful salesman. Short, stout, and stubborn, with a flattop haircut and glasses that magnified his light blue eyes, Cannard resembled a badger, if one that was affable and gregarious. He was always smiling and talking, his conversation interspersed with homespun jokes and analogies. He was content to enjoy the Gorge on drives with friends and family. Bower was Cannard's opposite. Tall, lean, and taciturn, he ran his family's trucking company and was an avid backpacker who enjoyed solitary hikes in the Gorge. Both men considered the Gorge an important resource for the Vancouver community, and both sacrificed substantial time to the effort, especially Cannard, who devoted most of his free time and untold work hours.

As the City of Portland drove Oregon's politics and philanthropy, so Seattle drove Washington's. In the fall of 1981, the Friends had opened an office in Seattle, just blocks from the Space Needle, where there was barely room for a desk and a chair for Kristine Simenstad, the Friends' Washington State coordinator. A psychologist by training, she possessed an outgoing and engaging personality epitomized by a laugh that was so constant and loud that the building's landlord moved her into a soundproof office.

Harriet Bullitt was central to the Friends' early success in Seattle. She chaired the executive committee for her family's media company, King Broadcasting, which owned radio stations and NBC television affiliates in Seattle and Portland. A conservationist and a philanthropist, she had attended the 1980 picnic at The Shire for the Coalition, where Russell had persuaded her

to become the Friends' honorary chair in Washington State.[44] Kristine Simenstad was close to Bullitt's son Stimson, who had recently retired as president of
King Broadcasting, and she arranged a series of successful Seattle fundraisers
and membership events for Russell with the assistance of the Bullitts, the Wil-
sons, Gretchen Hull, and others with Portland and Garden Club connections.

A friendly editor at the *Seattle Times* advised Russell and Simenstad to
get in touch with media in eastern Washington, whose editors and reporters covered the Gorge and where fewer stories competed for attention. So
with Russell at the wheel and Simenstad navigating, the two women began
biannual, multiday tours of eastside newspaper, television, and radio outlets,
punctuated by *Who Is Watching?* presentations to local colleges and organizations. Like golden leaves trailing autumn gusts, favorable editorials appeared
in the *Tri-City Herald*, the Walla Walla *Union Bulletin*, and the *Lewiston
Tribune* in Idaho. Russell and Simenstad had a close, easy rapport, and their
trips—in addition to building support for the cause in a conservative part of
Washington—restored Nancy's energy and gave her a break from the inces-
sant pressure to raise money.[45]

Before Russell could persuade Congress to even consider protecting the Gorge,
developers threatened to destroy much of what she wanted to save. The population of Clark County, which includes the City of Vancouver and the western
three miles of the Gorge, had grown by 50 percent during the 1970s, to almost
two hundred thousand residents. High-tech manufacturers sought out large,
undeveloped tracts of industrial-zoned land in the county's eastern section
and an attractive quality of life for their employees. Tektronix, an international
electronics manufacturer and one of Oregon's largest employers, invested $20
million in a plant just outside Camas, hired twelve hundred workers, and
anticipated employing almost nine thousand more by 2000. Hewlett Packard
built a computer assembly plant nearby with 450 workers and expected to
grow to 10,000 by the year 2000. Planners anticipated that workers would live
on Mount Pleasant or Mount Zion or in Cascade Villages, a proposed $1.3
billion city of forty-five thousand people just west of the entrance to the Gorge,
and commute to downtown Portland on the I-205 bridge—a "cocked gun"
pointed at the Gorge, attorney Gail Achterman warned.[46]

It was not new cities that would damage the Gorge, however, as much as
subdivisions and houses here, there, and everywhere. "This will not happen
instantly," John Yeon wrote in October 1981, calling such developments "an
insidious hazard."

> The total eventual effect of suburbanizing the Gorge, if proposed at one time, would incite such total opposition that protection would be decisive. Piecemeal nibbling, in bites of various size, at various times, is the way it will occur, to the obvious advantage of developers whose single operations may seem no major threat to the vast grandeur of the Gorge. Yet subdivisions, which spread like cancers, are the most hopeless afflictions of great natural landscapes. . . .The creeping transformations of suburbia are irreversible.[47]

The eastern reaches of the Gorge—where there were fewer trees to hide the effects of development on its grasslands and basalt plateaus—were also susceptible. Klickitat County's boundary started forty miles from the Gorge's western entrance and extended past its eastern portal near Maryhill Museum.[48] It was too remote for most metro-area commuters, but retirees were drawn to the county's affordable housing and wealthy Portland and Seattle residents had recreation homes there, attracted by a sunny climate and the steady winds that blew windsurfers across the Columbia at speeds exceeding thirty miles an hour.

One Klickitat County landowner wanted to develop over a thousand acres of prime agricultural land bordering a wildlife refuge and had asked county commissioners to change the land's open-space zoning to five-acre residential. The commission had agreed, reversing the recommendation of the county's planning director and Environmental Review Committee. "People shouldn't be told what to do with their land," Fred Holly, the chair of the commission said. Later, when the county considered a more restrictive overlay zone proposed by the Gorge Commission, Holly cautioned: "I want to be careful we don't adopt something that tells the landowner he's got to do this, this and this."[49]

New residences were not the only threat. In the western Gorge, the Stevenson family was preparing the Steigerwald Lake wetlands for heavy industry, and Skamania and Klickitat county commissions considered the I-205 bridge to be a significant advantage in their pursuit of industrial development. In the eastern Gorge, the community of Dallesport, across the Columbia from The Dalles, had a population of only a few hundred people in 1980, yet the local port was actively marketing six thousand acres for industrial development. A few years earlier, the port had promoted the zirconium plant that Barbara Bailey and other alarmed orchardists in The Dalles had stopped. The plant had moved to Utah, where its neighbors would blame it for causing major health problems. In the middle Gorge, the owners of Pierce Island and Ives Island near Beacon Rock and Wells Island in Hood River—large islands with important heron rookeries and wildlife habitat—were advertising their properties for industry, dredge spoils, or intense tourist development.[50]

State and federal agencies were facilitating or standing by the loss of some of the Gorge's most significant resources. The Oregon Department of Transportation (ODOT), for example, determined that the 1918 bridge that crossed the Hood River was inadequate for modern traffic and chose not to retain it for cyclists or pedestrians, as proposed by local groups. The graceful, four-hundred-foot-long bridge—the longest on the Historic Columbia River Highway and one of its foremost engineering features—was demolished in 1982. That same year, ODOT and Governor Atiyeh resisted Nancy Russell's demand to save popular sand dunes east of The Dalles, which deserved "special recognition," according to the Park Service's 1980 study of alternatives.[51] Instead the state carpeted the twenty-thousand-year-old fifty-acre dunes with a five-inch "blanket" of crushed rock to keep them from migrating, a solution that Russell described as "a sledgehammer approach that could be better handled with vegetation." The Army Corps of Engineers, when building the second powerhouse at Bonneville Dam in the late 1970s, obliterated an "undisturbed [and] significant archeological site." Eleven hundred cubic feet of artifacts were removed to make way for the new river channel, including "centuries-old stone tools and pottery." Farther west, the US Forest Service was entertaining a proposal—to be funded by state development loans—for a hydroelectric facility on Gorton Creek Falls, a dramatic 115-foot-high waterfall near Cascade Locks. Federal and state agencies, unwittingly but effectively, were making the case for federal legislation.[52]

No area in the Gorge was as endangered as the sixteen miles in Washington that stretched from the western entrance at the Steigerwald Lake wetlands to Beacon Rock. In December 1979, John Yeon had written a forceful letter to Governor Atiyeh that explained the need for federal legislation, the decades-long fight to provide it, and how the Gorge—particularly this sixteen-mile reach—was now at crisis stage.

On the fertile north shore lowlands in the foreground of the western view from Crown Point, the Port of Washougal is attempting to expand its industrial park over the whole of the Steigerwald Lake area. The high farmlands on Mt. Pleasant . . . are already in the subdivision process. From Cape Horn to Beacon Rock (the western core of the

Gorge) all of the vacant land with feasible contours, with the exception of perhaps half a dozen properties, is held for suburban subdivision. Even the lofty summit of Archer Mountain shares this fate. The new town of North Bonneville has recently attempted to acquire for an industrial park the Pierce Ranch area between it and Beacon Rock. The completion of the 1-205 bridge can only hasten the junking of an area which is not as grand as Yosemite Valley, but may be the next best thing.[53]

There were no public lands in this segment, and there was no public access to the river. Even Skamania County recognized this deficiency and called for public land purchases in its 1982 park plan. The land remained remarkably pristine, despite being slated for subdivision or industrialization.[54]

At noon on December 15, 1982, the two-mile-long I-205 bridge opened to great fanfare. Named for Glenn L. Jackson—former Oregon Highway Commission chair, behind-the-scenes powerbroker, and visionary leader who had died in 1980—the bridge also opened to some odd omens. Its first accident occurred within an hour, and among its inaugural travelers were Slinky Jones and fellow members of the Gypsy Jokers and Rude Boys motorcycle gangs. At the dedication a day earlier, the *Oregonian* reported, festivities led by Mabel Bishop of the Pendleton Woolen Mills family were "cut short by the near-gale-force winds howling down the Columbia Gorge."[55]

Twenty-seven thousand vehicles were predicted to cross the bridge every day, most from eastern Multnomah County, which had a population density of over a thousand people per square mile. But the boundary for western Skamania County, where the comparable density was only ten people per square mile, was now fifteen minutes from the new bridge, placing the county within easy commuting distance of downtown Portland. Realtors enthused that prices for farmland on Mount Pleasant and Mount Zion, with their extraordinary views, had doubled in two years. "It's just a matter of time," one celebrated, "before that area becomes part of the greater Portland-Vancouver area." George Rizor's Columbia Gorge Riverfront Estates in Skamania County was perfectly positioned to capitalize on the demand.[56]

It would be difficult to find two people more different than George Rizor and Nancy Russell. Rizor had spent his career in the army and retired as a full colonel, a title he still preferred. Conservative and deeply religious, he taught Sunday school classes at the Camas Nazarene Church. The initials of his corporation—Heritage Investment Services—paid tribute to God and formed the shape of a cross on the letterhead. "The Gorge is not my God. The God I worship made the Gorge," Rizor told the Skamania County Planning Commission the following summer, "and he made this earth for us to use."[57]

And use it Rizor would. "I'm not only within my legal rights," he had declared to a reporter a year earlier. "I'm within my moral rights." He labeled his opponents "Portland Communists," and chief among them was Nancy Russell. She also saw the situation in black and white. "The Gorge is one of the great features of the world" she told a reporter, "and this type of development will totally change its character." Russell concluded with a flourish: "to have it subdivided American-style is an insult."[58]

A few months after Rizor filed his subdivision, another was filed in western Skamania County. Rim View Estates replicated Rizor's strategy: split a large property into separately owned parcels whose owners would divide their parcels into individual lots and create a subdivision without notice or hearings. Rim View Estates, owned by a small real estate corporation with Clark County officers, consisted of sixteen lots on top of Cape Horn.[59] Most of the lots were narrow, running through pastures and wildflowers to the edge of the thousand-foot precipice, and offered spectacular views upriver to Beacon Rock. John Yeon's feared "piecemeal nibbling" was growing into large bites, and, if developed, Nancy Russell's dream of creating a park at Cape Horn would die.

Russell's ten-hour days lengthened as she scrambled to address the threats from both Rizor and Rim View Estates. Although both developments presented the same legal issue, with limited resources, she was forced to choose: try to save the view from Multnomah Falls, seen by over 2 million visitors a year, or try to stop the Cape Horn development, buy its land, and create a park. Russell chose to fight Rizor's subdivision, and the lots at uncontested Rim View Estates soon started selling for up to $50,000. Within months she had recruited five Skamania County landowners to serve as potential plaintiffs against Rizor, including John Yeon. She engaged a pro bono lawyer to represent the plaintiffs and raised enough money to pay for expert witnesses and file a lawsuit.[60] When the court ruled that the plaintiffs would need to post a $50,000 surety bond to proceed, she rallied seven others to underwrite the bond, including herself and Nani Warren, whose Prindle property was just downstream from the proposed development.

Six months later, in April 1982, Russell won her lawsuit. Her satisfaction was tempered by the loss of Cape Horn—where a quarter of the sixteen lots at Rim View Estates would sell by the end of the year—by the inexorable industrialization of the Steigerwald Lake floodplain, and by the realization that Rizor could still subdivide his land by refiling his application, this time following the minimal state rules. But she had bought time and had focused attention on the Columbia Gorge. The Vancouver *Columbian* had been perceptive, in late 1980, when it editorialized that there had been "limited success in stirring widespread concern about the gorge" but that Rizor's proposal could provide "a foundation on which to build."[61]

John Yeon had acknowledged that a miracle would be required for federal legislation to overcome the resistance of both governors, all but one of the six counties, and now President Reagan. Despite the daunting odds, he believed this was the last opportunity. "There is no chance of choosing a better time," he said. "The time is set by the I-205 bridge, the development of a new city between Vancouver and Camas (as big as Vancouver) and the present Skamania County government which is tripping over its own regulations in its haste to encourage and expedite subdivisions in the Gorge . . . it is now or too late." Yeon might have added that without federal legislation, the industrialization of Steigerwald Lake, Pierce and Wells Islands, Dallesport, and potential new subdivisions on Klickitat County vistas would overwhelm much of the Gorge.[62]

The situation worsened early in the Reagan administration. Instead of buying and protecting land to preserve the nation's heritage, Secretary of the Interior James Watt called for the Land and Water Conservation Fund, the federal government's main source of funding for new parklands, to be reduced by 75 percent, from an annual average of $284 million during President Carter's last three years in office to $76 million. Secretary Watt then declared a moratorium on the federal purchase of parkland. In February 1982 he announced that the federal government intended to sell 35 million acres of the public domain.[63]

The secretary's message resonated in Skamania County, which had been dominated by the federal government since its inception in 1854, when more than three-quarters of its land was in the public domain. The federal government had withdrawn most of that land from general development in 1893 when it created, with broad public support for protecting scenic values, the Pacific Forest Reserve, much of which later became the Gifford Pinchot National Forest.[64] Although Skamania County extends north almost sixty miles from the Columbia River, most of the county's population and private lands are in a narrow band in the south, one to three miles wide, of relatively flat, developable land. That band, between the river and the rim of the Gorge, stretches upriver for almost forty miles, from Skamania's western boundary with Clark County to its eastern boundary with Klickitat County. It is where the towns are located and where most of its economic development must occur. Any regulatory encroachment on that narrow band would be resisted.

The remote, rugged terrain of Skamania County had fostered a culture that prized hard-scrabble independence and resented outside interference. By the early 1980s, however, outside forces—pressure from the Glenn Jackson Bridge, agitation for Gorge legislation, and double-dip recessions—started to rock the county. Skamania's economy was handcuffed to the timber industry, and housing starts and timber harvesting plummeted as economic recessions pushed average mortgage rates above 16 percent in 1981 and 1982. In February 1982, the unemployment rate in Skamania County hovered at 30 percent, the highest in Washington. The county received a quarter of its revenue from the Gifford Pinchot National Forest, and like many dependencies, this one bred contempt. The Reagan administration intended to double the harvest in Northwest national forests, despite decades of unsustainable cutting that was destroying the region's old-growth forests. Rumblings over the fate of the northern spotted owl, a small bird that was dependent on the forests, had started a decade earlier, and pressure to protect the owl's habitat, especially in the national forests, soon added to the county's sense of victimization by conservationists and the federal government.[65]

"Skamania County isn't just a place—it's a way of life, an ethic," Ed McClarney, editor and publisher of the *Skamania County Pioneer*, told a Seattle reporter. "Our way of life is indeed being threatened. The environment is not," he continued in an editorial that castigated federal legislation. "We are an endangered species, little counties like ours," he thundered,

> and as God-created biological creatures (people), we should be offered the same protection as the grey whale or the sea otter or the tufted-ear dingbat. . . . With the advent of the recent Columbia River Gorge control issue, we are seeing the kinds of actions which may destroy city and county government through potentially illegal, unethical, and totally un-American means.[66]

County residents piled on. "Only the tourister and downstream flatlander will benefit" from federal legislation, said one. "We don't need another thumb on our necks," said another. And lest any ambiguity remain regarding the depth of the chasm between Skamania County and the City of Portland, one woman told Nancy Russell that "you Portland people don't know how we think. You don't know how Skamania County people are. You come stepping on our toes, and you've bitten off more than you can chew. You can't love it (the gorge) and live in Portland."[67]

One of Russell's strengths was a laserlike focus on her objective. Like many strengths, however, it also could be a weakness. Politicians like Don Clark would empathize with the plight of county residents and point out that a national scenic area designation would boost tourism and allow Skamania County's economy to expand. Russell had crafted that argument—in fact, locals criticized her for supporting the construction of a hotel in the town of North Bonneville—and she knew the economic advantages of an NSA better than anyone. But she was not empathetic when it came to Skamania County's economic distress. She viewed its plight through the lens of logic and practicality, not emotion, and she was certain that her legislation would improve the local economy. The county's reliance on the timber industry had brought it 30 percent unemployment, Russell reasoned. If county leadership and many of its citizens chose not to recognize this, then it was their own fault. Residents "would pull up their socks" and "clean up their act," she told the *Pioneer*, when they saw the economic development potential of tourism.[68]

Some accused Russell of being elitist, and in a way she was. While her childhood was modest and itinerant, and she had relied on scholarships to gain an education, her marriage to Bruce had conferred a measure of wealth and prominence. It gave her the ability to immerse herself in the Gorge, nurturing a love of nature that had been kindled at Dundee and Elk Lake. Mostly, however, charges of elitism were levied against Russell because she was an outsider who insisted on a benchmark of beauty for the Gorge that, as with any definition of beauty, was subjective. Skamania County generally mistrusted outsiders, especially those seeking to impose change. But change was coming, as the expanding metropolitan area brought new interests and influences along with new houses and subdivisions. Anyone carrying Russell's message would have been pilloried, but her social status, relentlessness and sometimes impolitic responses made her already difficult path steeper and rockier.

Most of those benefitting from Russell's actions were not elite. While her mentor John Yeon viewed the Gorge landscape through the eyes of an artist and preferred The Shire's meticulously manicured and secluded grounds, Russell emphasized the "public" part of public parks. She believed that public needs—as well as the landscape—should be served, and she saw hiking, sightseeing, and enjoying nature as causes for celebration. Russell did not dismiss the need for jobs, but she wanted them to be compatible with resource protection, preferring, for instance, agriculture, forestry, recreation, and tourism—all essential Northwest industries—over mining and rural factories that might provide well-paying jobs but erode the Gorge's natural economic advantage. She was more offended by mansions with multiple garages—and their outsize impact on the landscape—than by mobile homes. And she knew whose interests she represented. "I am aware the people who benefit the most from Gorge preservation will certainly be those who use it so fully now," Russell wrote a friend, "the young and the working people who can't afford to go further afield to enjoy wild, magnificent nature."[69]

In the early 1980s, Skamania residents were represented by a three-person county commission chaired by Bill Benson, Nani Warren's caretaker for her Prindle estate. The county's real power, however, was in a long-ruling pair: Bob Leick, the prosecuting attorney and head of the Republican Party, and Rudy Hegewald, a businessman and former leader of the Democratic Party. Both had economic interests at stake, and both opposed Gorge legislation. Leick's office placed stickers on county envelopes that proclaimed, NO FEDERAL LANDGRAB IN THE COLUMBIA RIVER GORGE, and he threatened to sue Southwest Washington Health Systems Agency when Russell was scheduled to give a presentation there, backing away only when asked to put his reasons in writing. More ominously, Leick promised that as the county's top prosecutor he would not enforce "federally-imposed land use regulations." Almost a dozen organizations—including the Columbia Gorge Protection Council, the Gorge Defense League, the Protect the Gorge Committee, and Columbia Gorge United—were created in the early 1980s to fight for "local control." Most were headquartered in Skamania County. All shared misleading names, anti-legislation missions, and often Leick's and Hegewald's leadership and timber industry funding, including, it was assumed, from the Stevenson family.[70]

In early 1981, Charles Cushman, a fire-and-brimstone rabble rouser who took pride is his press-bestowed nickname "Rent-a-Riot," was paid $22,000 by Leick's Gorge Defense League to oppose legislation. Chuck Williams wrote the most extensive and detailed exposé of Cushman for *Not Man Apart*, the Friends of the Earth magazine. Cushman had been a successful Beverly Hills insurance salesman—selling over a million dollars of insurance a year for thirteen years, Williams reported—until he retired at full disability due to headaches. His father had been a seasonal interpreter at Yosemite National Park and owned a cabin in the park, which Cushman claimed the Park Service had forcibly acquired. Apparently in retaliation, he had filed a Freedom of Information Act request for the names of inholders in the National Park system and had used those thirty-four thousand names to create the National Inholders Association, which paid him to crusade against the Park Service. When Cushman's insurance company learned about his strenuous travel schedule, it stopped paying for his disability, but he was undeterred. He was close to Interior Secretary Watt, who appointed him to the National Park System Advisory Board, which was charged with overseeing land acquisition for the agency. Also appointed to the board was Ric Davidge, Cushman's close associate who once called the National Park concept "feudalistic colonialism."[71]

Before long, Cushman was making presentations about the Gorge to standing-room-only crowds, including a capacity crowd at the Portland Chamber of Commerce, a hundred people in Cascade Locks, and audiences in Hood River, Stevenson, and The Dalles. His strategy was simple and effective. Using a film that featured interviews with landowners from the Cuyahoga National Recreation Area near Cleveland, Ohio, Cushman painted a vivid, and inaccurate, portrayal of what the National Park Service would do in the Columbia Gorge if Nancy Russell's "incredibly radical proposal" was adopted. Her proposal, he told audiences, "wipes out families," would result in "mass displacement," and could forcibly relocate up to fifteen thousand families, a wild claim, since only forty-one thousand people lived in the Gorge, half of them in urban areas that would be exempted from regulation. Russell's legislation, Cushman continued, would cost taxpayers a half-billion dollars. He compared the National Park Service to "Nazis," Williams wrote, and called Gorge legislation "the final solution." When Russell and others enumerated the landowner safeguards contained in the draft legislation, Cushman responded that the law did not matter as it could always be changed.[72]

While whipping up Skamania County residents and bashing federal land management agencies, Cushman reached for a broader audience by claiming to support some form of Gorge protection. His strategy seemed transparent: stop federal legislation by supporting weak state measures that maintained local control. Skamania County commissioner Benson adopted Cushman's approach, and a local state senator introduced two bills in the Washington legislature. One called for a commission, dominated by local elected officials, to craft an advisory management plan for the Washington side of the Gorge while the other would fund conservation easements purchased from willing sellers. The internal inconsistencies of Cushman's strategy—that is, incite the locals while seeking palliative legislation—became apparent when both the Klickitat and Skamania county commissions, responding to constituent outcries against *any* legislation, reversed course and urged rejection of their own management-by-commission bill. Neither bill passed. The county commissioners successfully requested, instead, that the legislature send a memorial to Congress demanding local control.[73]

Washington's new Republican governor, John Spellman, had a fallback plan. He created a ten-person select committee—composed of several outspoken opponents of federal legislation, including county chairs Benson and Holly—to recommend how the Gorge should be managed. It was no surprise when six months later the committee recommended that state legislation be drafted to create a thirteen-member commission, composed mostly of local elected officials and residents. The proposed commission, guided by vague goals and uncertain authority, would help local governments "maintain the unique qualities of the Gorge," at least in Washington. Oregon's governor was invited to appoint three nonvoting "observers." To explain the absence of meaningful Oregon participation, Bill Benson likened Oregonians to starlings: "Well, they lay their eggs in other birds' nests, and then when they hatch, they kick the other birds out and take over."[74]

Others had different views. The Vancouver *Columbian*, which initially favored local control, editorialized that "after straining at a lion of a plan, the committee gave birth to a mouse," and the *Skamania County Pioneer*, perhaps realizing that even mice have teeth, wailed that "legislation which could destroy the people of the gorge is in the wind." The Gorge Defense League mobilized against the committee's recommendation. With no public support and plenty of opposition, legislation to create a commission never advanced. Russell and Friends of the Columbia Gorge, inadvertently aided by the Skamania and Klickitat county commissions, now had a clearer path to federal legislation. A state legislator who represented Washington's counties in the Gorge and shared their antipathy to federal legislation remarked: "I'm afraid if they (county commissioners) resist everything, at some point they're going to lose everything."[75]

In 1981 and 1982, Russell and the Friends of the Columbia Gorge—with help from attorneys Gail Achterman and Borden Beck—drafted legislation for Congress to consider. Given the political complexity of the Columbia Gorge and Russell's legal and legislative inexperience, progress was slow. Nancy Russell, Don Clark, John Yeon, Chuck Williams, and other supporters agreed that a federal agency needed to manage the Gorge, and that cities—where the bulk of the population lived and where scenic, natural, and cultural resources had already been disturbed—should be exempt from legislation, but key questions remained: How far upriver would the boundaries of the protected area extend? Would the Columbia's major tributaries be protected? Would there be a regional commission, and if so what role would it play? Most importantly, which agency should lead, the National Park Service or the US Forest Service, and how should private lands be managed? These questions needed answers.

The boundary question was perhaps easiest to resolve. Three of the four alternatives in the Park Service study extended the protected area to the eastern Gorge; the fourth reached only west of Hood River, where extensive blocks of public land ended. Chuck Williams was the most forceful advocate for protecting the eastern Gorge, where fish runs at Celilo Falls and the Long Narrows had sustained Native people for millennia. John Yeon, however, believed that including the eastern Gorge would create new burdens for a campaign that had consistently failed for over seventy years, and under more favorable political conditions. It meant adding two counties—Klickitat and Wasco—that opposed legislation and whose land was mostly private and owned by opponents to regulation. There was no federal precedent, moreover, for designating an area with so much private land. "I cannot envision a plan for saving the full length of the Gorge," Yeon stated. "The penalty price of past neglect may be that such a plan is not now possible." Russell disagreed. Adding the eastern Gorge would create new challenges, but it would also protect a landscape with no parallel in the United States—a rainforest linked to desert through an eighty-five-mile-long canyon that cleaved a mountain range, embraced incomparable beauty and history, offered recreational opportunities for a growing metropolis, and boasted extraordinary natural diversity and significant cultural landscapes.[76]

While Yeon did not disagree with Williams's desire to protect the major tributaries in the Gorge, he opposed their inclusion in the legislation, which he believed should concentrate on protecting beauty more than fisheries. And he continued to worry about additions that made passage problematic. "I am convinced that the sheer size and weight of the encumbrance of these irrelevant appendages," he said, "would crush the life out of the Gorge effort." Although Russell wanted all of the Gorge's attributes protected—scenic, natural, cultural, and recreational—she agreed with Yeon and the Park Service study, which excluded the tributaries because of their size and complexity.[77]

Some supporters favored a role for a commission in Gorge management, if it had limited powers and was well defined. Constitutional provisions discourage the federal government from directly zoning private lands, so a regional commission would be useful if the entire Gorge was protected, especially in the east where public lands were few. Again, Yeon disagreed. He preferred an easier-to-pass, compact national recreation area in the western Gorge, where a commission was not needed and land purchases would provide protection. "Zoning can reduce subdivision density," he said, "but cannot preserve intact the natural open spaces which are now so important to the Gorge landscape. It is not possible to zone for no use. Zoning cannot provide areas or facilities for public use along the shores or among the heights. Zoning cannot preserve the remarkable wilderness scenery still surviving in the Gorge." Both Russell and Yeon were wary of zoning, which they believed could be undermined by litigation and variances. Public ownership was more durable. Russell recognized, however, that zoning was essential if the entire Gorge was to be protected.[78]

A representative commission, in any case, with members appointed by leaders at all levels of government, could ensure that all perspectives were considered, and perhaps even gain broader support over time. Russell and the Friends proposed that a regional commission serve as the lead federal agency's "chief advisor" and share some power. Local representatives—whose appointers were beholden to developers' campaign contributions and who might be susceptible to a neighbor angry over a denied a permit—should not constitute a majority on the commission. That approach, supporters of legislation believed, had been tried and had failed at Lake Tahoe.[79]

The lead federal agency would fund and craft a single management plan for the Gorge. That plan would supersede the fifty-plus divergent plans governments used in the two-state, six-county region, plans that promoted economic development, industry, residential housing, farming, and forestry but rarely conservation. Only a federal agency could pull together the expertise to manage such complexity. The federal government already had a significant presence as the largest landowner in the Gorge, owning one-fifth of the area, and its works—two federal dams, two national forests, and an interstate highway—had left their mark. Moreover, only the federal government had sufficient funding to acquire parks at the scale necessary in the Gorge. "Parklands remain the major device for preserving the shores and summits of the Washington side," Yeon emphasized, "just as public ownership elsewhere in the Gorge is responsible for what has so far been permanently saved." Russell concurred. "Public ownership," she said, "will last for future generations."[80]

The question, therefore, was not whether a federal agency should lead Gorge protection, but which one? On pure merits, the answer was the National Park Service. After observing both agencies operate in the Northwest for over a half century, Yeon had a stinging assessment of the Forest Service, saying it had "done virtually nothing" to expand its holdings in the Gorge. "Content within its nineteenth century boundaries," he said, the Forest Service was "aloof from the twentieth century problems besetting the Gorge." Its "historic attitudes make it singularly unmotivated and ill-equipted [sic] to become an aggressive lead agency for Federal action in the Gorge."[81]

By comparison, Yeon concluded, "if the Forest Service has been traditionally isolationist, the Park Service has been traditionally interventionist," as confirmed by its 1980 Study of Alternatives and its 1981 report that studied the Historic Columbia River Highway's historic and recreational resources and recommended conservation opportunities. The Park Service was also more experienced than the Forest Service in managing large popular parks near urban areas, parks that often contained significant private inholdings, such as the Golden Gate National Recreation Area in San Francisco and the Gateway National Recreation Area in New York City. The mission of the National Park Service was precise and oriented to conservation: "to conserve the scenery and the natural and historic objects and the wild life therein and to . . . leave them unimpaired for the enjoyment of future generations." The multiple-use mission of the Forest Service seemed muddier and more focused on timber harvesting, which could lead to "multiple abuse of exceptional areas," Yeon wrote. The agencies' different missions affected staffing as well. "The Park Service has the largest pool by far of the talents and experience required to execute and manage a project such as a Gorge Recreation or Scenic Area," Yeon noted. "These talents in the Forest Service are in short supply since such activities are peripheral to [its] main mission." Russell, Yeon, and Williams agreed, but other considerations were at play.[82]

Charles Cushman had successfully demonized the National Park Service, particularly in Skamania County, and claimed to have a "much easier time dealing with the Forest Service." Skamania was a timber county, and Oregon was a timber state, with 12 million acres in eighteen national forests. As a consequence, the timber industry dominated state and local politics and, some would say, the US Forest Service. The industry reflexively opposed new Park Service units, especially those proposed for national forests, where logging was mostly encouraged; the Park Service typically prohibits commercial logging. If there was to be a lead federal agency in the Columbia

Gorge, most residents, local officials, the governor of Oregon, and many members of the Oregon delegation, including Senator Hatfield, preferred the Forest Service. A simple tally of the national parks and Park Service-managed national recreation areas in the two states demonstrates how the timber industry dominated land and politics in Oregon, while agriculture, airplane manufacturing, atomic weapons and aluminum competed for influence in the State of Washington. Washington had three national parks and three national recreation areas managed by the National Park Service, for a combined 1.8 million acres, while Oregon had one national park, Crater Lake, with 160,000 acres.[83]

In any case, under President Reagan and Secretary Watt, both agencies proved to be reluctant suitors for a Columbia Gorge bride. The Park Service's new director opposed a national park or recreation area for the Gorge. It was too controversial, and a high-ranking Park Service official said that creation of a national scenic area was "unlikely." The Gorge was "worth preserving," he said, but no new Park Service units were contemplated anywhere. Even John Yeon had to admit that his favorite agency was "paralyzed . . . they can't acquire anything and are afraid to stick their neck out."[84]

Meanwhile, the Forest Service hardly acknowledged the problem. Responding to the Park Service study, a top Forest Service official accused the Park Service of painting "a more gloomy picture" and having "an overly pessimistic view" of the situation than was warranted. In fact, he said, no additional controls were needed in Oregon, and a boundary expansion of the Gifford Pinchot National Forest in Washington would suffice as long as protection extended only to Hood River. "The Forest Service should not be forced to undertake a project it perceives as unnecessary," an irritated Yeon responded. "Neither should it be permitted to be a dog-in-the-manger preventing another agency from executing a job it doesn't itself want." After Russell raised the Gorge's profile, however, Yeon's dog in the manger bared its fangs. In territorial remarks reminiscent of its response to the Park Service sixty-five years earlier, the Forest Service asserted that it was not just willing to serve as the lead agency, if Congress requested, "but would expect to do so." The Gorge's largest landowner, responsible for forty-four thousand acres, would not give up its land or its management authority without a fight.[85]

Russell wrestled with the decision. She knew the Park Service, with its experience, conservation mission, and innovative staff, would be the best manager, and she admired the agency for how it had managed the Oregon Trail. But she also believed—thanks to Cushman, Secretary Watt, and the influence of the timber industry—that the creation of a Park Service–led national scenic area could make a nearly impossible challenge actually impossible. She was not as uncomfortable with the Forest Service as Yeon was, having been familiar with the agency since childhood at Elk Lake, and the agency was courting her, telling her that a Columbia River Gorge NSA represented a historic opportunity for it to evolve into a more relevant, twenty-first-century agency—an agency that would promote miles of hiking trails, not just board feet of lumber.[86]

She considered the options, including joint management of the Gorge by the Park Service and the Forest Service, and asked the attorneys to leave blank, until the last moment, the section in the Friends' legislation that named the lead agency. Yeon also considered creative alternatives, including a Park Service–managed NSA in the western Gorge that allowed the Forest Service to retain its lands and a bifurcated NSA where the Park Service managed everything west of Bonneville Dam and the Forest Service managed everything to the east. Chuck Williams advocated for Park Service management but saw it as a political chit that could be bargained away to secure an NSA, telling a key Oregon congressman that Forest Service management would be "a big compromise, but one worth at least trying."[87]

When Russell submitted the draft legislation to the Oregon delegation, she named the Forest Service as the lead agency.[88] Oregon senators Mark Hatfield and Bob Packwood introduced the Friends' bill on March 31, 1982, and Oregon representatives Les AuCoin and Jim Weaver introduced the same bill in the House. The Forest Service would manage the eighty-five-mile-long scenic area, and the legislation required that a regional commission with thirteen voting members—six appointed by the six counties, four by the two governors, and three by the secretary of agriculture—would advise the agency.

Senator Hatfield remained cautious, perhaps surprised by the depth of opposition to federal legislation, especially in Skamania County. He introduced a second, less protective bill, without the support of Senator Packwood, who was more willing to push for a strong conservation solution. Hatfield's second bill replaced the Forest Service with an eleven-member regional commission, with six county appointees outnumbering four governor appointees and a Forest Service appointee. The Friends disagreed with his approach, Hatfield acknowledged, but many Gorge residents saw the first bill as a "federal takeover of private property," and he wanted "a complete public forum for these ideas to be discussed."[89]

No member of the Washington delegation supported either bill, but legislation had finally been introduced in Congress, where the power of national
conservation organizations and the Garden Club of America could be influential. Russell and Gretchen Hull had visited each Garden Club affiliate in
their four-state zone, and by January 1982 they had the support of all eleven
of them. In April, before the GCA's Zone XII meeting in Portland, Russell
guided its president and seven other luminaries through the Gorge. The next
month, the Garden Club of America endorsed the Friends' legislation.[90]

In Washington and Oregon, however, neither governor supported
federal legislation. The recommendation for state legislation by Governor
Spellman's Select Committee had withered under an onslaught of opposition from Skamania and Klickitat counties. As the spotlight shifted to Capitol Hill, Governor Atiyeh, who had changed his position three times over
fifteen months, was isolated. Meeting with John Yeon in June 1981, Atiyeh
perfunctorily professed his love for the Gorge. Yeon could no longer contain
himself, and shouted furiously, accusing the governor of hypocrisy and abys-
mal leadership. Alarmed by the commotion, Atiyeh's chief of staff raced into
the office and separated the two men. Yeon later apologized. "In a long life,
I have accumulated lots of regrets," he wrote Atiyeh, "but now the day I most
wish I could live over differently is the day I came to your office. I am terribly
sorry about that. The regret is persistent." Russell once described Yeon as "a
star up there in the sky, a pure point of view," and like a star Yeon burned hot.
Not Nancy Russell, although she could be less circumspect in private and
once wrote Yeon that "when I smash a ball" when playing tennis "I am going
to pretend it's Atiyeh."[91]

Attacks on Russell intensified as she became the public face of the
Gorge campaign. Skamania County's history and culture made it difficult
for anyone to bring change to the area, especially a woman and especially a
woman from Portland's West Hills. At first, the criticism tended to be generic.
Skamania prosecutor Bob Leick, for example, dismissed the Friends as the
"wine and cheese" set or as "limosine [sic] liberals from Portland." The *Pioneer* editorialized against "rich backpackers with oversized calves," and some
residents railed against "Portland socialites." Then it got personal. Bumper

A popular bumper sticker.
FOCG archives

Russell debating Skamania County protesters picketing the Friends' first winter picnic
fundraiser, Portland 1982. FOCG archives.

stickers screamed, "Save the Gorge from Nancy Russell," and Leick gave
Russell his "Looking for Love in All the Wrong Places" award. A candidate for
county sheriff ran a chilling political ad in the *Pioneer* warning that "Nancy
Russell wants us to disappear." The attacks would worsen, but the hostility
never seemed to bother her. If anything, it emboldened her. When Skamania
County protesters picketed the Friends' Winter Picnic in downtown Portland
with signs demanding "No Nancy Russell Ziggurat," she walked into the
crowd, eager for debate.[92]

Russell reacted in much the same way to hostility from others. In 1981,
the director of the Western Forestry Center in Portland, John Blackwell, called
her days before she was scheduled to talk to The Nature Conservancy there.
The center received considerable funding from the timber industry, and
he had been approached by a delegation of Forestry Center members who
opposed Russell and Friends of the Columbia Gorge. Blackwell demanded
that her presentation be confined to botany and wildflowers and forbid her
to discuss Gorge protection efforts. Russell asked who was in the delegation.
Blackwell refused to answer. Russell persisted. Finally, he acknowledged that

the delegation was composed of timber interests, including the Stevenson family. Unwilling to disappoint The Nature Conservancy, Russell acquiesced and gave the talk as directed. As she ended, she told her audience that she had been forbidden to discuss efforts to protect the Gorge. If anyone was interested, however, they could join her outside, where she would be happy to explain the campaign. With that, the entire audience donned coats and scarves against the blustery spring weather and followed Russell to the Portland Zoo parking lot, where she gave a spirited explanation of why federal legislation was needed. She asked everyone to join the Friends and write their congressman.[93]

It was not the last time Russell would encounter the Stevensons. One afternoon at home her doorbell rang. Russell opened the door to find an angry Eloise Stevenson, a family matriarch, on her doorstep. Out of breath from her long walk up Westwinds' steep driveway, jabbing her finger and raising her voice, Stevenson harangued Russell about the Gorge and warned that her family "will fight you!" The attempt at intimidation shook Russell, but not for long. Secure in her belief that she was right and the Stevensons were not—and that her visitor had exhibited exceedingly poor behavior—Russell carried on as before, except, perhaps, with a bit more incentive to win.[94]

With progress came increased opposition. New organizations—the Committee to Preserve Property Rights in the Columbia River Gorge and STOP (Stop Taking Our Property)—bobbed in Cushman's wake and singled out Russell with increasing vitriol. Skamania County, the timber industry, the Stevensons, and other members of Portland's business and political elite continued to assail her. John Yeon did not. Russell was his protégée, and his disagreements with her on important elements of the legislation must have been especially painful for him. "She had to knock herself out," Russell's life-long friend Marie Hall observed about Russell's relationship with Yeon. "She had to go way more than halfway with John."[95] Yeon, who typically lacerated those with whom he disagreed, acknowledged his respect for Russell in early 1982, when their differences were acute. "My association with Nancy has been an exceptional, once in a lifetime experience for me, as seeing Halley's Comet might be, and I don't expect to observe such a phenomenon again," he wrote. "No wonder then if I seem awestruck; I am." Yeon explained why he so admired Russell:

> With long experience in this field, I have never previously observed the devotion, energy and skill which have fueled her monumental effort. To an exceptional degree, she has been responsible not only for

grand strategies, but for the detailed execution of them: raising funds, enlisting supporters, filling brutal schedules of lectures and meetings over much of the region, contacting newspapers, conferring with legislators, guiding tours and hikes in the Gorge, and participating in talk shows on radio and television. In these, the volleys of clear answers to challenging questions suggest the athletic skills which made Nancy the longtime . . . women's tennis champion of Portland.[96]

While Yeon would continue to disagree with Russell, neither lost respect for the other. And despite their disagreements, he bolstered Russell's efforts by welcoming her to use The Shire, one of his most private possessions, "as her own."[97]

Russell had become a formidable and resilient advocate. No one knew the Gorge's resources better than she did. No one better understood the extent of the problem and the merits of possible solutions. No one cared more or worked harder. And no one was better positioned to protect the Gorge. Friends of the Columbia Gorge now had a thousand members and had won the support of three hundred influential sponsors.[98] Its finances were growing. Media from Portland and Seattle, eastern Oregon and Washington, and soon across the country were highlighting threats to the Gorge, endorsing the Friends' position, and writing favorable editorials.

But as 1982 drew to a close, time was running out. The Glenn Jackson Bridge had been completed. The metropolitan area was flowing east, turning country to city and pastures to pavement and sloshing against the Gorge's doorstep. Land values were soaring. And while Rizor's subdivision was temporarily stymied, Rim View Estates lots at Cape Horn were selling. The Stevensons' plans to industrialize Steigerwald Lake's wetlands were proceeding. After three years of effort, with no support in Washington's congressional delegation and the Reagan administration's antipathy to parks and public lands, federal legislation seemed further away than ever.

Chapter 4
The Berthing, 1983–1985

Six weeks after the Glenn Jackson Bridge opened, Jeff Breckel, the executive director for the two Gorge commissions, released a study of land use trends that found "substantial land division" within Skamania County from its western boundary (near the Gorge entrance) upriver to Beacon Rock. "Encouraged by lax land use and platting controls," the study emphasized, "land divisions have occurred in a leapfrog, haphazard manner, affecting nearly one-third of the land within the study boundary." The report refuted one Skamania County official's contention that "God has zoned the Gorge."[1]

Legislation to protect the Gorge, if it came at all, was years away, and litigation was proving to be an imperfect tool. It was expensive, time-consuming, and rarely conclusive, primarily because Skamania County had few land use laws. Buying critical land could help solve the problem, but that required experienced negotiators, stewards, and money. Russell had tried to entice The Nature Conservancy to buy land in the western Gorge, but its Washington state director told her that his donors were focused on Puget Sound.[2] The conservancy's Oregon director was enthusiastic, but the north bank of the Columbia was outside his jurisdiction. Besides, the conservancy's mission was to protect threatened and endangered species and, while abundant in the Gorge, those species did not exist on all critical land.

There was another possibility. A decade earlier, Huey Johnson, the president of The Nature Conservancy, had concluded that the organization's mission was too confining and had left to create a new organization. He founded the Trust for Public Land (TPL) in San Francisco and gave it a broad "land and people" mission.[3] Now TPL was looking to expand its work of purchasing private land for public parks, recreation, vistas, and habitat.

The US Forest Service had already worked with TPL to complete a complicated land transaction near Cascade Locks in 1979. Under local pressure to develop tourist-oriented recreational opportunities, the Forest Service had identified a five-hundred-acre inholding in the Mount Hood National Forest. A grove of old-growth trees grew on the property, which could link the

Columbia River with high-country trails, but the parcel was privately owned and advertised for development.[4] A congressional appropriation would be needed to purchase the land, but that could take years and the property would likely be sold and developed by then. The Trust for Public Land was called in to help.

The trust's strategy was to buy the right to purchase private properties that federal agencies wanted, usually in the form of long-term, low-cost option agreements. Once that right was secured, TPL lobbied Congress for funds so the federal agency could buy the property. The trust typically would not purchase the property until Congress had appropriated the funds and the agency had agreed on a price, and it rarely purchased and held property in advance of congressional appropriations. Owning land was expensive and risky: land management and property taxes were costly, the land could lose value through market or natural forces such as forest fires, and appropriations could fall through. More commonly, TPL and the cooperating agency might disagree on the property's fair market value, leaving TPL holding property for which it had overpaid. So the Trust for Public Land optioned land, rarely buying before it reached agreement with the agency on price and before funds were available.

Unlike The Nature Conservancy, TPL did not have a membership or a large donor base, and it did not permanently own land as reserves. Most of the organization's funding came through its transactions, as landowners were generally required—if they used TPL's nonprofit services—to donate a tax-deductible percentage of the value of their property to the organization, a gift that would turn to cash when the land was sold to the agency. The model was efficient, allowing TPL to fund itself while fulfilling its parks mission, but it required a public agency to buy and manage the land. The trust also had to negotiate good deals and skillfully predict land values and costs in fluctuating markets and politics, or it would go broke.[5]

The trust's need for a public agency to buy land was problematic in Washington's western Gorge, where there were few federal lands. Nevertheless, Nancy Russell arranged to meet Harriet Burgess, TPL's Western Region director, at The Shire in early 1980, soon after she had completed her Cascade Locks transaction with the Forest Service. Forty-five years old, Burgess was tall, long-limbed, and charismatic, with a persistent squint earned from years spent in the sun, cross-country skiing, hiking, and whitewater rafting. She had run the Colorado River through the Grand Canyon nineteen times. As a former congressional staffer and campaign manager, she knew Congress as well as Russell knew the Gorge, and she too was adept at building alliances. Parks were popular, and Burgess knew how to direct favorable publicity and the support of grateful constituents to members of Congress as they campaigned near election day. She also did favors for government agencies, discounting land costs when an agency was over budget or using TPL funds to pay for unfunded trailheads and rights of way. The people she worked with were devoted to her, and she counted on that to create more parks.[6]

Burgess and Russell developed an instant rapport. Both were dedicated to protecting western landscapes, and both were persuasive advocates. Burgess was "indominable . . . a real risk-taker," Russell said, a person who shared her passion for the Gorge, who could cultivate landowners—most of whom saw Russell as the enemy—and who could develop relationships with agencies and appropriators. Although there was little hope that the federal government would acquire land in the imperiled sixteen-mile segment of the western Gorge from its entrance to Beacon Rock, Russell supplied Burgess with lists of key landowners and maps, some taken from John Yeon's 1935 land acquisition report. She sent her a book of Oregon foundations, identifying prospects with red stickers, and flew to San Francisco to show *Who Is Watching?* to Marty Rosen, the president of the Trust for Public Land. Russell also met with the editorial board of the *San Francisco Chronicle* "to sell the Gorge in the Bay Area," she wrote to a friend. "At the moment I feel small and provincial, but I shall overcome."[7]

As Russell encouraged Burgess to scout for opportunities in the western Gorge at the close of 1982, she and the Friends board hired me as executive director. Twenty-eight years old and two years out of law school, I had limited experience and a broad charge: to ensure that Gorge legislation passed. Over the next six years, I would lobby Congress, negotiate statutory language, coordinate with national conservation groups, and make the case for legislation through the media. I also would oversee the Friends' response to development, especially if litigation was required. My work would free Russell, who remained involved in lobbying and held critical relationships with key congressmen, to spend more time raising funds, building membership in the Friends, and guiding the trust's efforts in the Gorge.

Russell's hard work seemed to pay off in January 1983 when Governor Atiyeh announced in his State of the State address that "before I leave office . . . I want to see our unmatched Columbia River Gorge preserved and protected for future generations"—a line, he acknowledged, that drew the speech's greatest applause. But Russell now believed that Atiyeh's positions were as capricious as the Gorge winds, and those winds were not stirring Washington State's delegation.[8]

In February, Bob Packwood held a hearing in Hood River on the Gorge. Field hearings typically represent the beginning of the legislative process after a bill is introduced, followed by hearings before House and Senate committees in Washington, DC, and votes by both houses. Senator Packwood would stand for reelection in 1986, and he knew that Oregonians were mostly enthusiastic for Gorge protection—and, luckily for Packwood, Skamania residents could not vote in Oregon. He was less cautious than Hatfield and unabashedly advocated for Gorge protection. Packwood had championed other environmental legislation—most notably a national recreation area for Hells Canyon, on the boundary between Oregon and Idaho—and would soon chair the Senate Committee on Finance. A top committee staffer referred to Packwood and Hatfield as "two 1,000-pound gorillas,"[9] although none of Packwood's committees had direct jurisdiction over Gorge bills.

Packwood invited more than a dozen people to testify. Nancy Russell spoke about the history of protection efforts and threats, especially in the western Gorge, which she said was "up for grabs." Having guided hundreds and presented to thousands, she explained, she knew that people loved the Gorge once they experienced it. Skamania County commissioner Bill Benson complained that his constituents were "accused of being backward hillbillies" and announced that Clark, Skamania, and Klickitat counties had "signed an interlocal agreement to develop a plan and guidelines for the Washington side of the gorge," a tactic that Chuck Cushman had proposed. Outsiders should have no say as to how an area was managed, Benson said, which caused Packwood to observe that such a policy would have prevented the creation of America's national parks.[10]

After three and a half hours, Senator Packwood gaveled the hearing to a close. No minds in the audience appeared to have been changed. Days later at a Skamania County commission meeting, Benson moved to support the interlocal agreement that he had testified had already been approved. As if to emphasize the deadlock, his motion—and the interlocal agreement—died when no one provided a second.[11]

Less than a month after the hearing, Oregon's senators and representatives reintroduced the Friends of the Gorge bill in the first session of the 98th Congress. Senator Packwood cited his "renewed commitment and an increasing sense of urgency," while Senator Hatfield cautioned that many Gorge residents remained concerned about the federal government's role in local land use planning. "That concern and divergence of opinion continues," Hatfield said, "and a great deal of discussion and cooperation with State and local governments, as well as gorge residents on both sides of the Columbia River, will have to take place before the legislation moves forward."[12]

The discussion Hatfield sought boiled over two weeks later in mid-March, when Governor Atiyeh and Governor Spellman, amid great fanfare and media interest, announced that they had reached an agreement on Gorge management. In essence, the governors proposed that a twenty-three-person commission manage the Gorge and that twenty-two general "principles" and eight "key elements" be incorporated into federal legislation. While the Friends was unhappy with the weak proposal, its response was measured. Russell was pleased, she said, that the State of Washington recognized the need for federal legislation, and she emphasized that many of the principles and elements had been incorporated in the Friends' bill. She was concerned, however, by the absence of a lead federal agency and the unworkability of such a large commission.[13]

Meanwhile, Mark Hatfield scheduled a second hearing on the legislation on March 25 in Portland, this one before his Energy and Natural Resources Committee, which had jurisdiction over Gorge bills. The hearing scheduled dozens of witnesses and required considerable scrambling by Russell and the Friends, who needed to make sure that their most effective representatives testified, opponents' testimony was countered, the audience was packed with supporters, and the media favorably covered the event. A large, hostile crowd was expected. Skamania mill workers were given the day off to testify, and the county was bussing them to the Bonneville Power Administration building, where the hearing would be held. The best witnesses, the ones most respected by Hatfield, had the most challenging schedules and the least time to prepare, so Nancy Russell and I spent days drafting their testimony and preparing them for questions.[14]

Several hundred people attended the hearing, where fifty-four witnesses testified over seven hours and dozens of people outside picketed against "federal control." Half of those who testified—all of whom Russell knew and most of whom she had personally recruited—supported the strongest possible legislation. National conservation groups, including the Sierra Club, National Audubon Society, Wilderness Society, and National Wildlife Federation, turned out in force. Those who opposed legislation of any kind—county and port officials, timber industry representatives, grange members, and Gorge residents—were also well represented. "Are boarded-up storefronts,

abandoned homes, dead and decaying communities 'scenic'?" asked Chuck
Cushman, in testimony submitted for the record. "Is unemployment 'scenic'?" The arguments replicated those made three years earlier, even seventy
years earlier. To the extent that there was consensus, it was over the governors'
agreement, which almost no one liked. Skamania's Bill Benson labeled it a
"misbegotten agreement" that

> seems an innocuous document that harms no one, makes some partly
> happy. However, when it reaches the Houses of Congress, the Sierras,
> Audubons, 1000 Friends of Oregon, the garden clubs, the Friends of
> the Columbia Gorge, to name a few, and they finish cutting, slashing,
> and amending it, they will have accomplished their original goal: To
> put Skamania County under an onerous, unreasonable, unheeding,
> uncaring, unfeeling, unthinkable bureaucracy, which will toll the
> death knell for life as we know and love it.[15]

At the hearing's conclusion, Senator Hatfield said that he had heard
"loud and clear" that the Gorge was "one of the great resources of the nation."
Even the two governors had agreed that federal legislation was needed, he
said, emphasizing that "the Federal government is inexorably involved in the
gorge and its future and management." He lamented how many witnesses
had portrayed the federal government as "they" versus "we" and reminded
the audience that the federal government was "nothing more than a collection of the people of this country" and that some of the same people who
opposed federal involvement regularly came to his office requesting federal
funds for port development and commerce in the Gorge.[16]

It was when Hatfield—unscripted and heartfelt—spoke of his personal
philosophy regarding land ownership that Russell's misgivings over his cau-
tion began to evaporate. "I don't believe we own anything," the senator said.
"I believe we are but stewards of a great creation. We have a responsibility
to administer the land in a way that's going to pass on to generations upon
generations."[17] Russell wrote Hatfield the next day:

> You put into such eloquent words; you expressed so gently and fairly
> what those of us who love the Gorge's wonderful beauty feel—that
> we are but briefly here and gone and must be careful stewards of the
> great works of creation. It has been hard for me, having such great
> passion for this magnificent landscape . . . to listen again and again

to the diatribes against our government in the name of patriotism, property rights, and religion. Your moving words and expression of commitment have affected me greatly.[18]

She then wrote thank you letters to all who had testified in support of legislation. And while the record remained open, she drafted additional testimony for the consideration of those unable to attend.

Whether inspired by the Glenn Jackson Bridge or alarmed by signs of legislative progress, developers buffeted the western Gorge with proposals during the spring and summer of 1983. In April, the Port of Camas-Washougal announced plans to triple its industrial footprint by expanding east of the Gorge entrance onto twelve hundred acres of wetlands, most of it owned by the Stevenson family. With that expansion, Steigerwald's intermittently inundated land, already zoned for heavy industry, would be drained and industrialized and Gibbons Creek would be relocated. The port acknowledged that its plans would generate "stiff opposition" from wildlife agencies and environmental organizations. Gorge commissions in both Washington and Oregon questioned the need to expand the port and declared that the proposal would "radically alter" the views from Crown Point and other iconic places. Friends of the Gorge studied litigation options, but even stalwarts like John Yeon considered the industrialization of the western portal a "certainty." "The negatives are not just the loss of an excellent wildlife refuge," Yeon rued, "they include damage to a famous landscape on the scale of a national scandal." Smokestacks and factories, not marshes and a celebrated vista, would soon greet Gorge visitors.[19]

Other development proposals proliferated in the sixteen-mile stretch from the Gorge entrance to Beacon Rock. At Cape Horn, Russell's vision of a park to mirror the one at Crown Point was shattered, shard by shard, as a quarter of the lots at Rim View Estate were sold by early 1983. Her litigation against George Rizor two years earlier had proven that the short-platting of Rim View Estates was illegal, but she did not have the resources to also pursue Rim View, and it was given a pass. In October, the Friends received an anonymous tip that an enormous house was being constructed on a lot just feet from the edge of the cliff. When it was completed, the house was visible for miles upriver, even at night. It nagged at Russell as she drove the Gorge each day, reminding her of what she had been unable to prevent.

PROPOSED HIDDEN HARBOR SUBDIVISION
located two miles west of Beacon Rock, directly
across Columbia River from Horsetail Falls

"Before and after"
rendering by Friends of
the Columbia Gorge
of the 83-lot Hidden
Harbor subdivision
approved by Skamania
County in September
1984. FOCG archives.

In June 1983, a California developer announced plans for the largest subdivision yet. Hidden Harbor, equidistant between Rizor's subdivision and Beacon Rock, would convert seventy-eight acres and a mile of natural shoreline into eighty-three residential lots and a marina. A two-hundred-foot-wide entrance to the development would be dredged into the riverbank to access a meadow, where a three-acre harbor would be excavated. One hundred seventy thousand cubic yards of spoils left from digging the meadow would be used to raise part of the subdivision above the hundred-year floodplain. Sewage would be handled by individual septic tanks, except for houses built on fill, which would be served by a communal septic system.[20]

The editor emeritus and columnist for the *Skamania County Pioneer*, Roy Craft, endorsed the project, predicting that most of the opposition would come from "well-heeled Portlanders." The World War II veteran warned that "if extremists have their way," Skamania residents "will be herded into a few incorporated enclaves." In the developer's promotional material, Gertrude Glutsch Jensen regained the spotlight, calling the proposal a "welcome addition" and decrying "over-zealous crusaders" and "fanatics [who] hope to keep people out . . . [by] convert[ing] the Gorge into one huge federal reserve."[21]

As Hidden Harbor was announced, George Rizor submitted new plans for twenty-one houses, three fewer than in his short plat in order to meet Washington State subdivision requirements. On July 12, 1983—a summer evening made warmer by klieg lights from Portland television stations and a standing-room-only crowd in a cramped courtroom—the Skamania County Planning Commission deliberated the new proposal for four hours. Rizor led with a slide show that began with Nani Warren's expansive compound, one property downriver, as "an example of what we will not do." He testified that his subdivision would more resemble the property owned by "my millionaire neighbor friend John Yeon . . . a single man [who] has evidently enough money to hire a full-time gardener." Rizor continued:

> I feel, most of all, that property is to be used. Most of the people on the
> other side of this issue don't want to use it. I think God made us and he
> made this earth for us to use. . . . I don't believe that conservancy of the
> entire Gorge is an appropriate use from our standards and particularly
> not from God's standards.[22]

The planning commission unanimously endorsed Rizor's preliminary plat, and in October the board of commissioners agreed, also unanimously. A week after the board's action, both Gorge commissions called, to no avail, for a development moratorium in unincorporated Skamania County until zoning could be adopted.[23]

The Friends tried to find legal grounds to stop the subdivision, but there were no zoning regulations for Rizor to violate, and he had complied with the few statewide rules that applied. Motivated by God and profit, he did not seem the type to retreat, and final approval of his subdivision was inevitable. The near-pristine sixteen-mile stretch of river would soon be transformed. Twenty-one houses would be built across from Multnomah Falls, sixteen on top of Cape Horn, eighty-three more upriver at Hidden Harbor, and—at the Gorge's threshold—heavy industry would expand into a thousand acres of wetlands. This onslaught made Russell's case for federal legislation even more compelling. Regional newspapers, including the Vancouver *Columbian*, the *Oregonian*, the *Walla Walla Union–Bulletin*, and the *Daily Astorian* editorialized for federal legislation and against the Skamania County subdivisions. In September, the Gorge received national attention when the *Chicago Tribune* ran a thousand-word article whose penultimate paragraph quoted Colonel Rizor's new marketing twist: "this is your last chance to buy lots in the gorge." The publicity seemed too late for the western Gorge, however. "It's going," a Washington Gorge commissioner said. "We're going to be the generation that lost."[24]

In the summer of 1983, Senator Hatfield and Washington senators Henry M. "Scoop" Jackson and Slade Gorton—but not Senator Packwood, who preferred stronger legislation—introduced a bill drafted by Governors Atiyeh and Spellman. They introduced the bill "at the request" of the two governors, which often is congressional code for "this isn't my idea—I'm doing it as a favor." The bill essentially substituted a fourteen-member, bistate commission in the role played by the Forest Service in the Friends' bill. Ten members of the commission were required to live in the six Gorge counties, and conservationists worried that a commission with a local majority would serve short-term economic over long-term conservation interests. At Lake Tahoe, which straddled the California-Nevada state line, a similar commission had approved 96 percent of all development proposals during its first ten years. There was not a place in the country, environmentalists argued, where a commission had protected a nationally significant landscape. "Our greatest danger" with the governors' bill, Russell said, "is having a piece of legislation that promises to protect the Gorge but in reality, changes nothing." She understood that her campaign could be defeated by legislation that gave the appearance but not the substance of protection. Even Chuck Cushman's acolytes did not support the governors' bill. Columbia Gorge United, now the main opposition group, stoked Cushman's fire by comparing the Friends and the governors' bills to whether one preferred being dragged to a concentration camp by Russian or Polish troops.[25]

If a single senator could have derailed Gorge legislation it was Scoop Jackson, a Democrat. In an illustrious, forty-three-year-long congressional career that included chairing the Senate Interior and Insular Affairs Committee, Jackson had helped guide some of the nation's most important environmental laws through Congress. But he had just seen his colleague of four decades, Warren G. Magnuson, lose an election and, according to committee staff, had "not yet recovered" from tangling with Chuck Cushman over a wild-and-scenic-river bill aimed at protecting rivers on Washington's Olympic Peninsula. Jackson had urged Governor Spellman to lead on the Gorge—to take the heat, really—while he remained noncommittal and, behind the scenes, personally conflicted. Nancy Russell arranged for Jackson's good friend Charles Luce—a former undersecretary of the Interior Department and the chair of Consolidated Edison—to push the senator to support rigorous legislation, but longtime Jackson backer and southwest Washington political powerbroker Bob Schaefer, who owned development land in the western Gorge and represented Gorge developers, was lobbying him vigorously to oppose legislation. "Senator Jackson is between a rock and a hard place," explained Don Bonker, the congressman who represented southwest Washington. "He will choose between Bob Schaefer and his friend, Charles Luce; his decision on the Gorge will be based on that."[26]

Ultimately, Senator Jackson did not choose. He died suddenly on September 1, 1983, and a week later Governor Spellman appointed former three-term Washington governor Dan Evans, a Republican, to fill his seat. In a special election two months later, Evans was elected to serve Jackson's remaining five-year term. Friends of the Columbia Gorge was delighted. Evans was environmentally inclined, an avid backpacker who had been instrumental in creating Washington's Alpine Lakes Wilderness. A moderate at a time when his party was turning conservative, especially on the environment, Evans had been an honorary sponsor of the Friends because of his friendship with Tom McCall.[27]

In order to serve in the Senate, Evans had to resign from the Northwest Power Planning Council (now called the Northwest Power and Conservation Council). Congress had authorized the eight-person regional council three years earlier, following disastrous efforts to build five nuclear power plants in Washington State. Its goal was to balance the Northwest's energy and environmental needs, paying particular attention to energy conservation and the protection of fish and wildlife in the Columbia Basin. The council, which Evans chaired from its inception, shared power-planning authority with the Bonneville Power Administration (BPA). Before the Northwest Power Planning Council was created, Evans wrote years later, BPA had "dominated the power planning of the Northwest and there was no involvement of the states of the Northwest, for the people in the Northwest, in that power planning." The council represented, Evans recalled in language that would have chilled Russell at the time, "the ideas and the desires of those who live here, rather than having them imposed from the top by someone who is heading Bonneville, a federal agency that may or may not really be sensitive to the needs of each part of the Northwest."[28]

Colonel George Rizor at his Skamania County press conference, October 25, 1983. Beth Campbell Hovee, Vancouver *Columbian.*

On October 25, 1983, George Rizor called a press conference at the Skamania County courthouse, presumably to announce that his lots were now for sale. "The retired Army colonel was at his military finest," John Harrison reported in the *Columbian*, "calmly facing a firing squad of television cameras pointed like cannons at his head. In a commanding, unwavering monotone . . . Rizor . . . briefed reporters armed with tape recorders and note pads on the 'Battle for the Gorge,' as he called it." Using a white board propped on an easel, Rizor launched into a remarkable exposition, which Harrison captured:

> The Battle for the Gorge, as Rizor saw it, clearly was one of good against evil. Those who would stop him lived on the "asphalt plains" of the Portland/Vancouver area, he said. In contrast, his property was "the green garden of Eden." . . . He diagrammed all of this on a chart for the assembled reporters and spectators. There were "AGRESSOR [*sic*] FORCES," also called "REDS," and "FRIENDLY FORCES," or "BLUES." The chart showed red and blue arrows converging on a green zone — Rizor's property. The red forces included "Litigation, Media Assault," and "Legislative Envelopment." They clearly outnumbered the blue forces, which included Skamania County officials.[29]

The dual threats of litigation and potential legislation, Rizor explained, had driven away buyers and investors and left him with a "flood of financial problems." But God had sent him an angel, he said. On cue, he introduced Harriet Burgess and made what Harrison called "his bombshell announcement": the sale of his property to the Trust for Public Land. Burgess thanked Rizor, explained the trust's role to facilitate the transfer of conservation properties into public ownership, and expressed anxiety over how long TPL could hold the property, since there was no federal legislation and no public agency to transfer the property to. "I feel like George climbed down off the limb," Burgess concluded, "and I've climbed onto it."[30]

The purchase and the controversy over Gorge management made national headlines as the *New York Times* followed the *Chicago Tribune's* reporting with an extensive article. The purchase delighted Russell, who had asked Burgess to prioritize Rizor's property as early as 1981, but she and the Friends cautioned that legislation was still needed. The Trust for Public Land could not buy every endangered property in the Gorge. An *Oregonian* editorial reiterated the point three days later, calling the transaction "a momentary respite [given the] many more subdivisions . . . on speculators' drawing boards." Although Rizor acknowledged that his sale had been motivated by potential litigation and legislation, Skamania Commissioner Bill Benson said it proved that "left to our own devices, we can work things out without Big Brother coming in." Others were not so sanguine. A *Pioneer* editorial accused the Friends of trying to destroy Rizor and other "little people" who "offend the egos of wealthy Portlanders who feel the Gorge is simply too good for us," and Skamania prosecutor Bob Leick told the *New York Times* that federal legislation "was nothing more than urban snobbery," warning that "we're not going to knuckle under just because somebody doesn't want to look at one of our homes."[31]

Russell did everything she could to convince TPL to make the Gorge a priority, even if it meant giving up contributions that otherwise would have gone to the Friends. She asked Northwest foundations and Friends donors to contribute to the trust, and when the occasional landowner offered to donate property to the Friends, she arranged for TPL to be the beneficiary. When the nephew of Dorthea Gilbert, a Maryland resident who owned land in Skamania County, heard Russell interviewed on Portland's KEX Radio, he called her about his aunt. Russell arranged for Gilbert to donate her two-acre, riverfront property, valued at $30,000, to TPL. This came at a time when the Friends' finances were precarious, with growing expenses and expanding challenges at every level: legislation, litigation, and now land acquisition. At times, the Russells had to dip into the family bank account to meet payroll for the Friends, which often had less than a month's operating funds available. "That is the very worst part of this job of mine," Russell lamented to a friend about fundraising. "It's never enough. It goes on and on."[32]

When Dan Evans saw how land acquisition could assist legislation by removing contentious land and landowners from the debate, he told Harriet Burgess to "buy everything in the Gorge that she could lay her hands on." Buoyed by his encouragement, Russell redoubled her fundraising efforts on TPL's behalf and in 1984 secured her biggest prize yet: a $600,000 no-interest loan from Oregon's largest foundation, the Fred Meyer Charitable Trust (later called the Meyer Memorial Trust), to help purchase land in the Gorge. With more funds available, at least temporarily, Burgess met with landowners whose property Russell had ranked by importance, vulnerability and, occasionally, the landowner's ability to oppose legislation or undermine her fundraising.[33]

The Stevensons' Steigerwald Lake wetlands were at the top of Russell's list. At her July 1979 dinner at The Shire, John Yeon had called Steigerwald "the most supremely difficult problem in the entire Gorge." Four years later, the problem became exponentially more difficult when the port announced expansion plans. The crisis intensified in November when the Stevensons obtained a permit to clear-cut a thousand two-hundred-year-old cottonwood trees on the property, essential habitat for roosting bald eagles and great blue herons but an obstacle to industrialization.[34]

The Stevensons would cash in on Steigerwald Lake, but Russell believed that if the land could be acquired then perhaps the family's opposition to legislation might lessen, and they might stop undermining her to potential contributors, especially corporate donors.[35] If Burgess could build a relationship with the family, then other important properties they owned in the Gorge might also be acquired. In addition, Burgess had discovered that the Army Corps of Engineers was required to mitigate environmental damage from the construction of the second powerhouse at Bonneville Dam. If she could option the Steigerwald Lake land and convince the Corps and Congress that its wetlands constituted suitable mitigation, then federal funds might become available.

Burgess cold-called Wally Stevenson and began to negotiate. He threatened to cut all of the cottonwoods on the Steigerwald property and place mobile-home pads in the wetlands if the zoning was changed from its high-value industrial designation. Burgess had the property appraised, as did Stevenson. They were $4 million apart. Burgess made an offer, and Stevenson rejected it but agreed to postpone clear-cutting the cottonwoods during negotiations. They developed a close rapport. "She was just like my sister," Stevenson later recalled. "I could talk with her." It was difficult to say no to her.[36]

The Stevensons signed an option agreement on April 20, 1984. The Trust for Public Land paid $5,000 for the right to buy, within sixty days, seven hundred acres of industrial-zoned wetlands for just under $6 million. The sixty days would give Burgess an opportunity to present the property to federal agencies as a candidate for mitigation and to meet the Appropriations Committee's annual deadline. If Senator Hatfield could add the property to the appropriations bill at the last second, then TPL could extend its option another ten months for $95,000, allowing time for the purchase funds to wind through the system. Since Steigerwald was in Washington, Hatfield wanted support from that state's congressional delegation, which was not anticipated to be difficult, as there appeared to be no opposition to the transaction. In fact, there was considerable public support from the National Audubon Society to conservatives rallied by the Stevensons, who were major contributors to the Republican Party. Burgess executed a quick and successful campaign that brought the federal agencies and Washington's delegation on board. Except for one person.[37]

Two weeks before the appropriations deadline, Dan Evans announced that he would oppose the Steigerwald purchase. Russell was furious. Evans had not met with the Friends after his appointment, despite many requests, and he still would not. Why was he standing in the way of the chair of the Appropriations Committee, she fumed, and why was he undercutting his own directions to the Trust for Public Land to buy whatever it could? Evans, an Eagle Scout who had been nicknamed "Straight Arrow" during his three terms as governor, told the media that Steigerwald was too expensive and that land acquisition opportunities in the Gorge should be prioritized before money was spent. Such a process, of course, would outlive the cottonwoods, and probably the wetlands too. Russell called leaders of the business community, national environmental groups, Governor Spellman's staff, and the media—everyone she knew who might influence Evans. The senator "seems to feel no sense of urgency about the Gorge," she complained to Weyerhaeuser chair Bob Wilson. "If he were in my shoes he would."[38]

Russell's actions triggered an avalanche of protest. Governor Spellman wrote Evans. Business leaders from Weyerhaeuser, Pendleton, and Pacific

Power and Light called him, along with every national and local conservation group. Calls from the public jammed his phone lines. After Russell and
I met with editorial boards, a Sunday *Oregonian* editorial entitled "Don't
Block Gorge Purchase" urged Evans to reconsider. The next day, the *Columbian* chastised Evans for being out of touch with southwest Washington and
warned that his continued opposition would "blot . . . his admirable record
of concern for the environment." Under pressure, Evans relented and did
not oppose the purchase, but he refused to endorse it. That was enough for
Hatfield, and the appropriations bill passed in the Senate with Steigerwald
funds intact. Oregon Congressman Les AuCoin, who represented the Portland metro area west to the coast and was a senior member of the Interior
Appropriations Subcommittee, maneuvered the bill through the House.[39]

   When he heard the news, John Yeon wrote Harriet Burgess that her
achievement was "earth shaking, like Mt. St. Helens . . . I cannot possibly
tell you of my joy and wonderment . . . I am literally struck dumb." Russell sent a laudatory telegram to Hatfield, "full of joy and gratitude," and
within weeks did three things that would not have occurred to her even a
year earlier. First, she cut a television commercial for AuCoin's November
re-election campaign. "Hello, I'm Nancy Russell," she began, "and I want to
tell you that Les AuCoin knows how much Oregonians love the Gorge." She
then explained how he had used his power to ensure that "an industrial park
across from Crown Point" would be purchased so it could become a national
wildlife refuge. Second, she drafted a letter for Hatfield's campaign, extolling
his efforts to protect the Gorge and Steigerwald Lake. The campaign sent
copies of the letter out to ten thousand Oregonians. Third, she held a reception at Westwinds to honor Mark Hatfield. "Senator Hatfield is responsible
for the likely success of the most positive accomplishment in the Gorge since
Simon Benson donated Multnomah Falls," she told two hundred guests, and
his "accomplishment is far more complicated."[40]

   The successful protection of the Steigerwald wetlands demonstrated how
effective an activist Russell had become and how high her profile had risen.
Politicians sought her endorsement, and she was eager to help, or hinder,
their careers. Hatfield's willingness and ability to direct $10 million of federal
funding to the Gorge at a moment's notice and Russell's endorsement of him
when environmentalists were increasingly disenchanted with his ties to the
timber industry strengthened the bond between them.[41]

   Another important relationship grew out of the Steigerwald transaction.
The purchase by the Corps of Engineers and the transfer of the land to the

US Fish and Wildlife Service, as directed by Hatfield's appropriations bill, would take eighteen months from passage of the appropriations bill. Ordinarily, the Trust for Public Land would have bought the property once federal funds were available, but the Corps had disputed the property's fair market value and dragged out negotiations. After three option extensions and several price reductions, the trust's contract with the Stevensons lapsed, and it lost $100,000 in option payments, two years of staff time, and tens of thousands of dollars in expenses. Crucially, TPL also lost its right to buy the property, convey it into public ownership, and receive a donation. Nevertheless, Wally Stevenson, who credited Burgess's tenacity for the success of the transaction and recognized a good deal when he saw one, moved forward as though the contract remained in place. He conveyed the wetlands into public ownership and donated $200,000 to the Trust for Public Land.[42]

The Rizor and Steigerwald properties were not the only ones Russell sought to protect in the western Gorge. In 1982, she had asked Charles Luce to contact Bob Schaefer, the owner of the St. Cloud Ranch, and encourage him to sell his ranch to TPL. Schaefer was a Clark County attorney and Scoop Jackson confidant. He was also a Democratic kingpin who represented large development interests in eastern Clark County, and Russell believed he was behind much of the organized opposition to legislation. Schaefer had told Luce that he was not interested in selling. "If he can be taken out of the Gorge," Russell told Burgess in 1983, "the politics of protection will be so much easier." She asked Burgess to approach Schaefer again, but he remained uninterested in a deal. Within a year, however, Dan Evans had replaced Jackson, and Schaefer's influence was waning. After reading about the Rizor purchase, he called Burgess. His heavily forested, 120-acre ranch, four miles downriver from Beacon Rock and just above the Rizor property, included two-thirds of a mile of river frontage with views of Oregon's Horsetail Falls. It contained two creeks, one with a thirty-foot-high waterfall, and part of Arthur Lake, an important rearing area for juvenile salmon where hundreds of tundra swans overwintered, attracted by an unusual and healthy stand of arrowhead, called wapato by Native people. Schaefer had planned to subdivide the ranch into small lots but recognized that legislation, if it passed, would reduce profits. Now he wanted to know if the Trust for Public Land was still interested in purchasing it.[43]

Burgess was, but she knew that TPL's board was worried about being financially overleveraged in the Gorge. Russell had escorted members of the board through the Gorge in the spring of 1984,[44] and they had been impressed, but they remained concerned about the cash outlays required by the Rizor purchase and the Steigerwald option. What if legislation did not pass? Whom would they sell the Rizor land to? Another developer? And what if Burgess had miscalculated its value and TPL was forced to sell at a loss? As conservationists, trust board members understood the importance of the Gorge and its vulnerability, but as fiduciaries they worried about finances. Nevertheless, Burgess negotiated an option with Schaefer, believing it would give her leverage with her board.

In June, Russell proposed a solution: she and Bruce could take out a $200,000 bank loan and transfer it to TPL at no interest. Her proposal carried risks, as bank loans were expensive—in June 1984, the federal prime rate was 13 percent—and there was some chance that TPL could default. If all went well, the loan would be paid back after legislation passed and the federal government bought St. Cloud from the trust. Otherwise, the loan would have to be repaid within five years. The Trust for Public Land's executive committee remained skeptical, but Russell and Burgess soon persuaded them to agree to the arrangement. Burgess exercised TPL's option to buy the ranch for $500,000, with a $50,000 donation to the organization from Schaefer, and by mid-August TPL had acquired St. Cloud Ranch.[45]

By the end of the year, the Trust for Public Land owned nine properties in the Gorge and, for $100,000 consideration, had extended its option on Steigerwald Lake, which would be transferred to the US Fish and Wildlife Service in thirteen months. On New Year's Eve, TPL acquired a small but important property from Yvonne Montchalin, whom Russell had introduced to Burgess. Montchalin's six acres linked the Rizor and St. Cloud properties, west to east, to form over a mile of continuous river frontage. If The Shire, which bordered the Rizor property, could also be conveyed to a federal agency, then the public would have access to over two continuous miles of the Columbia River in an area where public ownership was nonexistent. Steigerwald would add another three miles of river frontage, which gave TPL the opportunity to save, by the end of 1984, more than a quarter of the sixteen-mile shoreline from the Gorge entrance to Beacon Rock, even without The Shire. But these achievements came at considerable risk, as Burgess and Russell had persuaded the organization to largely ignore its proven model of not buying and holding property, opening up TPL to financial and reputational peril. For TPL to come out whole, federal legislation would have to pass soon and the lead federal agency would have to buy the properties at a price that was consistent with TPL's assessment of their fair market value. The Trust for Public Land now joined Harriet Burgess out on the limb that Colonel Rizor had recently climbed off.[46]

At the end of 1984, passage of federal legislation remained unlikely. The Washington delegation had been preoccupied by a bill to protect Mount St. Helens, which had erupted in 1980, and then on a bill to designate over a million acres as wilderness in the state. The wilderness bill, enacted in the summer of 1984, had taken much of Evans's attention. Slade Gorton was less engaged in environmental issues, deferring to Evans because of his interest in conservation and his seat on the relevant committees. Gorton confided to a timber industry lobbying group that he had received more mail about the Gorge than any other issue. So, he probably thought, good riddance.[47]

Russell badly wanted to meet with Evans, to show him the Gorge and persuade him to support legislation, but he had not responded to her or to John Yeon's invitation to The Shire. She tried intermediaries, drafting a letter for Audrey McCall to send and admitting to a "certain guilt" in asking for help, since McCall's husband Tom had recently died. Her draft letter reminded Evans of an April ceremony two years earlier where the three former governors dedicated land in the eastern Gorge to Governor McCall. It described Mrs. McCall's shock during a recent trip to the park, looking across the Columbia, and seeing "two gravel pits, a hillside with junked cars, and a large white mobile home with a garbage dump in front of it—the garbage spilled down over the cliffs." While the letter tactfully left unspoken Evans's pledge at the dedication to support the Friends' effort, it expressed the "hope [that] you can give this issue some real leadership. The Columbia Gorge very much needs your help."[48] Evans remained silent.

While Washington's senators were concentrating on wilderness, Oregon's senators had pushed for Gorge legislation and in January 1984 announced that forty-two of their colleagues had agreed to cosponsor the Friends' bill.[49] The list of names included neither of the senators representing Washington State.

On Memorial Day, the Friends turned out over four hundred members on a blistering hot day at Rooster Rock State Park to greet Bob Packwood, who gave a rousing speech that reaffirmed his support for the bill.[50] In the House, Les AuCoin and Jim Weaver worked on a strategy developed by the Friends and national conservation organizations to first pass legislation in the Senate, where Hatfield and Packwood presided and where environmental legislation was more difficult to pass. The bill could then be strengthened in the Democrat-controlled House, where Oregon's House delegation should be supportive, except for Republicans Denny Smith and Bob Smith (whose district included the eastern Gorge).

The outlier in the Oregon delegation was Ron Wyden, who had been elected to the House in 1981. As a candidate, he was an early and vociferous voice for strong Gorge protection. His district, which included inner eastside Portland, was Oregon's most environmentally inclined and was so liberal that it often was referred to as "the Kremlin," but it also included conservative east Multnomah County, which extended into the Gorge. Since taking office, Wyden had equivocated on tough protection, a position Russell attributed to his interest in higher office, which required support from the timber industry. At a "stormy" meeting in 1982, Wyden yelled at Russell for a quarter of an hour, trying to budge her off of the Friends' bill. The yelling did not especially bother her—she remained calm and firm, and the congressman later apologized. What did bother her—and, she said, "violates my sense of fairness"—was her belief that Wyden was drafting a weak bill in secret. Two years later, when Wyden promoted the governors' bill, the Friends commissioned a poll in Wyden's district and released its findings at a press conference. The poll found that his constituents—after listening to descriptions of the Friends' and the governors' bills—preferred the Friends' by a 74 to 20 percent margin. Within a week, the *Oregonian* published an editorial entitled "Wyden Out of Step," castigating the media-sensitive congressman for being on the side of "special interests who won the compromise but lost the environment at Lake Tahoe." The Friends sent a volunteer to Wyden's frequent town hall meetings to berate him on his position.[51]

Even with its fissures, the Oregon delegation could deliver comprehensive legislation if Washington's delegation acquiesced. By 1984, the Friends had made inroads, especially with Democrat Don Bonker, the representative from southwest Washington who saw the conservation and economic benefits of legislation and whose support was made easier when Bob Schaefer sold the St. Cloud Ranch to the Trust for Public Land. A changing coterie of Seattle representatives was also supportive. Republican Sid Morrison, whose district included the Washington side of the Gorge, recognized his constituents' overreliance on the timber industry and sought a fair solution that included federal legislation. In the Senate, however, where rules and culture aspired to collegiality, senators would not run over a colleague on an issue that meaningfully affected his state. And Dan Evans was not moving.

To coax support from Evans and his delegation, the Friends raised the Gorge's profile—especially its vulnerability—to new levels in 1983 and 1984. To promote the sense that the Friends was a bistate organization, Dave Cannard from Vancouver was named cochair in early 1983. At the same time, as executive director, I started spending a portion of each week in Seattle, meeting with conservation organizations, media, and donors. Kristine Simenstad's efforts had resulted in the Friends' Seattle office receiving many inquiries for showings of *Who Is Watching?*, sixty-eight in the first half of 1983 alone.

In February, the *Seattle Post-Intelligencer* credited the "persistent Friends of the Columbia Gorge" with making progress and concluded: "Saving the Gorge is a common cause of Washington and Oregon. Oregon has done its part. It is past time for Washington to contribute its share." Next to the editorial was a political cartoon depicting Russell, backed to a cliff edge by a giant bulldozer, her pleas for help to Washington's governor and delegation echoing off the bulldozer's looming blade. A month later, the *Post-Intelligencer* warned that "if Skamania County sets policy for all Washington on this issue, it will be a case of the tail wagging the dog." When field hearings come to the region, the editorial continued, "true friends of the gorge should line up with the citizens lobby of the same name."[52]

In October 1983, 125 people attended a fundraiser at Stim Bullitt's home that raised $7,000 for the organization (about $19,000 in 2021 dollars). Russell's Gorge tours were so popular that Simenstad started marketing "A Day with Nancy Russell in the Gorge" bus trips to Seattle residents. They sold out. When almost 250 Seattleites joined as members of Friends of the Gorge the following June, the office computer crashed. The software to track its thirty-five hundred members was moved, thanks to Brot Bishop, to computers at Pendleton Woolen Mills.[53]

In 1984, the Friends' Hiking Weekend focused on the north bank of the Gorge so people could learn more about and hopefully advocate for Washington trails. Russell selected each of the forty-three hikes for the weekend, ranked them by difficulty, and trained leaders for them. She designed the brochure and hand-distributed it to dozens of outlets in Portland, Seattle, and the Gorge, arranged entertainment and media coverage, and procured insurance. She raised money to subsidize the event and persuaded twenty-seven other organizations to assist with and publicize it. She also led hikes, gave speeches, and asked everyone she met to join the Friends, sign its petition supporting the national scenic area—fifteen thousand people had already done so, mostly at *Who Is Watching?* presentations—and write

Congress. A record thousand people, including hundreds of Washington-ians, participated.[54]

A month after Hiking Weekend, in July 1984, Congress passed the Washington delegation's wilderness bill, freeing Senator Evans to focus on the Columbia Gorge. Developers had been under no such constraint. Five months earlier, Hidden Harbor's owners had submitted a draft environmental impact statement for their marina and eighty-three-lot subdivision. Located on flatter land with fewer trees, the development would dwarf Rizor's pro-posal in size and intensity. The Washington Gorge commission opposed the development, noting its negative impact on open space and wildlife habitat, and questioned why it was needed at all, since only a third of the ninety-eight lots in the adjacent Woodard Marina Estates subdivision, platted in 1964 and now called Skamania Landing, were occupied. Gertrude Glutsch Jensen criticized her successors on the commission, saying they had "turned into a lobbying arm for environmental extremists who seek federal control." The Skamania County Commission unanimously approved Hidden Harbor in September.[55]

In August 1984, the Klickitat County commission approved a twenty-four-lot subdivision by short plat east of White Salmon on Burdoin Moun-tain, an open plain that slopes southeast for over a mile to the Columbia River and drops hundreds of feet on the west from a natural stone arch to talus fields. The commission overruled its own planning director, who had found that the proposal violated state requirements, and disregarded near-unanimous local support for a moratorium on short plats until their effect on wildlife and the water table could be assessed. Two wells had already run dry on the mountain, but, the local paper reported, "the commission felt it couldn't deny approval . . . based solely on logical evidence presented in testimony." The Friends was stretched too thin to challenge the Klickitat County subdivision but managed to halt attempts to transfer to private owner-ship a state-owned park on Ruthton Point west of Hood River, federal lands at the Gorge entrance near the Sandy River, and forty forested acres in Beacon Rock State Park.[56]

Nancy Russell sometimes abandoned her fundraising grind to engage a proposal that she felt particularly strongly about. On the Oregon side of the western Gorge, a developer wanted to divert Gorton Creek for hydroelectric power. Russell protested, noting that the project would block Gorton Creek Falls, a robust waterfall that plummeted 115 feet into a pool of basalt boul-ders surrounded by a thick rainforest canopy and shrouded in mist. It would endanger an endemic plant with yellow, daisy-like petals and broad green leaves that grew along the Gorge's waterfalls and wet cliffs—and nowhere else in the world. The Forest Service had listed the wildflower as sensitive, along with three other plants that grew nearby.[57]

It was clear to Russell that the developer was exploiting loopholes in state legislation and the Forest Service's land classification order, both passed in 1915 to protect Gorge waterfalls. He needed state economic development funds to move forward, as well as Forest Service approval, since the project was planned for federal land. In late 1984, Russell contacted a friendly state legislator who chaired the committee that controlled the funds, and she explained the problem to Forest Service Chief Max Peterson during a tour and reception she arranged for him. Peterson was courting Russell, determined that if any federal agency was to manage the Gorge, it would be his and not the Park Service. The Forest Service soon denied the project, and the state refused to provide funds. To close the loophole, in the next legislative session the Friends persuaded the Oregon legislature to protect nine waterfalls that had eluded protection in 1915. When the organization proposed similar legislation in Washington for its Gorge waterfalls, Skamania County objected and the bill failed. Although refusing to safeguard its waterfalls, Washington's legislature—to Russell's annoyance—considered making Woody Guthrie's "Roll On, Columbia" the state's official folk song. That initiative passed two years later.[58]

As Russell wrestled with the Gorton Creek project, the Oregon Department of Transportation was maneuvering to build a port of entry for trucks on the east bank of the Sandy River, which traditionally had kept Portland's ever-expanding urban growth from entering the Gorge. The plan was to locate the port of entry next to Lewis and Clark State Park, partly on public land and partly on the old Martin Ranch, still owned by Reynolds Metals. If the project moved forward, visitors' first impression of the Columbia Gorge would not be the Corps of Discovery's Quicksand River or the basalt cliffs named for Lt. William Broughton or the Sandy River Delta or even the farms on Mount Pleasant. Instead, they would see a massive truck stop squatting on ten acres of asphalt, with towering stadium lights illuminating the industrial paraphernalia—scales, ramps, office quarters—required to inspect trucks for violations. The twenty-four-hour glare, the odor of diesel, and the sound of grinding gears and revving engines, Russell wrote a friend, was something "I can't IMAGINE!"[59]

By January 1984, a year after Governor Atiyeh had pledged to make the Gorge his top environmental priority, the Oregon Department of Transportation was accelerating toward approval of the port of entry like a runaway eighteen-wheeler. ODOT's head engineer told reporters that he hoped the Sandy River site would be authorized in less than three weeks with permission to start construction three weeks later. To gain public support, a Gorge interpretive center had been added to the proposal, mixing education with development and cars with trucks. "What good is the gorge," asked state representative Glenn Otto, a truck stop booster who represented the area, "if we do not have an interpretive center to brief people before they enter?" Otto had been trying for years to push infrastructure east of the Sandy River and into the Gorge to increase jobs in his district, and he offered to extend water and sewer to the site if it was chosen. Truck stops typically attract other commercial development, and the Friends worried that strip malls would follow an expansion of infrastructure across the Sandy.[60]

Russell blitzkrieged the media. She rallied her members and made the truck stop a part of her evening presentations. She met with the *Oregonian's* editorial board and wrote an opinion column for the paper, calling the truck stop "unthinkable." A subsequent *Oregonian* editorial was headlined "No truck port in the gorge." She appeared on a morning radio show where "we talked truck stop . . . and it *was* spirited," she wrote a friend. The Friends warned it would sue to compel the federally financed project to meet National Environmental Policy Act standards. But what most changed the outcome was that Russell reached out in January to the manager of the port of Cascade Locks, imploring him to find an appropriate alternative in his town. The Cascade Locks site was added to the possible locations for the truck stop, and—"bow[ing] to political pressure and environmental pressures," according to the mayor of Troutdale—the Highway Commission approved the Cascade Locks site in October 1984.[61]

By late 1984, threats to the Gorge had come from the sale of public lands, industry, houses, a hydroelectric project, and a truck stop, and they had occurred on both banks of the Columbia, east and west of the Cascades, and on state, federal, and private land. The greatest danger, however, was still the subdivisions proposed for the western Gorge, particularly in Skamania County. Days before the Highway Commission approved the port of entry for Cascade Locks, the Skamania County Commission unanimously approved the Hidden Harbor subdivision. A month later, the Friends sued the county, alleging that it had violated Washington's Shoreline Management and

Environmental Policy Acts. The Shorelines Hearings Board would schedule a hearing the following year and—if the Friends could persuade it to do
so—a site visit.

By November 1984, Russell and the Friends had built considerable support
for Gorge protection in Washington State, especially in Seattle and Puget
Sound. With Mount St. Helens legislation and Washington's wilderness bill
out of the way, the hope was that the Gorge would become a priority for
Senator Evans. Interior Secretary James Watt had resigned a year earlier, and
Ronald Reagan had been elected to a second term as president on November
6. But the election's most immediate impact on the Gorge was when Booth
Gardner—county executive for Puget Sound's Pierce County, the second
most populous county in the state—beat incumbent John Spellman in the
governor's race. Environmentalists had supported Gardner, who had taken
an aggressive stand in favor of Gorge protection and had called Atiyeh's and
Spellman's bill "an open invitation to bulldozers and land speculators."[62]

   Two days after the election, Evans convened a congressional field hearing in Skamania County, where opponents to legislation had been preparing
for their homefield advantage for more than a month. Local newspapers
carried full-page ads depicting a gap-toothed bulldozer menacing a pleasant
suburban home, its second-story windows trimmed with neat shutters, asking
readers, "Do you want this to happen in the Columbia River Gorge?" and
urging them to testify and "Send a message to Congress." IT'S YOUR FUTURE,
the ad warned. ISN'T IT TIME YOU SAID SOMETHING?[63]

   An hour before the hearing began, four hundred angry people crammed
into and spilled out of Stevenson's Rock Creek auditorium. Many of the
vehicles in the filled-to-capacity parking lot had bumper stickers broadcasting "Save the Gorge from Nancy Russell," a sentiment echoed on buttons
worn by most audience members, along with "No Federal Control" and
"Thou Shalt Not Covet Thy Neighbors' Gorge." By nine o'clock, when Boy
Scout Troop 321 presented the colors to start the hearing, the tension had
not subsided. Evans began by announcing his position, which put him in
direct conflict with his state's governor-elect and explained why he had been
avoiding Russell. "The initiative of the Governors of Oregon and Washington, together with the cooperation of local governments, should represent the
prime effort for preservation of the gorge," Evans told the crowd. "Only if this
effort falters should the Federal Government consider legislation to ensure
protection of this unique natural resource." His position was alarming as well

as confusing, since even the commission-based initiative sponsored by Atiyeh and Spellman required federal legislation. Evans acknowledged that a "clean slate" would start in January with the 99th Congress and said he was "seeking new ideas."[64]

Over the next fourteen hours—with a twenty-minute break for lunch and thirty minutes for dinner—few new ideas materialized. Most Gorge residents and local officials continued to resist federal efforts—"the issue is not scenery, it is survival," said one—while others, typically from outside the area, promoted legislation at least as strong as that supported by Oregon's senators. Chuck Williams, representing the Columbia Gorge Coalition, called the Friends' bill an "unwise 'compromise'" and urged improvements.[65]

Almost two hundred people testified, but John Yeon was not among them. He and Russell were still friends, but Yeon continued to favor a smaller, traditional national recreation area in the western Gorge primarily managed by the National Park Service. He declined to testify, he later said, because his public disagreement with Russell "would have given no end of aid and comfort to the enemy." He wrote an acquaintance that he

> had hoped that she might consider a midcourse correction. But she is stubborn; in a way, thank God. Otherwise, she would have given up long ago. Her land-use plan remains the only official game in town. Nancy's constituency is strong and follows her with gospel faith. . . . I think it is a suicide course for the Gorge effort. I have thought so all along."[66]

Although Evans received few new ideas at the hearing, he may have gained an appreciation for the emotions and the division the issue generated, as he repeatedly had to bang his gavel to quell outbursts and at times threatened to adjourn. The testimony of Governor-elect Gardner, a Democrat who had won working-class Skamania County's vote by an almost 20 percent margin, was particularly explosive. He urged that the federal government play the "primary role" in Gorge management, that any commission represent "the broad interests of all Washington and Oregon citizens, as well as the interests of local gorge residents," that key tributaries be protected, and that a moratorium on development be instituted until a management plan could be adopted. When Gardner's representative concluded that the governor-elect was "on the side of taking action now to protect the gorge and urges strongly that legislation . . . be enacted without further delay," the mutters and groans from the Stevenson contingent erupted into a cacophony of boos, hisses, and catcalls. During the lunch break, Evans told reporters that he "hoped to forge a compromise on the gorge that would not result in 'bitterly fought' stances or 'acrimonious division,'" but by midnight, when the hearing concluded, that path was difficult to see.[67]

above: 1. Western Gorge. Crown Point and Vista House with Beacon Rock in the background. Image by Peter Marbach.

below: 2. Central Gorge. Dog Mountain looking west. Image by Peter Marbach.

Above: 3. Eastern Gorge. Dalles Mountain Ranch. © Darrell Gulin / DanitaDelimont.com

Below: 4. The Shire, with Multnomah Falls in the background. Image by Craig Collins.

5. Vista House, Reed Island, and—at the Gorge entrance—the Steigerwald Lake wetlands, zoned for heavy industry when purchased by TPL in 1986. Factories and the Camas paper mill's smoke plume are downriver from the Gorge. Image by Craig Collins.

6. Mount Pleasant and Mount Zion farmlands in unzoned Skamania County (pre-Act), seen from Crown Point. Image by Craig Collins.

7. River frontage from Cape Horn to Beacon Rock in unzoned Skamania County (pre-Act), seen from Cape Horn. Image by Peter Marbach.

8. Sandy River flowing into the Columbia at Oregon's entrance to the Gorge. The 1,380-acre Sandy River Delta—purchased by TPL in 1991—is on the right. Camas factories are across the Columbia, just downriver from the Gorge's Washington entrance. Image by Craig Collins.

9. Land adjacent to the 83-lot Hidden Harbor subdivision and marina; approved by Skamania County in 1984, defeated by Friends of the Columbia Gorge, and acquired by TPL in 1987. Image by Peter Marbach.

10. Doetsch Ranch (partially obscured by Beacon Rock), with 1.5 miles of shoreline, was acquired by TPL in 1987. Image by Craig Collins.

bove: 11. Six-thousand-acre Dalles Mountain Ranch, acquired by TPL in 1993. © Jamie and Judy Wild / DanitaDelimont.com.

elow: 12. Rim View Estates subdivision was approved for the top of Cape Horn (in foreground of meadow on right). Most of s lots were acquired by TPL in 1986, and the Cleveland house (below the meadow to the left) was acquired twenty years later y TPL and FOCG Land Trust. In 1994-95, TPL acquired the Grams' pastures in the background. Image by Craig Collins.

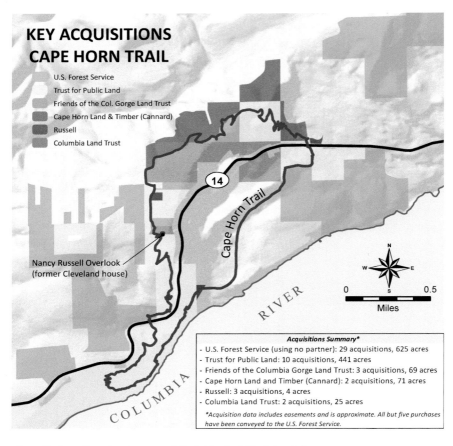

KEY ACQUISITIONS
CAPE HORN TRAIL

U.S. Forest Service
Trust for Public Land
Friends of the Col. Gorge Land Trust
Cape Horn Land & Timber (Cannard)
Russell
Columbia Land Trust

14

Cape Horn Trail

Nancy Russell Overlook
(former Cleveland house)

RIVER

0   0.5
Miles

COLUMBIA

Acquisitions Summary*
- U.S. Forest Service (using no partner): 29 acquisitions, 625 acres
- Trust for Public Land: 10 acquisitions, 441 acres
- Friends of the Columbia Gorge Land Trust: 3 acquisitions, 69 acres
- Cape Horn Land and Timber (Cannard): 2 acquisitions, 71 acres
- Russell: 3 acquisitions, 4 acres
- Columbia Land Trust: 2 acquisitions, 25 acres

**Acquisition data includes easements and is approximate. All but five purchases
have been conveyed to the U.S. Forest Service.*

Above: 13. Cape Horn Acquisitions and Trail. Map by Mike Schrankel

Below: 14. A popular postcard from 1992. FOCG archives.

bove left: 15. Camas Patch near Carson, WA. Acquired by TPL in 1992 with assistance from the Portland Garden Club.
Conveyed to Friends of the Columbia Gorge Land Trust in 2019. Image by Peter Marbach.

bove right 16. Two-thousand-acre Lauterbach Ranch at Catherine Creek, one of the Gorge's premier wildflower properties,
acquired by TPL in 1985. © John Barger / DanitaDelimont.com

elow: 17. Bruce Russell painting the view from South 40, purchased by the Russells in 1988. Russell archives.

Above: 18. Nancy Russell at South 40 in 2004. © Thomas Patterson—USA TODAY NETWORK

Below: 19. View from Nancy Russell Overlook, looking east. Image by Peter Marbach.

Chapter 5
The Landing, 1986

Since Russell's first Portland Garden Club press conference four years earlier, men—and occasionally women—had tried to intimidate her. Yelled at by a congressman, censured at the Forestry Center, rebuked by bumper stickers demanding that the Gorge be saved from her, Russell was familiar with the tactic. But the attacks were getting worse, and more personal. If Russell had not been a woman, it is doubtful that opponents would have described her as Don Clark's "front" or given her a "Looking for Love in All the Wrong Places" award. And they probably would not have circulated a "Columbia Gorge Primer" based on "The House that Jack Built" nursery rhyme. The twenty-eight-page illustrated book began with Jack proudly surveying his newly built cottage in the Gorge, a "Home Sweet Home" sign over the entrance. A drawing of Russell appeared seven pages later: "And this is the lady that spotted the flowers, that grew by the trail, that led through the pasture, that fed the cattle, that lived in the barn, that sat in the trees, that grew in the Gorge, that stretched for miles, behind the house that Jack built." At the instigation of "the lady that spotted the flowers," the tale continued, Congress passed a law, "written by the committee to save the view," that led the Forest Service—represented by a surly, salivating, cigar-chomping Smoky the Bear—to close trails in the Gorge and condemn Jack's house. "This is a true story," the last page warned. "It hasn't happened here yet," but "only you can prevent a National Scenic Area."[1]

The personal attacks did not bother Russell, at least not by the end of 1984, and she never attributed them to gender, but she also did not dwell on things that were beyond her control. She had too much to do and too little time given the pace of development in the Gorge. Hers was a practical approach that concentrated on issues that she could influence. She looked ahead to the next challenge, believing that other issues would resolve themselves, for better or worse. Russell's strengths were her intelligence and her focus; she always charged forward and never retreated. Sometimes gender worked to her advantage. Just as in tennis, Russell was often underestimated

by male opponents. Gorge commissioner Vera Dafoe thought that her "gen-
teel . . . attractive" appearance "was ideal for the role she was playing." Some
men initially viewed her "as a housewife, as lesser," Dafoe explained. "Nothing about her looked threatening or aggressive . . . you wouldn't expect her
to be a really powerful force, so that was good camouflage."[2] And, as tennis
professional Mike Metz remembered, Russell particularly liked beating men.

Women comprised a critical constituency for Russell's movement. When
Paul Pritchard, the president of the National Parks and Conservation Association, a Washington, DC–based national conservation organization, was
scheduled to speak at the Portland Garden Club, he asked Russell for suggestions on his speech. "I probably have over-suggested, as usual," Russell replied
in a detailed letter. "As those principally responsible for raising children," she
explained about her generation, "it is women who are especially aware of the
beneficial effects" of the outdoors, and "parks often directly affect their lives
and their children's lives." She continued:

> Business and businessmen represent themselves very, very effectively
> and are active in the political process where the important decisions
> are made. If parks are contrary to a business interest, they will oppose
> them. Who, then will support and help the parks? People who believe
> in park values—women like Portland Garden Club and Garden Club
> of America members. They are an important constituency for parks.[3]

Russell did whatever she could to build that constituency, and it responded
to her.

As her strategy to bring people to the Gorge matured, she focused on
women's groups. These included Delta Kappa Gamma (a women teachers' organization), Fir Grove Garden Club, Alpha Delta Kappa (a teachers'
honorary society), Methodist Church Women's Auxiliary, Gresham Christian
Women's Club, the women's auxiliary of the Oregon Museum of Science
and Industry, General Federation of Women's Clubs of Washington, and one
hundred women from the spring convention of the P.E.O. Sisterhood, whose
motto is "women helping women reach for the stars."[4] Russell asked each
group to sponsor Friends of the Columbia Gorge and to sign petitions endorsing Gorge legislation. She wanted their members to become her members, to
donate to the cause, and to write their congressmen.

She asked more of other women's groups, including the League of
Women Voters, which testified at hearings and lobbied Congress for Gorge

protection. She cultivated garden clubs in Zone XII through tours and presentations, even after they and the Garden Club of America had endorsed
legislation. The bond between Russell and the Portland Garden Club grew
even stronger as legislative and development challenges arose, and she continued to devote substantial hours to her horticultural group. The Portland
Garden Club and its members responded by generously donating to the
Friends and supporting its legislation.

Russell was appointed to the Garden Club of America's National Affairs
and Legislative Committee, where she briefed colleagues on the Gorge. Calling legislation one of its highest priorities, the Garden Club sent teams of
women to Capitol Hill to promote it. Each team knew the Gorge and how
to lobby, and they also knew their congressional targets. A "Dear Colleague"
letter sponsored by Senators Packwood and Hatfield inviting senators to join
their bill was signed by almost half the Senate, thanks in no small part to
GCA efforts. A senator from Texas might not care much about the Columbia
Gorge, and he likely would oppose anything compromising private property
rights or promoting an intrusive federal government. At the same time, he
cared about his relationships with Oregon's senators, the chairs of the Appropriations and Finance Committees who could influence most issues important to Texas. And he damn sure cared about the determined, well-informed,
well-connected, campaign-contributing women from Houston's River Oaks
Garden Club, San Antonio's Alamo Heights Garden Club, Beaumont's
Magnolia Garden Club, Dallas's Founders Garden Club, and the Garden
Club of Houston, who scheduled appointments with him to discuss saving
the Columbia River Gorge. "When the next history of parks is written," Russell wrote Paul Pritchard, "the Garden Club of America and the Portland
Garden Club should be in its pages, recognized for the[ir] work . . . to create
a Columbia River Gorge National Scenic Area."[5]

Russell wanted every woman to join her army. Some, like Harriet Burgess,
would command their own troops, while others, like Evelyn Nokes, would be
soldiers. Nokes was a member of the Friends who was active in politics, married to the long-time editor of the *Oregonian*, and the mother of a reporter.
She loved the Gorge—particularly the petroglyphs and pictographs in the
eastern Gorge—and introduced Russell to the editor of the *Seattle Times*,
which would soon support Russell's effort. She also arranged for her husband
to give Russell a thousand copies of a section of the paper that the *Oregonian*
had devoted to the Gorge. When Russell sent one to Congressman Weaver,
she noted Nokes's role and credited "WOMAN POWER."[6]

Many other women enlisted, and most of the Friends' financial support came from women, as individuals and as leaders of foundations, with the exception of a small group of Portland businessmen led by Brot Bishop. In Seattle, Harriet Bullitt and her family led the way, with assistance from Kristine Simenstad. In Portland, Russell relied on her network of friends, Portland Garden Club members, and tennis players. Occasionally, when their husbands' business interests were aligned against the Friends, they donated their own funds. Mary Bishop, Russell's friend and tennis partner, who sat on several nonprofit boards, recalled almost thirty years later that she had never been involved with an organization where women were more important. And when Russell needed to decompress from the constant demands of her work, she went to the Gorge to hike with any of a dozen or more close friends, including her childhood friend Marie Hall, Nancie McGraw from her "hort group," and botanical expert Barbara Robinson.[7]

Russell could become frustrated with women who did not advocate for parks and other issues that were important to their children. As she wrote Paul Pritchard before he addressed the Portland Garden Club,

> establishment women (many of whose husbands are captains of industry) are uncomfortable with controversy and with taking strong stands, because their familial roles are as peace-makers. As wives and mothers they have always looked for ways to keep things running smoothly and peacefully. With this urge to keep peace, women often look for compromise and forget that there is a time to be an advocate. Women can be effective advocates, and they *should* be advocates of issues dear to their hearts. Others are not going to do it for them, because they do not care as much. Women must do it for themselves.[8]

She was an advocate, but also a wife and mother. She benefitted from Bruce's help and pride in her accomplishments. He had supported making regular donations to the Friends—using family funds to prop up the organization when money was tight—and borrowing money so TPL could purchase the St. Cloud Ranch. But Bruce could tire of Nancy's preoccupation, sometimes demanding that talk about the Gorge be banned during family dinners. He also insisted that Nancy be home to prepare that dinner each night at six o'clock. "Dad didn't want to be alone all of the time," their daughter Sally observed. "He really did want somebody to cook his meals," and that was one of the areas where Nancy "knew she had to toe the line." She rarely confronted Bruce directly and managed to turn his edict into more of a request that would be breached when necessary. As one family member noted, Nancy Russell was adept at "plowing around the stumps." More often than not, however, she returned from a full day in the Gorge, cooked dinner for the family, washed the dishes, and then headed out for an evening presentation to audiences populated mostly by women.[9]

The family was changing too. Sally and Wendy had graduated from college, and Alison was in her first year at Williams College in northwest Massachusetts. With only sixteen-year-old Aubrey at home, Russell's day-to-day responsibilities as a mother lessened. Bruce spent his free time keeping up Westwinds and the family house, researching history, painting western scenes, and penning letters to his children. He left Merrill Lynch in 1984 to form his own business and bought into a few companies whose histories he knew as well as his own and whose officers he called by their first names. His clients prospered from his advice, as did his family, which continued its frugal lifestyle—not caring about fancy cars and clothes, expensive vacations, or living in a mansion—as Bruce made a small fortune bigger.[10]

As her husband focused inward, Nancy attended events alone. Family vacations became less frequent, perhaps a few days at Elk Lake or a week at Eaton's Ranch. On a rare break from the Gorge, she served as a delegate to an international conference—titled New Directions for Conservation of Parks—in Hamburg, West Germany, to study the European park system. As the conference concluded, it passed a resolution at her behest, quite off topic, calling for Gorge protection. The morning after she returned home—having awoken at two o'clock in the morning to catch a flight, then traveled for twenty-four hours—Russell led a hike in pouring rain and spoke to "USA Blue Bird lovers" that evening. She took mechanical engineers on a bus tour the following day, lecturing them on "their responsibility for changing the face of the earth."[11]

Russell had never found maternal responsibilities particularly daunting, except with regards to Alison. As a young girl, Alison had been sweet and self-contained, a talented artist who preferred to draw and read, much like her father. As she grew older, however, her mental health deteriorated, and she became isolated and listless, and by late 1984 she was asked to leave Williams. Nancy accompanied her to specialists and re-enrolled her in college, first at Scripps and later at Portland State University. At home, Alison refused to take her medicine and became disruptive, particularly toward her mother. She accused Nancy of hating her because she could not replace her brother Hardy, who had died eighteen months before she was born. Alison worshipped her father and resented her mother, while Nancy adored Alison but could not relate to her. Remembering the depression she had suffered after Hardy's death, Nancy wondered if she could be responsible for Alison's behavior.[12]

Alison became more belligerent as her illness progressed. Bruce, nurturing and attentive by nature, had a close relationship with her and became her primary caregiver. Nancy approached her the only way she could, logically and pragmatically. She struggled with her daughter's irrationality and at times with the charges that Alison levied at her, but she understood that there were limits to how she could help Alison and that medical professionals and Bruce could better assist their daughter than she could. Eventually, they came to terms with her illness and the care it required, and Alison was committed to facilities for the care of the mentally ill. Kristine Simenstad was a clinical psychologist and Nancy's confidante during their long trips to eastern Oregon and Washington. "I know the [situation] with Alison killed her," she later observed, "but there was nothing that she could do about it. . . . Losing a child to mental illness, is like losing a child."[13]

Although the Trust for Public Land was financially overextended in the Gorge by February 1985, Russell urged it to increase its commitment and provided landowner leads and funds whenever possible. Because of Harriet Burgess's push to buy and hold critical properties, TPL now owned nine properties in the Gorge, worth $1.25 million, and had optioned five others valued at $7.5 million, including Steigerwald Lake. Almost all of the properties were in the western Gorge, including four miles of shoreline within the sixteen unprotected miles from the Gorge's entrance to Beacon Rock. Burgess was negotiating to buy fifteen more properties, even though the Meyer loan was already fully obligated. The trust had identified an agency owner, known as a take-out, for only one property, Steigerwald Lake. Worse, the Friends' legislation—which would establish a Forest Service take-out for most of its properties—was not moving, blocked by Senator Evans's insistence that the Gorge be managed by a commission. The Friends had been reminded of the flaws of a commission structure just months earlier, when a federal court determined that Lake Tahoe's regional commission was so ineffective that it had violated its own federal compact. Russell worried that a Gorge commission would become similarly politicized, capitulate to powerful developers, or be led by appointees like Nani Warren, who would resist the public purchase of private land. Even if the commission wanted to acquire land, it would not have the Forest Service's eighty years of acquisition experience and its established funding sources.[14]

There were no assurances, of course, that the Forest Service would buy TPL properties, and at prices consistent with what the nonprofit had paid. The regional lands officer had assured Burgess as early as 1979 that "public ownership in the gorge was clearly the direction of the future," but John Yeon had long seen the Forest Service as unwilling to acquire key Oregon lands, "safe, aloof, and spared controversy . . . atop its ramparts." Yeon's criticisms seemed clairvoyant in March 1985 when the new regional lands officer told TPL that he saw no role for it in the Gorge. If there were going to be any purchases in the Gorge, he seemed to suggest, his agency would proceed by itself, thus dooming TPL's future and perhaps current efforts. But both Burgess and Russell were used to going over the heads of reluctant bureau-crats, especially now that Forest Service chief Max Peterson was courting the Friends and Senator Hatfield supported land purchases in the Gorge.[15]

In early 1985, three months after the Friends had filed its lawsuit against Hidden Harbor, the developer approached Burgess on an "extremely con-fidential" basis to see if TPL would be interested in buying the property. Within three weeks, she had hired an accredited third-party appraiser who determined the land's value to be $269,200. The trust made an offer of $220,000. A second appraiser, hired by the owner, valued the property at $390,000. Dueling appraisals were so common that Bob McIntyre, TPL's chief financial officer, once sketched a five-paneled cartoon entitled "The Typical Project as Seen by." The first panel depicted a nice house "as seen by TPL's project manager." The next showed the same house, except much smaller and presumably less valuable, "as seen by TPL's appraiser." Then the house, larger and more valuable, appeared "as seen by the landowner's appraiser." Next the house was depicted as a mansion, "as seen by the land-owner." And finally the house was reduced to rubble, "as seen by the public agency review appraiser."[16]

Meanwhile, at the Friends' request, the Washington State Shorelines Hearings Board was scheduled to tour the property in early May, followed by a picnic lunch at The Shire. The morning of the tour a dreary canopy of clouds covered the western Gorge, spitting rain. The top of Archer Mountain, two thousand feet above the property, was shrouded in fog, and the Oregon shore and its lattice of waterfalls were hidden. The only part of the property that could be seen was muddy and overrun by canary grass and clumps of blackberries. It looked like a disaster for the Friends, since the purpose of the tour was to appeal to board members' sense of aesthetics, not just their legal duty. As the board members stepped off the bus, however, the weather changed. Shafts of sunlight pierced the drizzle, bathing the property in a soft glow, and waterfalls emerged from the mist across the river. A rainbow formed, and two eagles swooped out of the clouds, gliding so close that the group could see their heads, radiant white, swiveling left and right. The board would deliberate for the rest of the year, but the signs were propitious.

"The only positive real actions now going on are the land acquisition work of TPL," said Russell, "and Friends of the Columbia Gorge keeping the finger in the dike with lawsuits stopping illegal developments." Harriet Burgess was pushing forward despite legislation being stymied, her board expressing fresh reservations, and the Forest Service apparently opposing TPL's work in the Gorge. Russell introduced Burgess to one of her tennis partners, Andrew P. Kerr, who owned twenty-seven acres at the west entrance to the Gorge, zoned for heavy industry and surrounded on three sides by land owned by the Stevenson family. Gibbons Creek flowed through the property and provided fresh water to Steigerwald Lake, essential if its salmon habitat was to be restored. Burgess negotiated a one-year option to purchase the property for $450,000.[17]

Upriver, she used a more complicated strategy. Conservationists wanted the high farms and pastures on Mount Pleasant and Mount Zion, a thousand feet above the Columbia and squarely in view from Vista House at Crown Point, to continue as farmland. Burgess intended to buy the land, sell the right to further develop it—a conservation easement—to the federal government, and then sell the farm to a farmer. In 1985, relatively few acres of land were protected by conservation easements nationally, and none in the Gorge. A respected farmer who owned over three hundred acres on Mount Pleasant, Rolf Jemtegaard, asked to meet with TPL. His parents, Bendikt and Gertrude, had come to the Gorge from Norway when he was two years old, attracted by its similarity to the fjords back home. While Bendikt cleared the land of wildfire snags and "7-foot-tall ferns," Rolf's brother Marvin lived off the wilderness, trapping mountain lions and earning bounties and money for their pelts. Rolf was now seventy-eight, a widower, and in declining health. His children, he felt, did not understand or share his love of the land. Most of the two-thousand-acre Mount Pleasant area was owned by a handful of patriarchs like Jemtegaard, with deep ties to the land but too old to farm, their children drawn to the city. Their generation had seen the western Gorge change from a wild place dominated by mountain lions to a pastoral landscape shaped by farmers; the next few years would determine whether it would become urban sprawl, transformed by the Glenn Jackson Bridge.[18]

In transactions this complex, involving a complicated conservation easement, a land purchase, and two dispositions, TPL insisted on long-term options to allow time to fit the pieces together. But Rolf Jemtegaard had a serious heart condition, and he co-owned the farm with his daughter, who had terminal cancer, and his son-in-law, who had recently been hospitalized. He knew he could make more money selling the farm on the open market, where it would be subdivided into five- and ten-acre lots, but, as Burgess told TPL's executive committee, "the farm is his heart and soul." He did not have time for a long-term option, and he wanted certainty. The trust needed to act now. So it initially bought 166 acres for almost $400,000, believing it could sell the land to another farmer within a few months—partially recouping the cash outlay—and retain an easement for future sale to the Forest Service if federal legislation passed. Part of the agreement was that Rolf could live on the farm for the rest of his life. The headline in the *Columbian* got it right: "Washougal family sells their farm to save it."[19]

At the same time that Burgess was negotiating with Jemtegaard, she offered a one-year option to buy the twelve unsold lots at Rim View Estates, two miles to the east on top of Cape Horn, for $266,400. The owners countered at $350,000. The trust said it could not go higher "unless some benefactor came along," but the landowner agreed not to sell additional lots while discussions continued. Farther east, above the proposed Hidden Harbor subdivision, Burgess purchased four hundred acres on Archer Mountain for $314,000. The property bordered Washington State's Columbia Falls Natural Area Preserve and provided habitat for nine Gorge-endemic plant species and the Larch Mountain salamander, which had been listed as threatened.[20]

That summer, Russell met with Mark Hatfield about TPL's increasingly untenable position. She asked him what could be done about trust land in the western Gorge that was not suitable for mitigation (like Steigerwald Lake) and outside the Gifford Pinchot National Forest farther east, where the Forest Service was authorized to buy land. The appropriations chair laughed and said that he could be "wonderfully creative." Hatfield then asked Russell to work with him directly, starting with a prioritized list of properties.[21]

Encouraged by Hatfield's support, Burgess moved forward. While still concentrating on Washington's western Gorge, she scouted properties farther upriver near the Gifford Pinchot National Forest boundary, where she optioned two properties valued at just under a million dollars: Dog Creek Falls, seven acres just off the highway with a thirty-foot-high waterfall, and over six hundred forested acres at Dog Mountain. The Dog Mountain property, which contained a trail that gave the public access to stunning fields of wildflowers, was held by the Stevensons for logging. Wally Stevenson, who had been pleased with Burgess's work at Steigerwald Lake, allowed her to craft a traditional, and safer, "back-to-back" transaction, where the trust optioned the property and simultaneously bought and sold it to the Forest Service, which it did in August.

In 1985, there was little public land in the eastern Gorge other than a sprinkling of Oregon state parks next to the Historic Columbia River Highway. Almost all of that dramatic, arid landscape, with its culturally significant land and bountiful spring wildflowers, was privately owned. There were few places where the public could hike on the north bank to savor the scenery or admire early spring stands of wildflowers—grass widows (*Olsynium douglasii*), smooth prairie stars (*Lithophragma glabrum*), and mock orange (*Philadelphus lewisii*). Perhaps the most remarkable property was owned by the Lauterbach family, sixteen miles upriver from Dog Mountain between White Salmon and Lyle, far past the Gifford Pinchot's eastern boundary. The two-thousand-acre ranch on Catherine Creek gained two thousand feet as it sloped three miles up from the river, offering spectacular views of the Gorge and the Cascades. Many considered the ranch to be the Gorge's "premier wildflower property," where over two hundred and fifty plant species flourished, several of them rare, threatened, or endemic. A natural basalt arch curved hundreds of feet above Catherine Creek, and Native people had built elaborate rock walls, trenches, and pits on the talus slopes. The formations were described in 1954 in *American Anthropologist*, which noted a similar site across the river near Mosier. Twenty years later, just before the Mosier property could be evaluated as a state park, a rock crusher reduced those formations to gravel for resurfacing the interstate highway.[22]

Russell had been urging TPL to buy the ranch at Catherine Creek for years, and Burgess was enthusiastic. She offered the owner almost a million dollars, structured as a five-year installment purchase, with interest payments adding another $250,000 to the price. She hoped to sell the property to the Forest Service—if legislation passed—or the State of Washington. The trust's executive committee usually approved purchases routinely, as the transactions were first vetted and authorized by senior staff, including the president. After having approved more than a dozen Gorge transactions, this time the committee balked. Concerned about dwindling acquisition funds and the daunting prospects for Gorge legislation, it demanded that Burgess raise at least $150,000 in financing, with a "strong recommendation" to raise $300,000. Two months later, just days before the purchase agreement would lapse, Burgess presented a financing list that was long on wish and short on cash: a nonbinding, verbal "assurance" from Union Pacific Railroad to donate two properties near Cascade Locks that she believed were worth $113,000 (if and when TPL could sell them); the likelihood of the Meyer Trust approving a second $600,000 loan, as the application had been "warmly received"; "informal assurances" that the Mazamas mountaineering club in Portland would approve a $10,000 grant; and, most importantly, a second five-year, interest-free $200,000 loan from the Russells to be used for the Jemtegaard and Lauterbach purchases. "We have no cash in hand," Burgess wrote Marty Rosen, but she believed the gifts were "solid" and the Russell loan was "gold-plated." The Russells' loan met the executive committee's terms, and TPL bought the ranch at Catherine Creek.[23]

By the fall of 1985, TPL's financial position in the Gorge was more precarious than ever. Of the eighteen properties it had purchased, seven had been conveyed to the Forest Service, including Burgess's first Gorge transaction in 1979 and Dog Mountain and Dog Creek Falls, all within national forest boundaries. One property, near Rooster Rock, had been transferred to Oregon State Parks. The ten remaining properties, mostly in Skamania County and all but two in Washington, were valued at more than $3 million. In addition to its purchase costs, TPL was paying property taxes, maintenance expenses, and interest charges of between 10 and 14 percent on many of the properties. And Burgess was not slowing down: she had also optioned several other properties, valued at more than $6 million.

The board was close to shutting down TPL's operations in the Gorge. The financial and reputational risks of being stuck with nearly $10 million in land were simply too high. There was little progress in Congress and less confidence that President Reagan would approve the legislation if it passed. And finally, even if the NSA was established, there was no certainty that public agencies would agree that TPL's lands were priorities, or worth $10 million. The board took their CFO's cartoon seriously: if TPL's valuations were off by only 15 percent, then that $1.5 million represented close to half the organization's annual budget.[24]

Burgess knew that her board was close to stopping her work in the Gorge and believed that it would act at its next meeting, in mid-October. That gave her and Russell several days to plan. Almost all of TPL's revenue at the time came from selling land to the federal government, so they turned to the person who could most influence the trust's transactions, the chair of the Senate Appropriations Committee. Russell was used to drafting letters and testimony for others, so why shouldn't she draft a letter for Senator Hatfield to send to Marty Rosen? She wrote a one-page letter that captured Hatfield's understated and unthreatening style, but with implications that were hard to miss. "I want to express my appreciation for the role that your organization has played" in the Gorge, Russell began for the senator. "I am very much aware of the significance of your work. I am also aware of the national scope of your concerns and the myriad demands made upon TPL. That you have favored the Columbia Gorge with such a generous quota of your resources during the last few years, I assure you, has not gone unnoticed by me." In the penultimate sentence, perhaps to bolster her own hopes as much as to reflect reality, Russell wrote for Hatfield: "the commitment of TPL to the Gorge and the willingness to remain steadfast and determined while waiting for legislation is, in large measure, why legislation is forthcoming." The senator agreed to send it, and the board allowed Burgess's gamble to continue, understanding and perhaps fearing that the Senate's most powerful appropriator was keeping his eye on their commitment to the Gorge.[25]

Congress did not match TPL's pace. No bills to protect the Gorge would be introduced in 1985, and no hearings held. But both Oregon senators remained committed to legislation, with Packwood continuing to press for the strongest conservation outcome and Hatfield pledging not to settle for less than federal agency management. Under the leadership of Les AuCoin and Jim Weaver in Oregon and Don Bonker in southwest Washington, the Democrat-controlled House was primed to improve legislation. Senator Evans continued to insist on management by commission, however, and his colleague, Slade Gorton, the most conservative of the four senators, became more involved. In one hurried meeting that Russell and I had with Gorton off the Senate floor, he raised his voice to emphasize: "There will be no federal zoning in the Gorge, Nancy!" He did not need to elaborate. For him and most Republicans, especially conservatives in the Intermountain West, the prospect of the federal government managing private lands was anathema.[26]

To our surprise, during a lobbying trip in early 1985 senior Interior Department staff—the acting assistant secretary, the acting director of the National Park Service, and the head of land acquisition for the Park Service—appeared eager to manage the Gorge. They likely had seen Senator Hatfield's interest, and any interest in land protection shown by the chair of the Appropriations Committee interested them as well. Their newfound interest also might have reflected a concern that a Forest Service–managed national scenic area could siphon off Land and Water Conservation Fund money destined for national parks. In addition, the director of the Park Service—who had opposed adding the Gorge to his agency's portfolio—had just resigned, and William Penn Mott, celebrated for doubling the size of California's park system under Governor Reagan, was rumored to replace him.[27]

As the Park Service encouraged the Friends of the Columbia Gorge, Chuck Williams—the original proponent of an NSA managed by that agency—was becoming more volatile. He had always struggled to raise funds and attention, and in February 1985 a "distraught and desperate" Williams approached Friends' associate director Marie Pampush and accused Russell and the organization of having "financially ruined" him and his mother. "Call it blackmail call it anything you want," Williams charged, "but unless the Friends of the Columbia Gorge start giving us some money I will not restrain my anger and resentment of the Friends and Nancy Russell." He suggested a payment of $3,000 to $4,000. In mid-March, in a rambling, five-page letter to Mike McCloskey, the executive director of the Sierra Club, Williams complained about the Friends' strategy, and demanded that Jim Blomquist, Sierra Club's Northwest representative, be "immediately terminated" for helping craft it. If not, Williams warned, he and others would resign, "and the Club will almost surely lose much of its leadership in this region." Marie and I, with cochair Dave Cannard and others, met with Williams to offer help but no money.[28]

Also in March, all four Washington and Oregon senators sent a joint letter to the Friends and fifty other agencies and organizations extolling the Gorge's beauty and other attributes and recognizing its economic significance and the "right of residents . . . to continue enjoyment of their homes." They conceded that the fifty planning and regulatory bodies that already existed could not protect the Gorge and pledged "to work together to develop legislation." While acknowledging that they did not agree on a legislative solution, the senators invited those who received the letter to identify three areas on Gorge maps: residential and commercial areas to be exempted from federal legislation, areas of "scenic, cultural, and natural resource concern" that deserved protection, and areas appropriate for "special protection, including federal acquisition." The boundaries favored by the Oregon senators resembled those in the National Park Service's 1980 study that extended past The Dalles; Dan Evans wanted to exclude almost twenty thousand acres, including Maryhill Museum and the entire six-thousand-acre Dallesport peninsula.[29]

Before Russell could take on the mapping task, however, the Friends needed to resolve the question of who should manage the Gorge. The organization had decided two years earlier to back the Forest Service; there had been little congressional support in Oregon for the Park Service, which did not want to manage the Gorge, and Chuck Cushman had successfully vilified the agency among residents. While Russell preferred the National Park Service, she liked Forest Service Chief Max Peterson, who she believed was eager to manage the Gorge, and she thought the Gorge would be "a great addition to the Forest Service domain—a crown jewel where there are few." But things had changed. The Park Service showed renewed interest in managing the Gorge, Cushman was no longer as involved, and residents were fighting the Forest Service as hard as they had fought the Park Service. Dan Evans was not budging in his support of management by commission, and perhaps advocating for the Park Service as the lead agency might give the Friends a way to pressure him. In May, the Friends' board announced its support for the National Park Service.[30]

That same month, Evans's staff sent out maps showing tentative boundaries for the three areas that the senators had outlined earlier: urban, protected, and those deserving special protection. The last area, labeled "areas of potential acquisition," ignited a firestorm among many people who lived there. Chuck Cushman had warned them that they would be thrown off their land, and it seemed that their houses, like Jack's, were in danger of being condemned by a cigar-smoking Smoky the Bear prodded by "the lady that spotted the flowers that grew by the trail."

In June 1985, the four senators convened public workshops on the mapping project. Russell had reservations about the process, fearing that the workshops would turn into "just one more destructive dog and pony show." As she wrote one of her National Park Service contacts, "We need rational discussion, not more emotion."[31] But the process presented her with an opportunity. She understood the Gorge's resources and vulnerabilities better than anyone. She knew where the best vistas were located, where wildflowers flourished, and where endemic species grew. She knew where hidden waterfalls and geologic wonders like razor-thin ridges, basalt arches, and notches between cliffs could be found. She knew where Lewis and Clark and the Corps of Discovery had slept, where battles had been fought between white settlers, US soldiers, and Indians. She knew where fishwheels had scooped salmon from the Columbia and where wagons had left deep ruts along the Oregon Trail. She knew where deer paths, historic highway remnants, and obsolete logging roads could be converted into public trails. She knew where stands of old-growth Douglas-fir and ponderosa pine grew side by side, which hillsides were prone to summer wildfires, and where winter winds made hiking treacherous. She knew which roads could accommodate busses, where bathrooms were well maintained, which restaurants could host large groups, and where milkshakes with local berries and homemade ice cream were served. She knew which taxes applied to forestland and the source of Skamania County's revenue down to the dollar. And if someone knew more than she did about something in the Gorge, chances were that she knew them and that they admired her. And chances were that they would be willing to drop everything to help her.

Doug Macy was such a person. Gregarious and smart, he was a landscape architect who had cofounded the Portland firm Walker Macy in 1975. He loved to fish and hike in the Gorge and often drove through it on the way to his central Oregon childhood home in Madras. He was devoted to Russell and her cause, and when she asked him for help, he readily agreed. He lent the Friends an accomplished employee, Bennett Burns, to help prepare for the workshop; donated $30,000 of staff time, much of it his own; and provided computing, drafting, and technical expertise. By June 12, Macy had supplemented the Friends' five-hundred-page response to the mapping project with twenty-six 7.5-minute quadrangle maps, each with two mylar overlays, that plotted the Gorge's scenic, natural, historic, cultural, and recreational resources. The document combined obscure data Russell had unearthed—such as Henry Biddle's archeological survey in the 1920s near the Deschutes River—with new studies submitted by experts she had recruited. It was the most extensive analysis ever produced of the conservation and historic resources in the Gorge and was completed in less than two months. In the end, the three days of workshops gave the senators critical information and cooled the scalding temperature of debate. A surprised Russell conveyed her "intense pleasure" to Evans's staff that issues were "discussed at the rational level."[32]

But her pleasure did not last, as she and the Friends again turned their attention to Evans's preference for a commission. Two weeks after the workshops, the Friends wrote and circulated "Management Alternatives for the Columbia Gorge," which reviewed each management structure proposed for the Gorge—local, state, federal, and commission—and challenged Evans. The report explained why commissions had failed at Lake Tahoe and in the Columbia Gorge. It was too soon to judge Evans's five-year-old Northwest Power Planning Council a success, it said. The council had not yet made difficult, localized decisions, such as whether a coal-burning plant, with its job benefits and environmental problems, should be located in Montana or Oregon. The council had been formed around a consensus that a regional energy plan was needed, the report continued. No similar consensus existed in the Gorge for land use, so dissident counties would inevitably push for commissioners who opposed the purpose of the legislation. The report also noted that regional commissions had historically struggled with funding for management and land acquisition. This was not just an academic concern, as Skamania County had urged the governor to disband the Washington Gorge commission a year earlier, and in April a key committee in the state legislature had voted to defund the advisory commission. Evans was "frustrated and depressed" by the Friends' opposition, his staff told Friends cochair Dave Cannard, and the senator accused the organization of creating a rift between him and his colleagues.[33]

In the weeks after the workshops, Russell launched a single-handed campaign to expand the "areas of potential acquisition." Her knowledge of the Gorge, her vision of how it could be transformed, and her ability to implement her vision ensured that thousands of additional acres were included— or at least considered—for special designation: the Sandy River Delta, where Paul Martin's family lived and the port of entry died; the High Valley Farm commune, started fifteen years earlier by seven adults with twelve children to protect a narrow, 183-acre meadow high on Archer Mountain from logging, their members now aging and scattering to cities; the historic but withering towns of Dodson, Warrendale, and Bridal Veil, which offered access to a celebrated waterfall; Oregon Trail ruts west of the Deschutes River; petroglyphs and pictographs near Horsethief Lake on the Washington side; and the stunning section of the Historic Columbia River Highway between Hood River and Mosier with twin tunnels that had passed into private ownership and disrepair. Each place offered a resource that would be considered exceptional anywhere in the world. And they shared another characteristic: all had decayed over the decades and would further deteriorate, even disappear, without attention and funding.[34]

In mid-August, Governor Atiyeh and Governor Gardner sponsored a closed-door, two-day retreat in Lacey, Washington, to try and break the

legislative impasse. Only their staff, senior Senate staff, and the Gorge commissions' Jeff Breckel were invited to participate.[35] They agreed to support any
consensus worked out by the four senators, which was a step back for Governor
Gardner, who had been jolted by Skamania County's reaction to his tough,
pre-inauguration position. The discussions focused on a proposal presented
by Evans's lead staffer, Joe Mentor Jr. Mentor was intelligent, hard-working
and hard-driving, an attorney in his late twenties whose features reflected
his personality: a fixed, often defiant gaze and a square, forward-jutting jaw
that, like volcanic basalt, suggested an explosion could be imminent. Over
two days, Mentor pushed, prodded, and pulled his colleagues into an accord
to create a hybrid national scenic area, partly managed by commission and
partly by a yet-to-be-named federal agency.

The agreement carved the Gorge into three areas. Urban areas, where
most of the 41,000 Gorge residents lived, was the first. Those represented
the smallest portion—perhaps 10 percent of the proposed NSA—and economic development consistent with resource values would be encouraged
and lightly regulated there. Second, "special management areas," which
contained some of the Gorge's most important and threatened lands, would
be managed by the unnamed federal agency. Those areas had started out, in
the spring workshop maps, as "areas of potential acquisition" and included
only 37,500 acres. Two months later, after Russell's drive to expand them,
acre by precious acre, they totaled over 100,000 acres, more than 40 percent
of the proposed national scenic area. Third was the rest of the Gorge, later
called "general management areas," which would be managed by a regional,
twelve-member commission. Half of the commissioners would be appointed
by the two governors (three apiece) and half appointed by the six counties
(one each).[36]

The so-called Lacey accord addressed other key points but, to proponents
of legislation, unsatisfactorily. It gave the federal agency authority to veto the
commission's management plan but did not spell out policies and goals for the
two management plans. The commission and federal agency were required
to adopt guidelines for interim protection (before management plans were
adopted), but the accord offered no guidance on what the guidelines should
include. Enforcement was addressed in a single sentence and provided only
civil, not criminal penalties for violations. When Russell learned about the
accord, her anger was evident in her scribbled notes: "Need to make a speech
& *soon*; Env Grps have to *scream*; need letter writing campaign; Evans

doesn't care about Gorge or he'd meet . . . Evans doesn't value input. Month of intense activity; Hold press conference; FOCG & Env orgs."[37]

Both Packwood, who consistently had supported a strong federal role, and Hatfield indicated that they would work to strengthen the accord as it developed into legislation. In Russell's meeting with Hatfield two weeks later, however, he seemed satisfied with the Lacey results. He wanted a bill, any bill, to come to his Committee on Energy and Natural Resources, where he believed he could shape it to his liking. His tone then shifted, and "in a gentle way" he "upbraided" Russell for supporting the National Park Service as the lead federal agency. He spoke "*very* strongly" against the agency, Russell wrote in her notes, stating that it was "*totally* unacceptable." In a speech to Capitol Hill Republicans a few weeks later, Interior Secretary Donald Hodel also nixed any management role for the Park Service in the Gorge, calling his own agency a "far-away, insensitive bureaucracy."[38]

The Friends, and Russell, were in a difficult position. Legislation could not pass, they believed, if Hatfield was not fully supportive and without acquiescence from Evans and Gorton, yet they also believed that the Lacey principles would not protect the Gorge. Their challenge was to improve those principles without losing Evans and Gorton and upsetting Hatfield. Jim Blomquist, a seasoned and respected advocate who had led the Sierra Club's efforts in the Gorge, had some advice: who managed the Gorge was less important than how it was managed. If the standards in the legislation were specific and clear and demanded conservation, and if they were enforceable, then the manager—whether a commission, the Forest Service, or the Park Service—became less relevant.

The Friends agreed and circulated a position paper a few weeks later that detailed eleven priorities that "must be resolved to prevent our organization from *actively opposing*" legislation based on the Lacey accord. Like a Jenga game, where wooden blocks are removed and added to a teetering tower, the Friends hoped its priorities would not cause the legislative structure to collapse. In exchange for accepting the two-tiered system, the Friends insisted that protective language be added to the standards that would govern how the Gorge would be managed and that there be ways to enforce them. Russell and the Friends staff then began a "month of intense activity," with letter writing, media visits, and enlisting support from members and other environmental groups. The Friends was well-positioned to affect the debate. Its membership, now at thirty-eight hundred, was thriving and responsive. Hiking Weekend had attracted fifteen hundred hikers, bikers, and even kayakers that summer, triple the number two years earlier. And Russell's tours were continuing at a furious pace with increasingly influential groups; on a tour in September, she led a hundred and twenty mayors from the United States and Japan through the Gorge.[39]

Reporters relied on the Friends to help them determine whether the Lacey accord was workable. They knew Russell—she had guided most of them on tours—and they trusted her and the Friends staff to provide accurate information. Distilled to its essence, the Friends' message was that while it did not prefer the two-tiered system, the Lacey framework might work if its standards and enforcement were improved. Columbia Gorge United's message was even more distilled, judging that the Lacey accord was akin to "cleaning house with an atom bomb." The media supported the Friends' position. "The best that can be said of that division of power is that it might work," wrote Phil Cogswell, the Oregonian's associate editor, "but only if the goals and standards for the bistate commission to use in preparing the plan and for the secretary of agriculture to use in judging it are clearly set forth in the federal legislation." Both the Seattle Post-Intelligencer and the Columbian urged Washington's senators to strengthen the Lacey accord, and to do it quickly. Shelby Scates, a respected columnist for the Post-Intelligencer, called the Gorge campaign one of the "best lobbied and publicized" causes in the Northwest.[40]

Chuck Williams did not agree. He wanted the National Park Service to manage the Gorge and believed the Friends' support for the US Forest Service had destroyed that possibility. And because of Hatfield's opposition, it had. But Williams had signaled his willingness to accept management by the Forest Service years earlier, and his resentment of Russell—not support for the Park Service—now seemed to be motivating him. When the Friends declined to join other conservation organizations in a press conference if Williams participated, worried that he would use that platform to criticize the organization and its position in front of the media, he called the decision "bullshit." He charged: "you 'Friends' have fucked me and the Coalition constantly for almost five years now, and we suffer politically and financially every day because of your group."[41]

But Williams had isolated himself, and the national environmental groups supported the Friends' position. In a confidential memorandum to environmental leaders in mid-December, the National Audubon Society's vice president for national issues, Brock Evans, gave his perspective on the Lacey accords. If improvements proposed by conservationists were adopted, he wrote, it would be "almost impossible to have any development" on the more than a hundred thousand acres of special management areas. And, while the commission was "weaker than we would like, [it] must also meet standards in the legislation." Legislation could not pass without Hatfield's, Gorton's, and Dan Evans's support, he reminded his colleagues, and those senators were opposed to the protection of Columbia River tributaries and to a meaningful role for the National Park Service, which itself now opposed any role. Park Service management, he emphasized, was a *dead issue for now.* To improve on the amendments offered by conservation groups, Evans estimated, might take four more years of fighting, additional resources, and a more favorable political climate. Even if that effort was successful, he asked, what additional losses would the Gorge suffer? Legislation based on the Lacey accord, as amended, he concluded, should be accepted. The plan gave environmentalists most of what they want, and the rest "we can get later."[42]

Congress usually passes environmental legislation in even-numbered years, during each session's second year, when members stand for reelection. The bills on the Columbia Gorge launched early in 1986. On February 6, the four senators—with Evans as the official sponsor and Packwood vowing to seek strengthening amendments—introduced S. 2055, which codified most of the Lacey accord. Two days earlier, Congressman Weaver, who represented southwest Oregon and Eugene, and Congressman Mike Lowry, who represented Seattle and its suburbs, had introduced the original Friends' bill that identified the US Forest Service as the manager for the Gorge. Also on February 6, Congressmen AuCoin and Bonker introduced a bill that employed a two-tiered management system but mandated clear, protective standards and strict enforcement provisions. The same day, Congressmen Wyden and Morrison introduced yet another bill, intended to be identical to the bill introduced in the Senate. After a year in which no legislation on the Columbia Gorge had been introduced, four separate bills were submitted in the opening weeks of the last year of the 99th Congress.[43]

Russell and I met with editorial boards around the region, especially in Washington State. The response was immediate. The *Oregonian*'s Clark County edition called Evans's proposal "barely . . . an improvement over the dismally unsuccessful bistate commission established to plan for Lake Tahoe." The paper supported the "promising" AuCoin-Bonker bill because it toughened enforcement and added development standards. "The best that can be said of the senators' bill," the *Columbian* suggested, "is that it might survive the legislative process to become a framework upon which real Gorge protection could be hung." A *Seattle Post-Intelligencer* editorial embarrassed its state's senators by encouraging Bob Packwood to improve the Senate bill and echoing the Friends' concerns about enforcement and development standards. The *Bremerton Sun* called the Senate bill "an empty shell when it comes to Gorge protection" and urged citizens to tell Evans and Gorton to improve the bill's standards and enforcement. The Friends, with five other local and national conservation groups, then sent out an "Action Alert" that quoted extensively from the *Oregonian* and *Columbian* editorials, calling the Senate bill "An Empty Promise of Protection" that "quite simply, will not protect the Columbia River Gorge." The appeal asked members to demand that their senators improve the bill.[44]

Senator Evans was stung, and furious, especially at me. He phoned Friends Washington cochair, Dave Cannard, and demanded that I be fired. Cannard was caught off guard by a call from a United States senator, particularly one who was so angry. Perhaps to appease him, or believing that the legislation's chances could be improved, he agreed, and recommended to Russell that I be fired. Russell disagreed. She had been actively involved in the campaign to pressure Evans and was pleased that it seemed to be working.

Evans's backers also responded. Doug Jewett, Seattle city attorney (and Kristine Simenstad's brother-in-law) had been an early supporter of the Friends while running against Scoop Jackson for the Senate. He was close to both Washington senators, and he scolded Russell in a five-page letter that he copied to them. Evans and Gorton, he wrote, were "two of the finest public servants I have known," and he accused the Friends of ignoring their "extraordinary efforts and good faith concerns," insisting that they were acting on "principles and judgment—not political expediency." Jewett instructed Russell that instead of criticizing the two senators, the Friends should "focus on the positive and possible" and "believe in the good faith of our Governors and several of our Counties to appoint people [to the commission] who care." Try to improve the senators' bill by working with them, he urged, but if that is unsuccessful, then support it. "They know more about it than we do," he continued, and in any case "Congress meets every year," so the bill could be strengthened in the future.[45] It is unlikely that Jewett would have counseled fellow politicians to focus on the positive, to follow others' judgement on what is possible, to believe in the good faith of the governors—one of whom had consistently undermined his pledge to protect the Gorge—and to return to Congress in the future, if necessary, hoping that public support would not recede. But then Russell was not a politician. Nor a fellow.

Jewett received Russell's answer a week later when over three hundred volunteers, organized by the Friends and a dozen other organizations, spread out across Vancouver and hung forty thousand fliers on front doors. "Won't you spend five minutes today to help protect the Columbia Gorge forever?" the flyer asked, followed by quotes from supporting editorials and urging Clark County residents to push Evans and Gorton to strengthen their bill.[46] Vancouver and Portland media, especially television, covered the event extensively. Volunteers—some racing between doors, some using walkers, others pushing babies in strollers or accompanied by toddlers on tricycles—were portrayed carrying the same message: strengthen enforcement and development restrictions or lose the Columbia River Gorge. Calls and letters flooded the senators' offices.

Senator Evans wrote Jewett a week later, copying Russell, Washington cochair Cannard, and treasurer Bower. "I don't believe I have ever been involved in an issue in my political career where we have been so tortured by friends," he complained. "Although I have held my tongue, I fear that the well has been so poisoned that there is little hope that a bill will pass during this Congress." The Friends responded by inviting Evans to a board meeting on May 6 to clear the air. He sent Jewett in his place. During a "lively discussion," board members dispelled any sense that they were not completely behind Russell and staff. In a follow-up letter to Evans, the board explained that the organization had not questioned his or Gorton's good faith and that it appreciated the substantial time and effort they had invested in the Gorge. It then reiterated the Friends' belief that Evans's two-tiered approach could work. "However, our organization has stressed from the outset," they continued, "that the considerable management authority of the regional commission inherent in the two-tiered approach must be balanced by clear and reasonably protective legislative standards and enforcement provisions, among other elements, in order to assure the long-term protection of the Columbia River Gorge."[47]

While neither party retreated, resentments had been vented. The catharsis was therapeutic and timely, as the 1986 legislative calendar had been shortened so incumbents could campaign. Hearings on the Gorge were scheduled in Washington, DC, for June 17 and 19, which signified that the issue was ripe for legislative attention. The hearings were challenging for West Coast residents who needed several days to travel back and forth and to testify, and to pay for flights, accommodations, and meals. Russell and I scrambled to enlist effective witnesses. She asked Millard McClung, the associate director of the Oregon Historical Society, which now supported the legislation, to testify. Almost thirty years later, McClung recalled their conversation. He had not wanted to spend hours preparing his remarks, an afternoon delivering them, and two days traveling, and he told Russell that he simply could not testify. She told him she would write his testimony. "But they'll ask me questions that I won't know the answer to," he countered. "They won't ask you any questions," she replied. "And the next thing I knew," McClung recalled with a chuckle, "I was on a plane to Washington to testify. I could never figure out a way to say 'no' to Nancy."[48]

Nor could others. On June 17, eighty witnesses testified before a sub-committee of the Senate Committee on Energy and Natural Resources. The hearing was chaired by Wyoming senator Malcolm Wallop, who did not hide his disdain for a national scenic area in the Gorge. He complained to Governor Atiyeh, who had arrived to give his support, that too often "the Federal Government when it is the court of last resort becomes . . . the court of first resort," and he estimated that the NSA could cost taxpayers $100 million.[49] Wallop then mostly deferred to committee members Hatfield and Evans to lead the questioning.

Senator Packwood testified first, describing the bill as "an outline for protection rather than . . . a final product." He recommended, as did scores of other witnesses, that enforcement be made mandatory, not discretionary; that development standards be strengthened; and that interim protection—after enactment of legislation but prior to adoption of a management plan—be improved. Peter Myers, the deputy secretary of agriculture representing the Reagan administration, followed and was chided by Wallop for the "intolerable insult" of not providing an advance copy of his testimony, as was customary. Myers apologized and then—presumably to Wallop's pleasure—denounced the bill, inveighing against its "overriding Federal presence" and potentially unconstitutional provisions that "amount to Federal zoning of private lands." He concluded: "We cannot support S. 2055 in its present form."[50]

Opponents and proponents to the bill followed well-worn paths. Tribal representatives, the Garden Club of America, and over a dozen national conservation organizations and their local affiliates—ranging from the Sierra Club, the Audubon Society, and the American Rivers Council to the National Parks and Conservation Association—asked for stronger development standards, mandatory enforcement, and protection for tributaries. Senator Evans often challenged these witnesses, including Dick Benner, senior staff attorney for 1000 Friends of Oregon. Evans preferred discretionary enforcement—the commission "may" enforce violations rather than the mandatory "shall" enforce—saying that everyone needs and wants discretion. He read examples of enforcement language from unnamed sources and asked Benner for his opinion. When Benner rejected all of Evans's examples, saying that discretion in implementing the act was proper but that the commission must enforce the law if a violation occurred, Evans responded that he was "astonished" at Benner's position and called it "totally inappropriate."[51]

Senator Evans was gentler with those who opposed the bill. After Skamania County officials denounced "dilettante nongorge residents and nongorge taxpayers who wish to steal our own birthright by making the gorge their scenic playground" and blamed draft legislation for the county's 20 percent unemployment rate, Evans suggested that the high unemployment rate might be attributable to changes in the timber industry. Wouldn't a national scenic area attract tourists, he asked. One commissioner replied that the county was "inundated with the surf sailors now" and besides, had only one motel. Timber industry representatives testified against legislation, although several suggested amendments to mitigate its impact.[52]

Residents of the Gorge were divided, even families. Lois Jemtegaard, who did not mention in her testimony her brother-in-law's land sale to the Trust for Public Land, was overcome with the anxiety that Chuck Cushman had so ably stoked. "Through the years, we have fought forest fires, bears, bobcats, coyotes, cougars, wolves, and killer dogs that have endangered us, our home, and our animals," she began. "But I have not been as scared of any of these threats as I am of this Senate Committee." She continued: "This is not conservation. It is the destruction of everything my husband and I, and his parents before us, worked a lifetime to conserve. This bill should not be dignified with your vote. My husband is fighting for his life and when this hearing came up, he said, damn the cancer; protect our land." A resident who lived at Rim View Estates agreed. "Do you think we are going to destroy property or views that we have spent our own hard-earned money to acquire?" asked Edgar Cleveland, who had built the floodlit mansion on Cape Horn that Nancy Russell detested. "That does not make sense."[53]

Nine and a half hours after the hearing began, Evans brought it to a close. "We have precious little time left" to pass the legislation in the current election year, he warned, "and we have got to work fast." After the congressional session ended, any unresolved legislative efforts would have to begin anew in the 100th Congress. He had already expressed his appreciation for the Trust for Public Land, especially Harriet Burgess, and now he paused to recognize

Nancy Russell, "who over the years has been a stalwart constantly working toward . . . preserv[ing] the gorge." He then asked those who supported the legislation to recognize the legitimate concerns of Gorge landowners, many of whom were "frightened." Finally, in a stern rebuke that left little doubt that he was addressing Chuck Cushman, he admonished those who carried "outrageously wrong information" to landowners about the legislation. "I have no truck for those who do that," he said. "I think they are damaging in the utmost to the very people they are trying to attract."[54]

Two days later, across the rotunda, a House Interior subcommittee took testimony, mostly from the same witnesses. The Senate's collegiality, even from someone who despised "federal zoning" as much as Malcolm Wallop did, was absent in the House. Conservation-minded Democrats like John Seiberling from Ohio and Bruce Vento from Minnesota jousted with Republicans from the West, and Idaho Republican Larry Craig assailed conservationists and exhorted Skamania County officials to resist:

> So fight. You have the right to, especially when the taking of property is at hand. We fought a revolution over that. So fight. Don't give in. Land management is best at the local level . . . [The Gorge] is beautiful today as it has always been beautiful. It is not damaged; it is not destroyed; it is vibrant and alive, not because of a Federal bureaucrat, or a national environmental group telling you how to do it. For the last 200 years you have done it your way . . . and Easterners just do not understand this.[55]

Oregon's Denny Smith, a member of the Interior Committee whom Russell had accused years earlier of violating Teddy Roosevelt's conservation heritage, called all three House bills "unnecessary, unwanted, and probably unconstitutional." He demanded an "economic impact study" of the bills—a common delay tactic—and predicted that "private land will be condemned. Citizens, some of whom have lived in the area for generations, will be forced off their land. Logging operations and other businesses will be forced to close. Thousands of acres of land will be yanked from the tax rolls." Jim Weaver, a senior member of both the House Interior and Agriculture Committees, observed that markup—when committees review and amend draft legislation—"will be most interesting."[56]

John Yeon testified at neither hearing, still preferring a traditional national recreation area for land west of Hood River, although he had begrudgingly suggested a role for the Forest Service east of Bonneville Dam if the Park Service managed the lands to the west. "I don't agree with the strategy of present legislation," he wrote an acquaintance, Jim Gardner, "and I doubt that it will fly. But it is the only game in town, and I don't want to be, or appear to be, a saboteur." Then Yeon revealed the depths of his anguish:

> I have felt that while legislation is pending, it would be the worst of times for it to be known that I might be parting with The Shire. It has been a sort of keystone of the preservation effort. Paradoxically, I have long been known for advocating public acquisition and consolidation of parklands in the Gorge. I could easily appear to be a turncoat for obstructing it; a traitor or worse. I am not concerned about the consequences to me, but to the Gorge effort; undercutting it at a crucial time, or demoralizing it.[57]

He told Gardner that he likely would have donated The Shire to the National Park Service if it had been chosen to manage the Gorge. As all pending bills named the Forest Service as the lead federal agency, however, protection of The Shire now "involves the sale of it to you."[58]

As Yeon considered selling The Shire, Skamania County was tense over other events. In July, angry at the Gorge commissions' testimony that the Senate bill provided a "reasonable balance" between protection and economic development, the county evicted the commissions' staff from its offices in the old jail. The *Oregonian* accused the financially struggling county of ruling by "temper tantrum." "How seriously can a reasonable politician take a government that deals with people it disagrees with by making them go away," the editorial asked Senator Evans, "even when such exile is against the government's own interests?"[59]

A week later, those interests worsened when the county's oldest timber company, Broughton Lumber, which owned two mills and maintained a nine-mile-long wooden flume to float logs to its mill near the river, announced it would close. Washington State officials predicted that losing Broughton's ninety-five full-time and ten part-time employees might push the county's unemployment rate to 35 percent. Broughton's general manager attributed the closure to "economics," specifically the several million dollars needed to retool its Willard mill to accept smaller logs, as fewer old growth trees were available. But in a letter to its employees, the company blamed "pending legislative efforts" for the closure, even though its mills were located in areas exempted from the legislation, its timber sources were almost entirely outside the Gorge, and its flume was a historic resource that the legislation would protect. Although a timber official admitted that an "infinitesimal" amount of commercial timber still grew in the Gorge, the industry was wary of anything that might increase the federal government's oversight of private timberlands and often distorted the impact of legislation. In a letter to Washington congressman Sid Morrison, Russell accused Broughton of "irresponsible and cowardly scapegoating."[60]

On August 1, four members of the US House of Representatives flew to Stevenson for the only hearing the Committee on Agriculture would hold on the bill. More than one hundred forty witnesses had asked to testify, and three hundred people crowded into the Rock Creek Recreation Center to watch. Subcommittee Chairman Charles Whitley from North Carolina warned the audience that "no disturbances would be tolerated," an admonition that was ignored more than observed, especially when supporters of the legislation spoke. Governor Gardner's representative was greeted with boos, which intensified when he urged Congress to prioritize national scenic area legislation, especially since the 99th Congress was scheduled to adjourn in two months. Recent hearings had brought the Gorge issue to a fever pitch, with most of the vitriol directed at Russell. Worried about her safety, I drove her to the hearing in her sister Betsy's car, which was unknown in the Gorge. At nine o'clock that night, we walked out to the parking lot to discover that three of the car's four tires had been slashed.[61]

Three days after the hearing and a continent away — pressed by Bob Packwood, conservationists, the media, and the public — Senator Evans brokered amendments that were acceptable to his three colleagues. The amendments made enforcement mandatory, gave the Forest Service the authority to stop development before management plans were approved, added protection for Gorge tributaries, required federal and state activities to be consistent with the act, and toughened development standards in the special management areas managed by the Forest Service. The new standards banned residences and related structures from being built on any unimproved parcel smaller than forty acres in a special management area, adding to the prohibition of multifamily residential, commercial and industrial development, subdivisions, and short plats. The senators' amended bill now protected the Gorge more than any of the House bills and had the Friends' enthusiastic support.[62]

In February 1986, as the four bills were introduced in Congress, the Trust for Public Land continued to struggle financially in the Gorge. Mark Hatfield's commitment and his estimate that legislation would be "forthcoming" had somewhat eased the concerns raised by the board or were outweighed by the board's anxiety that the Senate Appropriations chair was examining its own commitment. Russell had stepped up her fundraising on behalf of TPL, organizing tours for foundation heads and for the Friends' major donors and asking them to donate to the organization. She equated the trust's role in the Gorge with John D. Rockefeller Jr.'s land acquisitions at Grand Teton, Great Smoky Mountains, and Acadia National Parks during the first half of the twentieth century. Still, with few agency take-outs for its land holdings, TPL's financial situation had deteriorated. In late February, Harriet Burgess wrote Bob Schaefer to remind him of his unfulfilled donation on St. Cloud Ranch, telling him that the trust was "facing a serious cash flow crunch right now and needs to call in all of its outstanding pledges." The cash crunch, however, did not deter her from increasing TPL's gamble in the Gorge.[63]

Just a month earlier, Burgess had extended an option TPL held on Doetsch Ranch, a 228-acre property at the base of Beacon Rock State Park. The option cost $20,000 and would allow the trust to acquire the ranch for $363,000. Although the state park encompassed over four thousand acres, it included just a half mile of river frontage, the north bank's only public access to the Columbia in the sixteen miles from the entrance to the park. Most of the ranch comprised lush, open meadows that stretched west along the river for a mile and a half, with forested uplands rising above Highway 14. The property offered sensational views of Oregon's cliffs, the Columbia in front and Beacon Rock behind. Its level terrain, river access, and unrestricted views had once drawn Native people, who built a large village there named Nimisxaya, which likely was abandoned after diseases took their toll on its population.[64] Lewis and Clark had called the village Wahclellah. The same attributes that attracted those early residents to the site—flat land, unrestricted views, river access—were prized by developers seven generations later, along with no zoning restrictions and a reasonable commute to Portland. If Doetsch Ranch could be protected, it would snatch a prime site away from developers, triple the land available for public access to the river, and preserve property of incomparable aesthetic, cultural, and historic significance.

In February, the Army Corps of Engineers used $5.45 million of Bonneville Dam mitigation funds to buy the Stevensons' seven hundred acres of wetlands at Steigerwald Lake. The following month, the US Fish and

Wildlife Service purchased TPL's twenty-seven-acre Kerr property, which was surrounded on three sides by Stevenson land and was bisected by Gibbons Creek. It was hard for Russell to believe that Steigerwald Lake, at long last, was protected and would become a national wildlife refuge. Once her success registered, she organized another reception to thank Senator Hatfield.[65]

More good news came in March when Washington's Shoreline Hearings Board ruled in favor of Friends of the Gorge and reversed Skamania County's approval of the Hidden Harbor subdivision. The county's Shorelines Master Plan prohibited marinas and excavation, the board concluded, and the developer's plan to dig a three-acre harbor and use the spoils to raise houses above the hundred-year flood plain was not allowed. The victory stopped the subdivision, at least temporarily, and demonstrated to Congress that Skamania County was not enforcing its own laws. It also tilted, in TPL's favor, the confidential negotiations the developer had opened with the organization a year earlier.[66]

The trust now turned its attention to the last twelve unsold lots in the subdivision on top of Cape Horn. Four of the sixteen lots at Rim View Estates had been sold, and two had been developed, including Edgar Cleveland's sprawling residence at the edge of the cliff. Cleveland had testified in June that landowners would neither destroy property nor views, although his own house was visible for miles up the Gorge. Russell's lawsuit against Colonel Rizor had established that the county's subdivision-by-short-plat process violated state law, and Rim View Estates—especially the Cleveland house—reminded her of what had been lost when she had been unable to challenge the development in 1981. In late July, the Russells made their third, no-interest loan to the Trust for Public Land, this time for $300,000 to help buy the twelve remaining lots. The loan also served an additional purpose. "Your commitment has inspired our Board to be steadfast in TPL's efforts to acquire what we can," TPL President Marty Rosen wrote Russell, "so that when the Columbia Gorge legislation is finally in place it will not be too late."[67]

By the fall of 1986, TPL was betting heavily that legislation would soon be "in place." It had already conveyed eleven Gorge properties, valued at over $9 million, into public ownership. But the organization that relied on long-term, low-interest options, and rarely owned land still held fifteen properties valued at over $4 million—an amount that exceeded the organization's annual operating budget—and had placed four other properties, totaling six hundred acres, under option. Most of the properties were in Skamania County. Harriet Burgess needed a federal agency to buy them, and soon.

Even with the three Russell loans, now totaling $700,000, and a $600,000 loan from the Meyer Trust, the trust carried an additional $700,000 in debt on the land and had significant transaction and holding costs. If federal legislation failed, the trust would be forced to resell most, perhaps all, of its properties on the private market for pennies on the dollar, a financial and reputational disaster. Burgess was betting the house—TPL's house—that legislation would pass.[68]

By mid-August 1986, just over a month remained in the ninety-ninth congressional session. The White House and conservative Republicans were furious at the level of federal control over private land proposed by the Gorge bills, and the nonpartisan Congressional Research Service had found scant support in the Constitution for such authority. Unlike other legislation—the Cape Cod National Seashore Act, which relied upon condemnation, or the Coastal Barrier Resources Act, which used economic sanctions—the Gorge bills sought to "impose direct coercive controls" through civil and criminal penalties to enforce federal land use standards. Those controls were needed, the Friends argued, because the Gorge was larger and had more private land than areas like Cape Cod and civil and criminal penalties were more effective. Such authority was "unlikely" to be authorized by the Property Clause of the Constitution, the Research Service concluded, and "a step beyond" what courts had held the Commerce Clause permitted. To the extent that the Commerce Clause could be construed to allow such authority, it might be due to the substantial federal presence in the Gorge, although only 20 percent of the Gorge was owned by the federal government.[69]

In other words, the federal activities that had defaced the Gorge for so long—two dams that destroyed Celilo Falls, the Long Narrows, and the world's largest salmon runs; two railroads that dynamited both shorelines to lay track through the Gorge; the interstate highway that obliterated culturally significant rock formations and brought thousands of cars through the Gorge each day; the interstate bridge that threatened Mount Pleasant and Mount Zion with suburbia—might now be its salvation. The irony was lost on conservative Republicans and officials of the timber, mining, and other extractive industries, who saw an "unnecessary, unwanted, and probably unconstitutional" federal land grab.[70]

On the morning of August 14, a week after the four senators had agreed on strengthening amendments to the proposed legislation, the Committee on Energy and Natural Resources planned to consider it at the committee's last

meeting of the congressional session. The bill had just been reprinted, however, and arrived too late to be placed on the agenda. The three-week August
recess began in seventy-two hours, and Republicans, expecting an intense
Democratic effort to recapture the Senate, were eager to resume campaigning. Afternoon committee meetings had been prohibited, and the chances
of getting the bill through committee and then passed were "almost extinct,"
Senator Evans said. But Senator Hatfield marched to the Senate floor and
requested unanimous consent to allow the committee to meet that afternoon.
Unanimous consent is a Senate procedure that permits its petitioner to move
forward with an uncontroversial action as long as no one disagrees. But the
Gorge bill was not uncontroversial, and the *Oregonian* reported that such
a motion—assuming it succeeded—would take a full day. Hatfield accomplished it in twenty minutes. The committee met that afternoon, and the bill
was approved unanimously in a brief, hurried session. Members broke into
applause. Idaho Senator Jim McClure, one of the Senate's most conservative
"old bulls" and the committee chairman, called the process "extraordinary"
and cautioned that staff would review the bill during the August recess and
amendments could be offered later on the Senate floor.[71]

Six weeks later, after Congress had reconvened, the *Oregonian*'s Washington, DC, correspondent David Whitney reported on Monday, September
29, that chances for Gorge legislation were deteriorating "as Congress rushed
toward its Friday adjournment" and "as Republican opposition mounted."
Chairman McClure and subcommittee Chairman Wallop wanted "substantial revisions," Whitney wrote, and the legislation "face[d] a solid wall
of Republican opposition" in the House, where Northwest Democrats had
united behind a new bill that was similar to the Senate's but even stronger.
The best news for conservationists, Whitney wrote, was that Congress might
miss its Friday adjournment, "meaning the potential for another week for the
gorge bill to work its way through its convoluted legislative obstacle course."[72]

Two days later, the situation had worsened, improved, then worsened
again. McClure and Wallop remained opposed, and the Forest Service
hardened its opposition, calling the senators' bill "unacceptable" because of
its estimated $100 million in costs over five years and the degree of federal
authority over private lands. Bruce Vento, chairman of the House Interior
Subcommittee on National Parks, nonetheless agreed to take up the legislation on Thursday. Republicans—led by Denny Smith from Oregon, Don
Young from Alaska, and Ron Marlenee from Montana—threatened to delay
until the 99th Congress expired. Gorge legislation had become a "cause

célèbre" among right-wing House Republicans, according to a congressional aide, reinforced by a guest editorial in the *Wall Street Journal* entitled "Stop Congress's National Adjournment Park." If the bill passed, the editorial forecast, there would be "far-reaching regulation of private land use and extensive purchases and condemnations of privately owned land" that would kill jobs and lead to a "population exodus" in the Gorge.[73]

On Thursday afternoon, Republicans on the Interior subcommittee offered amendment after amendment, called for recorded votes, disallowed proxies, and insisted that quorums be present. After taking three hours to review the first two pages of the seventy-page bill and just six of Denny Smith's eighty amendments, a frustrated Vento gaveled the subcommittee closed. "We've only got time on our side," Smith rejoiced. But debate on an important spending bill, arms control measures, and raising the debt ceiling continued, and Congress delayed adjournment by a week, to October 10. Vento vowed to take the bill to the full Interior Committee.[74]

The Interior Committee met on Tuesday, October 7. Encouraged by their victory at the subcommittee the week before, Republicans planned to "use committee rules to delay and obstruct until majority Democrats quit in frustration," the *Seattle Times* reported. But Jim Weaver had prepared his own strategy and moved that the committee substitute a "blank-check" bill—that is, a bill that contained only a title—for the full bill under consideration, giving Republicans nothing to amend. Republicans objected to a lack of quorum, and the vote was rescheduled for that afternoon. Denny Smith was the sole Republican attending the afternoon meeting, intending to object to the expected absence of a quorum, but he arrived fifteen minutes late. The Democrats pounced on his blunder. Still absent a quorum but with no Republican present to object, they passed the bill out of committee. Smith arrived in time to see jubilant Democrats whooping, hugging Jim Weaver, and yelling "Save the Gorge." He turned on the ranking Democrat, John Seiberling, and shouted, "Is this that important to you, to railroad it through like this?" Seiberling replied, "If you didn't get here, that's tough."[75]

That evening, the Department of Agriculture informed the four senators that the amendments negotiated by their staffs, mostly procedural in nature, had addressed its objections to a considerable extent. Although uncertain whether they had overcome McClure's and Wallop's "federal zoning" concerns, the senators took the amended bill to the floor the next day. Finding a gap in the Senate calendar, Senator Hatfield asked for unanimous consent to take up the bill. His request was approved, and for forty-five minutes the four senators spoke in favor of their bill and responded to questions. Deliberations concluded, Hatfield asked the Senate to vote. McClure and Wallop had agreed not to block the bill, since it was a "vast improvement" over earlier bills, but they still voted against it, as did Idaho's Steve Symms. Nevertheless, the bill passed on a voice vote.[76] The same day, a subcommittee of the House Committee on Agriculture—which shared jurisdiction with the Interior Committee because of the Forest Service's potential role—approved the bill and a handful of amendments proposed by Bob Smith.[77]

Now, with just two days remaining before adjournment, Mark Hatfield sent Bob Smith what political correspondent Steve Forrester called an "extraordinary letter," pleading with him not to upset the Senate's "delicately-balanced compromise" by delaying and amending the House bill. Rumors swirled through the Capitol that adjournment would be delayed for an additional week in order to pass an enormous spending bill that allocated funds for every state and which Hatfield happened to be shepherding through the Senate. "For the Northwest delegation, this extended work period has given the Columbia River Gorge protection bill new odds for passage," Forrester reported. "Had Congress left on schedule, or even one week late, the gorge bill would be dead. But a second, added week might do the trick."[78]

Adjournment was delayed until October 17. Using the reprieve, the House Agriculture Committee met to consider Gorge legislation and met with the same fervent Republican opposition the Interior Committee had encountered. In a rebuke to Hatfield, Bob Smith had prepared eight amendments. Congressman Marlenee offered eighty, fumed that the bill had been "ram-rodded, bulldozed, and railroaded" in Interior, and continually called for a quorum. After suffering through several quorum calls, Chairman Kika de la Garza, a Democrat from Texas, slammed down his gavel and adjourned the committee without forwarding the bill to the floor.[79]

The week of October 13, everyone knew, was going to be the session's last. "Incumbent senators in tight races are climbing the walls," Forrester reported. House Republicans who opposed the Gorge legislation would prevail if they could force a stalemate through Friday. Their task became easier on Tuesday, when the Department of Justice harshly criticized both the House and the Senate bills, warning that "our concerns . . . are fundamental and serious enough to warrant consideration of a veto recommendation." Bruce Vento had contrary concerns and wanted to strengthen the bill. A battle on the floor of the House—the only refuge in the gathering storm—was certain, but only if a bill could reach the floor.[80]

During the last weeks of a congressional session, getting a bill to the floor is challenging. The path is often through the Rules Committee, but the Rules Committee was not scheduled to meet during the session's final days. By Wednesday morning, however, Congressmen Weaver, AuCoin, and Bonker—after agreeing to a series of conservation-oriented amendments with Bruce Vento—had buttonholed Chairman Claude Pepper, a Democrat from Florida, and persuaded him to convene his committee. Weaver proposed a "closed rule," where the full House would vote the legislation up or down, with no amendments. Bob Smith objected, wanting to debate ten amendments. Republican committee members backed Smith, and Pepper, seeing the disagreement, adjourned the meeting. Opponents rejoiced. The bill was dead, Weaver acknowledged.[81]

I had spent the past month on Capitol Hill negotiating bill provisions and conferring daily with Russell in Portland while she called allies and presented to groups, ratcheting up pressure on Congress and keeping TPL's Gorge efforts and the Friends afloat through constant fundraising. Now Congressman Weaver told me it was time to return home, as no bill would pass this session. I made plane reservations for late that afternoon, returned to the hotel, and called a cab for the airport. While waiting in the lobby, I received a message from Don Bonker's staff. The situation had changed. Representatives AuCoin, Bonker, Wyden, and Weaver, with the support of Sid Morrison—who represented Skamania County and favored legislation to diversify its economy and end uncertainty for its residents—had asked House Majority Whip Tom Foley to intervene. Foley, who had represented his district in eastern Washington for twenty years, was one of the most influential and knowledgeable members in the House and would soon be elected speaker. He asked Chairman Pepper to have the Rules Committee move the Gorge bill to the floor. And he wanted the bill to be debated the next day, on Thursday, not on Friday, the session's last legislative day, when many members would be returning to their districts.[82]

Seconds before midnight on Wednesday, the Rules Committee—after not having been scheduled to meet at all that week—met for a second time to consider the Gorge bill. Bob Smith was livid and again told the committee that he had ten amendments to offer. When Sid Morrison stood to support the bill, his fellow Republicans walked out. At one o'clock in the morning, the committee voted to send the bill to the House floor later that day, where Bob Smith could offer three amendments. The chairman described the committee meeting as an "unusual circumstance."[83]

Twelve hours later, the House of Representatives convened to debate the future of the Columbia Gorge. Debate was scheduled for two hours. It lasted over four. The Republican floor manager from Tennessee opened by calling the bill controversial, labeled the Rules Committee decision a "gag rule," and announced that he had received nearly one hundred telegrams in opposition. Debate then deteriorated. Alaska's Don Young suggested that Congress design a red flag, with hammer and sickle, for the Gorge. Mike Strang from Colorado charged that the bill had "slithered through the process here during the dark of night, a slimy travesty, a rip-off of the American taxpayer," and California's Bob Lagomarsino called it a "complete perversion of the legislative process." Bob Smith, after comparing the federal government to the eighteenth-century British Empire, warned that British actions had led to war and offered his three amendments. The first and third would have gutted the bill and were quickly voted down; the second, requiring one of each governor's three commission appointees to live in the national scenic area, was accepted. After four hours, debate closed. Congressman Smith insisted on a quorum and a roll call vote. The legislation passed by a three-to-one margin: 290 yeas to 91 nays.[84]

Because the House bill differed from the Senate bill and there was no time for the two chambers to reconcile their differences, the Senate needed to pass the exact bill the House had passed—and by the next day, the session's last. Worse, since Senate passage a week earlier, the Department of Justice had threatened to recommend a presidential veto and the chair of the powerful Senate Committee on the Budget, Pete Domenici from New Mexico, had expressed alarm over the costs of implementing the bill. Worse yet, the *Oregonian* reported that Malcolm Wallop had agreed earlier not to block Senate approval only because he was sure the bill would die in the House. He was now expected to oppose Senate consideration of the House bill. "The situation is perilous," said Hatfield's press aide. "We don't have any clear signals as to how anyone who has problems with the bill will proceed. . . . It won't take much to kill the bill." Even Hatfield disagreed with portions of the House-passed bill, especially a provision, inserted at Representative Vento's request, that withheld federal funds from Gorge counties if the Oregon and Washington legislatures did not ratify the legislation and create the commission.[85]

At four o'clock on Friday morning, Hatfield and Evans "conceived a plan," the *Oregonian* reported, "to skirt potential floor amendments from McClure and Wallop by introducing 'colloquies'—that is, prepared exchanges between members—in an effort to establish a legislative record protecting those senators' concerns." Jim McClure agreed to the proposal that morning, but Malcolm Wallop remained undecided until late that afternoon. When Wallop finally relented, Hatfield rushed to the Senate floor and was granted permission to interrupt its proceedings. He introduced the colloquies and asked for unanimous consent to pass the House bill. A single senator could stop Gorge legislation, and several were so inclined. Yet to do so would anger the chair of the Appropriations Committee. The Columbia River Gorge National Scenic Area Act passed with no objection. House passage had taken more than four hours; in the Senate, Hatfield needed less than two minutes. Congress met briefly on Saturday and adjourned.[86]

Immediately after the bill passed, I tracked Nancy Russell down by phone, finding her at a friend's house. She was ecstatic, almost speechless. Congratulatory calls from friends and congressmen flooded her phone, a television news team interviewed her, Don and Shirley Clark delivered an azalea, and Senator Evans sent her the bill's front page with the inscription: "Nancy, this is your bill." That evening, she spoke at a Trust for Public Land fundraiser. After talking about TPL and the enormous risks it was taking in the Gorge, donors rose in a standing ovation. The next night, she received an award from The Nature Conservancy, scheduled before the legislation had passed, at the Western Forestry Center.[87] Unlike five years before, she did not have to lead the audience out to the parking lot to speak. Bruce stayed home to write Aubrey about the week's events.

> I am sure you cannot grasp the significance of this. . . . Even I, on the sidelines, found the tension of the last week almost unbearable. In fact, it *was* unbearable: I forbid Nancy telling me the developments of the day because they were so often disappointing and frustrating. My God, what a series of crevices, hurdles and banana peels were put in the way of the bill! . . . The story is an amazing one to me—a wild mixture of big egos, low motives, parliamentary procedure, strategies and remarkable luck at a number of junctures when all appeared lost.[88]

He reminded his son of his mother's attributes. "It would be nice to think that you had inherited your mother's basic character, her modesty yet self-assurance, her iron determination yet gentility and her fundamental intelligence and good sense. A rare combination, really." A week later, Nancy

Russell sent her own letter to Aubrey. It contained just two sentences about her accomplishment: "It has been an awfully exciting time for me. All my friends are excited about the Gorge bill's passing Congress and have been calling right and left." She did not mention the calls from congressmen, the ovation at the Trust for Public Land, The Nature Conservancy award, or the *Oregonian* headline that spanned its front page in inch-high type: "Gorge bill sent to Reagan." She was already focused on ensuring that President Reagan signed the bill.[89]

The president had to sign the bill in thirty days, by midnight on November 17, or it would die of a pocket veto. As a former western governor—who famously declared in his first inaugural address that "government is not the solution . . . government is the problem"—Reagan was inclined to veto the bill. The Departments of Justice and Interior agreed, and both recommended a veto to the Office of Management and Budget, which was pulling together the various cabinet department positions. OMB staff "overwhelmingly opposed" the bill, Hatfield was told. Only the Department of Agriculture was supportive.[90]

Skamania County passed a resolution declaring a week of mourning "for the loss of principles upon which this nation was founded" and ordered the American flag flown at half-mast. The front page of the *Skamania County Pioneer*, above the fold, featured a photograph of the lowered flag at the courthouse and a blood-red headline declaring "A Time of Mourning." Gorge residents organized a letter-writing campaign to encourage a presidential veto, a cardboard box on the *Pioneer*'s counter was labeled "veto letters." Every day, the newspaper's advertising director bundled the letters and mailed them to the White House.[91]

The Friends wanted the bill sent to the president before the November 4 election, thinking that Reagan might sign the bill—despite agency recommendations and his own inclination—to help reelect Slade Gorton. The bill was popular in Washington's large urban areas, where Gorton's support was weakest, and Reagan's party retained only a slim majority in the Senate. But another delay at the Government Printing Office resulted in the bill getting to the president a day after the election. Gorton lost, as did the Republicans the Senate. A member of Don Bonker's staff lamented that backers of the Gorge bill "have lost leverage since the election." Other congressional staff fretted that a veto could dash future hopes for legislation, pointing out the "political chemistry" and "unique set of circumstances" that had gotten the bill this far. They also knew that with the Democrats achieving a majority in the Senate, Senator Hatfield would lose his chairmanship of the Appropriations Committee and, with it, some influence.[92]

Nancy Russell marshalled support for the bill. She called leading Republicans, including Pendleton's Brot Bishop, Weyerhaeuser's Bob Wilson, and Don Frisbee from Pacific Power and Light, and asked them to write the president. She asked Nani Warren, who now backed the legislation, for help. New supporters such as lumberman Peter Murphy from Eugene, a Republican national committeeman who was close to Reagan, called the president on her behalf. She reached out to Vice President George H. W. Bush, who had met with Russell in 1982. Oregon's attorney general got in touch with the Department of Justice after talking with Russell.[93] She asked everyone she knew to write the president, and members of the Friends inundated his office with letters.

But the White House was quiet. Rumors swirled. Fifteen days elapsed, then twenty, then twenty-five. After talking with his White House contact, Peter Murphy reported back to Russell that "it does not look good." Then he asked: "Does the name Stevenson mean anything to you?" Fearful that they were sabotaging the bill, Evans's staff called the family's attorney and learned that its patriarchs were supportive but that several family members remained loudly antagonistic. So two Stevenson timber companies, along with three other companies, sent a letter to President Reagan, expressing their worry that "gorge legislation will become law either this year or next" and urging him to remove uncertainty by signing the bill. Hatfield was the only Northwest senator who remained at the capital after the election, and he pressed the head of the Office of Management and Budget, with whom he had just guided a record $575 billion spending bill through Congress, to lobby the president. Then, "with the odds running heavily against turning the White House around," the *Oregonian* reported, "Hatfield called in some political debts."[94]

On Friday, November 14, three days before the bill would die, Senator Hatfield wrote the president: "I regard the Columbia Gorge Act as my highest personal priority, and I urge your approval today." President Reagan retired to Camp David for the weekend. But Mark Hatfield knew that President Reagan was eager to fund his Strategic Defense Initiative—"Star Wars" to its detractors—and his staff had advised the White House that there was a connection between Gorge legislation and SDI's budget. "Typical Hatfield," Don Bonker recalled years later, "not a threat or asserting his authority as chairman, but subtly letting the White House know a veto may have consequences."[95]

On Sunday evening, President Reagan phoned Senator Hatfield to tell him that he was going to veto the bill. Hatfield's wife Antoinette overheard her husband's part in the conversation. The president, she later said, "wasn't going to sign it. . . . I heard [Mark] say 'No, I understand . . . do what you have to do. I understand perfectly.' And he [repeated] that, it seems, about five times." Then he became less subtle: "'But you know we're very busy up here and I would suggest you don't waste any paper sending up your budget.' . . . Mark wasn't mad about it. He just said 'you have to do what you have to do, and I have to do what I have to do.'"[96]

The next day, just hours before the bill would have died, President Reagan signed the Columbia River Gorge National Scenic Area Act into law. In a statement that accompanied his signing, the president expressed "grave doubts as to the constitutionality" of portions of the bill and reiterated that he was "strongly opposed to Federal regulation of private land." Nevertheless, he signed the bill because of the "far-reaching support in both States for a solution to the longstanding problems related to management of the Columbia River Gorge." According to Mark Hatfield, the president signed the bill with one hand and held his nose with the other.[97]

Chapter 6
Roll On, Columbia, 1987–2003

Although overjoyed by passage of the Columbia River Gorge National Scenic Area Act, Russell spent little time celebrating. There was still too much to do. Behind the scenes, Forest Service leaders had implored Russell not to walk away if legislation passed. Too often, they warned, advocates believe they are no longer needed once laws are enacted, and agencies are deprived of crucial support. Russell didn't need much encouragement. "I know from my own experience that without a determined and effective public interest group, the Congress and the agency does nothing," Russell told one audience. "You have to hit the politicians." But a watchdog also needs food, and the all-out lobbying effort in 1986 had left the Friends' larder depleted. It was $25,000 in debt, and its bank account was empty. Worse, Russell had to convince the public and donors, several of whom questioned why the Friends was "still in business," that the new law did not solve all of the problems in the Gorge.[1]

"I am not crazy about fundraising," Russell told one donor, "but I am committed to getting a job done." Russell soon secured an $11,000 loan for the Friends from her cochair Dave Cannard and loaned funds herself. She overhauled the board, replacing members who had been chosen for their geographic diversity with those who were both committed and connected. A new advisory board attracted more donors who gave larger gifts, thanks in part to Russell's prominence. When Friends associate director Marie Pampush left to pursue a career on Capitol Hill, a professional development director, Margaret Donsbach, was brought in to help. Without "constant pressure" from a watchdog organization the law "would never be implemented and would be constantly weakened," Russell told audiences, exhorting them to hold the new commission and the Forest Service accountable and to join the Friends, whose membership had swelled to almost four thousand. To protect a landscape, she wrote in her presentation notes for one conference, you needed to "build a constituency, raise money, provide reliable information, get your solution in place, and MOST IMPORTANTLY, REMAIN VIGILANT FOREVER." The fight was not over, she told editorial boards of regional newspapers, and they agreed. "Gorge Job not Done," the *Oregonian* editorialized just days after President Reagan signed the act, repeating Russell's warning that "passage of the law allows protection, but only vigilant implementation of that law will ensure protection."[2]

As Russell stabilized the Friends financially, the Forest Service faced its first test in implementing the new law: enacting interim guidelines that would regulate development in the NSA outside urban areas. The guidelines — released in two stages, in draft and then in final form — would clarify some of the broad provisions of the law and specify what and where development would be allowed until a management plan was adopted. In February 1987, a month before the guidelines were to be released, the Forest Service's NSA manager met with the Friends board and advised them to "watch and understand the implementation of the Gorge Act carefully and constantly." Weeks later, the release of the guidelines was delayed, and his advice seemed portentous. "There are whispers that administration opposition to the legislation is finding an outlet," the *Skamania County Pioneer* reported in April, "and that concerns about the rights of private property owners are uppermost in Washington minds." The guidelines were "under intensive internal review in Washington, D.C.," the Forest Service acknowledged, "due to policy conflicts with the current administration." One reviewer was Undersecretary of Agriculture George Dunlop, who oversaw the Forest Service for the Reagan administration. Russell had met Dunlop the summer before, and he had used the occasion to quote passages from Genesis and Exodus to her, "justifying the virtues of local control."[3]

The draft guidelines, when released in April 1987, reflected President Reagan's animosity to "federal zoning." Only seven pages long, they were littered with qualifications — "as appropriate," "where practicable," and "generally" — leading the Friends to declare that the "National Scenic Area will be turned into the National Litigation Area." Even the timid state Gorge commissions, which would be disbanded when the new bistate commission was formed, maintained that the guidelines' deficiencies were "so widespread and fundamental as to make [them] of little or questionable value."[4]

Nancy and I visited with editorial boards and returned to Washington, DC, to meet with Dale Robertson, chief of the Forest Service, and with the Northwest delegation. "Rewrite Gorge Rules," the *Sunday Oregonian* editorialized, beseeching Oregon and Washington delegations to "insist on" regulations that were consistent with the delegations' hard work. The four senators complained to Secretary of Agriculture Richard Lyng: "At worst the draft is contradictory. At best it is confusing."[5] Chief Robertson agreed.[6] The guidelines were rewritten, and the final version, released in June, was much improved, but the Forest Service had failed its first test. John Yeon and Nancy Russell had been prophetic. Squeezed by the Reagan administration's political appointees, the Forest Service appeared to be "singularly unmotivated and ill-equipted [sic]" to lead Gorge protection, as Yeon had warned. Yet, the movement Russell had built and her demand for eternal vigilance had prevailed.

While the Forest Service was drafting its interim guidelines, the act came before both state legislatures for ratification, as required of all bistate compacts. The National Scenic Area Act was different from most compacts, however, as it had been initiated by Congress, its standards directed by Congress, and painful federal penalties were prescribed by Congress if either state did not comply. Ratification was eased considerably by Congressman Vento's last-minute amendments to withhold certain federal funds and permits from NSA land if ratification failed.

After each state had ratified the act, the Friends turned its attention to the Columbia River Gorge Commission. Who sat on the commission had always been Russell's greatest concern, and its authority had been her greatest compromise. Half of the twelve voting members would be appointed by the two governors and half by the six counties, two-thirds of which had opposed the National Scenic Area Act.[7] Neil Goldschmidt had just been elected governor in Oregon and Booth Gardner was governor of Washington—Democrats whom Russell had cultivated and supported financially—and with overwhelming public support for the legislation outside the Gorge in both states, conditions seemed promising for the governors' appointments.

Russell had a short list of candidates, most of whom she had met through her campaigning. Governor Goldschmidt appointed her mentor Don Clark; her friend and fellow board member Barbara Bailey, from The Dalles; and Stafford Hansell, a former legislator and chair of Oregon's Land Conservation and Development Commission. Hansell and Russell had bonded when he attended her inaugural showing of *Who Is Watching?* as a board member of the Oregon Historical Society, and the relationship had flourished on her visits to his home in eastern Oregon.[8] In Washington, Governor Gardner appointed Dave Cannard, the Friends' cochair, and two others: a member of the state Shorelines Hearings Board who had ruled for the Friends against the Hidden Harbor subdivision, and a former University of North Carolina land use professor. Skamania County, to the surprise of many, appointed a former VISTA volunteer who confessed to having been a socialist while a student at the University of Vermont. Klickitat County, less surprisingly, appointed a conservative rancher who had opposed the act. Hood River and Wasco counties also appointed conservatives, while Clark County appointed an employee of the local public utility district.

In Multnomah County, Russell met with County Chair Gladys McCoy to propose several Portland attorneys for consideration, all of whom had worked closely with Friends of the Columbia Gorge. But McCoy had another idea: Russell should be the county's appointee. She wanted Russell to be the last appointment, concerned that her nomination would cause other counties to appoint more conservative members. Still, word got out, and two hundred and fifty residents of Corbett—the county's largest town in the National Scenic Area—signed a petition opposing Russell's appointment. As quickly as McCoy had promoted Russell, she abandoned her. Russell was disappointed but not surprised, having doubted that the county commission would "have the nerve" to appoint her, and McCoy's sensitivity to political pressure reinforced Russell's opinion that "you have to hit" even supportive politicians. Instead, the county selected Kristine Olson Rogers, an attorney and advocate for conservation and Native American rights. Russell was impressed and arranged for the two of them to take a tour of the Gorge together.[9]

The commissioners elected Stafford Hansell chair and Dave Cannard vice-chair and then considered their consequential first test: hiring an executive director. The position was advertised nationally, and over a hundred candidates applied. The Friends' clear favorite was Dick Benner, a senior staff attorney for 1000 Friends of Oregon, the nonprofit organization that monitored implementation of Oregon's pioneering land use laws. Benner was known as a smart, experienced litigator whom even opponents described as fair minded. He had helped the Friends review language for the bill and had testified on its behalf on Capitol Hill, advocating that enforcement be mandatory, not discretionary, an opinion that rendered Senator Evans "astonished." Benner had been one of three finalists for the Multnomah County position on the commission, but Russell asked him to withdraw his application and the Friends campaigned for him to be selected executive director. The commission made the unanimous decision to hire Benner in September 1987, but not everyone was pleased. Columbia Gorge United, which called Benner a "visible and vocal advocate of federal control," complained that the commission had "shot itself in the foot," and the *Pioneer* blamed the selection on "Chicago ward-heeler" tactics, a "massive lobbying effort," and a "barrage of phone calls."[10]

By the end of the year, Benner had hired four staff members, and the commission was up and running. A year earlier, one of Russell's greatest concerns had been a commission dominated by local interests that would try to unwind the act and ignore its responsibilities. Instead, the executive director and the majority of commission members embraced the act and supported the Friends' positions. The Friends had overestimated the Forest Service's ability to implement conservation regulations, at least during the Reagan administration, but had underestimated the commission—the first commission anyway, when the political stars were perfectly aligned.

By the spring of 1987, the Trust for Public Land was facing a financial crisis in the Gorge. The trust owned twenty properties, most of them in Skamania County, valued at over $4.5 million, and it owed $2 million, including $700,000 to the Russells and $600,000 to the Meyer Trust. The expense of holding the land—interest payments, property taxes, and appraisals—was also rising by hundreds of thousands of dollars. The trust's continuing risks in the Gorge, even with the Forest Service available as a potential take-out, dwarfed the cost of running the organization. Only a significant boost in revenue, TPL's board chair wrote Russell, "will enable it to continue working in the Gorge." To address these risks, TPL needed to sell its holdings to the Forest Service at a price, including landowner donations, that exceeded its costs. To do so, the Forest Service had to establish the trust's properties as purchase priorities, federal appraisers had to decide that each property's fair market value (the agency's purchase price) was consistent with TPL's purchase price, and Congress had to appropriate funds.[11]

The first step—prioritization—was problematic. The Forest Service had received more offers to sell than it had funding, and it assigned highest priority to "physical or financial hardship cases," which did not include TPL. George Dunlop, the Bible-quoting undersecretary of agriculture who oversaw the Forest Service, now tried to use the act he had crusaded against to his advantage. TPL's land was no longer threatened, he figured, since it was now protected by some of the nation's toughest restrictions on development. Why, then, should this land be acquired? "We are going to have to force the Forest Service," Burgess wrote Russell, "thanks to Dunlop." Since federal agencies consider "congressional directives" when prioritizing land acquisitions, Burgess and Russell alerted Senator Hatfield and Congressman AuCoin to the trust's precarious position and sidestepped the administration. The Forest Service was soon directed to acquire TPL lands, at times waiving oversight requirements that would delay the purchases. Hatfield's and AuCoin's enthusiastic support also solved the trust's third obstacle, securing appropriations.[12]

It was the second hurdle, the appraisal process, that tripped up TPL. Before purchasing land, TPL hired qualified, independent appraisers—preapproved by the take-out agency—to determine fair market value. Their appraisals then underwent rigorous review by the agency when it was ready to buy—often years later. The appraisal process was inherently uncertain, especially for the one-of-a-kind properties that attracted the trust, which is why it rarely bought and held land and had been uneasy making exceptions in the Gorge.

The Forest Service had transferred professional staff from around the country to its NSA office in Hood River, and by the end of 1987 it had spent over $4 million to purchase three thousand acres in the Gorge, the majority owned by TPL. Most of the properties were uncomplicated, but they also included the twelve undeveloped Rim View Estates lots at Cape Horn, a four-hundred-acre parcel at Archer Mountain (above The Shire), and the 1,909-acre Catherine Creek Ranch. Although TPL had incurred substantial expenses while holding those properties, some for years, the sales to the Forest Service produced positive net revenue for the organization. The sales outraged the *Skamania County Pioneer,* however, which accused the Forest Service of favoring TPL over other landowners and calculated, down to the penny, how much the nonprofit had "profited" and how much the county would forfeit in future property taxes.[13]

In 1988, TPL's favorable revenue flow reversed. Skamania and Klickitat counties were furious that the trust and conservationists were succeeding, at county expense, and retaliated. Led by prosecutor Bob Leick, the counties revoked tax benefits on the agricultural and forest land TPL had bought. The two counties also imposed steep fines on the trust when it sold land to public agencies, ignoring precedent and other counties' interpretation of similar tax provisions. The penalties imposed on three properties in Skamania County cost the trust almost $150,000.

Other factors also contributed to TPL's financial losses. Forest Service appraisers, knowing that the *Pioneer* would dispute any gains made by the trust, may have been more conservative in their estimates. Burgess's and Russell's refusal to lose key lands—even if TPL paid more than it should—created more financial reverses. Whatever the reason, TPL's list of losses became long and painful. The trust, for example, had paid $515,000 to buy and hold the St. Cloud Ranch for three and a half years. The Forest Service paid just $335,000 for the property. The trust expected to gain $1,500 in net revenue from selling the Montchalin property to the Forest Service; instead, a low agency appraisal and high costs contributed to TPL losing $40,000. "Sell it and weep," Burgess directed an associate. Particularly painful for Burgess was the Forest Service purchase of Columbia Gorge Riverfront Estates, Colonel Rizor's subdivision that had kick-started the drive for legislation five years earlier. TPL had paid $540,000 to buy and hold the property. Five years later, the Forest Service paid only $245,000. Land transactions were TPL's primary revenue source, and it had lost over half a million dollars on just three properties.[14]

Of all the properties purchased by TPL before the National Scenic Area Act passed, Rolf Jemtegaard's Mount Pleasant farm proved most challenging. Using the Russells' second interest-free loan, the trust had bought the farm in the summer of 1985 with the intention of preserving the bucolic landscape on Mount Pleasant and Mount Zion. The strategy was simple in concept—sell the land to a farmer and a conservation easement to the Forest Service—but complicated in execution. In June 1987, TPL's realtor, who had been hired to find a farmer, insisted that "the economics are simply no longer there" for a farm. He suggested that Burgess subdivide the property into four forty-acre parcels that could be sold for ranchettes and mansions. Burgess scrawled "NO, I *won't agree*" and "forget it" across the realtor's recommendation and attached a sticky note: "*No way*. We are going to sell a 160-acre *farm*. No 40-ac stuff!!"[15]

In November, Skamania County ratcheted up the pressure by removing the property's timber and agricultural classifications, which cost the trust thousands of dollars. In December, the county vacated the road that provided the only access to the farm, preventing emergency vehicles, school busses, and snow plows from reaching the farm and damaging its marketability. The trust persevered, however, and in 1988 sold the land to a young farmer and an easement to the Forest Service. Instead of holding the property for three to six months and netting $70,000 as expected, the process took three years, and TPL's net revenue plunged. And Skamania County was not finished. After the sale, the county penalized the trust almost six thousand dollars for selling the easement to the Forest Service, even though it facilitated farming, which was the purpose of the tax provisions. But Rolf Jemtegaard had lived to see his farm protected, and Russell and Burgess, unintimidated, were scouting nearby farms.[16]

Burgess understood the need for more parks in the Gorge and was eager to generate positive net revenue to keep working there. One plan involved property named for General Philip Sheridan, who as an army lieutenant in 1856 had led troops in a bloody battle against Yakama warriors near Cascade Locks.[17] Burgess had persuaded the Union Pacific Railroad to donate Sheridan Point, twenty-two acres of sloping Douglas-fir forest that the railroad considered surplus, to TPL. Bordered on three sides by national forest, the land offered beautiful views of the Bridge of the Gods and included a popular, low-elevation trail that connected to the Pacific Crest Trail.

Although the Forest Service was required to offer "just compensation" (that is, fair market value) to landowners, the trust often discounted prices to public agencies, passing along the benefit of some of the donations it had received. Given TPL's financial situation, however, Burgess proposed selling the donated property to the agency for its full fair market value, which would generate almost $81,000 in net revenue and, no doubt, headlines in the *Pioneer*. The Forest Service balked, and Burgess flew to Washington, DC, to meet with Forest Service Chief Robertson. Over the past dozen years, she reminded him, TPL had saved the Forest Service almost $400,000 on the sale of $2.4 million of land in the Northwest. She then took an exceptional step and revealed TPL's net revenue on all Gorge projects since the National Scenic Area Act had passed. Those projects—even if Sheridan Point's full revenue was recognized—resulted in an aggregate net loss of $70,000. Robertson relented, and in mid-1988 the Forest Service paid fair market value for Sheridan Point.[18]

By the end of 1988, TPL had conveyed twenty-one properties into public ownership after President Reagan had signed the act, bringing its total number of Gorge conveyances to thirty. Most were located in Skamania County, and most were in the western sixteen miles of the Columbia River Gorge National Scenic Area. Instead of subdivisions at Cape Horn and across the Columbia from Multnomah Falls, there now were parks and public access to the river. At the end of this stretch, TPL had added Doetsch Ranch—with its emerald meadows, sylvan uplands, and a mile and a half of shoreline—to Beacon Rock State Park, Washington's only accessible state park in the western Gorge.[19] The ranch tripled the park's access to the river and included the Chinookan village site of Nimisxaya. In the same sixteen-mile segment, TPL bought Hidden Harbor, Skamania County's largest proposed subdivision. By year-end, the trust had conveyed 5,559 acres of land into public ownership, valued at almost $13 million. Its gamble in the Gorge had paid off, although by the slimmest of margins. Two of the Russells' three loans had been repaid; the third would be returned in eighteen months, when TPL sold Hidden

Harbor to the Forest Service. And TPL was not finished: in 1988, Russell joined its board.

As TPL persevered, Russell and Friends of the Columbia Gorge faced an internal crisis that threatened the organization's existence. Passing the National Scenic Area Act had "nearly sunk the ship," Russell told one contributor, but her fundraising had righted the organization.[20] By the end of 1988, most of our energy—Russell's and mine—had been spent getting the act passed, implementing it, and fighting development, and we had relied on our longtime treasurer to monitor the organization's finances. Costly safeguards, including audits, had been unnecessary when the organization was small, but they became essential as the Friends grew. Still, by February 1988, when I announced my resignation as executive director to open a Trust for Public Land office in Portland, effective later that summer, we thought we were passing a robust organization over to the new director. My replacement, Brad Jones, an attorney from Virginia, was hired in June. In July, I was elected to the Friends' board, replacing Russell as chair so she could dedicate more attention to substantive Gorge issues and less to board matters.

A month after Jones started, the Friends development director, Margaret Donsbach, discovered financial irregularities. Staff suspected that the treasurer, Mitch Bower, had been making unauthorized withdrawals from the Friends' account. He soon broke down and admitted that, in a series of loans he had made to the Friends, he had inadvertently overpaid himself $10,000. I secured the books and accepted Bower's resignation and his promise to repay the missing money. Russell and I alerted the Friends board, which approved hiring an accounting firm to perform an audit. Within a month, Bower had repaid the Friends $24,612—the total amount taken, it turned out—and had agreed to pay all costs of the financial review. By the following spring, he had reimbursed the Friends an additional $17,000 for the full cost of investigating and resolving his misappropriations, and the board had adopted the financial procedures recommended by the accountants.[21]

Bower's actions received extensive publicity, and Russell and I worried that the organization's mistakes would cause donations to drop, even as we implemented new procedures and recovered the missing funds. At the same time, Brad Jones was behaving oddly. In September, he wrote the *Oregonian's* Gorge reporter and accused her of inaccurate and unfair reporting, including making up his quotes. He copied her editor on the letter, which he had sent without consulting committee members, who had known and respected the reporter for years. In October, Brot Bishop, the new treasurer for the Friends, arrived late for an executive committee meeting. A generation older than Jones, Bishop was chairman of the board of Pendleton Woolen Mills, which his family owned, and had been a crucial Friends supporter from the beginning. Because he was late, Jones refused to allow him to ask questions, causing Bishop to resign as treasurer (although he remained on the board). In November, Margaret Donsbach said she could not work for Jones and was looking for another job. I asked her to stay and met with executive committee members to discuss firing Jones. Earlier that day, he had approached Friends vice-chair Debbie Craig to demand my resignation. The executive committee decided to fire Jones that afternoon, and Donsbach was named interim director. Three days later, the board unanimously reaffirmed the decision and reelected its officers.[22]

Jones then engaged in a series of actions, all of them seemingly calculated to destroy Friends of the Columbia Gorge. When the board granted his request for a December meeting to discuss his termination, he failed to appear. He demanded an investigation of the Friends by the Oregon attorney general, who declined, and got in touch with a foundation to accuse the Friends of misusing its grant. He demanded that the Friends pay him $100,000 or he would file a lawsuit for wrongful termination; the Friends declined, and he filed. He appeared before the Gorge commission to "fulfill moral obligations," he said, and testified that Dave Cannard had intentionally misled the commission about his loan to the Friends. Neither the commission nor the governor acted, and Jones went to the media, accusing the Friends' leadership of acting "illegally and unethically." He wrote letters to the editor, demanding an "independent investigation" and claiming that the Friends were being investigated by the state attorney general. The Friends were close to running out of money, he said, prompting Russell to assure members that "not one penny of their donated funds" would be lost in the Bower affair. "And I mean that," she told the Gresham Outlook.[23]

Jones continued his vendetta into the spring. He demanded that the Friends pay him $250,000, and he put together a small group called "Friends of the Friends," which sent out mailings to members, donors, and foundations, emphasizing the negative publicity the organization had received. One mailing showed a Friends check Bower had written to the "Don Bonker Campaign," which appeared to be illegal, as nonprofit organizations are prohibited from donating to political campaigns. The memo section of the check, which showed it was a legitimate expense written for attending a "tourism conference," was covered up. Another mailing accused the Friends' board of not cooperating with the district attorney in Bower's prosecution, a claim the district attorney personally refuted. The Friends believed it had successfully addressed Jones's allegations, but his campaign had sown confusion. A Vancouver *Columbian* editorial in early February described the Friends as being in its "death throes," and charged that it should have disbanded when the National Scenic Area Act was passed. Three weeks later, the paper acknowledged that its call had been hasty and that "further consideration suggests that the problem lies mostly with the irate ex-employee."[24]

In early March, Jones demanded that the Friends hold a special membership meeting to approve three measures: launch an independent investigation "of the Friends' problems"; audit the Friends books, which was already underway; and impose term limits on the board, which seemed directed at removing Russell.[25] The meeting was set for three o'clock on Sunday, March 19, at the Westminster Presbyterian church in northeast Portland. By three-twenty, four hundred members—many of whom had been personally asked by Russell to join the Friends and had received her handwritten thank you notes over the years—had jammed the pews and were spilling into the aisles. I chaired the meeting, and presentations were made by the organization's attorney, Brot Bishop, vice-chair Debbie Craig, and Nancy Russell. Brad Jones and a former Friends employee represented Friends of the Friends. Reporters were in attendance.

"In some respects," the *Columbian* reported, "the debate Sunday was cast as a choice between Jones and Russell, now director emeritus [*sic*] of the organization. By midway through the meeting, there was no mystery about who was more popular." When Russell was introduced, she received a standing ovation, while Jones was greeted with "jeers and hissing." Russell reviewed the organization's accomplishments over the past two decades and the challenges that it still confronted. "I've been jeered in Skamania County, I've seen my name on bumper stickers, I've had stickers on my mail box, I've had my tires slashed while attending a Congressional hearing," she confided. "But I never thought I would go to the door twice and find a process server delivering Brad Jones's lawsuits. One of them to dissolve YOUR organization." The board is "asking [for] your support," she continued. "We deserve it." Three hours after convening, the membership overwhelmingly approved three motions. First, it expressed its "complete support and confidence" in the board, and then it urged Jones to drop his litigation "as a sign of his good faith." Russell rose to second the last motion. She recounted her high hopes for Jones and her sadness as to what had transpired. She declared, her voice growing firm, "I don't want any more harassment." Another standing ovation. The motion, to permanently expel Jones from the organization, carried. Four hundred members approved, five opposed.[26]

The organization was fully insured for Jones's lawsuit, and the case was settled when its attorneys recommended settling for a "nuisance amount." Russell and Friends of the Columbia Gorge moved forward; Jones moved back to Virginia. In a letter to his children, Bruce Russell distilled the past four months into two sentences: "The whole episode has been an exceedingly nasty and emotionally draining distraction, expensive and time-consuming and maddening in a strangely upsetting way. But your mother—and you both, too—cannot but be deeply moved by the overwhelming personal tribute paid to her." Nancy wrote a friend: "The sorriest thing about it all is the time it takes away from what I really want to get done in life."[27]

Over the next fifteen years, Russell worked on what she wanted "to get done in life": make sure the Columbia River Gorge National Scenic Area was protected. "Endless pressure, endlessly applied," as National Audubon's Brock Evans put it.[28] When Portland's regional government, Metro, decided to truck its garbage through the national scenic area to Arlington, Russell fought to keep three hundred garbage trucks a day off Gorge roads, preferring that the waste be barged or transported by rail.[29] When the Stevenson family proposed a destination resort—ultimately 245 condominiums and townhouses—alongside their Skamania County riverfront mill west of Bingen, Russell and the Friends organized successful resistance.[30] And when Skamania County chose not to enforce its own conditions of approval for a large house built on the cliff west of Cape Horn, the Friends objected. The *Los Angeles Times* reported that Brian and Jody Bea's house had become a "rallying cry in the debate over public versus private property rights," and the *New York Times* called the controversy "a major test of a 13-year-old Federal law." *People Magazine* and *Reader's Digest* delved into the controversy, often with sympathetic portrayals of the Beas, and the conservative Pacific Legal Foundation helped pay the couple's legal bills. After five years of litigation, the Beas settled, screening their house with large trees and an earthen berm and lowering the roof by ten feet while the commission and county paid damages.[31]

Russell and the Friends also fought off challenges to the National Scenic Area Act and to its management plan, which laid out, in minute detail, how the commission and Forest Service would manage the Gorge. A lawsuit filed by Columbia Gorge United and the Pacific Legal Foundation had challenged the act's constitutionality and sought remedies for other grievances, including commission bias toward the Friends, conflicts of interest, taking land without compensation, and violations of due process. Russell had persuaded the Sierra Club Legal Defense Fund to represent the Friends pro bono and had signed an experienced former Forest Service attorney, Gary Kahn, to a two-year contract. In 1990, Owen Panner, the chief judge for the US District Court of Oregon, found for the Friends and the federal government on all counts. The US Supreme Court refused to consider an appeal, and Judge Panner's decision stood. With Kahn addressing legal issues and Russell rousing the public and lobbying commissioners, the commission also approved the management plan in October 1991, overcoming resistance from the administration and litigation by a Stevenson-family company and other Gorge corporations.

County resistance continued through the 1990s. Klickitat County sued to hold the State of Washington liable for its costs in implementing the National Scenic Area Act, but lost. When it refused to adopt an ordinance to implement the plan, the commission took over its NSA responsibilities. Skamania County's ordinance included a "sunset clause" that would allow protection to lapse, as well as other provisions inconsistent with the act. The Friends threatened litigation, and the county eventually complied. The two counties also lobbied the state legislature to defund the commission and appointed commissioners to roll back the management plan. Commission funding had to come equally from the two states, so a cut to the commission's budget by one state had to be matched by the other. In 1997, Washington's senate reduced the commission's budget by almost three-quarters. Russell and the Friends redoubled their lobbying and halved the cut, and the Forest Service restored the balance through a grant. Normal funding was resumed the following biennium after Russell and the Friends rallied Washington members.

As Skamania, Klickitat, Hood River, and Wasco counties continued to appoint commissioners to undercut the plan and hire weak staff, Russell fought back. She was straightforward and clear eyed about how politics worked. "Politicians pay attention to people who give money to their campaigns," Russell explained in a *Portland Monthly* interview. "You may think, 'Oh dear, how nasty,' but boy is that the truth. It's not something that's spoken about a lot, but it's the way this democracy works." She and Bruce became Portland's third largest political contributors during one election cycle, giving

One irate landowner supported the counties' resistance in 1996 when he erected several billboards along Gorge roads. FOCG archives.

over $95,000 to candidates, committees, and campaigns that affected the Gorge. But her power was not confined to donations. The environmental vote was important to Democratic governors, and neither Washington nor Oregon had elected a Republican governor since the mid-1980s. Protection of the Columbia Gorge was a motherhood-and-apple-pie issue to many Northwest residents, who saw Russell as its matriarch and master chef. Her constituency was large and devoted, and her stature was rising.[32]

In the late 1990s and early 2000s, Russell's profile was boosted by a string of awards, including the Conservation Award from Chevron/Times Mirror Magazines and the American Land Conservation Award from the Land Trust Alliance, which came with $50,000. While she appreciated the spotlight on the Gorge, and the cash—which she turned over to the Friends and TPL—awards did not really matter to Russell. When the Trust for Public Land planned to recognize her, they asked me whether a stone bench on a hill overlooking a nine-acre field of camas lilies that Russell had recently protected would be appropriate. When I asked her what she thought, she nixed the idea, saying she was trying to get the Forest Service to halt public memorials because they cluttered the view. Besides, she continued, a bench with her name on it in Skamania County would soon be riddled by bullets. She wanted TPL to spend its money on land and suggested a simple plaque that she could hang in her laundry-room office instead.

Russell's awards and high profile did affect others, however. Chuck Williams raged at her, writing that she had left him a "broken man [and] put me through a living hell that I sure don't deserve." He demanded the $50,000 prize for himself and another activist. "You launched an evil war against me," he said, "and now only you can end this war." Mutual friends warned Russell that Williams could be dangerous, and she worried that he might harm her. Others also tried to intimidate her. An irate protester, shouting and shaking a large sign, shadowed Russell as she shopped at her neighborhood grocery, leaving only when the store manager threatened to call the police. An anonymous Skamania County caller told the *Oregonian* that Russell was the most hated person in the Gorge and warned she was not safe there. The paper received death threats against her.[33]

But Russell was not deterred. She continued to lead tours and hikes, make presentations, attend commission and Forest Service meetings, distribute Hiking Weekend brochures, and take advantage of chance encounters, as witnessed by a reporter one afternoon:

> Hiking near Multnomah Falls, she is visibly embarrassed when spotted by an ecology professor leading students on a field trip. "There's the mother of the Columbia River Gorge National Scenic Area, the subject of yesterday's lecture!" he trumpets, as though she were some rare form of wildlife. Nevertheless, she allows herself to be hoisted onto a picnic table and delivers a crisp, two-minute lecture, which includes a plea for continued vigilance—and funds.[34]

Part of Russell's success was that she wasn't against all development. She believed people would want to protect the Gorge if it was shared with them and made sure the National Scenic Area Act authorized $10 million for a conference center in Washington and an interpretive center in Oregon. She thought the centers could help rural areas in the Gorge, especially Skamania County, transition from dependence on the timber industry to a balanced economy that valued scenic, natural, cultural, and recreational assets. When Congress was slow to appropriate the funds, Russell lobbied hard for them, and she resisted when Multnomah County wanted the interpretive center on its land, a location that she believed would not help Gorge residents or its economy. "It is certainly for the best that I am not Multnomah County's representative on the Commission," she told one congressional staffer, "for I absolutely could not represent such a parochial attitude." Russell supported locating the conference center in Skamania County, despite its opposition to the national scenic area. When the county presented its proposal to the Gorge commission, Don Clark likened the county to "the kid in the neighborhood who keeps throwing rocks at your house and then for some reason ends up marrying your niece. . . . You are a little bit uneasy about the relationship. . . . On the other hand, if this marriage is going to prosper, [then] awarding . . . a wedding present to this strange combination [may be] worthwhile."[35]

It was worthwhile. In early 1993, John Gray, a Friends supporter, philanthropist, and resort developer, leveraged the federal funds to build Skamania Lodge in the urban area west of downtown Stevenson. The four-story, Cascadian-style lodge nestled into a wooded hillside—its location chosen by landscape architect Doug Macy—and used recycled timber columns from a Bumble Bee cannery and andesite rock from a nearby abandoned quarry. In just two years, the lodge became Skamania County's largest private employer and generated almost $14 million in payroll and benefits for the county. The Columbia Gorge Discovery Center and Museum was built in Wasco County, just west of The Dalles, and its grounds were also designed by Macy. A thousand people attended the grand opening, and in less than a year the museum had ninety-three thousand visitors.[36]

As the years unfolded, other changes came to the Gorge. In May 1994, Russell's close friend and ally Stafford Hansell died. When he was diagnosed with brain cancer and his declining health forced him to leave the commission, she wrote him that she could never find a way to thank him for his service and for being the "only responsive member . . . [to] my housewifey presentation to the OHS [Oregon Historical Society] Board in 1981." She continued: "I imagine that both of us will be at this with all we can give until the time finally does come for us to cash in our chips." Signing off, she teased Hansell, noting that he no longer was bound by the commission's conflict-of-interest regulations. "Perhaps now . . . you can renew your Friends membership!"[37]

As their terms expired, other inaugural commissioners—Clark, Cannard, Bailey, and Olson Rogers—left the commission. Dick Benner moved on in 1991, and Forest Service managers came and went. Russell educated their replacements. In 2001, she took the Forest Service's third manager, Dan Harkenrider, on a daylong tour. "She was able to work in a few interrogatories for me concerning what my land ethic was and whether I understood the conservation responsibilities that were handed to me," Harkenrider chuckled years later. "I very much felt that I was being interviewed for the position that I held." She "was always kind, respectful, and oh, so very persistent in ensuring that I understood her point of view," he continued. "I suspect she knew fully well that eventually I would agree with her."[38]

Politicians also came and went. Washington's Dan Evans left the US Senate in 1989, lamenting its "bickering and protracted paralysis,"[39] and Slade Gorton—reelected in 1988—made peace with "federal zoning" and guided land acquisition funds to the Gorge from his position on the Senate Appropriations Committee. Oregon's Les AuCoin left the US House of Representatives in 1992 to unsuccessfully challenge Bob Packwood for his seat in the Senate. Packwood retired under pressure three years later, and Representative Ron Wyden, who had patched up his relationship with Russell years earlier, was elected senator.

Russell suffered a setback in 1995 when Senator Hatfield decided not to run for reelection. She and the senator had grown close, a testament to her hard work and support for him and to the senator's influence on appropriations, his heroics in passing the act, and his belief—Russell felt—that the Gorge was "his baby." Intangibles also had helped. Once, while driving the Historic Columbia River Highway, Hatfield's car was buffeted by cold rain and thirty-mile-an-hour east winds. Between slaps of his windshield wipers, he could barely see what looked like a roadside prison gang ahead, stooped against the wind. When he stopped to speak to the trusty in charge, he discovered Nancy Russell with a group of Friends volunteers who were spending their weekend picking up trash on the senator's favorite road. When Russell heard in the summer of 1995 that Hatfield might not run for reelection, she urged him to "stay where you can do the most good on earth" and offered to hold a fundraiser. The senator expressed his gratitude for her efforts in the Gorge, but he retired in 1997. The cover of his memoir, *Against the Grain*, published three years later, shows the senator with the fields of Mount Pleasant and Mount Zion, the Columbia River, and Crown Point in the background. After forty years of public service, he called the National Scenic Area Act one of the most contentious issues he had ever faced.[40]

The Friends' staff changed too. Kristine Simensted left to pursue a career as a therapist, and the Seattle office closed. Margaret Donsbach resigned in 1990 to write a book, and two executive directors followed her over the decade. In 1993, Michael Lang was hired to address timber harvesting in the Gorge, and—like Gary Kahn—he remained with the Friends a quarter century later, employed as its director of conservation. The Friends hired professional development staff, including Jane Harris in 1998, the same year it hired Kevin Gorman as executive director.

Gorman and his wife Michelle had moved from Detroit four years earlier, and he joined the combative Oregon Natural Resources Council (ONRC) as associate director, overseeing fundraising and much of the nonprofit's management. ONRC had filed the first spotted-owl lawsuit, and its director, Andy Kerr, was a brilliant and fearless strategist. When Kerr heard that Gorman was interviewing with the Friends, he had some advice: "You need to know" that Russell is a competitive athlete, "and she hates to lose." In Gorman's first meeting with Russell, she confided "I love to win."[41]

Amid the changes, Russell focused on her goal of Friends being effective and vigilant. Professional staff had to be secure, and Friends needed an engaged membership that could "hit the politicians" when necessary, which—in Russell's mind—was pretty much always. All of that required money, more than she had ever raised before, and the organization needed a core of donors to give year after year. So in 1993 she started the Columbia River Gorge Conservators, whose members would donate at least a thousand dollars annually. She employed the strengths that had worked so well for her in the past: her passion and enthusiasm for the Gorge, her knowledge of its history and landscape, and the example of her own hard work and generosity. She stayed in touch with conservators, hosted events at interesting places, and expressed her appreciation through handwritten notes. Thirty conservators attended its annual event in 1996; over a hundred showed up in 2001.[42]

In 1998, the Friends started an endowment, something Russell was not initially keen on. She wanted the money she raised to be *used*, not to just sit there. But staff convinced her that some donors would like the idea, and by the next year Friends had raised $80,000 for the endowment; they raised $400,000 the following year. With a hundred conservators contributing at least $1,000 a year, over three thousand members paying at least $35 a year, and the endowment spinning off its share, the organization's budget grew. By 2000, the Friends had an operating budget of $530,000 and ten employees, more than the Columbia River Gorge Commission.[43]

Russell received the Outstanding Volunteer Fundraiser award from the Association of Fundraising Professionals several years later. "I'll tell you what it takes to be so-called 'outstanding,'" Russell told the audience. "Persistence. Just that. . . . What makes me persist is the full knowledge that we can't keep the Gorge beautiful without money to support Gorge work. . . . If you care enough you *will* fundraise."[44] Russell wanted more people to care, to join the Friends and defend the Gorge. She created an audio tape tour to educate visitors and continued to run Hiking Weekend, which would attract over two thousand participants to forty-four hikes in 2000. The event became so popular that the Friends added thirteen spring wildflower hikes that year, drawing another six hundred hikers, many of whom became members.

A large membership and endowment offered stability, but Russell wanted members to be active and funds used proactively. The membership was her army, and she would muster her troops when needed. In 1998 they were needed as a new crisis erupted just east of Hood River, one precipitated by an important ally, the Confederated Tribes of Warm Springs.

Although it includes three tribes—the Warm Springs, Wasco, and Paiute—with four thousand citizens, the Confederated Tribes of Warm Springs is recognized by the federal government as a single entity. In the nineteenth century, when white settlers encroached on tribal land in central Oregon, the federal government ordered the removal of Native people. The Warm Springs and Wascos ceded 10 million acres of their homeland to the United States in the Treaty of 1855 but retained a 578,000-acre reservation more than forty miles south of the Columbia River. "Government agents reported to Congress that the [retained] land was mountainous, rocky, had poor soil, and was covered with timber," wrote the tribe's longtime attorney and future federal judge Owen Panner, "so that it was unlikely the white settler would ever wish to occupy it." The tribe also reserved certain off-reservation hunting, fishing, and gathering rights in the treaty for its citizens, including the right to fish at Celilo Falls. A century later, the federal government built The Dalles Dam, flooding Celilo Falls. With $4 million in compensation that it had never sought—and whose portion Celilo chief Tommy Thompson never

(*Left*) entrance to the Mosier Twin Tunnels' west tunnel, circa 1921; (*right*) entrance to the Mosier Twin Tunnels' west tunnel, circa 1954. Images from Library of Congress.

accepted—the tribe invested in economic projects on the reservation, buying a timber mill, land, and hot springs along the Warm Springs River.[45] The tribe built a small resort, Kah-Nee-Ta, at the hot springs, and added a casino in 1995, but a confluence of factors—especially Kah-Nee-Ta's isolation—conspired against it. So, three years later, the tribe announced its intent to build a seventy-five-thousand-square-foot casino in the Gorge, much closer to major population centers.

The tribe is a sovereign nation, and its forty acres of land near Hood River had been held by the United States in trust for the tribe since 1923 and was therefore exempt from the provisions of the act and from state and local laws. The tribe planned to build the casino along a five-mile stretch of the historic highway that had been abandoned in the 1950s and sold to multiple landowners. The stretch included twin tunnels, now filled with rubble, that spanned almost five hundred feet and a cliffside walkway and two eight-by-ten-foot windows that had been cemented shut. Russell had hoped to revive this abandoned section of the historic highway as a linear park for hikers and cyclists, with the twin tunnels as its centerpiece.[46]

The Russells frequently hiked the roadway, which was intact although interrupted by rock slides. Otherwise, the roadbed was wide and smooth, flanked by rock walls and pits that early Native people had forged in the nearby talus slopes, by stone guardrails that Italian masons had mortared in the early 1900s, and by wildflowers, including Almeta Hodge Barrett's penstemon, found only in the Gorge. The views from five hundred feet above the Columbia—across the river to Mount Adams and the Bingen Anticline—were spectacular. But the tunnels were impenetrable and blocked

hiking between Hood River and Mosier. Russell had made sure that the
National Scenic Area Act directed the Oregon Department of Transportation
to "restore the continuity and historic integrity of the remaining segments of
the Old Columbia River Highway for public use." The act authorized $2.8
million for restoration, and in 1987 ODOT announced that its highest priority for those funds was to assess whether the tunnels could be reopened.[47]
Russell asked the Trust for Public Land to start buying the land.

Protecting the tunnels put Russell on a collision course with the tribe
and, because its land was held in trust, the tribe only needed permission
from the secretary of the interior and a waiver from the governor to build a
casino along the five-mile-long segment. Warm Springs citizens had endured
difficult times as Kah-Nee-Ta withered, timber revenue fell, and salmon runs
declined. Per capita income was just over $9,000,[48] and the tribe saw the
casino as an employment opportunity for tribal members and a source of
desperately needed revenue. Nancy Russell saw it differently. The casino, she
wrote Governor John Kitzhaber, is "far and away the most damaging proposal
I have seen for the Columbia Gorge since I became involved in 1979."[49] But
she could not rely on the act to stop it. Instead, she and the Friends would
spend the next several years doing the hard, unglamorous work that Russell
had perfected over two decades—building public support and political coali-
tions, person by person and organization by organization.

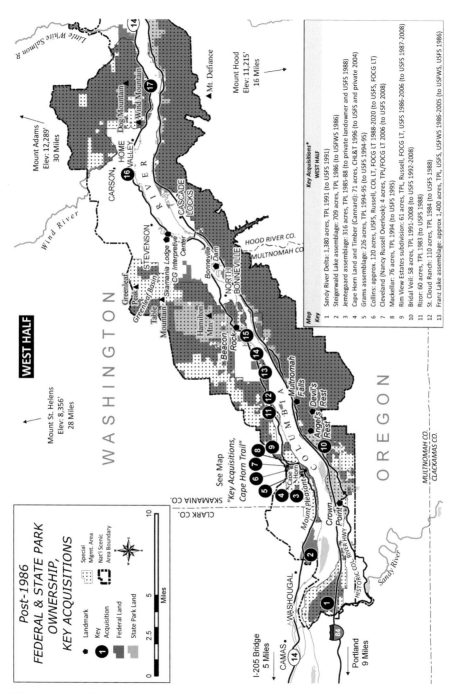

Western National Scenic Area: Post-1986 Federal and State Park Ownership, Key Acquisitions.
Map by Mike Schrankel.

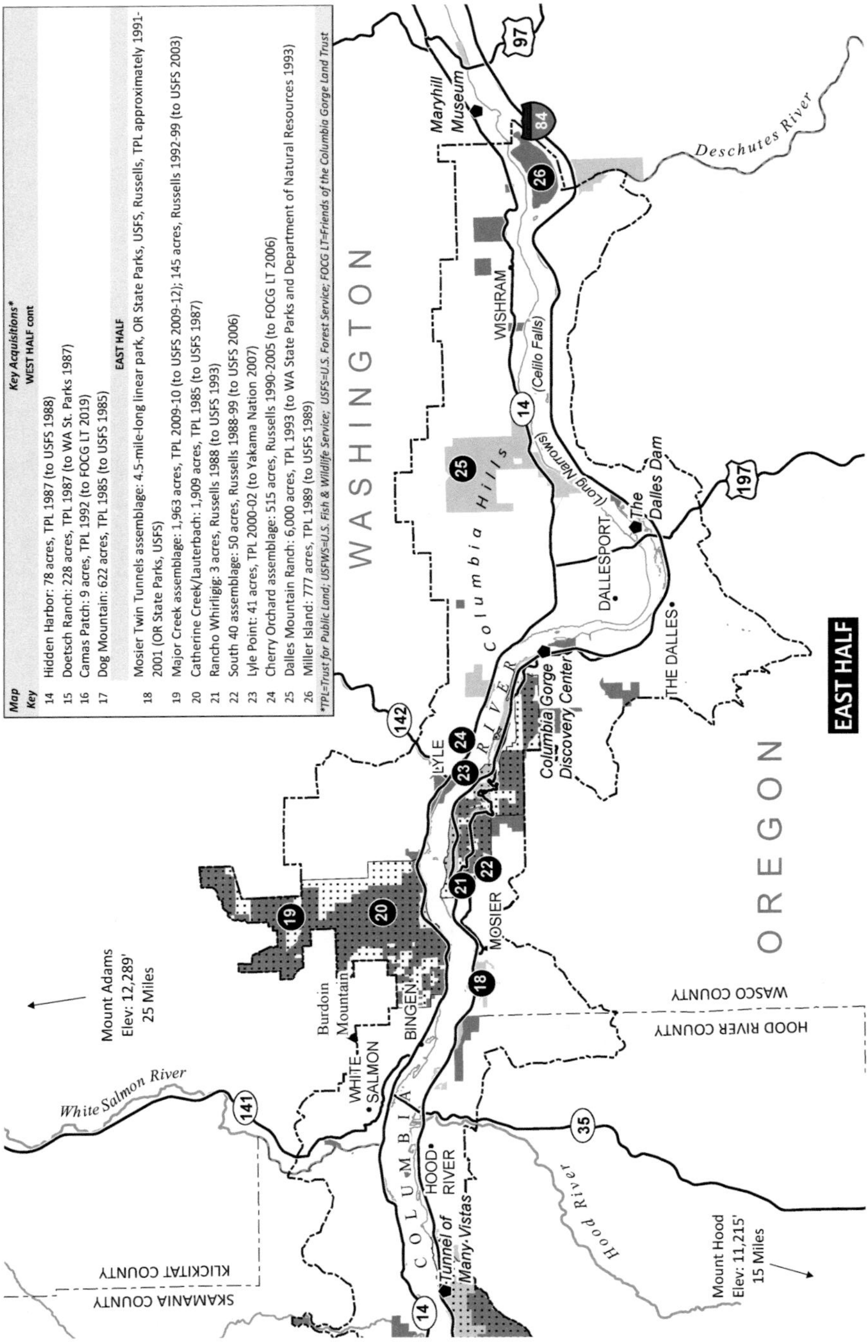

Map Key	Key Acquisitions*
	WEST HALF cont
14	Hidden Harbor: 78 acres, TPL 1987 (to USFS 1988)
15	Doetsch Ranch: 228 acres, TPL 1987 (to WA St. Parks 1987)
16	Camas Patch: 9 acres, TPL 1992 (to FOCG LT 2019)
17	Dog Mountain: 622 acres, TPL 1985 (to USFS 1985)
	EAST HALF
18	Mosier Twin Tunnels assemblage: 4.5-mile-long linear park, OR State Parks, USFS, Russells, TPL approximately 1991-2001 (OR State Parks, USFS)
19	Major Creek assemblage: 1,963 acres, TPL 2009-10 (to USFS 2009-12); 145 acres, Russells 1992-99 (to USFS 2003)
20	Catherine Creek/Lauterbach: 1,909 acres, TPL 1985 (to USFS 1987)
21	Rancho Whirligig: 3 acres, Russells 1988 (to USFS 1993)
22	South 40 assemblage: 50 acres, Russells 1988-99 (to USFS 2006)
23	Lyle Point: 41 acres, TPL 2000-02 (to Yakama Nation 2007)
24	Cherry Orchard assemblage: 515 acres, Russells 1990-2005 (to FOCG LT 2006)
25	Dalles Mountain Ranch: 6,000 acres, TPL 1993 (to WA State Parks and Department of Natural Resources 1993)
26	Miller Island: 777 acres, TPL 1989 (to USFS 1989)

*TPL=Trust for Public Land; USFWS=U.S. Fish & Wildlife Service; USFS=U.S. Forest Service; FOCG LT=Friends of the Columbia Gorge Land Trust

Eastern National Scenic Area: Post-1986 Federal and State Park Ownership, Key Acquisitions. Map by Mike Schrankel.

Chapter 7
So Roll On, Columbia, Roll On, 1988–2003

Both John Yeon and Nancy Russell believed that regulations, unlike public ownership, could ebb and flow with political tides. "We must be very cautious not to fall for the idea that land-use planning can accomplish what ownership can," Russell had told her board in 1981, years before the act passed. "Planning may accomplish nothing. Lawsuits may destroy and delay protection, variances can emasculate it," she continued. "Public ownership will last for . . . generations."[1] More public land also meant more trails and more hikers, which meant more converts to the Columbia Gorge. The Trust for Public Land and public agencies had to be even more aggressive.

After the National Scenic Area Act passed, Russell inspired audiences with a vision of how the Gorge should be protected, a vision that became a lodestar for the Friends and a shopping list for TPL. Her vision generated two Friends reports, submitted to the Forest Service and the Columbia River Gorge Commission, that specified where parks, overlooks, and hiking trails were needed. Croplands and orchards should be protected through easements; "historic wagon roads that skirt the Gorge's steep slopes" should be turned into trails; scenic overlooks at Mount Zion and Cape Horn should emulate those at Chanticleer Point and Crown Point; Paul Martin's ranch on the Sandy River Delta should become a park; the Historic Columbia River Highway should be restored for hiking and biking; a "string of pearls," composed of parks, should be established along roadways as Lancaster, Hill, and John Yeon's father had once done; wildlife refuges should be established at Franz and Arthur Lakes and at Steigerwald; new trails should be built along the Columbia Hills ridgeline and from Memaloose to Tom McCall Point; Native cultural sites, including Miller Island above Celilo Falls, should be protected; and thousands of acres in the eastern Gorge should be acquired.[2]

Vision without results seemed frivolous to Russell. Marty Rosen, the president of the Trust for Public Land, often declared that its achievements were so tangible that they could be walked on, and Russell had been drawn to TPL by its results-driven culture. When she joined TPL's board in 1988, her vision for the Gorge became its vision; and to execute it she and Burgess wanted a land acquisition fund that would revolve in perpetuity—that is, money taken out to buy land would be returned when the land was sold to a public agency—and would commit TPL to the Gorge. A million dollars would have a lasting impact, Burgess believed—Gorge land prices averaged about a thousand dollars an acre at the time—and Russell thought she could raise that, maybe more. In 1989, they proposed a $1.3 million Columbia Gorge Protection Fund, with $1 million to buy land and $300,000 to defray TPL's acquisition and holding costs. Washington and Oregon senators endorsed the proposal, as did the Forest Service.[3]

Russell's first stop was the Meyer Trust, Oregon's largest foundation, which had already loaned TPL $600,000, scheduled to be repaid in 1989. Russell proposed that Meyer now contribute $400,000 toward the fund and grant an interest-free, five-year loan of $300,000. Her request came just months after the unfavorable publicity generated by Mitch Bower's misappropriations and the removal of Brad Jones, and Russell was concerned about donors' reactions, but Meyer approved the request, subject to its grant being matched dollar-for-dollar by other donations. Russell worked nonstop for eighteen months to cobble together the match, relying on $10,000 to $15,000 gifts. One ally who had been at her side from the start, however, was not there to celebrate Russell's success. Harriet Burgess had left TPL in 1990 to form American Lands Conservancy, where she would have to ask for neither permission nor forgiveness. Her achievements would be extended, though, by TPL's expanding Oregon staff.

Guided by Russell's priorities and supported by a substantial war chest, TPL acquired some of the most iconic properties in the Gorge from 1991 to 1995. It was soon possible to travel the eighty-five-mile length of the Columbia River Gorge National Scenic Area and never lose sight of a trust property. At Washington's western entrance, visitors were greeted by Steigerwald Lake National Wildlife Refuge. Across the river, at the confluence of the Sandy and Columbia Rivers, TPL bought Paul Martin's ranch from Reynolds Aluminum and sold it to the Forest Service. The 1,380-acre floodplain—where Indigenous people had hunted, Lewis and Clark had visited, and Oregon Trail travelers had disembarked—was finally protected, having survived fluoride poisoning, a hulking port of entry, and, more recently, a proposed thirty-six-hole golf course and marina. Easily accessible from the Portland-Vancouver metropolitan area, the Sandy River Delta became one of the Gorge's most popular parks. Two hundred years after William Clark complained of not being able to sleep nearby due to "emensely numerous" waterfowl, "their noise horrid," artist Maya Lin designed an elliptical bird blind on the property to commemorate the Corps's journey past the site and to "bear witness" to the property's restoration. The ten-foot-tall wooden slats that comprise the blind are inscribed with the names, both common and Latin, and the current status of the more than one hundred animal species recorded by the Lewis and Clark Expedition.[4]

Just upriver, Russell pushed TPL to buy Bridal Veil, a derelict timber town that she thought blighted visitors' views and blocked access to one of the most beautiful waterfalls in the Gorge. She had persuaded Senator Hatfield to redraw special management area boundaries to make Bridal Veil eligible for federal purchase, and when local preservationists insisted that the town's buildings were historic and should be preserved, she enlisted John Yeon and won. The *New York Times* covered the controversy, and the *Oregonian* endorsed her vision,[5] but the Forest Service refused to buy a town with sixteen rented homes, a cemetery, a church, a post office, and asbestos and oil contamination from an abandoned timber mill. Even the Trust for Public Land balked. But when Russell raised $400,000 from a donor to offset anticipated costs, TPL bought the town and after a year was permitted to raze many of the buildings, clean the property, and sell much of it to the Forest Service. Soon after, a former renter bolted a large wooden sign to the top of a telephone pole, where it remained for months: BRIDAL VEIL: POPULATION 21 was crossed out in red paint, replaced by RUSSELLVILLE: POPULATION 0.

Farther upstream and across the river was Franz Lake, the largest lake in the Gorge. The lake teemed with juvenile salmon and whistling swans during

"Russellville" sign at Bridal Veil. Russell archives.

winter migrations, and environmentalists considered it magical. "Lovely water-front beaches, views of Horsetail Falls across the river, a very large shallow lake with kingfishers . . . wonderful plants," Nancy Russell had written Harriet Burgess in 1980, "and the most vigorous display of Wapato I have ever seen . . . fringing the lake, ducks floating serenely on the water, Archer Mountain's cliffs looming up behind."[6] By 1992, TPL had assembled eight properties, 670 acres, and conveyed them to federal agencies to create the third national wildlife refuge in the Gorge since Russell had started her campaign.

Russell found another favorite property a few miles upriver, which she named the Camas Patch for the delicate, blue-violet camas lilies that filled its meadows each May. The nine-acre property was in a general management area, where federal purchases were discouraged, so Russell sought help from the Portland Garden Club and Russ Jolley, an old friend and botanical expert. She had proposed and helped raise money for Jolley's field guide on Gorge wildflowers, *Wildflowers of the Columbia Gorge*, which was published in 1988 with the Camas Patch — in full blossom — on its cover.[7] In 1992, Russell inspired a Garden Club fundraising effort and persuaded TPL to buy and indefinitely manage the Camas Patch using the proceeds. When Skamania neighbors routinely tore down the fences to ride ATVs through the fragile meadows, she and Jolley donned work gloves to repair the fields and rebuild the fences.

There were few properties that Russell loved as much as Dalles Mountain Ranch in the eastern Gorge, owned by Pat and Darlene Bleakney. "I adore that place—all of it," Russell wrote a friend. "When I'm there I am in heaven on earth."[8] Pat Bleakney had opposed federal legislation and had been Klickitat County's first appointee to the commission, but he also was open-minded and had succeeded Stafford Hansell as commission chair. He managed Dalles Mountain Ranch with care, lightly grazing his seven hundred head of cattle on fields brimming with balsam root, lupine, and paintbrush. At six thousand acres, the ranch was one of the Gorge's largest and most varied properties, five miles long and extending from the Columbia to Stacker Butte, thirty-two hundred feet high at the crest of the Columbia Hills, with views of seven Cascade peaks, from Mount Rainier in Washington to the Three Sisters in Oregon. The diverse topography created several microclimates and supported dozens of rare and uncommon plant and animal species, including the Dalles Mountain buttercup—found nowhere else in the world—black bear, elk, mountain lions, and the endangered western pond turtle. Bleakney enjoyed guiding visitors across the ranch's footpaths, packed firm over thousands of years by families traveling between river fishing sites and hunting and huckleberry grounds on Mount Adams, often through Devil's Pass, a hidden gap in the rimrock that could barely accommodate a horse and rider. He pointed out pictographs, petroglyphs, hunting blinds, and sites where Native people had chipped arrowheads for generations, their glassy, remnant flakes still gleaming after morning showers. Stands of black walnut trees and patches of yellow roses marked the homesteads of early white settlers. Russell and Bleakney formed a fast friendship, grounded in their love of the land and its history and reinforced by hours spent hiking the ranch's trails. He granted her unlimited access to the ranch so she could lead Garden Club and native plant tours, which he often joined.

It was not surprising, then, that Russell was one of the first people to whom Bleakney confided when he considered selling the ranch. Nor was it surprising when Russell called me, asking the Trust for Public Land to buy it. Or when she called a week later, asking if TPL had succeeded. But buying Dalles Mountain Ranch would be complicated. The Forest Service was not interested because the ranch was designated a general management area and was located far from Portland and Seattle, where most park and natural area advocates lived. Pat Bleakney wanted top dollar, and—assuming another agency could be found—the ranch would be expensive and difficult to appraise given its size and unusual qualities. Pat and I negotiated over the next year and eventually agreed that TPL would pay one dollar for the option, on which Pat wrote "this dollar bill tied down my $2.4 million ranch for eighteen months," which he framed and hung in his office. Meanwhile, Russell pressed the head of the Washington Department of Natural Resources to fly with senior staff to nearby Dallesport and join us to tour the ranch. She led other tours, called the director and members of the Washington State Parks Commission, and asked Friends members to call. She hired an ornithologist to identify the bird species on the ranch—which included bald and golden eagles, peregrine falcons, and wild turkeys—and sent the list to agencies. In late 1993, TPL bought and sold the ranch to Washington State in two back-to-back transactions: the 2,900-acre upper ranch became the Columbia Hills Natural Area Preserve, managed by the Department of Natural Resources to protect rare plant communities, and the lower 3,100 acres became Dalles Mountain State Park. At the dedication the following May, during the height of the wildflower bloom, Russell and Russ Jolley led hikes to celebrate the purchase.

Russell wanted visitors to experience an epiphany when they entered the Gorge, a world where the protection of scenic, natural, cultural, and recreational resources was paramount. While residential and commercial development did not threaten the sparsely settled eastern entrance, Russell knew they could. And they have. Drivers approaching the National Scenic Area from the east now pass hundreds of power-generating windmills—forty-one stories high with blades the length of a Boeing 747—in what used to be wheat fields. Crossing into the National Scenic Area where they are prohibited, the windmills vanish, giving way to the basalt cliffs and rolling prairie of the Gorge's largest island. Miller Island's cactus-studded landscape, a thousand acres reaching over two miles, harbors golden eagle nests, ring-bill gull and blue heron rookeries, and rare and endangered species. Located in Washington at the mouth of the Deschutes River, six miles east of Dalles Mountain Ranch and upriver from Celilo Falls, the island was once the site of a Sahaptin village. In the mid-1920s, Henry Biddle sponsored a University of California archeological expedition that documented the island's cultural importance, including remnants of 132 house pits. Pictographs, brightly colored in red and white, mark the island's dark cliffs; and while pre-NSA gravel mining and agriculture have erased signs of the village, Miller Island is sacred to the four treaty tribes. Worried that the island might be further damaged, Russell led small parties of major donors there to assist the trust. She asked Senator Hatfield for federal funds when TPL optioned the island. The trust conveyed Miller Island to the Forest Service in 1989, and it is now guarded by tribal law enforcement.[9]

Russell was delighted by TPL's successes but not content. She believed TPL was too dependent on generating revenue from land transactions. Where it saw an efficient way to raise money, Russell saw limitations that kept the organization from buying land where net income could not be realized or where there was no public agency take-out. TPL's model also made it difficult to pursue important but less expensive properties. These were lands that Russell wanted purchased, so she did it herself.

After the National Scenic Area Act passed, a friend asked Russell what she planned for an encore. Russell wrote back:

> Advocacy . . . will never be over. While the political component of Friends of the Columbia Gorge's work will always be there as development interests continue to press against the NSA Act, I hope to focus my own efforts on making parks and open space for people to enjoy, and to permanently protect significant Gorge landscapes.[10]

Beacon Rock Tavern, acquired and razed by TPL circa 1989; conveyed to Washington State Parks. Russell archives.

By permanent protection, Russell meant ownership. Among the gaps in TPL's model was one that particularly galled her: TPL rarely purchased properties where developments were so misplaced or jarring that they spoiled the landscape, at least for her. That land included Ed Cleveland's estate on Cape Horn; the Starr property above the confluence of the Klickitat and Columbia Rivers, where seventy-seven junked cars sat on the rim and tons of garbage had been pushed down the cliff face; and a deserted 1950s gas station, rusting just yards from the interstate at Dodson. With her help, TPL had bought and razed some of Russell's nemeses, most notably the town of Bridal Veil and a tavern at the entrance to Beacon Rock State Park, where light from a red neon sign had shimmered against the monument like a rogue aurora borealis.[11] But those purchases were exceptions to TPL's rule that transactions should cover costs and provide net revenue.

Barbara Robinson, who loved Gorge wildflowers as much as Russell, would help her friend address TPL's perceived shortcomings. Robinson had been drawn to the eastern Columbia Gorge since she was a student at Reed College in Portland. In 1985, she had tried to raise $29,000 to purchase and save sixty-four acres at the Rowena Plateau whose views and wildflowers were threatened by residential development. The Nature Conservancy owned a nearby preserve and agreed to manage the property if Robinson's campaign was successful, but she was discouraged by her lack of progress and cold-called Russell for advice. Nancy was happy to give it, along with an unsolicited $5,000 donation, as long as Oregon State Parks provided the balance. Robinson was inspired to complete her goal, and the property was purchased and named after Governor Tom McCall's family. Along the way, the two women formed a close friendship. "My job," Robinson later recalled, "was to get her away from the [pressure of] meetings and fundraising and out hiking in the east Gorge."[12]

Three years later, Robinson approached her friend about a three-acre property along the historic highway east of Mosier that she considered her "favorite eyesore."[13] High above the Columbia, it offered exceptional views of the river, the Washington shoreline, cherry orchards, and Mount Adams, but neither woman liked the white double-wide trailer or the six shiny outbuildings whose reflected sunlight could be seen for miles. Nor did they like the dozens of sun-bleached Clorox bottles, mounted on fence posts, that clattered and whirred in the breeze.

Robinson proposed that they buy the property together, remove the buildings and bottles, paint the double-wide brown so it better blended into the landscape, then resell it, a plan she believed could break even financially. Russell declined, predicting that new owners would build new structures, repaint them white, park recreational vehicles in the driveway, and "re-eyesore" the property. Instead, she proposed they buy the three-acre property, tear everything down, and sell it to the Forest Service.[14] Robinson could not afford to buy into the plan, but Russell could. She christened her property Rancho Whirligig after the Clorox bottles, tore down the outbuildings and fences, painted the double-wide earth tone—including its metal roof, which baffled the painter—and rented it while negotiating with the Forest Service. Five years later, after the double-wide had been hauled away, Russell and Robinson scoured the ground for lingering plastic and wire and sowed wildflower seeds. Within a few days, the Forest Service owned Rancho Whirligig, which adjoined Memaloose State Park to the east and north and federal land to the south. The property would soon have the eastern Gorge's newest wildflower trail, Memaloose Overlook Trail.

At about the same time, in April 1988, Robinson presented Russell with another opportunity, a forty-acre property across the historic highway, just up the hill from Whirligig. The property had "Albert Bierstadt views," Russell told Bruce, and on their way back from a weekend at Elk Lake the couple stopped to see it. At the pinnacle of the property were views that exceeded even Whirligig's. "The view to the west is spectacular with the cherry orchards of Mosier below and the gorge extending away to the west beyond," Bruce wrote his son Aubrey. "One can see all the Washington shore, the Oregon side for most of the distance to Hood River and . . . both Mt. Hood and Mt. Adams." When Nancy asked Bruce what he thought, his response was short and enthusiastic: "Buy it!"[15]

The site's "ugly 'improvements'" attracted Russell as much as its beauty. She particularly disliked a section of roof that peeled off several feet from the mobile home to cover a makeshift porch. "This part of the roof consisted of sheets of galvanized, corrugated metal," Aubrey remembered, "and it shone in the evening sun with such brilliance that it stood like a lighthouse visible from miles around. . . . In Mom's parlance, it stuck out like a sore thumb."[16] The Russells bought the property less than two months after purchasing Whirligig. They named it South 40 and registered both properties in Bruce's name to avoid harassment. Then they removed the mobile home, tore down the wellhouse, and cleared the property of knapweed, an invasive noxious plant.

Of all of the land the Russells bought, South 40 would remain Bruce's favorite. His oil painting of the view from its crest—the sun's early morning rays lighting up the landscape from the distant palisades to the orchards below—hung for years in their Westwinds living room. Soon after buying South 40, he wrote Aubrey that he had "told Nancy that I had had a lot of pleasure out of owning various stocks over the years and I thought it wholly appropriate that she own something in the way of an investment that she would enjoy . . . [Both] pieces of property have eye-sores on them the removal of which will be worthwhile. That your legacy will be somewhat reduced is regrettable," Bruce continued, with tongue firmly in cheek, "but not likely to make much difference if you remember to marry [well]."[17]

Two years after buying Whirligig and South 40, Russell bought one hundred and eleven acres east of Lyle, within a designated general management area (GMA), midway between White Salmon and Dallesport. The property rose above the Columbia to grassy benches choked with wildflowers and an abandoned cherry orchard that erupted in blossoms each spring. The south-facing escarpments of the eastern Gorge in Washington have some of the best wildflower displays anywhere, but in 1990 there were no public lands and few prospects. No public lands meant no opportunities for people to hike without trespassing. Russell changed that.

For three years, Barbara Robinson built a trail through the Lyle property, moving rocks, killing poison oak, and dodging rattlesnakes and ticks. When she suggested a more favorable course for the trail, Russell bought more land, eventually spending $800,000 to assemble almost five hundred acres that would connect the trail to the town of Lyle, two miles away. When floods washed out sections of the trail, she paid a professional trail builder to buttress it with wooden supports, and when Robinson found arrowhead flakes Russell paid $8,000 for an archeological survey. She hired a local artist to engrave a four-foot square redwood sign, inlaid with brightly painted yellow bells and poet's shooting stars, that welcomed the public to the Cherry Orchard Trail and Nature Preserve, and she left waivers at the trailhead, hoping hikers would sign them and protect her from liability. While the sign's designer was an excellent artist, she proved to be a poor proof reader. After the sign had been fastened to a large oak tree, Russell noticed that a letter had been omitted and wanted it corrected. The sign was removed—its lower portion sawed off and swapped out to edit the errant word—and rehung while a deluge of ticks rained down on the hapless workers. The loop trail, which gained fourteen hundred feet in elevation over its four miles, opened in April 1997 to glowing reviews.[18]

Six miles downriver, also in Washington, were other properties that Russell wanted protected. Located in the Major Creek drainage, these lands

Bruce Russell at the Lyle Cherry Orchard Preserve, over 500 acres that he and Nancy acquired from 1991–2005, now owned and managed by FOCG Land Trust. FOCG archives.

bumped up against Catherine Creek Ranch to the west, the premier wild-flower property that the Trust for Public Land had sold to the Forest Service four years earlier. Major Creek was also covered with spring wildflowers, and Lewis and Clark had camped at its mouth in 1806. "It's a beautiful piece of property," Bruce wrote Aubrey, "a really magnificent panorama . . . of the cherry orchards east of Mosier and . . . a beautiful view of Mt. Hood above them." Major Creek had deep springtime flows and steep fifteen-foot-high banks, and Nancy and her daughter Wendy often swam in the six-foot-deep punchbowl at the base of its waterfall.[19]

Russell bought the forty-acre property in early 1992 and assembled four adjacent properties over the next seven years. By 1999, she had paid almost $900,000 for 145 acres at Major Creek. As at Whirligig, her intention was to rent out the buildings while she worked on a sale to the Forest Service. If successful, she would raze the two houses, a barn, a garage and shop, and a storage shed on the property, fill in the swimming pool, and reseed the land with wildflowers and native grasses. But there were two substantial challenges to overcome: Klickitat County's opposition to reducing its private land base and the reluctance of the Forest Service to buy half of the property, the portion located in a general management area.

The county and many of its residents remained unhappy with the National Scenic Area Act and, by extension, with Russell. She had her share of typical landowner problems, including tenants filing insurance claims and having to evict one renter for $12,000 in back rent. Some of her difficulties, however, came from being Nancy Russell. When a tenant, with Russell's approval, wanted to temporarily turn one of her Major Creek houses into a bed and breakfast, seventy Lyle-area landowners fought back, petitioning against "certain purveyors of the Scenic Act . . . reaping their plunder [by] buying up pristine land to exploit, [and by] bringing in more 'naturalists, botanists, bird watchers, wild flower enthusiasts, artists and writers as well as hikers and bikers and tourists' to run rampant over our properties." When Russell leased her land for grazing to keep down weeds and continue the property's agricultural tax deferment, the cattle were poisoned and the county yanked her deferment, charging her $16,000 in back taxes and penalties. She developed ties to the community—hiring local contractors, realtors, and handymen to gain relationships as well as expertise—but she also stood up for her principles. One politically influential local family asked to buy back some of the land it had sold her when they realized their remaining property would be less developable. Russell refused, saying that she was "not in the business of promoting development" and then later opposed the family's application to mine gravel on adjacent property. They never forgave her and would fight many of her future efforts.[20]

Russell's plan to sell her Major Creek properties to the Forest Service was similarly contested. The Forest Service only wanted half of her land, the part designated special management area (SMA) and adjacent to the Catherine Creek property it had bought from TPL. Russell refused to sell only the SMA lands, noting that her GMA lands provided the same resources. When she applied to the Gorge commission to demolish the structures on her property, the commission received 138 letters in opposition. Russell persevered, however, and the Forest Service relented, worried about the scenic impact on its land if Russell's GMA land was ever developed. In late 2002, the Forest Service offered Russell $1,217,000 for her five-property assemblage, contingent on congressional funding. She led several congressional tours of the properties, pointing out their relevance to the upcoming Lewis and Clark Bicentennial celebration, and funding was appropriated. When the Forest Service asked her to preserve just one building so it could store equipment, Russell declined.

"Buy land," Mark Twain once said, "they're not making it anymore." Russell agreed. She often overpaid rather than lose a key property and took on difficult transactions, including complicated assemblages, general management land, and properties that had been developed. Rural counties continued to single her out for unfavorable treatment. As a result, she rarely made money when she sold land to public agencies, and there was no public agency take-out for many of her properties. Whether she made money, as at Major Creek, or lost it, she plowed all of the proceeds into buying more land. Her objectives were to protect the landscape and promote public access, and her methods became increasingly sophisticated, using tax code provisions enacted to benefit real estate investors and developers, for instance, to lower her capital gains. With the money saved, she bought more land. By the late 1990s, as Friends of the Columbia Gorge prospered and became less reliant on her, Russell bought even more land.

Her campaign could not have succeeded without Bruce's enthusiastic support, usually as a silent partner. In addition to buying their own land, the couple often contributed to other land purchases, including a nine-and-a-half-acre Mosier property that Barbara Robinson saw advertised on the cover of a local real estate magazine. She alerted Russell, who loved its wildflowers—prairie stars, monkey flowers, and *Douglasia laevigata*, a pink primrose named for botanist David Douglas—and its two-tiered waterfall, separated by a plunge pool that locals used for a swimming hole.

Russell asked a friend in Mosier to apply for an Oregon State Parks grant to cover the property's $240,000 cost, but the grant required a 40 percent match and its application window expired in thirty days. Bruce also felt a connection to the property, particularly to an adjacent pioneer cemetery, and offered to pay the $96,000 match. At the property's dedication in 2002, he dressed as a pioneer—to his grandchildren's joy—and spoke about his great-grandparents' journeys over the Oregon Trail, their settlement in Oregon, and the care his grandmother, at age fifteen, had given to the settler who had left much of his estate to her. It was the first time that Bruce's role had been publicly recognized. A plaque on the property dedicates the park to Bruce's mother Helen Wortman Russell, "Granddaughter of four Oregon Trail Pioneers of 1852."

Of all of Russell's projects, few were as important to her as two assemblages at either end of the National Scenic Area: Cape Horn and near Mosier. She had spent years laying the groundwork for opening the historic highway's twin tunnels between Hood River and Mosier, not knowing if it would be physically possible. She had supported a 1981 National Park Service study of the highway that promoted reopening the tunnels, the highway's listing on the National Register of Historic Places in 1983, and its recognition as a National Historic Civil Engineering Landmark a year later. She had insisted that the National Scenic Area Act direct the Oregon Department of Transportation to spend $2.8 million to restore and reconnect the historic highway. At her encouragement, ODOT announced that its highest priority for those funds was to assess whether the tunnels could be opened. She promoted a vision to acquire the five-mile segment from private owners, restore the tunnels, and buy enough land on either side of the roadbed to create a wide linear park, not just a narrow trail. Believing it would encourage his support, she suggested that the park be named for Governor Neil Goldschmidt. Above all, Russell insisted that cars be banned from the park, so everyone could safely enjoy the striking views.

In 1989, the Trust for Public Land executed an agreement with Oregon State Parks to lead negotiations with the dozen landowners who owned the roadway and adjacent land. Land assemblages are notoriously difficult to put together, as neighbors share negotiation details and compete not just with the buyer but also with each other to get the best deal. Prices increase as ceilings become floors when information leaks after sales close. Russell had already met with several landowners, including Beulah Hand, who had picked up her forty-acre property in a tax foreclosure while serving as a state legislator in the 1960s. Between 1985 and 1995, Hand had offered to donate her forty acres to the trust, to bequeath it, and to sell it at a discount, but in the end she refused to sell to TPL at all, believing that she could make more money dealing directly with the state. The trust had better luck with her neighbor, who agreed to donate his five-acre property before selling it to the organization for $600 in back taxes and $750 in cash. With TPL's ownership, the state was able to determine that the tunnels could be stabilized, once the rubble was removed, to allow public access. The project gained momentum, but largely without the trust, which realized that negotiations like Beulah Hand's were unsustainable. An agency with the authority to condemn the property or a buyer willing to lose money was needed instead.

Russell, meanwhile, was building a coalition. The Historic Preservation League of Oregon played a lead role, as did state and federal agencies, and Russell brought in new advocates as well, most notably Shared Outdoor Adventure and Recreation (SOAR), a group that worked to provide recreational opportunities to people with limited mobility. Russell led tour after tour to the twin tunnels' blocked entrances, including a volkswalk for seven hundred people during the Friends' 1991 Hiking Weekend. When positive reinforcement failed, she pursued other options. The Friends, for instance, filed notice to sue Hood River County for mining gravel at the twin tunnels' west entrance, and—at the Friends' urging—the Gorge commission rejected the county's plan. The Forest Service then completed a complex land exchange involving six federal and state agencies, trading timberland in two national forests for the county quarry, and ODOT replaced Hood River's lost gravel. Russell guided Senator Hatfield around the tunnels in 1993, and within months Congress had appropriated $2.5 million to restore them for hiking and biking. Work began the next year on what Russell started calling the "Mark O. Hatfield State Park."[21]

With congressional appropriation came a new challenge, finding the required 20 percent local match. Oregon planned to meet the $500,000 requirement with state gas tax funds, but those funds could only be used for automobile-related projects. Russell pushed the state to provide a match from other sources, and she asked her coalition, now twenty-two groups, to push as well. The Friends sent an alert to members in mid-August 1994, just months before federal funding would lapse, asking them to pressure the state. She hoped that occasional use of the road by vintage cars would meet

Oregon's legal standard, but the state's attorneys said automobiles would need to access the restored section at least one weekend a month. Russell was convinced, if that kind of access was allowed, that pressure would mount for unrestricted car use. The state refused to budge, so Russell completed an emergency application to the Meyer Trust, asking it to match the funds. She called its trustees at home. Meyer declined. She asked it to reconsider. No luck. Then Bruce proposed that they provide the $500,000 grant themselves, anonymously, and with conditions. Russell had always wanted visitors to the twin tunnels to experience "an outing replete with revelations and discovery . . . dependent on an individual's imagination, [not] something resembling a museum with a sign every several hundred yards." Nature, beauty, and history were what mattered to her. The Oregon Trail's water route, the Corps of Discovery's journey, rare plants, and Native American cultural sites all lent themselves to interpretation at the park—"signs commemorating every politician and citizen who had something to do with the project," not so much. The state accepted the Russells' gift, along with their conditions that the park be open to hikers, bikers, wheelchair users, the occasional antique car tour, and that interpretive signs, benches, and restrooms would be confined to the trailheads.[22]

As quickly as that problem was solved, another arose. ODOT offered to buy only a tiny sliver of TPL's five-acre parcel, interested in protecting the roadbed and nothing else. TPL refused to sell, insisting that the agency buy the entire property, including a large, flat bench with sweeping views that was ideal for side trails and overlooks. ODOT responded by threatening to condemn just the roadbed. TPL held firm while Russell directed her megaphone at Oregon's governor, reminding him of the need to create a broad, linear park that transported visitors to 1921, the year the tunnels had been completed. The governor agreed, and ODOT soon acquired TPL's entire property, and other landowners' as well.

In August 1996, Senator Hatfield was the first person in forty years to drive the historic highway from Mosier to the twin tunnels' west portal, beyond which the roadway was still closed. The tunnels were dedicated that November, and Russell arranged for a 1923 Pierce Arrow touring car to transport the senator to the celebration. Before he left office, he told Russell, he would get Congress to fund the project, from "trailhead to trailhead."[23]

Three years later, the Warm Springs tribe announced plans for their seventy-five-thousand-square-foot casino on forty acres of tribal land, five hundred yards inside Russell's five-mile-linear-park and just two miles from the

Senator Mark O. Hatfield with Nancy Russell at the dedication of the Mosier Twin
Tunnels, November 1996. FOCG archives.

twin tunnels. But Russell's coalition was strong, and off-reservation casinos
were controversial in Oregon and in Washington, DC. The act could also
prevent infrastructure that the casino needed on adjacent lands from being
built. Facing these challenges and resounding public opposition, especially in
Hood River, the tribe proposed Cascade Locks as an alternate location. When
Governor Kitzhaber vetoed that location, the tribe returned to their original
proposal and upped the ante by buying 160 acres adjacent to their Hood
River trust land. "Everybody thinks we're bluffing," said tribal representative
Rudy Clements, "but we're going to build a casino on our Hood River trust
property." By October, however, the Forest Service had weighed in, notifying
the Bureau of Indian Affairs that converting the 160 acres to trust status—as
requested by the Warm Springs—would be inconsistent with the act. Once
again the tribe turned to Cascade Locks. Over the next several years Russell
and the Friends led the opposition to a casino in the Gorge. They were joined
by the Confederated Tribes of Grand Ronde, which feared competition for
its Spirit Mountain casino near the coast, the Garden Club of America, and
dozens of environmental and faith-based organizations and small businesses.[24]

Meanwhile, in July 2000 the Mosier Twin Tunnels park held its grand
opening. For the first time in half a century, people could walk between
Hood River and Mosier on the "king of roads . . . a poem in stone."[25] But

Restored Mosier Twin Tunnels, looking west. Image by Cate Hotchkiss.

Russell was not finished. She bought a four-acre property at the Mosier end of the park that she considered an eyesore and that Oregon State Parks had long wanted but had resisted because of its buildings and complicated ownership. After buying the property, Russell razed a house that was under construction, removed a double-wide trailer, and conveyed the land to the state nine months later. When Governor Kitzhaber, an opponent of off-reservation casinos, was reelected to a third term in 2010, the tribe dropped its plans for a casino in the Gorge. A year later, it opened a smaller facility on their reservation in the town of Warm Springs.

At Cape Horn on the opposite end of the Gorge, Russell faced a different challenge. Several hundred feet above where she, Bruce, and John Yeon had stopped to take in the views on their way to The Shire in 1979, the cliffs reach a high plateau. Almost a square mile in size, the Cape Horn plateau lies east of Mount Pleasant, just below Mount Zion's summit. On the south and east, the plateau plummets thirteen hundred feet from its four-mile-long ridge to the Columbia and riverine meadows below. Silver Star Mountain rises above the Washougal River valley to the north. The Rim View Estates subdivision—twelve of its sixteen lots conveyed by TPL to the Forest Service in 1987—sits on the eastern edge of the plateau, the nucleus of a park that Russell hoped would match Crown Point.

In the early 1990s, Russell asked TPL to approach the Grams and Mackellar families, who owned hundreds of acres stretching several miles upriver, shoreline to rim, from Mount Pleasant to Cape Horn. These were the properties that had compelled Russell, standing at Crown Point in 1980, to fight for the Gorge. They afforded outstanding views, and the Mackellar land—which contained a prominent waterfall—bordered the southernmost Rim View lot. Both properties were ideal for TPL: adjoining high-value special management properties, prominently visible, and owned by families who supported public ownership. By 1994, TPL had optioned both properties and turned to Congress for funding. Russell got in touch with Senator Hatfield and flew to Washington, DC, to seek appropriations. John Yeon had marked the properties for purchase in his 1935 report, and he celebrated their optioning from a hospital bed after a serious fall. Worried about her friend and mentor, Russell wrote Yeon, on a card featuring Wyoming wildflowers, that she thought about him every day. He died two weeks later. The next spring, sixty years after Yeon had first pushed for their purchase, TPL transferred the Grams and Mackellar properties to the Forest Service.[26]

John Yeon left a long record of successful Gorge advocacy, starting in the early 1930s and continuing through the mid-1990s, when he resigned in protest from a citizens advisory group that oversaw master planning for Multnomah Falls when he only achieved 90 percent of what he wanted. "Compromise," said his longtime partner Richard Brown, "was not part of his make-up or vocabulary." He carried grudges but was as devoted to Russell as she was to him. "It was one of the greatest pleasures of my life," Russell said at a memorial for Yeon at The Shire, "to have known him."[27]

The year that John Yeon died, Russell met thirty-five-year-old Dan Huntington, a financial broker who would help her transform Cape Horn. The Pacific Northwest—particularly the Columbia Gorge, which he had read about but not seen—had drawn Huntington across the country. He had flown from Wisconsin to Portland on a Saturday in May 1987, hiked Henry Biddle's trail to the top of Beacon Rock on Sunday, and was interviewed and hired by E. F. Hutton on Monday. He spent most of his free time in the Gorge, often hiking to Angel's Rest early in the morning and arriving at his downtown Portland desk by eight. Tall and lanky, Huntington was apt to wear khaki pants, loose-fitting short-sleeved shirts, and hiking boots when away from work. He walked with a forward-leaning tilt that glided over obstacles. At rest, his body kept its tension, especially his eyes, alert and challenging like the peregrine falcons that sailed above Cape Horn.

It was at the base of Cape Horn where Huntington saw a for-sale sign in 1989, bought his house in Prindle, and—consistent with Russell's nightmare of the consequences of the I-205 bridge—began commuting to Portland. Huntington, his wife and two young boys, were now living where they hiked, and he soon tired of his coat-and-tie corporate life. "No one understood real estate in the Columbia Gorge," he came to realize, especially how the act had created value through its national scenic area designation. With some qualms about the financial impact of his decision, he became a realtor, joined a Vancouver-based firm, and aggressively pursued listings within a ten-mile radius of his home. He bought assessors' maps and cornered the real estate market around Cape Horn. But he cared more about the environment than selling real estate, and he later acknowledged that his real estate license often was a front for his advocacy efforts. In 1994, he approached the Forest Service about a forty-two-acre forested property below Cape Horn. The agency was uninterested, so he called Nancy Russell, and the two met with Chris Beck, TPL's project manager. In short order, TPL had negotiated an option on the property and persuaded the Forest Service to buy the land. Russell and Huntington, who shared similar goals and many personal qualities, formed a close relationship.[28]

Russell was determined to create more trails and overlooks in the Gorge, especially on Washington's sunnier, gradual slopes. The challenge was formidable, as the National Park Service's 1980 study had revealed that Washington had only four miles of trails and two public overlooks in the Gorge, including the perilous pullout at Cape Horn. Oregon, even with its National Forest lands, had just twenty trail miles and eight overlooks. Before the Trust for Public Land arrived, there had been no public land at all on Mount Pleasant, Mount Zion, or Cape Horn and none on the shoreline upriver to Beacon Rock. By the mid-1990s, however, Russell had inspired and prodded TPL to buy a dozen properties around Cape Horn, totaling five hundred acres, for conveyance to the Forest Service. The land from Mount Pleasant to Cape Horn became the agency's top acquisition priority, and the Forest Service independently bought dozens of smaller properties there, including two of the remaining lots at Rim View Estates. That left two lots in private ownership, both with houses.[29]

Dan Huntington was the first to recognize the possibilities created by the trust's acquisitions. If another handful of properties could be bought, a trail—perhaps four miles long—could be built over Cape Horn, offering incomparable views of Oregon's parks across the river. The trail would come close to fulfilling another of Huntington's dreams, a pathway over public land that extended forty-five miles from Washougal's Steamboat Landing to the town of Stevenson. Cape Horn, with its legacy of no zoning, was the bottleneck, a mishmash of steep topography and residential development on large and small lots. Huntington envisioned that the Cape Horn Trail would start near the forty-two-acre property that TPL had sold to the Forest Service and climb north and west across private land and other public land TPL had bought, reaching the plateau by way of a 180-degree-view promontory the Forest Service had acquired in 1991. From the promontory, the trail would follow the rim south, cross more private land, skirt the two developed lots at Rim View Estate, and descend over the Evergreen Highway to the trail's terminus, a viewpoint on the Mackellar property above an eighty-foot-high waterfall.

Because the northeast portion of the plateau ended at a sheer thirteen-hundred-foot cliff and the NSA's boundaries extended from the river to cliff-edge, portions of the trail would have to be on land outside the national scenic area. Four private properties—two outside the NSA along the rim, and two inside the NSA but designated as general management area—would need to be acquired. Buying those properties presented enormous challenges: the Forest Service rarely purchased GMA lands and had never bought land outside national scenic area boundaries.

Before those problems could be addressed, more arose. The owner of a narrow ten-acre parcel on the plateau that paralleled Rim View to the west and was bordered on three sides by federal land offered to sell to the Forest Service. In a draft decision sent out for public comment, the agency declined the offer, rating the property a low priority. If the agency did not change its decision, then the property would revert to general management area status and a house could be built. Russell expressed her "great disappointment" to the Forest Service. She acknowledged that the property had no significant resources but noted that it was suitable for parking and restrooms, which large parks needed. "It has always been obvious that [this] parcel was important as an adjunct to recreation because it was not important for protection of resource values," she admonished the NSA manager. The Forest Service listened and bought the property.[30]

A greater crisis unfolded yards away. After the Forest Service had bought fourteen of the lots in the Rim View subdivision, it had leased the southern four lots to Ed Cleveland for grazing. Cleveland fenced the lots, so his horses could enjoy the public land but the public could not. To save money, the Forest Service then decided to sell those lots, subject to a conservation easement that permitted grazing but prohibited development. Russell knew that Cleveland was the only logical buyer, but his purchase would make it less likely that the public could ever buy his property and more likely that a Cape Horn Trail and park would have an entrenched opponent living next door. She wrote the Forest Service a diplomatic letter. "It is often said that there is no institutional memory," she started. "We hope herewith to provide that memory and revive the vision." She traced how the Friends had not had the resources in 1980 to fight both George Rizor's and Rim View's illegal subdivisions, how a "supporter" had lent TPL the money to buy the twelve unsold lots, and how it was "clear to all" that the subdivision should become a "magnificent, large overlook park" comparable to those in Oregon. "We feel that the CRGNSA has unintentionally dropped the vision for a great park," she concluded. "We hope that this history . . . will help to clarify that vision." She copied her letter to Senator Mark Hatfield and asked Harriet Burgess at the American Land Conservancy to reach out to former Senator Dan Evans. "This job," she wrote Burgess, "is *never* done, is it?" Russell's job may not have been done, but the Forest Service's effort to sell Rim View Estates was. The agency reversed course.[31]

While Russell was securing land around Rim View, Huntington was concentrating on the four properties necessary to create the Cape Horn Trail, three on the rim and one at the trailhead. He had procured one listing, talked another landowner into selling, and was cultivating a third. In the spring of 1996, he put his job on hold for six weeks to address the puzzle. He approached the Forest Service, but the agency said no, emphatically. The Trust for Public Land declined as well, judging the four properties to be high risk, low return transactions. Even the Russells declined to buy the land.

Huntington called Dave Cannard, whom he had met two years earlier. Cannard wanted to help create the trail but possibly profit at the same time. While well-intentioned, Cannard could be naïve, especially when it came to politics, and insisted that his identity be kept secret. He was worried, he said, that his name might stir up opposition in Skamania County. So Cannard formed the Cape Horn Land and Timber Trust and tapped his retirement fund to buy the two properties on the plateau's rim for $474,000, one inside the GMA, and one outside the NSA. He then surveyed the property, at considerable cost, and cleared brush to open up the views. Huntington, it turned out, had negotiated a very good deal. He was surprised, though, when Cannard—through his corporate shield—offered the properties to the federal government for their fair market value, potentially $1.5 million.[32] As an incentive, Cannard's trust offered to donate a quarter of the sales price to build the Cape Horn Trail. As Henry Biddle had done generations earlier at Beacon Rock, Cannard intended to do well by doing good. But as Biddle had also demonstrated, private profit mixed with public funds and lack of transparency can be a volatile brew. If successful, he would help create the Cape Horn Trail and receive a net profit, anonymously, of half a million dollars.

With two of the critical properties secured, Huntington built a coalition under Russell's guidance. She introduced him to Russ Jolley, who suggested that people would more likely rally around a place that had a name. Evoking the nineteenth-century wagon road that crossed Cape Horn—which he planned to incorporate into the trail—Huntington named the cliffside promontory, recently purchased by the Forest Service, Pioneer Point. Then he organized tours, leading reporters, politicians, donors, and activists on hikes. Soon newspapers were referring to Pioneer Point as though homesteaders had bestowed the name a century and a half earlier, and it was the descendants of those settlers in Skamania County whom Huntington was appealing to. If he could gain the county's support, then an irresistible coalition, from grassroots conservationists to conservative county leaders, would be created.

He knew how to appeal to Skamania County: he castigated the Forest Service. He blamed the agency for having bought fifteen thousand acres of land in the county but leaving some of the best properties—such as Pioneer Point—inaccessible, blocked by private land, or out of reach of existing trails. "To close it off from the people," he railed to the *Pioneer*, "is the truest form of ultra-elitism." The park and trail soon had endorsements from the Stevenson Chamber of Commerce and the Skamania County Economic Development Council and qualified support from the Skamania County Commission. The *Columbian* celebrated that there had been "no fiery protest, no threat of secession, no cry of 'communist'" and credited Huntington—"no greenie environmentalist"—with gaining that support.[33]

Then all hell broke loose. While Huntington was on a family vacation in Mexico, Cannard let slip to an acquaintance that he was the investor behind the Cape Horn Land and Timber Trust. Slade Gorton, now chair of the Interior Appropriations Subcommittee, found out and was furious. In a blistering press release, he accused Cannard of "blatant profiteering," and of hiding his involvement. The senator was "astonished" that the price sought by Cannard "would result in a $1,000,000 profit for a man who for years has worked systematically to restrict development in the Gorge Scenic Area . . . caus[ing] the devaluation of a great deal of private property and the loss of jobs." Nevertheless, he said, he would support an appropriation of $300,000 to acquire twenty-seven acres of Cannard's property inside the NSA, as long as Cannard sold for his cost, or donated, his land outside the NSA needed for the trail. While Cannard would have realized a modest profit, he decided to fight and gave public agencies a year to make a choice: buy the property or he would divide it into five homesites.[34]

Skamania County withdrew its support. Huntington resigned as trustee and turned to Russell for advice. She told him to donate to Gorton's campaign. Soon he had bundled $50,000 for the campaign and was invited to a meeting in Seattle of the senator's largest contributors. Gorton seemed appreciative that Huntington was representing broader public interests and later called him, again seeking to protect Cape Horn and create the trail without enriching Cannard. Huntington proposed that Cannard's NSA land become special management area, making it eligible for purchase yet limiting how much the portion not needed for the trail could be developed. He further suggested that Cannard's land outside the NSA be included in a new special purchase unit and that Cannard donate some land to the Forest Service. For good measure, Huntington proposed that other land outside the NSA needed for the trail—owned by Jack Collins on the rim—be included in the special purchase unit. Gorton agreed and oversaw passage of the necessary legislation. Cannard reluctantly approved the solution, but he wanted a better return on his investment and continued to fight the federal appraisal process.

With the two Cannard properties on a glidepath to public ownership, Huntington's efforts gained momentum. He secured a listing on twelve acres of Jack Collins's property—now included in the special purchase unit—that connected Cannard's properties to Rim View Estates, and he persuaded the Columbia Land Trust, a new organization, to buy the parcel in 1999. At his encouragement, the Columbia Land Trust then bought a thirteen-acre hiking easement over the fourth critical property, general management area land near the trailhead. In 1999, Russell bought one of the two remaining Rim View lots and tore down its modest house. Three years later, she sold the land to the Forest Service, losing more than $30,000. She used her temporary ownership to meet Ed Cleveland, whose six-thousand-square-foot mansion and outbuildings she coveted—not to live in, but to demolish.

With the essential four properties now controlled by supporters but not yet in public ownership, Huntington asked the Forest Service to start building a trail. When the NSA manager refused because the trail had not yet received the necessary permits, Huntington started building his own trail, using volunteer labor and avoiding sensitive plants under Russ Jolley's careful watch. Occasionally wielding a machete, he led hundreds of people over the trail to Pioneer Point "to stimulate the ever-latent bureaucracy," as Russell described it. "To let them know we are serious." Huntington asked supporters to lobby the Forest Service, but the agency was unreceptive. Instead, it ordered him to stop building the trail and to restore the land to its original condition. But pressure mounted on the Forest Service as the Trust for Public Land bought other special management area properties in the Cape Horn viewshed. In 2002, Russell—ever practical—bought a small parcel across the road from the proposed Cape Horn Trail trailhead for hikers to park their cars. The next year, one of Huntington's fellow trail builders discovered that from above the Mackellar waterfall he could hike down to the Columbia River and join up with a country lane that led back to the trailhead. Instead of an eight-mile, out-and-back trail, Huntington's friend had created a seven-mile loop. The Cape Horn Trail was going to happen.[35]

In January 2003, Russell celebrated her seventy-first birthday. She had spent a quarter-century fighting for her vision of the Columbia Gorge. There had been setbacks, of course, but she had addressed them head-on and had emerged stronger. Kevin Gorman, Michael Lang, and Jane Harris were guiding the Friends, including much of its advocacy, and its members had grown older, wealthier, and more committed to the organization—and to her. One member, for example, had alerted Russell to illegal grazing at Catherine Creek in 1987. She had investigated, fixed the problem, and formed a friendship, and his contributions grew from $35, to $1,000, to $2,000. When he died, he left the Friends $1.5 million. Beginning in 1993, other members started leaving bequests to the organization. The endowment continued to grow, and by 2003 Russell's Conservator Society was donating over $150,000 a year to the organization.[36]

Marie Hall once said that one of Russell's greatest gifts was her ability to attract and motivate talented people and organizations. She inspired and led fundraising efforts for Friends of the Gorge, the Columbia Land Trust, and the Trust for Public Land. She raised $1.3 million for TPL's Gorge Protection Fund and arranged for it to receive another million dollars in gifts. She encouraged others with influence and skills to help her, including Russ Jolley, Barbara Robinson, Doug Macy, and Dan Huntington. She set high standards and could stew when they were not met. In 2003, she wrote Dave Cannard that TPL and the Columbia Land Trust were "wimps" for not buying every property she wanted protected. "Only by taking risks and sometimes failing," she wrote, "can you protect the land that most needs to be saved."[37] But those moments of frustration were fleeting as she understood human imperfection and made allowances.

John Yeon may have understood human imperfection, but he rarely made allowances. His record of successful Gorge advocacy, nevertheless, spanned several generations. Although he did not fundraise or lead an army of supporters, he had recruited and inspired Russell. And Russell had achieved much of his dream, ensuring that the western Gorge was a national recreation area in all but name. By the close of 2003, a decade after Yeon's death and seventeen years after the act's passage, most of the Washington shoreline to Beacon Rock was in public ownership. The Trust for Public Land had bought three major subdivisions and conveyed the property to the US Forest Service.[38] Mount Zion, Mount Pleasant, and Cape Horn were protected by regulation, public ownership, and easements. Steigerwald Lake was one of three new federal wildlife refuges, preserving Yeon's goal of having a sudden transition from urban monotony to the farms, forests, and landscapes of the national scenic area.

By the end of 2003, Russell had built the framework for protecting the entire Columbia Gorge. The Trust for Public Land would ultimately purchase ninety properties, close to twenty thousand acres, in the national scenic area. More than a third of these properties were located east of Hood River, where Yeon's national recreation area would have ended. Most of TPL's lands were conveyed to the Forest Service, but many were transferred to other federal and state agencies. The Forest Service eventually acquired more than three hundred and fifty properties—almost twenty-two thousand acres—and easements over an additional two thousand acres. The agency protected another seventeen thousand acres through land exchanges, mostly with industrial forest landowners. In the seventeen years since the act had passed, the Forest Service—with assistance from the Trust for Public Land—had acquired, through purchase, easement, or exchange, over forty-one thousand acres in the national scenic area; other federal and state agencies had acquired an additional eight thousand acres.[39]

None of this included The Shire. John Yeon had clung tenaciously to his properties—The Shire, Chapman Point, and the Watzek house. Russell had wanted him to bequeath The Shire to the Friends, but Yeon—looking far into the future—was uncertain when he wrote his will that the organization would outlast Russell. Instead, working with its School of Architecture and Applied Arts, his executor Richard Brown donated The Shire and the Watzek house to the University of Oregon, along with an endowment created with proceeds from the sale of Chapman Point on the north Oregon Coast. Russell was generally pleased by Brown's decision but registered a concern that the university's management of The Shire "would emphasize educational, philosophical, and theoretical values" and "*not* necessarily stimulate activism in protection of the great Gorge landscape." The Shire had played an essential role in her campaign for legislation, and she requested access so she could continue to attract constituents to the Gorge in a contemplative setting of extraordinary beauty.[40]

In 1999, Russell had written Yeon's brother Norman to ask him to contribute to the Friends' endowment. Norman was eighty-three, a lifelong bachelor who spent half the year at his elegant Pacific Heights home overlooking San Francisco Bay and the remainder at Sunset Beach, north of Chapman Point, in a house set deep into a grove of seaside pines. Although Norman had joined the Friends' Conservators Society before John's death, Russell hardly knew him. In late September she visited him at Sunset Beach, where he was recovering from a broken leg. He had not walked his property for two years, but he reached for his cane to lead his visitor to a pond filled with mallards, through stands of wind-stunted pine, and across meadows of dune grass. They relaxed afterward in Yeon's house, reminiscing about John and the trips through the Gorge the brothers had taken with their father when he built the historic highway. In a letter to Norman Yeon a few days later, Russell described the visit as a "magical day," just as she had described her dinner with John at The Shire twenty years earlier.[41] Two weeks later, Norman Yeon revised his will.

By 2003, Nancy and Bruce Russell had bought over thirty properties in the Gorge—almost a thousand acres—and had facilitated the purchase of another dozen properties through cash donations. Their purchases surpassed those of 80 percent of the Northwest's land trusts.[42] Many of the properties— Rancho Whirligig and South 40, Major Creek and the Cherry Orchard—were in the eastern Gorge, where hardly any public land had existed in 1986. The acquisitions had been a team effort, and the experience changed the couple's relationship. They had drifted apart over the years, as Nancy concentrated on the Columbia Gorge and Bruce focused on Westwinds and investments. The process of buying those properties, along with the satisfaction of restoring the land and providing public access, had brought the couple close together again, as close as they had been exploring Lewis and Clark's trail twenty-five years earlier, bouncing along the rutted ranch roads of South Pass.

Bruce turned eighty that spring. Rheumatoid arthritis had turned his hands stiff, painful, and weak, and thinning trees at Westwinds became more chore than pleasure. He skipped the family's annual pilgrimage to Eaton's Ranch, unable to hold the reins of a galloping horse. Nancy's health was changing too. She first noticed it when she could no longer run down tennis lobs. "You're going to have to run a lot," she told her doubles partner before a match, "because there is something wrong with my legs."[43]

Chapter 8
Into the Sea, 2004–2008

Bruce's illness worsened in 2003 and through 2004. Rheumatoid arthritis is an autoimmune disease that attacks the lining of the joints and, in a small percentage of cases, causes tissue between the lungs' air sacs to scar. By early 2004, he needed bottled oxygen to breathe. He was stoic about his prognosis—less than a year to live—and focused on putting his affairs in order. Most of the couple's Gorge properties had been registered in his name to avoid vandalism and unfair county tax treatment, and Bruce transferred them to Nancy. He only asked that she not sell South 40 before his death. The Russells then set up the Columbia Gorge Environmental Foundation, chaired by Aubrey and endowed with $2 million to advance Gorge conservation and education along with Oregon's land use planning.[1]

Nancy's health also deteriorated. She lost stamina, at first almost imperceptibly. A less active person might not have noticed the difference, but it bothered her. Her hair turned almost completely gray, and her bearing, always erect and unbowed, became hunched. She stumbled occasionally. Tennis became impracticable and hiking difficult, even with the hickory staff she now used. She consulted her internist and orthopedists, and finally her stepbrother, a doctor, suggested that she see a neurologist. In the spring of 2004, after several months of tests, she was diagnosed with amyotrophic lateral sclerosis, commonly known as ALS or Lou Gehrig's disease, a neurodegenerative disease that progressively destroys the spinal cord and the brain's ability to signal and control the body's muscles. Only sixteen thousand or so Americans suffer from ALS, and their life expectancy after diagnosis is generally two to five years. In his biography about Gehrig, Jonathan Eig describes the progression of ALS from "stumbling and dropping things . . . [to when] the patient will be unable to walk, unable to sit up straight, unable to talk, unable to swallow and, finally, unable to breathe." He concludes: "While ALS leaves the victim's brain in perfect order, few diseases can so thoroughly bulldoze a person's spirit."[2]

Russell, now seventy-two, told family and friends about her diagnosis. To her closest friends, Marie Hall and her sister Betsy, Russell asked, "why me?" and was upset by her weakness, but that response lasted for the briefest of moments. Trail builder and native plant enthusiast Barbara Robinson best captured Russell's reaction, just days after the diagnosis: "It was like everything else; she was very pragmatic and practical-minded. If she was going to have ALS, she was going to get as much in order as she could in the Gorge, and she was going to continue as long as she could, and then she was going to try to set it up so that things continued."[3]

Passage of the Columbia River Gorge National Scenic Area Act and adoption of the management plan had created a framework for protecting the Columbia Gorge, but in Russell's mind uncertainty remained. Friends of the Columbia Gorge had proven to be an effective and resilient watchdog: Kevin Gorman had been executive director for six years, Michael Lang had led the group's conservation efforts for over a decade, and Gary Kahn had handled the Friends' legal work for almost twenty years. Membership was robust, and the Conservators' Society and endowment were growing. But nonprofit fundraising is primarily a peer-to-peer process, and potential donors are more likely to give a significant amount of money when a friend, not a staff member, asks. A future without Russell making the "ask" was difficult for anyone on the Friends' board and staff to imagine.

To better ensure Gorge protection, Russell knew that the Friends' funding had to rely on her less. And, she believed, it required something more. As early as 1983, Russell had wanted a land trust to focus exclusively on the Gorge. Regulation was important, but she had seen politicians ignore land use laws to avoid political heat or favor a campaign contributor. "Acquisition, acquisition, acquisition," Russell later told *Portland Monthly*, "it's the only way to preserve a place." She had considered having the Friends start its own land trust in 1987, but many believed—including some on her own board— that advocacy and acquisition seldom mixed well, as regulations sought by advocacy organizations can antagonize landowners who land trusts need to cultivate. If the Friends, for instance, prevented houses from being built in Rowena by encouraging land use designations to change from residential to grazing, land values could plummet. Few landowners would be amenable to selling their devalued land to the organization that promoted its devaluation. Russell had supported the creation of an independent land trust in the mid-1990s—the Gorge Trust—but it had bought no land and soon disbanded. Even if the advocacy and acquisition quandary was solved, some on her board wondered whether the Friends could raise sufficient funds to support both priorities, especially without Russell. And would acquisition get in the way of the Friends' primary work, which no other organization could do?[4]

Given the challenges to forming a Friends land trust, Russell had relied on the Trust for Public Land and to a lesser extent the Columbia Land Trust throughout the 1990s. TPL's perspective, however, would always be national, and Senator Hatfield's retirement in 1997 made federal funding for the Gorge harder to come by. TPL, moreover, had already acquired most of the large expensive properties that best fit its model. Russell's targets by this time were smaller and often had additional expenses such as razing buildings and removing driveways. When TPL's founder, Marty Rosen, announced his retirement in 1996, moreover, the organization accelerated its shift away from buying the iconic American landscapes that inspired Russell toward pursuing the inner-city pocket parks and parks programming that national foundations were increasingly funding. Russell left TPL's board after eight years of service. "I have watched TPL change its mission dramatically, becoming increasingly focused on smaller urban projects, [and] less focused on large open space," she explained at her last board meeting. "I think some of you have noticed, I have a passion for open space, the untrammeled landscape, [and] a particular passion for the Columbia River Gorge." Referring to her work on the Gorge, she added, "It's never going to be done."[5]

Russell had hoped that the Columbia Land Trust would focus on the National Scenic Area. She had helped the trust raise funds, donated her own, and considered leaving her properties to the trust in her will. She was pleased at its progress in the western Gorge, especially at Cape Horn, but by 2001 she believed that the trust had betrayed her. The problem had started three years earlier, when Russell and Dan Huntington were driving through the NSA's entrance at Gibbons Creek, on the north side of the Columbia. Instead of looking south across the Steigerwald Lake National Wildlife Refuge to Vista House, they looked north at a house, a barn, and a fifty-acre field where Nancy had often seen coyotes and blue herons. Wondering whether the property could be developed, Russell asked Huntington to investigate. He found that the land was owned by the Stevenson family and, as general management area, five houses could be built on it. The property was not for sale, but the Stevensons were buying a motel and looking for cash. If Russell could close a deal within three weeks, then they would sell her the field for a bargain price of $265,000. She wrote a $25,000 check to hold the property,

Huntington paid for a survey, and they and the Columbia Land Trust sought additional donors.[6]

Huntington and Russell met with a Clark County philanthropist, who agreed to have his foundation buy the property if Russell donated $25,000 and the Columbia Land Trust raised an additional $160,000. The foundation would then sell the property to the land trust for $160,000. All agreed to Russell's condition that proceeds gained from the trust's subsequent sale— presumably to the US Fish and Wildlife Service—would be used to buy other land in the Gorge. Another donor came forward, and the property was conveyed to the land trust and was sold to Fish and Wildlife for $500,000 three years later. The transaction expanded the Steigerwald refuge by fifty acres and increased the fund to buy Gorge lands more than tenfold, except the Columbia Land Trust changed its mind. It wanted leeway to spend the funds outside the national scenic area and, without notifying Russell or Huntington, asked the philanthropist to remove the condition that all proceeds be restricted to the Gorge. He did. "That's it!" Russell told Huntington. "Friends of the Columbia Gorge will create a land trust." And she changed her will to leave her properties to the Friends. If the Friends did not have a land trust in place at her death, then she would leave funds to create one.[7]

The Friends board investigated forming a land trust, but Russell's ALS diagnosis increased the urgency of both establishing the trust and growing the Friends' reserves. A land trust would need separate staff, trained in the intricacies of buying land, and a war chest to purchase property. The organization's reserves would have to be large enough to smooth the transition to a board that could raise $600,000 a year in operating costs. Russell was clear-eyed about the challenge. Several million dollars had to be raised. She had only a handful of years left and recognized that she was losing strength and stamina. To her surprise, and relief, the Yeon family intervened.

Norman Yeon died in early 2004, at age eighty-eight, from head injuries related to a fall, and Nancy Russell learned that he had changed his will just days after she had visited him five years earlier. Both the Friends and the Trust for Public Land received significant bequests: TPL was given Yeon's hundred and ten acres at Sunset Beach—"one of the largest pristine slices of private land on the Oregon coast," according to the *Oregonian*—to convey into public ownership, and the Friends received over $4 million, half of Yeon's remaining estate, reportedly the largest unrestricted gift to a conservation organization in Oregon history. "We need to use it [the gift] as efficiently as possible," Russell told the *Oregonian*, "but we also need to use it soon because the threats get worse every year." The Friends used the money to create Friends of the Columbia Gorge Land Trust, to build its endowment, and to fund "special projects." Russell was elected the first trustee of the land trust.[8]

Russell immersed herself in the work of the trust, which she believed should occupy a unique role of buying properties that other organizations and public agencies avoided—land that had high political or project costs or that risked bad publicity. To address the conflict between advocacy and acquisition, the Friends board adopted internal rules that prohibited the land trust from pursuing properties where the organization actively opposed development.[9] Russell saw an immediate need for the trust to act at Cape Horn, and continuing roles for the Trust for Public Land and, despite her recent irritation, the Columbia Land Trust.

By the spring of 2004, the US Forest Service, TPL, and the Columbia Land Trust had purchased thirty-five properties at or near Cape Horn, and most of the plateau's four-mile-long ridge was now publicly owned. Only three properties interfered with a seven-mile loop trail, two of them still owned by Dave Cannard, who continued to fight the federal appraisal process. His efforts to boost his properties' value ultimately failed though, and his finances deteriorated. The Russells loaned him $25,000 so he could hold on to the property and sell to the Forest Service in June. In lieu of interest, Nancy and Bruce asked him to donate to the Friends. In the end, Cannard made a modest profit on his sale and retained a small portion of land outside the national scenic area.[10]

While Cannard was closing on the sale, the Friends sponsored a hike on the still unauthorized trail. Toward the end of their trek, before the trail spilled out onto a country lane that led back to the trailhead a mile away, the hikers were confronted by landowners who accused the group of trespassing on their land for several hundred feet. The land was owned by Stevenson Heirs, a corporation that represented twenty-six heirs of the original Stevenson homesteading family (not related to the Stevensons who had owned Steigerwald).[11]

The attorney for Stevenson Heirs followed up with a warning letter, and several Private Property/No Trespassing signs were posted to deter hikers. Huntington arranged a meeting with one of the heirs, who told him that the family distrusted both the Friends and government and did not want the public crossing its land. He then met with more heirs to present his vision for Cape Horn in a slide show, but resistance continued. Huntington persisted, meeting with most of the heirs after a few weeks, but grim faces surrounded him and his audience was unmoved. On the spur of the moment, he offered $100,000 for a permanent, nonrevocable trail easement. "My rationale," he later explained, "was that there were countless ways to raise $100,000 but only one way to complete a loop trail at Cape Horn."[12] The owners agreed, and Huntington drafted the easement over an acre of land and three hundred feet of trail. The easement became one of the first purchases of the Columbia Gorge Environmental Foundation, the Russell family's foundation.

The seven-mile Cape Horn Trail was now entirely in Forest Service or nonprofit ownership, but neither Russell nor Huntington was satisfied. In two places on top of the plateau the trail was forced away from the rim by homesites, each developed with houses at the cliff's edge. Hikers could still enjoy what was now Washington's premier trail in the Gorge, but they had to detour several hundred yards inland for a combined half-mile. One detour skirted Ed Cleveland's residence; the other, a quarter mile north along the rim, was owned by the Collins family, long-time Cape Horn residents. Huntington warned Kevin Gorman that the Camas-Washougal real estate market was "VERY HOT" and was concerned that the Collins's modest house would be bought and developed into a mansion to rival Cleveland's. He worried that both properties might sell before they could be purchased for park and trail purposes. Russell worried that she would die before she could "put our trail where it belongs."[13]

Bruce died in September 2004. A few weeks earlier, he had sent "suggestions" to his family regarding his service, writing that having an unplanned wedding was "CHAOS, but think of an unplanned funeral!" Bruce had always been "bored to death by [the] cocktail party chit chat" that he believed funerals inspired, so he proposed that only immediate family be invited, along with a few favored nieces and two former secretaries. The small group gathered later that month on a cool fall afternoon under Westwinds' large pin oak near the gardens and pasture where Bruce had toiled each afternoon and where a few flowers still bloomed. At his request, some of the children's books he had written and illustrated were displayed, along with a favorite painting and a cartoon he had drawn for Nancy's fortieth birthday. In the cartoon, Nancy ascends, Phoenix-like, from flames of Ace bandages toward a tennis-racquet-shaped sun, a crown on her head and angel wings on her back. Bruce also had asked that his children read a selection of his writings, including one that recounted his first sail with Nancy, fifty years earlier, in a gale at Elk Lake.[14]

Perhaps it was Bruce's aesthetic sense and appreciation for nature that had drawn Nancy to him so many years earlier, or their shared interest in the region's history, from his great-grandparents' Oregon Trail journeys, to his stake in the Olds, Wortman and King department store, to the couple's research on the Corps of Discovery. Bruce's intelligence, curiosity, humor, and deep love for their children strengthened their bond, and they were proud of each other's accomplishments and enjoyed each other's company. Later in their marriage, buying land together—especially in the eastern Gorge, with its spring wildflowers and sunsets and where history and culture are visible and vibrant—had become a shared joy. Nancy had learned to work around the settled aspects of Bruce's personality just as he had accepted her round-the-clock concentration on the Gorge. "Bruce was strong enough for her," Marie Hall said. "They brought out each other's strengths . . . and were both born with gifts that they did not waste." Bruce's greatest regret in dying, he told Aubrey, was that he was leaving Nancy "alone to face her own certain fate in battling ALS."[15]

Throughout 2005, Nancy Russell remained active in the Friends and continued to spend time in the Gorge. "Nancy is committed to ensuring that our organization will be even stronger in the future than it is today," Kevin Gorman wrote in the Friends newsletter. She could still drive herself to the Gorge, where she walked short distances. On April 6, she and Barbara Robinson made it a third of the way up to Rowena Crest, finding native bunch grasses, glacier lilies, shooting stars, chocolate lilies, monkey flowers, and gold-backed ferns. Two weeks later, they walked at Catherine Creek to see early blooms of *Lewisia rediviva* and *Clarkia gracilis* and drove to the base of the Cherry Orchard preserve to see showy stands of death camas, grandma's pincushions with their pink, pinlike stamens, and the lavender stalks of Thomas Nuttall's larkspur. In May, Robinson and Angie Moore, a Friends volunteer recruited by Nancy, took her to the Upper Klickitat River, where they enjoyed lady slipper orchids and fields of paintbrush, lupine, and balsamroot, a kaleidoscope of orange, lavender, and gold. They drove to Dalles Mountain Ranch to see the red buds and yellow blooms of David Douglas's buckwheat and the snow-capped Cascade peaks. Nothing made

Nancy happier, Robinson later recalled, than visiting places that she loved with people she cared about.[16]

Later that year, Aubrey took his mother to the eastern Gorge. Her condition was worsening, and they toured by car except for a short walk near South 40 to admire the roadside flowers. As they prepared to return to Portland, Russell needed to use a restroom, but there were none in the area.

> But Mom was not worried about that as . . . there was a large sheltering oak tree just off of the road. I stopped the car and she got out and proceeded to conceal herself amongst the low limbs of the oak. Soon though, I heard her call out to me in a laughing voice that she couldn't get up! She was caught with her pants down and was laughing at herself and smiling because she didn't have the strength to stand back upright after 'watering' her tree. I discretely helped her get out of her ridiculous situation . . . and she took a good deal of pleasure from the silly situation that her ALS had gotten her into.[17]

Nancy Russell always wanted to be outside, where she was "happy, alive and well in the sunshine," her sister Betsy recalled, and the progress of the disease could be charted by how she maneuvered around Westwinds.[18] At Bruce's backyard service, she had leaned on a hiking staff, which she soon replaced with a sturdy cane, then a walker. When Westwinds' spongy lawn absorbed the walker's wheels, Nancy used a golf cart whose wide tires allowed her to float above the grass and visit the far reaches of the property, usually with grandchildren as company. Friends visited each day, and she drove them—the family's German shepherd Lexi trotting behind—to see the garden, a favorite peach tree Bruce had planted, or the flock of sheep that Aubrey tended. Kevin consulted her daily on Gorge business, and I checked in each week. After one autumn visit, we sat out on her patio by the front door. The air was warm, and we were laughing about the antics, thirty years earlier, of a pompous congressman who had opposed the National Scenic Area Act. Nancy then shifted the conversation and told me, without a hint of irony, how lucky she was and what a wonderful and full life she had led.

In November 2005, the Friends celebrated its twenty-fifth anniversary and honored Nancy at the Grand Ballroom of the Portland Art Museum. She had worried whether her voice muscles would allow a short speech and whether she could climb the stairs to the stage, but she was determined not to let anyone down. Four hundred and fifty people turned out, welcomed by businessman and philanthropist Al Jubitz, a family friend and Friends donor. After being feted by Senator Ron Wyden and Congressman Earl Blumenauer, she slowly climbed the steps. Her voice held. She explained how in 1980 she had "no idea that anyone would be opposed to 'saving the Gorge.' It seemed to me at the beginning that the road to federal legislation . . . would be as easy as pie." Her naiveté disappeared, she remembered, as opposition groups had sprung up, inspired by "a rabble rouser named Chuck Cushman." She explained how the Friends met the challenge and ended, as she had thousands of times before, with a plea:

> My fondest hope is that you will continue to be involved and that you introduce your children and grandchildren to the Gorge so they will be interested, too. All the public land and all the protective rules that we now have could be swept away very quickly, without the kind of active constituency you are a part of. Land preservation is always precarious. Fortunately, we have in Friends of the Columbia Gorge, a strong, fiscally sound, responsible organization with an outstanding staff that is well equipped to lead the Gorge effort for the *next* 25 years.[19]

Nancy received an extended standing ovation and was swarmed by admirers.

Seven years earlier, Congress had created a special purchase unit outside the national scenic area so that Dave Cannard's properties could be acquired. Dan Huntington had ensured that the boundary had been drawn widely and included lands owned by the Collins family. With Huntington's and Russell's assistance, the Columbia Land Trust had purchased a portion of the Collins property, which it sold to the Forest Service in 2001. While that property bridged a critical gap in the Cape Horn trail, it was located several hundred yards back from the rim and behind the home owned by Jack and Irma Collins. Russell and Huntington believed that an ideal trail would run on the edge of the cliff, thirteen hundred feet above the Columbia and through the Collins's homesite. In 2004, with the real estate market rising and her health failing, Russell urged Huntington to negotiate for this remaining property: thirty-six pastoral acres that included the Collins's modest home, two simple barns, and world-class views upriver to Beacon Rock and beyond. By late summer 2005, he had succeeded. The option terms favored the Collins,

Nancy Russell, with her sister Betsy Neighbor Hammond and supporter Al Jubitz on
November 12, 2005, celebrating Friends of the Columbia Gorge's twenty-fifth anniversary.
FOCG archives.

permitting them to live in their home for the rest of their lives. The agreement's initial one-year term could be extended for another twenty-four years,
as long as Russell paid the family $20,000 a year and covered their property
taxes. The purchase price was $2 million.[20] Russell pledged a million dollars
towards the purchase and committed herself to finding the other million.

With the option secure, Russell set her eyes on the last property required
for a perfect trail: Ed Cleveland's estate, located a quarter-mile to the south
and similarly perched on the rim. Of all the houses in the Columbia Gorge,
this was the one she most resented. The four-acre property included a
two-story, fifty-seven-hundred-square-foot residence, a thirty-six-hundred-
square-foot barn and attached apartment, a garage, a bomb shelter (with five
years of food), and several outbuildings. The property also demonstrated, to
Russell's continuing displeasure, why her conservation campaign had been
needed, year after year, for a quarter century. Cleveland's house was the
first one built at Rim View Estates, two years after Skamania County had
illegally permitted the sixteen-lot subdivision. The subdivision and house
had served—along with Colonel Rizor's development—as catalysts for legislation, which Ed Cleveland had opposed at the congressional hearings in
Washington, DC, where he had testified that it was not in Gorge residents'

Edgar Cleveland's deck. FOCG archives.

self-interest to ruin views. The Russells' loan had allowed TPL to buy the twelve undeveloped lots that surrounded the Cleveland house before the National Scenic Area Act passed and then to sell them to the Forest Service. Russell later had to stop the Forest Service from selling some of these lots to Cleveland for a private pasture. In 1999, Russell had bought the only other developed lot in the subdivision, tore down the house, and sold the property to the Forest Service. She was reminded of these events every time she drove through the Gorge and saw the house, its silhouette, or lights. She was concerned, she once confided to me, that she could not enjoy the Gorge as she once had, because she found herself focusing more on its blemishes than its beauty. And it was the Cleveland compound on which she most focused.[21]

Over the years, Russell had pressed the Trust for Public Land to buy the Cleveland house. It became a ritual in TPL's Portland office to assign this task to each new employee, emphasizing its importance but harboring little hope of success. After all, Ed Cleveland did not want to sell, and even if he did the cost of buying the property would be prohibitive. Those costs, moreover, would be lost in a sale to the Forest Service, which avoided buying developed property. By 1996 I was supervising TPL's region and would soon oversee its land acquisitions nationally, so the Cleveland challenge fell to Geoff Roach, Oregon's new state director. That March, Huntington heard that Cleveland wanted to sell, so Roach met with him. It was soon apparent, though, that he wanted nearly twice as much as his property was worth, so TPL decided to wait.[22]

Eight years later, at the end of 2004, Cleveland listed his property for sale at $1.5 million. Appraisers hired by TPL believed the fair market value was less than $1 million. Far apart on price, Cleveland stopped returning Roach's calls, and Roach stopped calling. Russell, now almost a year after her ALS diagnosis, called Roach periodically to offer encouragement. In May 2005, TPL discovered that Cleveland had just rejected a $1.35 million offer from a well-known California author. Cleveland—under pressure, he said, from his broker—had countered at $1.425 million, but the author was on a book tour and had not responded. When TPL offered $1.4 million, Cleveland rejected it.[23]

Meanwhile, Dan Huntington and Nancy Russell had taken Al Jubitz to see the property, where they explained their plan. If TPL's negotiations with Cleveland proved successful, then it would assign its contract to the Friends of the Columbia Gorge Land Trust, which would purchase the property, raze the buildings, remove the driveway, and restore the land. The land trust, however, would need money to buy the property, as Norman Yeon's estate was still in probate. Huntington called Jubitz the next day to ask if he would provide a bridge loan. Jubitz immediately agreed and pledged a $100,000 gift as well. With this new backing, Russell and Gorman pressed TPL to increase its offer. TPL proposed $1.5 million, and Cleveland accepted and signed the necessary documents. Two weeks later, he declared bankruptcy, which froze all transactions involving his properties. Cleveland's filings revealed that he had $35 million in liabilities, only $21 million in assets, and over sixty creditors. The deal appeared dead. The land trust's attorney advised it to "start looking at other properties." There were no properties as important as this one, however, and over several months TPL and the Friends' attorneys persuaded the bankruptcy judge to approve the transaction, allowing the land trust to make its first purchase.[24]

The Friends prepared a $4 million Cape Horn capital campaign to repay Al Jubitz's loan, match Russell's million-dollar pledge, and complete restoration of both properties. As long as the organization was engaged in the fundraising campaign, some board members suggested raising money to build an overlook below the existing Cleveland house and name it for Russell. The proposal, however, presented Gorman with a dilemma. People had wanted to celebrate Russell's achievements for at least eighteen years, but she did not want signs and memorials cluttering up the Gorge, especially if they called attention to her. So he approached Russell carefully about the idea. What if the Friends built a simple overlook, one that fit into the surrounding landscape, perhaps designed by Doug Macy? Maybe, he suggested, there could be a small plaque that told the story of Rim View Estates and Cape Horn. Russell had "lost a little feistiness by then," Gorman recalled, and he also may have "left a few things out." In any case, she agreed to an overlook and a small sign to educate future generations about Cape Horn's history. But naming the overlook after Russell? "I never asked her," Gorman recalled years later, "because I didn't want to hear the answer."[25]

Russell's health continued to deteriorate. By 2006, her walker had given way to a wheelchair, and while she could ride in the golf cart she no longer had the strength to drive it. Friends and family drove her to the Gorge, but she could only leave the car in a heavy, motorized wheelchair that she controlled with toggles. Catherine Creek's paved paths and the Mosier Twin Tunnels, with its level roadbed, were ideal, and Nancy visited the tunnels often, savoring them as she never had expected when she encouraged SOAR and other disability organizations to join the effort to restore them. One afternoon when Sally and her daughters accompanied Nancy to the tunnels, seven-year-old Isabelle requested a ride on her grandmother's lap. The wheelchair rocketed forward with its extra passenger, the family's laughter echoing off the canyon wall.[26]

Soon, even sitting for an hour became painful, and Russell was forced to curtail her outings. The family moved a hospital bed into a room that looked out over the garden and pasture and the Coast Range beyond. Aubrey hung birdfeeders outside the window so his mother could enjoy the nuthatches, warblers, and downy woodpeckers, and he got in touch with Bridger Konkel, a Wyoming artist and Eaton's Ranch neighbor whose work Nancy enjoyed. Konkel agreed to create ten paintings of her favorite Gorge scenes, and Aubrey was soon chauffeuring the painter to Cape Horn, then to Catherine Creek and Major Creek, up the Klickitat River, down to the Cherry Orchard Preserve, and over to Rancho Whirligig and South 40. Konkel worked quickly, and before long the Gorge had come to Nancy Russell.[27]

In 2006, Russell started using a BiPAP (bilevel positive airway pressure) device to help her breathe. By then, she was mostly housebound, usually in a hospital bed, attended by caregivers who were smart, interesting, and cared about her and the Gorge. Marie Hall and Russell's family—Betsy, Aubrey, Wendy, and Sally and their children—were there as well, with Aubrey so ubiquitous that Hall called him his mother's "second skin."[28] Betsy rented a piano for her sister's bedroom and invited friends who were professional musicians to perform the music of George Gershwin, Irving Berlin, and Cole Porter. Friends dropped by every day. Macy Wall, whom Russell had babysat in St. Croix, and his wife Pat sang, played the guitar, and reminisced about Cane Garden and island nightclubs. Pat Wall was on the Garden Club of America's conservation committee and was conservation chair for the Portland Garden Club, and she updated Russell on club activities. Barbara Robinson brought photographs of wildflower blooms in the eastern Gorge, and Kevin kept Nancy abreast of Gorge issues. Nancy and I shared laughs as I reminded her when she had a flat tire on the interstate on a stormy night and a good Samaritan—terrified by the trucks roaring by just inches away and blinded by headlights and spray—changed a tire, but the wrong one; and when only one person came to hear her presentation at an eastern Washington college and she assembled her projector, microphone, speakers, and screen, gave an enthusiastic presentation, then disassembled and packed everything away; and when we watched a medicine ball-sized boulder crash down the hillside toward us on the historic highway, snapping tree limbs and crushing saplings, only to bounce off the lip of the embankment at the last second and sail over the Volvo's hood as the boulder and Russell—unfazed—continued on their respective paths.

With help from friends and the Friends' staff, Russell spent time working on Gorge issues through late 2006 and into 2007. She discovered that Skamania County had been using property she had bought for Cape Horn trailhead parking as a park-and-ride facility so residents could leave their cars and catch a bus to Vancouver. While the county had never thought to ask her permission to use the property, Russell was happy to work out a deal. Dan Huntington negotiated a below-market sale that required the county to share the lot with hikers in perpetuity and implement $14,000 of trailhead-related upgrades, including an information kiosk, trailhead signs, sidewalks, a striped crosswalk, and a toolshed to store trail maintenance equipment.[29]

In 2007, the Friends staff helped Russell fit the final piece into the Cape Horn puzzle. Several years earlier, after learning of her diagnosis, Seattle businessman and veteran mountaineer Anthony Hovey—a vigorous eighty-one-year-old who still climbed the long steep trail on Dog Mountain—had written Russell to assure her of his continuing support. In February, with

Russell confined to bed, Kevin Gorman invited him to visit Cape Horn. At the plateau, Gorman and Jane Harris explained the history of Rim View Estates and the need to match Russell's million-dollar pledge so the trail could be located on the edge of the cliff. In a quiet voice, Hovey said, "I'd like to match that." They drove to Westwinds, gathered around Russell, and told her the news. It was the first time she and Hovey had met in person, and both were thrilled. "It always amazed her," Gorman recalled, "that some-body else would care as much as she cared." He continued: "It really started to hit her, the impact that she was having on other people."[30]

Russell was unable to leave her house for much of 2007 and 2008. After waking one morning in early September 2008, however, she told her lead caregiver, Polly Morrow, that she wanted to go to the Gorge. They had periodically discussed this possibility, and Morrow readily agreed, saying it would take a few days to arrange. "No," Russell responded. "I want to go today."[31] That afternoon—dressed in her nightgown, wrapped in blue and white blankets, her BiPAP machine helping her breathe—Russell was strapped into a gurney by two burly Metro West attendants and placed in their ambulance. Morrow and a colleague joined her in back, and Aubrey and his three-year-old son Everett followed in the family van. The caravan set off just before three o'clock.

Twenty minutes later, they crossed the Glenn Jackson Bridge, and were soon greeted by "Welcome to the Columbia River Gorge National Scenic Area" signs. Twenty-six years earlier, when the bridge was dedicated, the region was in the last leg of the race to protect the Columbia Gorge, a race that often seemed destined to be lost. But in 2008, instead of a landscape of factories and houses, Nancy Russell and her entourage saw grass fields opening to the north, sylvan hills and pastures ahead, and to the southeast a spectacular panorama of wetlands, river, basalt cliffs, and Douglas-fir for-ests, with Vista House and Crown Point in the distance, above Steigerwald Lake National Wildlife Refuge's marshes. During the final stretch of that long race, which had begun a century earlier when the Portland Chamber of Commerce proposed that the south bank be designated a national park, Russell had learned how to build and direct a major conservation move-ment. She had learned how to encourage cautious politicians, and when to use campaign contributions and endorsements—or repudiation—to persuade. It was over Steigerwald Lake that she had formed a close rela-tionship with Senator Hatfield, who would pass the National Scenic Area

Act despite determined opposition, force President Reagan's approval, and direct more than $75 million in federal dollars to buy parks and natural areas.[32]

The ambulance lumbered toward Cape Horn, passing through the pastures on Mount Pleasant and Mount Zion, and pulled into Rim Drive. The entire thousand-acre Cape Horn plateau, piece by piece, had been placed into public or land trust ownership, and the houses had disappeared, or would soon. The Cleveland house had been demolished, except for its foundation, and for the first time in twenty-five years Russell had an unimpeded view east. The ambulance attendants muscled her gurney down a steep, root-studded deer trail to where the overlook would be located. Morrow later recalled Russell's joy, her face glowing with delight at the view ahead and the bulldozed buildings behind. For several minutes the group was silent, out of breath and mesmerized, until Aubrey asked his mother what she thought. It is a "fabulous public viewpoint," she whispered. When he asked if they should return home, her answer was unequivocal. "East," she said. "Go east."[33]

They headed toward Beacon Rock, passing new signs pointing to Cape Horn trailhead parking and the county's park-and-ride. They passed the entrance to The Shire, where John Yeon had wooed Russell and where Russell had met Harriet Burgess and Don Clark and had cultivated donors, reporters, and politicians, showing them what the Gorge could become. Much like Thoreau's Walden Pond and Teddy Roosevelt's Pelican Island, The Shire was the epicenter for a movement that inspired an original type of protection for an area that was both complex and, as Yeon had constantly stressed, nationally significant.

The ambulance passed miles of riverfront where Skamania County subdivisions had been proposed or considered in the 1980s: Rizor's Columbia Riverfront Estates, Hidden Harbor subdivision and marina, and St. Cloud Ranch. All had been thwarted, usually by a combination of Friends' litigation and high-risk purchases by the Trust for Public Land. St. Cloud had been purchased with the Russells' first interest-free $200,000 loan, which they had borrowed. Serendipity played a role as well: Senator Jackson's unexpected death left St. Cloud's well-connected owner without political purchase, and the timely intervention of a rainbow and a pair of eagles had helped defeat Hidden Harbor. In many ways, Colonel Rizor and the Skamania County leadership had been ideal adversaries—uncompromising and belligerent. They had underestimated and belittled Russell, with Rizor labeling her a communist and the county prosecutor accusing her of "Looking for Love in All the Wrong Places."[34] They dismissed her, until it was too late.

At Beacon Rock, near the state park entrance where the neon light of the Beacon Rock tavern had once shimmered against the monolith, Polly Morrow and Aubrey gave Russell sunglasses and a hat, and the ambulance attendants wheeled her to the Columbia shoreline. Looming above, across the river, was the Mount Hood National Forest; Saint Peter's Dome, a large basalt pinnacle favored by rock climbers; Yeon Mountain, named for John Yeon's father; and four-thousand-foot-high Nesmith Point, which Russell had hiked dozens of times to admire its tiger lilies. The sixteen-mile shoreline from Steigerwald Lake to Beacon Rock had been the Gorge's most endangered segment during the 1980s, containing not a single public parcel and no public access to the river. After two decades of work by the Trust for Public Land—with Russell bolstering its board through fundraising, personal loans, and ghost-written letters from Senator Hatfield—most of the land was now owned by the public, including three national wildlife refuges. "In every project there was a constellation of partners, and in every one of those constellations, the brightest star was Nancy," TPL's senior vice president Alan Front said. "From the very beginning, we at TPL were foot soldiers, but she really orchestrated and inspired the campaign to protect these lands."[35]

The group drove east, past Bonneville Dam, where John Yeon's advocacy for a flat power rate had kept industrialization at bay, and past Skamania Lodge, built with federal dollars from the National Scenic Area Act and now the county's largest private employer. They cruised past the Rock Creek auditorium where Russell's tires had been slashed during a contentious congressional hearing, passed through the small town of Bingen, and stopped at Catherine Creek, one of Russell's favorite wildflower areas, whose path—built by the US Forest Service—was able to accommodate Russell's gurney. The Trust for Public land had bought the two-thousand-acre Catherine Creek Ranch in 1985 with another no-interest loan from the Russells, betting that legislation would pass. Morrow tucked an extra blanket around Nancy who, laughing and chatting, pointed out familiar landmarks as an evening breeze blew whitecaps on the river.

By six-thirty the caravan—which now seemed more like a parade—was back on the road, heading east with a quick stop at Major Creek Ranch, the five properties that Russell had assembled and then persuaded the Forest Service to buy. She had torn down all the buildings but one, where a ninety-year-old woman had retained a lifetime lease. The tenant had recently died, and the Forest Service was required — by its sale contract with Russell — to raze the house. The woman's sons did not want to leave, however, and had accused the government of being heavy-handed. It could take years to process the eviction. Knowing how much the property mattered to Russell, Barbara Robinson and Nancy's realtor had protested the situation to Dan Harkenrider, the NSA manager, explaining that Russell did not have long to live. Harkenrider was fond of Russell, and the agency moved quickly. The sons left, and the house was torn down days before the ambulance carrying Russell arrived.[36] The attendants opened the back doors and ratcheted up the gurney so she could take in a landscape that Lewis and Clark might recognize two centuries after they had camped at the mouth of Major Creek.

Continuing east across the Klickitat River, the ambulance entered the town of Lyle. To the south, Lyle Point jutted into the river, creating one of the narrowest sections of the Columbia in the Gorge. Lyle Point was sacred to the Yakama Nation, part fishing site and part burial ground where ancestors had been interred after smallpox endemics had swept through the region. Klickitat County had approved an East Coast real estate syndicate's request to build a thirty-three-house gated subdivision on the thirty-five-acre peninsula, and the developers had already built a massive bridge over the railroad and an extensive road system.[37] The Yakama Nation had fought back with litigation but were unsuccessful, as the proposed gated community was within Lyle's urban area and exempt from the National Scenic Area Act. Conservationists had organized protest marches at Washington's and Oregon's capitols and at the offices of the realtors who listed the lots. In 2000 and 2002, the Trust for Public land had managed to buy the entire subdivision. It held Lyle Point for over seven years before conveying it to the Yakama Nation, despite heated opposition from the Klickitat County Commission. When Russell had begun her Gorge campaign in 1980, there was virtually no public ownership in the eastern Gorge. By the time her ambulance rolled through Lyle in September 2008, her efforts — and her work through the Friends and TPL — had created a comprehensive public, tribal, and land trust base. In Washington, those lands included twelve thousand acres of some of the most important scenic, botanic, cultural, and historic lands in the Columbia Gorge, including Miller Island, Dalles Mountain Ranch, Catherine Creek Ranch, Major Creek, and the Cherry Orchard Preserve.

The caravan continued east a few more miles until the group reached the Columbia Hills, where the ambulance turned south, crossed the Columbia,

Nancy Russell with her son Aubrey at South 40 on her last trip through the Gorge. Mt. Adams in background. Russell archives.

and headed west along the Historic Columbia River Highway, motoring up Sam Lancaster's two sets of horseshoe curves—almost a perfect figure eight—to Rowena Crest at McCall Point. Russell and her gurney were again unloaded so she could see, across the Columbia and a thousand feet below, the Klickitat River, where she had bought several properties for parks, Lyle Point, and the Cherry Orchard Preserve.

Thirty minutes later, they turned into South 40, the last stop, climbing a steep hill on ruts that cut through native grasses, their stems caressing the sides of the ambulance. At the summit, Russell was helped out into the sun, which was slipping behind the distant palisades and casting the apple orchards, hundreds of feet below, in gilded light and long shadows. The snow-covered peaks of Mount Adams and Mount Hood jutted into the blue evening sky, but dusk held the day's warmth and the breeze had dissipated. They had left Portland four and a half hours earlier, but no one seemed tired. Russell had shed her hat but retained her sunglasses and her enthusiasm. Pointing from her gurney where the mobile home had stood, she described how its aluminum overhang had reflected a harsh glare for miles. She laughed as she described how Rancho Whirligig's chorus line of Clorox bottles would shake, rattle, and roll in the spring breeze. And she helped the group see where the Mosier Twin Tunnels bored through the basalt cliffs. Two years earlier, a hundred thousand people had visited the tunnels, on foot, bicycles, and in wheelchairs. The Oregon Department of Transportation, which had overseen the historic highway's destruction and had been John Yeon's and Gertrude Glutsch Jensen's most implacable foe, now wanted Mitchell Point's "Tunnel of Many Vistas" to be restored and supported designating the highway a World Heritage Site.[38]

The ambulance left South 40 at almost eight o'clock. An hour later, it passed the Sandy River Delta at the entrance to the Gorge, where Lewis and Clark had walked, where Paul Martin and his family had suffered, where Russell had defeated the port of entry, and which the Trust for Public Land had bought and conveyed to the Forest Service. By nine-thirty, they were back at Westwinds. Where, in sixteen days, Nancy Russell died.

A public memorial service was held a month later at the Portland Art Museum. By coincidence, the museum was showing *Wild Beauty*, an exhibit of Gorge photographs taken from 1867 to 1957 by legendary photographers of the American West, including Carleton Watkins and Edward Sheriff Curtis. These men knew that the scenes they were recording were vanishing; in the words of a newspaper critic, the loss was "simply the way things happen in this world." But in the museum's Grand Ballroom, six hundred guests celebrated one woman's efforts to reverse the trend, at least in the Columbia Gorge. They were welcomed by Nancy Russell's favorite songs, led by "Don't Fence Me In." In his eulogy, Aubrey described his mother's determination, enthusiasm, and knowledge of the Gorge, especially its botany, and he extolled her ability to organize, the physical strength and stamina that allowed her to plow through hard work, and her tenacity. "Mom could push and push like the River," he said, "her gravity was her belief in a special place, and she could wear down the hills that rose up in her path. She shifted her course enough to pass through, but she would not fail to move forward."[39]

Three years after Russell's death, in August 2011, a crowd gathered to dedicate the Cape Horn overlook, designed by Doug Macy and located just below where the Cleveland deck had stood. The design was modest and practical: two concentric walls, an outer loop enclosing an inner half-circle that opens to an extraordinary upriver view. Macy's design encourages visitors to sit on the waist-high walls, constructed of dry-stacked local basalt, while strategically placed blocks and pillars allow children to peek over the outer wall. At the entrance, a small sign recounts the efforts to protect Cape

Horn. The overlook was never formally named, but all the guidebooks and newspapers, and hikers and locals too, call it the Nancy Russell Overlook.

Nancy Russell Overlook, looking east. Image by Peter Marbach.

Acknowledgments

Ten years ago, a small group discussed how to present Nancy Russell's campaign to protect the Columbia Gorge to a wider audience. The group comprised Russell's longtime friends Nancie McGraw and Mary Bishop; 1000 Friends of Oregon founder Henry Richmond; Friends of the Columbia Gorge executive director Kevin Gorman; Nancy's son, Aubrey Russell; and myself.

After several meetings, the group—as a formal committee—asked me to write a book, assuming a two- or three-year commitment. A decade later, I'm grateful for their patience, as well as their stories, advice, and funding. I am especially appreciative of Nancie's kindness and generosity, Henry's unflagging enthusiasm, Mary's candor, Aubrey's objectivity and diligence, Kevin's diplomacy and insights, and everyone's goodwill and humor.

The committee's support allowed me to hire Marianne Keddington-Lang as an editor. Marianne was indispensable. She is superbly gifted, and her background—helping lead two Northwest presses and teaching at Stevenson High School in the Gorge—was ideal for this project.

Nancy Russell's extended family and dozens of friends illuminated her childhood and college years, her marriage and motherhood, and how she confronted ALS. Her sister, Betsy Neighbor Hammond, and Aubrey deserve special thanks for the innumerable hours that they spent with me, patiently explaining events that had occurred decades earlier. I am grateful for all of the afternoons that Marie Hall, one of Nancy's closest friends, devoted to answering my questions and recounting stories that were revealing, funny, and painful. I cannot thank Marie and Barbara Robinson, who was Nancy's confidant, hiking partner, trail builder, and "eyesore" scout, enough. Betsy, Aubrey, Marie, and Barbara—and many other friends and family members—painted an authentic portrait of Nancy that was neither adorned nor simplistic.

The Columbia Gorge is a complicated place. While my career was grounded there, I learned a great deal from Dan Huntington on the intricacies of the Cape Horn Trail; from Kathy Durbin on the Northwest's "timber wars" and on the Warm Springs tribe's efforts to build a casino east of Hood River in *Bridging a Great Divide: the Battle for the Columbia River Gorge*; from John Eliot Allen and Marjorie and Scott Burns on geology in their seminal book *Cataclysms on the Columbia: the Great Missoula Floods*; from the many people, mostly Native American, too numerous to list here—but certainly including Bobbie Conner, Antone Minthorn, and George Aguilar Sr.—who shared their histories of the Gorge, as well as Robert Boyd for *People of The Dalles: the Indians of Wascopam Mission*; from Roberta Ulrich for *Empty Nets: Indians, Dams, and the Columbia River*; from Katy Barber, for *Death of Celilo Falls*; and from my good friend Chuck Sams. Thank you all.

This book describes the work of Friends of the Columbia Gorge and the Trust for Public Land in the Gorge. Without generous assistance from Kevin Gorman, Michael Lang, Dan Bell, and Burt Edwards at the Friends, and from TPL's former staff, especially Geoff Roach, Nelson Mathews, Nelson Lee, Chris Beck, and Alan Front—and current staffer Tom Tyner—files would have remained inaccessible, foggy memories would not have cleared, and these stories could not have been told. Thanks also to Kerry Tymchuk and Sheri Neal at the Oregon Historical Society (which has its own compelling Gorge stories), for holding and dispersing the funds raised to make this book possible.

I am indebted to Aubrey Russell (again) and Richard Brown, who gave me access to basements full of information about Nancy Russell and John Yeon, shared their own stories, and never refused requests. Aubrey, in particular, spent countless hours searching through family correspondence, history, and images, and introduced me to distant relatives.

This book benefited from the work of other interviewers. Hillary Larson's extensive interviews with Nancy Russell in 2006 and 2007 were invaluable. Bob Peirce generously shared his research, including a dozen interviews. Kevin Gorman's interviews with Nancy Russell and others were essential, and his interview with Antoinette Hatfield is a treasure. Thanks also to Archives West and Archives of American Art's Northwest Oral History Project for their interviews with Chuck Williams and John Yeon and, again, to the Oregon Historical Society for its extraordinary collection.

Writing can be isolating. Fortunately, several friends reviewed drafts of the manuscript and encouraged me through a long process. In addition to committee members, I want to thank Janet Wainwright, Robert Liberty, and Rodger Nichols—fellow Gorge commissioners all. Janet, the movie is in your hands. Thanks also to Kerry Tymchuk and Steve Olson, writers whose own books I greatly admire, for their support at key moments.

Finally, I am eternally grateful for the diligence, skill, and enthusiasm of the entire staff at Oregon State University Press, starting with Tom Booth, whose advice at a Portland coffeehouse ten years ago was prescient. Kim Hogeland, the press's acquisitions editor, led me through a daunting (to me) and rewarding process with professionalism and cheer. Micki Reaman, the press's editorial, design, and production manager, produced a beautiful book. Micki also borrowed, from *Orion* magazine, Tara Rae Miner, who brought a keen eye and sharp scalpel to her copyediting responsibilities. And thanks to Marty Brown, the press's ever-diplomatic marketing manager, who worked overtime to find a title that resonated, created a solid marketing plan, and hired Erin Kirk to design a wonderful cover. When I was an outsider, I knew of Oregon State University Press's excellent reputation and relied on several of its books for my research. It is nice to confirm, now as an insider, that this reputation is well deserved.

Notes

PROLOGUE

1 G. Thomas Edwards, "The Final Ordeal: The Oregon Trail in the Columbia Gorge, 1843–1855," *Oregon Historical Quarterly* 97, no. 2 (Summer 1996): 136, 146.

2 "Management Plan: Columbia River Gorge National Scenic Area," Columbia River Gorge Commission, as amended through August 2016, I-3-1, http://www.gorgecommission.org/management-plan/plan/; Russ Jolley, *Wildflowers of the Columbia Gorge* (Portland: Oregon Historical Society Press, 1988).

3 Elizabeth Mylot, "The Landscape: Camas," *Metroscape* (Summer 2008), 4, https://pdxscholar.library.pdx.edu/cgi/viewcontent.cgi?article=1067&context=metroscape.

4 Jack Nisbet, *The Collector: David Douglas and the Natural History of the Northwest* (Seattle: Sasquatch Books, 2009), 41.

5 Earle E. Spamer, *Grand Canyon: Colossal Mirror* (Philadelphia: Raven's Perch Media, 2022), 34.

6 The place-name Wy'east is commonly used by both Natives and non-Natives. See, for example: Chuck Williams, *Bridge of the Gods, Mountains of Fire: A Return to the Columbia Gorge* (Portland, OR: Graphic Arts Center, 1980), 29–32; and Ella Elizabeth Clark, *Indian Legends of the Pacific Northwest* (Berkeley: University of California Press, 1953), 20–23.

7 "John Yeon (architect), interview by Marian W. Kolisch (photographer), American Art's Northwest Oral History Project," *Archives of American Art*, Smithsonian Institution, Washington, DC, December 14, 1982, January 10, 1983, https://www.aaa.si.edu/collections/interviews/oral-history-interview-john-yeon-12428.

8 John E. Tuhy, *Sam Hill: The Prince of Castle Nowhere* (Portland, OR: Timber Press, 1983), 140; Columbia Gorge Committee, *Land Program Recreation Project, Columbia Gorge, Oregon–Washington* (Portland: Pacific Northwest Regional Planning Commission, June 1935), 3. The Historic Columbia River Highway was completed to The Dalles by 1922. See National Park Service, *Columbia River Highway: Options for Conservation and Reuse*, prepared by Diane Ochi (Cascade Locks, OR: National Park Service, 1981), 19.

9 Yeon, directions to The Shire, n.d., in the author's possession.

10 John Yeon, letter to the editor, *Willamette Week* (Portland, OR), December 3, 1979; Columbia Gorge Committee, *Land Program Recreation Project*, 1–3; Columbia Gorge Committee, *Columbia Gorge Conservation and Development* (Portland: Pacific Northwest Regional Commission, January 1937); John Yeon, letter to Richard Giambardine, n.d. (c. 1980).

11 John Yeon, letter to Dan Evans (US senator, WA), September 18, 1984.

12 "Maintenance and Management of The Shire," School of Architecture and Allied Arts, University of Oregon, Eugene, n.d.; Richard Brown, interview by the author, July 11, July 16, 2013.

13 Nancy Russell, interview by Hillary Larson, January 2007. See also Nancy Russell, Steno 45. (From 1980 to 2006, Nancy Russell recorded in stenographer notebooks her thoughts, reminders, contemporaneous notes of conversations, and drafts of speeches and correspondence. When she died, she left behind 109 stenographer notebooks, each fifty to a hundred pages long. The notebooks, except for two that are missing for the periods from February 7 to June 18, 1990, and from April 23 to August 18, 1999, are found in the uncurated Nancy Russell collection managed by her son, Aubrey Russell, in Portland, Oregon.)

14 Nancy Russell, "Remarks at The Shire re: John Yeon," June 19, 2003, in the author's possession.

CHAPTER 1

1 "Revolution Feared if Taxes Stay Up," *Morning Oregonian*, January 11, 1932; J. P. Simpson and L. C. Swan, "Improvements in the Lumber Industry," *Annals of the American Academy of Political and Social Science* 193, no. 1 (September 1, 1937): 110–19; "Northwest Lumber Payroll Loses Sum of $93,000,000 in 1931," *Morning Oregonian*, January 11, 1932. See also E. Kimbark MacColl, *Growth of a City: Power and Politics in Portland, Oregon, 1915 to 1950* (Portland, OR: The Georgian Press, 1979), 369.

2 William H. Mullins, *The Depression and the Urban West Coast, 1929–1933* (Bloomington: Indiana University Press, 1991), 8; Lauren Kessler, *Stubborn Twig: Three Generations in the Life of a Japanese American Family* (New York: Penguin Books, 1993), 101.

3 "Bay City's Hardwood Industry," *Hardwood Record* 41 (January 10, 1916): 23, 41; "Bay County's Lumber, Salt and Coal Industries and Transportation Facilities," Michigan Family History Network, http://www.mifamilyhistory.org/bay/gansser_IX.htm; Steve McDonald, "Historic Logging and Milling Photos," *The Forestry Forum*, www.forestry-forum.com/board/index.php?topic=18781.280.

4 "Rejuvenated Pioneer Oregon Home," *The Spectator* 51, no. 22 (July 3, 1937); Betsy Neighbor Hammond, interview by the author, February 1, 2017. See also Nancy Russell, interview by Hillary Larson, November 2006; Charlie Mansfield, interview by the author, April 2017.

5 R. F. Präel, letter to Mrs. W. L. Bishop, August 14, 1936. See also "Rejuvenated Pioneer Oregon Home"; Betsy Neighbor Hammond, interview by the author, January 26, 2017. The 1928 amount was $700,000.

6 William Edward Neighbor Sr., "Elk Lake 1920–1942" (unpublished manuscript, July–September 1987), 8; R. Gregory Nokes, "Hard Times in the 1930s," OregonLive, https://www.oregonlive.com/century/1930_index.html; Nancy Russell interview (Larson, November 2006); Bob Neighbor, interview by the author, May 22, May 28, 2014; "College Students Must Pay Tuition," *Sunday Oregonian* (Portland, OR), March 6, 1927. The Neighbor cabin was the first cabin permitted by the US Forest Service on Elk Lake, although another cabin may have been built in 1920.

7 Mansfield interview.

8 Mullins, *The Depression and the Urban West Coast*, 136; Hammond interview, January 26, 2017.

9 "Rejuvenated Pioneer Oregon Home." See also Bob Neighbor interview.

10 R. W. Neighbor Jr., "Elk Lake Remembrances, 1904–1989" (unpublished manuscript, n.d.), 1, 5–6; Nancy Russell interview (Larson, November 2006).

11 Neighbor, "Elk Lake Remembrances," 7.

12 Bruce H. Russell, "Old Time Memories of Elk Lake" (unpublished manuscript, November 16, 2000), 6; Nancy Russell interview (Larson, November 2006).

13 Joan Gamble, interview by the author, September 5, 2013; Marie Hall, interview by the author, April 4, 2013; Sis Hayes, interview by the author, February 26, 2013; Susi Wilson, letter to the author, July 10, 2014;

14 Hammond interview, January 26, 2017; Aubrey Russell interview by the author, October 20, 2016. Nancy Neighbor, "The Good American Family," *Garrulous Pine* (Portland, OR: Catlin Gabel School, 1949), 2; Bob Neighbor interview.

15 Gamble interview; Hammond interview, January 26, 2017; Nancy Russell interview (Larson, November 2006).

16 Nancy Russell interview (Larson, November 2006); Bob Neighbor interview; Marie Hall, interview by the author, April 4, 2013.

17 "Stockings for Red Cross," *Oregonian* (Portland, OR), June 16, 1942.

18 Bob Neighbor interview; Barbara Robinson, interview by the author, November 18, November 20, 2013; Bob Neighbor interview; Nancy Russell interview (Larson, November 2006); Hammond interview, February 1, 2017.

19 Nancy Russell interview (Larson, November 2006); Catlin Gabel School, Portland, http://www.catlin.edu/page.cfm?p=768 (accessed September 20, 2017); Nancy Ann Neighbor, Application for Admissions, Catlin–Hillside Schools, June 12, 1945, in the author's possession.

20 Kate Mills, interview by the author, December 6, 2012; Nancy Russell interview (Larson, November 2006, January 2007); Susi Wilson, letter to the author, July 10, 2014.

21 Nancy Russell interview (Larson, December 2006).

22 Bob Neighbor interview.

23 Neighbor interview.

24 Nancy Russell interview (Larson, November 2006); Neighbor, "The Good American Family."

25 Hammond interview, February 1, 2017.

26 Russell, "Old Time Memories of Elk Lake," 3; Eve and Roger Bachman, interview by the author, March 5, 2013.

27 John Eliot Allen, Marjorie Burns, and Scott Burns, *Cataclysms on the Columbia: The Great Missoula Floods*, 2d ed. (Portland, OR: Ooligan Press, 2009), 68, 104, 153. Flood speeds were reduced when the water reached the Gorge, flowing at least thirty-five miles per hour.

28 Allen, M. Burns, and S. Burns, *Cataclysms on the Columbia*, 90, 100, 145, 153.

29 John Yeon, letter to Nancy Russell, n.d. (c. 1981), in the author's possession; Allen, M. Burns, and S. Burns, *Cataclysms*, 33, 159; William Clark, November 2, 1805, in Gary Moulton, ed., *The Journals of the Lewis and Clark Expedition*, vol. 6 (Lincoln: University of Nebraska Press, 1990), https://lewisandclarkjournals.unl.edu/item/lc.jrn.1805-11-02#n25110209 (accessed July 26, 2020).

30 Nisbet, *The Collector*, 60. There are several versions of this legend. See, for example, Clark, *Indian Legends*, 20–23; and Williams, *Bridge of the Gods*, 29–32.

31 "Cascade Locks, Oregon (351407), Period of Record Monthly Climate Summary, Period of Record: 09/01/1894 to 04/30/2016," Western Regional Climate Center, http://www.wrcc.dri.edu/cgi-bin/cliMAIN.pl?or1407 (accessed April 21, 2020). See also William G. Loy, Stuart Allan, Aileen R. Buckley, and James E. Meacham, *Atlas of Oregon*, 2d ed. (Eugene: University of Oregon Press, 2001), 154–57. Depending on moisture content, ten to thirteen inches of snow generally equal one inch of rain.

32 "Management Plan: Columbia River Gorge National Scenic Area," I-3-1. See also Russ Jolley, *Wildflowers of the Columbia Gorge* (Portland: Oregon Historical Society Press, 1988), 5.

33 Columbia River Inter-Tribal Fish Commission, "Salmon Range," http://www.critfc.org/fish-and-watersheds/columbia-river-fish-species/columbia-river-salmon/ (accessed April 21, 2020). See also Northwest Power and Conservation Council, "Salmon and Steelhead," http://www.nwcouncil.org:81/history/SalmonAndSteelhead.asp (accessed April 21, 2020); Roberta Ulrich, *Empty Nets: Indians, Dams and the Columbia River* (Corvallis: Oregon State University Press, 1999), 7.

34 Frederick K. Cramer, "A Fisherman's View," in *Celilo Falls: Remembering Thunder, Photos from the Collection of Wilma Roberts*, ed. Wilma Roberts and Carolyn Z. Shelton (The Dalles, OR: Wasco County Historical Museum Press, 1997), 15; Carol A. Mortland, "The Place," in *Celilo Falls*, 7; Francis Seufert, *Wheels of Fortune* (Portland: Oregon Historical Society Press, 1980), 40.

35 Katrine Barber, *Death of Celilo Falls* (Seattle: University of Washington Press, 2005), 22; Mortland, "The Place," 7; Daniel Lee, quoted in Robert Boyd, *People of The Dalles: The Indians of Wascopam Mission* (Lincoln: University of Nebraska Press 1996), 63–68; James P. Ronda, *Lewis and Clark among the Indians* (Lincoln: University of Nebraska Press, 1984), https://lewisandclarkjournals.unl.edu/item/lc.sup.ronda.01.07 (accessed April 21, 2020); Joseph B. Frazier, "A Way of Life Submerged under a Dam," *Los Angeles Times*, July 20, 2003, http://articles.latimes.com/2003/jul/20/news/adna-celilo20. See also National Congress of American Indians, "Inter-Tribal Free Trade Zone Re-Establishment," Resolution ABQ-10-055, annual session, 2010. Celilo Village has been moved at least

three times for new transportation structures—canal, railroad, and highway—but has remained close to the original village site.

36 This population estimate is a product of Lewis and Clark's estimate (as modified by Boyd's observations in *People of The Dalles*) plus Boyd's mortality estimates for the epidemics of the 1770s and 1801–1802. I increased this estimate by 15 percent to account for Boyd's admitted conservatism and his recognition that Columbia River tribal mortality was greater than that of the Northwest Coast populations in general. Finally, Boyd chose not to take into account mortality from an epidemic that started in the American Southwest in the 1520s, which some experts believe affected Northwest populations. See Robert Boyd, *The Coming of the Spirit of Pestilence: Introduced Infectious Diseases and Population Decline among Northwest Coast Indians, 1774–1874* (Seattle: University of Washington Press, 1999), 16, 17–20, 47, 232, 237, 262–3, map 13; Boyd, *People of The Dalles*, 50.

37 William Clark, October 24, 1805, in Moulton, ed. *Journals of the Lewis and Clark Expedition*; "Journal of Narcissa Whitman, July 18, 1836–Oct. 18, 1836," September 9, 1836, https://user.xmission.com/~drudy/mtman/html/NWhitmanJournal.html (accessed April 21, 2020); Edwards, "The Final Ordeal," 134, 146. See also Terence O'Donnell, *That Balance So Rare: The Story of Oregon*, rev. ed. (Portland: Oregon Historical Society Press, 1997), 31; Boyd, *Coming of the Spirit of Pestilence*, 16.

38 O'Donnell, *That Balance So Rare*, 59; Fred W. Wilson, "The Lure of the River," *Oregon Historical Quarterly* 34, no. 1 (1969): 7, 9; Michael S. Spranger, *Columbia Gorge: A Unique American Treasure* (Collingdale, PA: Diane Publishing, 1997), 43; Ivan Donaldson, "History of Skamania County" (unpublished manuscript, 1959–1960), 89.

39 D. W. Meinig, *The Great Columbia Plain: A Historical Geography, 1805–1910* (Seattle: University of Washington Press, 1968), 201; O'Donnell, *That Balance So Rare*, 64.

40 Ivan J. Donaldson and Frederick K. Cramer, *Fishwheels of the Columbia* (Portland: Binford and Mort, 1971), 7, 111, 113; "Columbia River Canneries," Smithsonian National Museum of American History, Washington, DC, http://americanhistory.si.edu/onthe-water/exhibition/3_6.html (accessed April 21, 2020); Gladys Seufert, quoted in George W. Aguilar Sr., *When the River Ran Wild! Indian Traditions on the Mid-Columbia and the Warm Springs Reservation* (Portland: Oregon Historical Society Press, 2005), 120.

41 *The Dalles Times Mountaineer*, June 7, 1890, 4; "Umatilla House, The Dalles, Oregon," *The Columbia River: A Photographic Journey*, http://columbiariverimages.com/Regions/Places/umatilla_house.html (accessed April 21, 2020).

42 Kessler, *Stubborn Twig*, 23, 24; William Clark, October 30, 1805, in Moulton, ed., *The Journals of the Lewis and Clark Expedition*, https://lewisandclarkjournals.unl.edu/item/lc.jrn.1805-10-31#lc.jrn.1805-10-31.02 (accessed August 18, 2020).

43 O'Donnell, *That Balance So Rare*, 100; Tuhy, *Sam Hill*, 129, 147.

44 Tuhy, *Sam Hill*, 136, 148, 212, 213; Oral Bullard, *Lancaster's Road: The Historic Columbia River Scenic Highway* (Beaverton, OR: TMS Book Service, 1982), 9; Peg Willis, *Building the Columbia River Highway: They Said It Couldn't Be Done* (Charleston, SC: The History Press, 2014), 31.

45 Tuhy, *Sam Hill*, 137; Paul Richert-Boe, "Gorge Road Constructed with Natural Beauty in Mind," *Oregonian*, February 7, 1978.

46 Bullard, *Lancaster's Road*, 19, 35; Oral Bullard, *Konapee's Eden: Historic and Scenic Handbook, The Columbia River Gorge* (Beaverton, OR: TMS Book Service, 1985), 28; Ronald J. Fahl, "S. C. Lancaster and the Columbia River Highway: Engineer as Conservationist," *Oregon Historical Quarterly* 74, no. 2 (1973): 101–44. See also State of Oregon, "Historic Columbia River Highway, Grading and Alignment," http://sos.oregon.gov/archives/exhibits/columbia-river-highway/Pages/design-grading-alignment.aspx (accessed April 21, 2020).

47 Bullard, *Lancaster's Road*, 11.

48 Richert-Boe, "Gorge Road Constructed"; Bullard, *Lancaster's Road*, 11. The highway was paved only to Multnomah Falls by the time of its dedication. See Nancy H. Gronowski and Jeanette Kloos, "A Study of the Historic Columbia River Highway," Oregon Department of Transportation (November 1987), 12, 13.

49 State of Oregon, "Historic Columbia River Highway, Grading and Alignment," http://sos. oregon.gov/archives/exhibits/columbia-river-highway/Pages/design-grading-alignment. aspx (accessed April 21, 2020); John Yeon, "Comments on the Role of John B. Yeon and Samuel Lancaster in Building of the Old Columbia River Highway," 1982, 2; Marguerite N. Davis, "Samuel Lancaster Engineered Columbia River Highway, But, More Than That, He Helped Others to Happiness," *Sunday Oregonian*, March 30, 1941; John Yeon, Testimony re Vista House, May 18, 1982, in the author's possession.

50 Lawrence Berlow, *Reference Guide to Famous Engineering Landmarks of the World: Bridges, Tunnels, Dams, Roads and Other Structures* (Phoenix: Oryx Press, 1998), 103.

51 Fahl, "S. C. Lancaster and the Columbia River Highway," 114; Willis, *Building the Columbia River Highway*, 70; "Columbia River Highway: Options for Conservation and Reuse" (Cascade Locks, OR: National Park Service, 1981), 23, 28. See also websites for Camp Crestview, http://www.campcrestview.com/ (accessed September 17, 2017), and Menucha https://menucha.org/ (accessed September 17, 2017).

52 "Columbia Highlands Scenic Homes Co.," photo in author's possession; Willis, *Building the Columbia River Highway*, 133.

53 MacColl, *Growth of a City*, 24; Richert-Boe, "Gorge Road Constructed"; Tuhy, *Sam Hill*, 151; Bullard, *Lancaster's Road*, 38, 48. The easternmost limit of the developed portion of Portland during this period was marked by Southeast 82nd Avenue, approximately twenty-three miles from Multnomah Falls. See Bureau of Planning and Sustainability, *East Portland Historical Overview and Historic Preservation Study* (Portland, OR: City of Portland, March 2009), 10, 26.

54 "Mt. Hood National Park: Chamber of Commerce Will Start Agitation for Project," *Morning Oregonian*, March 7, 1907. This concept was originally proposed by the Oregon Alpine Club almost twenty years earlier. See "To Preserve Mount Hood," *Morning Oregonian*, February 17, 1888.

55 Gifford Pinchot, quoted in Samuel P. Hays, *Conservation and the Gospel of Efficiency: The Progressive Conservation Movement, 1890–1920* (Cambridge: Harvard University Press, 1959), 197.

56 William C. Tweed, "Recreation Site Planning and Improvement in National Forests: 1891–1942," US Department of Agriculture, US Forest Service (November 1980), 5–6; "Reservation for Recreation Purposes of Lands within the Oregon National Forest Adjacent to the Columbia River Highway," Department of Agriculture Land Classification Order, December 24, 1915; Tweed, "Recreation Site Planning," 4; *Morning Oregonian*, January 5, 1916.

57 Land Classification Order, "Reservation for Recreation Purposes." Up to six months later, the *Oregonian* called this area a national park. See "Guide Maps Offered: Data on Columbia Gorge National Park Available," *Morning Oregonian*, June 13, 1916.

58 "Political Gossip," *Morning Oregonian*, February 25, 1916; "A Bill to Establish the Mount Hood National Parks in the State of Oregon," S. 6397, 64th Cong. (1916); "Mt. Hood Park Indorsed," *Morning Oregonian*, September 2, 1916; "High Official Due Today," *Morning Oregonian*, September 2, 1916; "Park Chief Heard," *Morning Oregonian*, September 3, 1916; "Head of National Park System Will Be Portland Visitor this Week," *Morning Oregonian*, November 13, 1916.

59 "Park Plan Is Opposed," *Morning Oregonian*, December 11, 1916.

60 National Park Service, *Study of Alternatives for the Columbia River Gorge*, (Denver, CO: National Park Service, April 1980), 7.

61 Clark initially called Beacon Rock "Beaten Rock" but later corrected his mistake. Beacon Rock was referred to as "Castle Rock" in the early 1900s. See Elliott Coues, ed., *The History of the Lewis and Clark Expedition*, vol. 3 (New York: Francis P. Harper, 1893), 939.

62 "Charles E. Ladd Buys Castle Rock," *Morning Oregonian*, November 27, 1904; "Blast Castle Rock," *Morning Oregonian*, March 26, 1906; "Court Notes," *Morning Oregonian*, December 31, 1902; "Work on River," *Morning Oregonian*, July 17, 1904; "To Rush Jetty Extension," *Morning Oregonian*, April 12, 1904; "Will Block the North-Bank Road," *Morning Oregonian*, March 25, 1906.

63 "Blast Castle Rock," *Morning Oregonian*, March 26, 1906; "Will Block the North-Bank Road," *Morning Oregonian*, March 25, 1906; "Castle Rock May Stand," *Morning Oregonian*, July 13, 1906.

64 "Castle Rock to Go," *Morning Oregonian*, March 16, 1906; "Blast Castle Rock," *Morning Oregonian*, March 26, 1906; "The Subjugation of Castle Rock," *Morning Oregonian*, March 17, 1906.

65 *Morning Oregonian*, March 26, March 28, 1906; "Mazamas Go on Record," *Morning Oregonian*, March 27, 1906; "Favors Judge Ellis," *Morning Oregonian*, March 24, 1906; "Castle Rock Saved," *Morning Oregonian*, July 19, 1906; "To Enjoin Ladds," *Morning Oregonian*, March 18, 1906.

66 John Caldbick, "James J. Hill and Associates Cross Columbia River," HistoryLink.org, January 13, 2016, https://historylink.org/File/8740 (accessed December 8, 2017); "Dynamite Used to Scare Crew," *Morning Oregonian*, April 13, 1906; "Will Block the North-Bank Road," *Morning Oregonian*, March 25, 1906; "To Enjoin Ladds," *Morning Oregonian*, March 18, 1906.

67 "Castle Rock Saved," *Morning Oregonian*, July 19, 1906; Henry J. Biddle papers, Ax 645, Special Collections and University Archives, University of Oregon Libraries, Eugene; Washington State Parks and Recreation Commission, "Beacon Rock State Park: Land Classification and Long-Term Boundary Plan, Skamania County, Requested Action," September 4, 1998, 2.

68 "Beacon Rock in the Gorge of the Columbia," *Skamania County Heritage* 3, no. 1 (June 1976); W. Duncan Strong, W. Egbert Schenck, and Julian H. Steward, "Archaeology of the Dalles–Deschutes Region," *University of California Publications in American Archaeology and Ethnology*, vol. 29 (1930–1932): 1; Henry J. Biddle to Lyd (sister), November 9, 1919, in the author's possession; "Biddle Home Ransacked," *Morning Oregonian*, January 9, 1910; Henry J. Biddle to Christine (sister), June 17, 1917, in the author's possession. Biddle would later become Columbia Contract Company's general manager.

69 Biddle, *Beacon Rock Legends*, 11; Margaret Riddle, "Hartley, Roland Hill (1864–1952)," HistoryLink.org, November 11, 2006, http://www.historylink.org/File/8008 (accessed December 8, 2017); Sam H. Boardman, "Recorded Events of How a State Park Was Acquired by Washington and Missed by Oregon," n.d., in the author's possession.

70 Boardman, "Recorded Events"; E. C. Hamilton (acting secretary, Cascade Pomona Grange No. 43), letter to Oregon governor Julius Meier, August 24, 1931.

71 Rebecca Biddle Wood and Spencer Biddle to State of Washington, Deed of Gift, April 15, 1935.

72 Oregon Driver and Motor Vehicle Services, "DMV Key Facts," https://www.oregon.gov/ODOT/DMV/pages/news/factsstats.aspx (accessed June 30, 2020); Edward M. Miller, "Super-Highway up Columbia Issue Facing State Commission," *Sunday Oregonian*, April 5, 1931. Hood River County accident reports show that 80 percent of people injured in county car accidents were from outside Oregon.

73 Leslie M. Scott, letter to John Yeon, April 1, 1933; Yeon, letter to Scott, April 1, 1933, in the author's possession.

74 Governor Julius Meier, letter to John Yeon, May 17, 1933, in the author's possession; Yeon interview, 47–50; Randy Gragg, Bowen Blair, Kenneth I. Helphand, and Susan Seubert, *John Yeon Landscape: Design Conservation Activism* (Andrea Monfried Editions LLC 2017), 40.

75 "Highways Utility Put before Beauty," *Morning Oregonian*, June 28, 1933; Columbia Gorge Committee, *Columbia Gorge Conservation and Development*, 31–32, C-3, C-4, C-7–C-8. According to Oregon State Parks' official history, the Parks Commission's perspectives "were not altogether satisfactory to the Highway Commission. . . . There is no record of further meetings or actions of the Parks Commission." See "History of The Oregon State Parks: 1917–1963," http://npshistory.com/publications/oregon/history/sec3.htm (accessed April 23, 2020). According to Yeon, "the whole commission resigned." See

Yeon interview. See also "Changes Sought in Highway Plan," *Sunday Oregonian*, September 16, 1934.

76 Yeon interview, 15.

77 O'Donnell, *A Balance So Rare*, 101; William F. Willingham, "Bonneville Dam," *The Oregon Encyclopedia*, https://oregonencyclopedia.org/articles/bonneville_dam/ (accessed May 7, 2020); William F. Willingham, *Water Power in the "Wilderness": The History of Bonneville Lock and Dam* (Portland, OR: US Army Corps of Engineers, Army Engineer District, 1984), 3, 4; MacColl, *Growth of a City*, 438, 447; Jim Marshall, "Dam of Doubt," *Collier's* 99 (June 19, 1937), 19–22. Three thousand people worked on the dam directly (Willingham, *Water Power in the Wilderness*, 9), and another two thousand were in industries supported by dam construction (MacColl, *Growth of a City*, 447).

78 Columbia Gorge Committee, *Land Program Recreation Project*, 6, 7, exhibit N(2); John B. Yeon, "The Issue of the Olympics," *American Forests* 42 (June 1936): 255.

79 Columbia Gorge Committee, *Columbia Gorge Conservation and Development*, 22, 95.

80 Columbia Gorge Committee, 28. As Yeon observed in his report (41–42), without the advantage of favorable electrical rates the Gorge would not have attracted industry on its own, so the federal government would have subsidized the Gorge's ruin.

81 Columbia Gorge Committee, 36.

82 Columbia Gorge Committee, 16–18, 36.

83 See John Yeon, letter to Richard Giambardine, n.d. (1980), in the author's possession; Columbia Gorge Committee, *Columbia Gorge Conservation and Development*, 28; MacColl, *Growth of a City*, 558.

84 MacColl, *Growth of a City*, 555, 558; Jewel Lansing, *Portland: People, Politics, and Power, 1851–2001* (Corvallis: Oregon State University Press, 2003), 341.

CHAPTER 2

1 Jewel Lansing, *Portland: People, Politics, and Power, 1851–2001* (Corvallis: Oregon State University Press, 2003), 341; Woody Guthrie, "Grand Coulee Dam," *This Land Is Your Land*.

2 Nancy Russell, interview by Hillary Larson, November 2006.

3 Nancy Neighbor, "The Good American Family," *Garrulous Pine* (Portland, OR: Catlin Gabel School, 1949); Nancy Russell, interview by Hillary Larson, January 2007; Nancy Russell, letter to Aubrey Russell, January 18, 1985, in the author's possession.

4 Blueprint Committee, "Scripps College Landscape & Architectural Blueprint," April 2004, 75, https://pdfs.semanticscholar.org/2d6b/c55cbc4d0a2a-b72a1f1d2c8d9804ec1e9371.pdf.

5 Blueprint Committee, 47.

6 Aubrey Russell interview by the author, October 13, 2016; Nancy Russell interview (Larson, November 2006).

7 Nancy Russell interview (Larson, November 2006); Jessie Scott, "The Grapevine," *Sunday Oregonian*, February 10, 1952; Hunty Wall, interview by the author, September 17, 2013.

8 Office of Counselor to Students, "Personal Rating Sheet," Scripps College, Claremont, CA, June 15, 1953, in the author's possession.

9 Susi Wilson, letter to the author, July 10, 2014; Hammond interview, January 27, 2017; Nancy Russell interview (Larson, November 2006). Although Susi Wilson was not fired, she left with Nancy, likely out of loyalty; her letter does not mention the incident and incorrectly states that both girls were "asked to stay."

10 Hammond interview by the author, January 26, 2017.

11 Nancy Russell interview (Larson, November 2006); Hunty Wall interview by author, September 24, 2013.

12 Aubrey Russell interview, October 13, 2016; Bruce H. Russell, "A Memo to the Fourth Generation of Oregon-born Test-Wortman-Russells," 1–2, 6. See also "Remarks of Bruce H. Russell: Dedication of Mosier Creek Pocket Park," April 28, 2002, in the author's possession.

13 Aubrey Russell interview, October 13, 2016.

14 Russell, "Old Time Memories of Elk Lake," 4.

15 Bruce Russell, letters to Nancy Neighbor, December 6, December 20, 1956, March 11, March 19, 1957, in the author's possession.

16 Bruce Russell, letter to Nancy Neighbor, April 5, 1957, in the author's possession; Nancy Neighbor, letter to Mr. and Mrs. R. W. Neighbor, April 25, 1957, in the author's possession; Nancy Russell interview (Larson, November 2006); Hayes interview, 2.

17 Nancy Russell interview (Larson, November 2006), 3.

18 Bruce H. Russell, "Some Russell Family History," July 17, 1992, 8. Westwinds was initially two acres, then later expanded through Bruce's purchases to 4.5 acres.

19 Nancy Russell interview (Larson, December 2006).

20 Laurie Rahr, interview by the author, January 28, 2013; Russell, "Some Russell Family History," 7; Hammond interview, January 26, 2017; Sally Russell, interview by the author, February 16, 2017; Bachman interview. Russell's daughter Sally believed that Nancy "always wanted to be a boy." See Gamble interview, 3.

21 Jean Henninger, "TLC Is Prescribed for Doctor's Band," *Oregonian*, May 15, 1964; photograph of Lendon Smith playing in "The Dumbwaiter," *Oregonian*, January 10, 1964; Rahr interview; Wall interview by author, September 24, 2013; Hammond interview, January 26, 2017.

22 Sally Russell, interview by author, February 16, 2017; Rahr interview; Hammond interview, January 26, 2017.

23 Nancy Russell interview (Larson, November 2006); Sally Russell interview, February 16, 2017.

24 "Pediatrics: TV Doctor, Friday," *Time Magazine*, June 16, 1967, http://content.time.com/time/magazine/article/0,9171,843960,00.html (accessed March 8, 2018); "Lendon H. Smith (1921–2001)" IMDbTV, http://www.imdb.com/name/nm1475360/ (accessed March 8, 2018); Stephen Barrett, M.D., "A Critical Look at Lendon Smith, M.D.," *Quackwatch*, March 7, 2009, https://quackwatch.org/consumer-education/lendonsmith/; Thomas V. Holohan, M.D., "Referral by Default: The Medical Community and Unorthodox Therapy," *Journal of the American Medical Association*, March 27, 1987, http://jama.jamanetwork.com/article.aspx?articleid=365219 (accessed March 8, 2018); http://www.digplanet.com/wiki/Lendon_Smith; "Dr. Lendon Smith, November 30, 2001: In Memoriam," http://www.iwr.com/ezine/dr.smith.htm. See also Scott Learn, "Lendon Smith: 1921–2001: 'Children's Doctor,' Author Dies at Age 80," *Oregonian*, November 19, 2001, http://www.digplanet.com/wiki/Lendon_Smith. See also Leslie L. Zaitz, "In Portland MDs Feed Drug Pipeline," *Sunday Oregonian*, January 14, 1979; Marian Burros, "Baby Doctor Recovers from 'Incident,'" *Oregonian*, May 5, 1980.

25 Rahr interview; Nancy Russell interview (Larson, November 2006); Aubrey Russell interview, November 6, 2012; Barbara Robinson, interview by the author, November 18, 2013.

26 Nancy Russell interview (Larson, December 2006); Aubrey Russell interview, October 20, 2016.

27 Aubrey Russell interview, October 13, 2016.

28 Aubrey Russell interview, October 13, 2016.

29 See Aubrey Russell interview, October 13, 2016. In 1958, a photograph of Nancy and a shirtless Bruce taken at the Rose Garden tennis courts appeared in the *Oregonian*. See "Summer in the City—It's Almost Like a Vacation Every Day," *Sunday Oregonian*, July 27, 1958.

30 Robin Lodewick, "Almeta Barrett: A Pioneer Woman Botanist in Oregon," *Oregon Flora*, newsletter, Oregon Flora Project, Oregon State University Herbarium, Corvallis (October 2003), https://archive.org/stream/oregonfloranewsl9132oreg/oregonfloranewsl9132oreg_djvu.txt.

31 "Don't Fence Me In," from *Hollywood Canteen*. Words and music by COLE PORTER © 1944 (Renewed) WC Music Corp. All rights reserved. Used by permission of Alfred Music.

32 Nancy Russell interview (Larson, January 2007).

33 Mike Metz, interview by the author, June 5, 2014; Mary Bishop, interview by the author, December 13, 2006.

34 Metz interview.

35 Jan Henderson, "'Back Door' Leads to New Vistas," *Oregonian*, December 11, 1979. See also B. J. Noles, "Veteran Women to Queen it Over Festival," *Oregonian*, June 5, 1970; Kasey Cordell, "Scenic Drive," *Portland Monthly* (August 2006), 24.

36 Sally Russell interview, February 16, 2017; "Distinguished Alumni Award Recipient Nancy Neighbor Russell '49," *Catlin Gabel School Summer Magazine* 40 (1998–1999); Nancy N. Russell, "Bio Data, Abbreviated" (July 19, 2002), in the author's possession.

37 Jan Henderson, "'Back Door' Leads to New Vistas," *Oregonian*, December 11, 1979; Aubrey Russell interview, October 13, 2016; W. Dan Hausel, "Guide to Prospecting and Rock Hunting in Wyoming," Information Pamphlet 11, Laramie, 2004, http://wsgs.wyo. gov/products/wsgs-2004-ip-11.pdf (accessed June 6, 2013).

38 Nancy Russell, letter to Randy Ravelle, January 28, 1980, in the author's possession; Sally Russell interview, February 16, 2017.

39 Mrs. Henry F. Cabell and Mrs. Benjamin M. Reed, comp., *The Portland Garden Club: The First Fifty Years; 1924–1974* (Portland, OR: Portland Garden Club, 1974), 9; Portland Rose Society, http://www.portlandrosesociety.org/index.html (accessed May 9, 2018); Maggie Drake, interview by the author, May 16, 2013; Phyllis Cantrell Reynolds, comp., *The Portland Garden Club: The Years 1975–2000* (Portland, OR: Portland Garden Club, 2000), 22.

40 William Seale, *The Garden Club of America: 100 Years of a Growing Legacy* (Washington, DC: Smithsonian Books, 2012), 6, 16–17, 24, 42–44; 50–53.

41 Reynolds, *Portland Garden Club*, 9, 14, 25; Cabell and Reed, *Portland Garden Club*, 13; Ira N. Gabrielson, "Wildflowers Give Charm to Garden," *Sunday Oregonian*, March 27, 1927; Seale, *Garden Club of America*, 203; Nancy N. Russell, "In Memoriam: Ivan Donaldson," newsletter, Friends of the Columbia Gorge (Fall 1989), 8.

42 Nancy N. Russell, "Taking on the Gorge," *The Gardeners*, newsletter, Portland Garden Club (December 1983); Nancy N. Russell, letter to Mrs. Lyman (Gretchen) Hull, September 3, 1980, in the author's possession.

43 "Draft National Historic Landmark Nomination, Aubrey Watzek House," US Department of the Interior, National Park Service, n.d., 15, 16, 17, 23; "Columbia Gorge's Vista Changed by Conservation," *Oregonian*, March 14, 2005; John Yeon, letter to Nancy Russell, n.d. (1981), in the author's possession; Randy Gragg, email to the author, May 14, 2018. See also Jamie Hale, "Oregon's 17 National Historic Landmarks, from Bonneville Dam to Wallowa Lake," *Oregonian/OregonLive*, https://www.oregonlive.com/ travel/2016/08/oregons_17_national_historic_l.html.

44 Elliott Coues, ed., *The History of the Lewis and Clark Expedition*, vol. 2 (New York: Francis P. Harper, 1893), 689–90; William Clark, November 2, 1805, in Moulton, ed., *The Journals of the Lewis and Clark Expedition*.

45 *Martin v. Reynolds Metals Company*, 224 F. Supp. 321, 224 F. Supp. 978. By March 1950, that amount approached four thousand pounds each day.

46 Trust for Public Land, "Prior Judgments Involving Reynolds Metal Land," memorandum, September 4, 1990, in author's possession; "Seven Enter Fluoride Case," *Oregonian*, October 15, 1957; "Appeal Set by Reynolds," *Oregonian*, February 26, 1960. See also "Appeal Won by Rancher," *Oregonian*, March 22, 1960.

47 *Martin v. Reynolds Metals Company*, 224 F. Supp. 978, 979; "Reynolds Loses Case Appeal," *Oregonian*, October 22, 1964; "Reynolds Buys Ranch to End Long Feud," *Oregonian*, August 7, 1968; "Judge Balks at Request," *Oregonian*, January 26, 1965; Don Bundy, "Gorge Feels Sting of Political Winds," *Oregonian*, March 17, 1980. See also National Park Service, *Study of Alternatives for the Columbia River Gorge*, (Denver, CO: National Park Service, April 1980), 73; Don Bundy, "Columbia Gorge Preservation Report Compiled," *Oregonian*, November 8, 1979.

48 "Yeon Lashes Road Policy," *Oregonian*, October 16, 1946; Gertrude Glutsch Jensen, interview by Roberta Watts, December 7, 1977. Jensen served on the Oregon Roadside

Council's board for twenty-five years. See Katrine Barber, "Gertrude Jensen (1903–1986)," *The Oregon Encyclopedia*, https://oregonencyclopedia.org/articles/jensen_gertrude/ (accessed September 1, 2016).

49 Jes Burns, "A War, the Chainsaw and the 2nd Great Cutting of the Northwest," Oregon Public Broadcasting, Portland, http://www.opb.org/news/series/battleready/chainsaw-history-world-war-2-forests-lumber/ (accessed April 23, 2020); Lansing, *Portland*, 357; Natasha Geiling, "How Oregon's Second Largest City Vanished in a Day," *Smithsonian Magazine* (February 18, 2015), https://www.smithsonianmag.com/history/vanport-oregon-how-countrys-largest-housing-project-vanished-day-180954040/ (accessed May 7, 2020). See also Lansing, *Portland*, 341; Carl Abbott, "Vanport," *The Oregon Encyclopedia*, https://oregonencyclopedia.org/articles/vanport/ (accessed April 23, 2020).

50 Connie Y. Chiang, with Michael Reese, "Evergreen State: Exploring the History of Washington's Forests," Center for the Study of the Pacific Northwest, University of Washington, Seattle, http://www.washington.edu/uwired/outreach/cspn/Website/Classroom%20Materials/Curriculum%20Packets/Evergreen%20State/Section%20II.html (accessed April 13, 2017); Oregon Department of Forestry, "Oregon's Timber Harvests: 1849–2004," 2005, file:///C:/Users/Owner/Documents/Biography%20-%20NNR/Research/History%20-%20General%20&%20CRG/OR%20Timber%20Harvests%20 1849-2004.pdf (accessed May 13, 2020); "Seeing the Forest for the Trees: Placing Washington's Forests in Historical Context," Center for the Study of the Pacific Northwest, University of Washington, Seattle, http://www.washington.edu/uwired/outreach/cspn/Website/Classroom%20Materials/Curriculum%20Packets/Evergreen%20State/Section%20II.html (accessed May 13, 2020); "Wood Use in US Housing," *Forest Research Notes* 13, no. 1 (2016): 3, http://www.forestresearchgroup.com/Newsletters/Vol13No1.pdf (accessed May 13, 2020).

51 Ted Mahar, "The Crusader of Columbia Gorge," *Oregonian*, September 18, 1966.

52 Jensen interview; Marshall N. Dana, "Operation Salvage," *Oregonian*, February 21, 1952.

53 Jensen interview; "McKay to Get Gorge Issue," *Oregonian*, May 4, 1952. Dana also chaired the Pacific Northwest Regional Planning Commission, which oversaw John Yeon's Columbia Gorge Committee.

54 "Governor Indorses Proposal to Preserve Gorge Beauty," *Oregonian*, June 22, 1952; G. E. Cannon (Recreational and Natural Resources Committee, Portland Chamber of Commerce), letter to Gertrude G. Jensen (Save the Gorge Committee), June 19, 1952; "For an Act Relating to the Establishment of the Columbia River Gorge Commission," SB357 (introduced February 24, 1953; not enacted); "Gorge Fund Sharply Cut," *Oregonian*, March 10, 1953; "Parks Budget Omits Gorge Recreation," *Oregonian*, March 22, 1953; Mervin Shoemaker, "Senate Votes Bill to Prohibit Billboards on All New or Relocated Throughways," *Oregonian*, March 29, 1953; "Gorge Fund Sharply Cut," *Oregonian*, March 10, 1953; "Parks Budget Omits Gorge Recreation," *Oregonian*, March 22, 1953.

55 "Gorge Board Okehs [*sic*] Study," *Oregonian*, September 14, 1953; Barber, "Gertrude Jensen."

56 "Highway Commission Accused of 'Indifference' Toward Plan to Save Columbia Gorge Beauty," *Oregonian*, August 8, 1953; "'Save Columbia Gorge' Group Refused on Land Purchase by Highway Officials," *Oregonian*, September 26, 1953.

57 Ted Mahar, "The Crusader of Columbia Gorge," *Oregonian*, September 18, 1966; Mara Stine, "History Lives On," *Outlook* (Gresham, OR), May 7, 2013; Gertrude Glutsch Jensen, speech, World Forestry Center, May 5, 1981; "Tree Cutting Causes Fuss," *Oregonian*, March 2, 1960; John Yeon, letter to Governor Spellman's Select Committee on the Columbia Gorge, October 26, 1981, in the author's possession. Jensen indicated interest in a Washington panel but did little to promote a bistate solution. See "Washington Joins Drive," *Oregonian*, February 5, 1958; Nani Warren, interview by the author, June 6, 2013.

58 "Mrs. Jensen, 'Angel of Gorge,' Wins First Oregon Conservationist Award," *Oregonian*, April 4, 1969; Ted Mahar, "The Crusader of Columbia Gorge," *Oregonian*, September 18, 1966; Gertrude Glutsch Jensen, speech, World Forestry Center, May 5, 1981; "McCall

Raps Opposition to New Oregon Plants," *Oregonian*, October 13, 1967; Yeon interview; Jensen interview. See also "Cascade Locks Panel Suggested to Advise Government Agencies," *Oregonian*, August 13, 1966; "Gorge Hassle Cools Down," *Oregonian*, April 1, 1967; "Gorge Group Loses Aide," *Oregonian*, March 16, 1969.

59 Frank Branch Riley, letter to the editor, *Oregonian*, November 18, 1954; Leslie Tooze, "Gorge Lovers Deplore Eclipse of Scenic Road; Age Demands Utilitarian Route," *Oregonian*, December 7, 1954; Lawrence H. Berlow, *The Reference Guide to Famous Engineering Landmarks of the World* (Phoenix: The Oryx Press, 1998), 103; "Boom . . . There Goes More of Mitchell Point," *Oregonian*, January 23, 1966.

60 Barber, *Death of Celilo Falls*, 4, 6; "Indian Drums, Voices Pay Homage to Chief Tommy Thompson," *Oregonian*, April 15, 1959.

61 US Bureau of the Census, "Washington: Population of Counties by Decennial Census: 1900 to 1990," https://www.census.gov/population/www/censusdata/cencounts/files/wa190090.txt (accessed April 23, 2020); Steve Campion, "WA-List," http://www.wa-list.com/?p=436 (accessed April 23, 2020).

62 Skamania Landing Owners Association, http://www.skamanialanding.org/about.html (accessed September 8, 2016); Donaldson, "Skamania County," 73; "Marina Due on Columbia," *Oregonian*, July 9, 1962; Skamania Landing advertisement, *Sunday Oregonian*, May 17, August 2, 1964. The 120 residential lots were reduced to 98, then 91; two decades later, only a third of the lots were developed. The marina and restaurant were never constructed. See Donald G. Jolly, "Final Environmental Impact Statement: Hidden Harbor" (July 1984), 74; "Firm Plans Marina Units," *Sunday Oregonian*, August 20, 1967.

63 Robert Caro, "The Power Broker, I: The Best Bill-Drafter in Albany," *New Yorker*, July 15, 1974, 35. See generally George Kramer, "Interstate 5 in Oregon," *The Oregon Encyclopedia* https://oregonencyclopedia.org/articles/interstate_5_in_oregon/.

64 Gragg, *John Yeon Landscape*, 40; Yeon interview, 48, 50.

65 "Henry Turrish Swigert, 1930– ," newsletter, World Forestry Center (January 2016), https://www.escocorp.com/MediaPressReleases/Hank%20Swigert%20World%20Forestry%20Center%20January%202016%20E-Newsletter%20and%20Bio_021716.pdf ; see also: http://www.oregonlive.com/business/index.ssf/2011/05/longtime_heavy_manufacturer_es.html; "Cascade President and CEO Leaves Behind a Legacy," news release, June 4, 2015, https://www.forkliftaction.com/news/newsdisplay.aspx?nwid=16179 (accessed April 24, 2020); Warren interview; Yeon interview, 51.

66 Yeon interview; Gragg, *John Yeon Landscape*, 48; Randy Gragg, "John Yeon (1910–1994)," *The Oregon Encyclopedia*, https://oregonencyclopedia.org/articles/john_yeon/ (accessed April 24, 2020); Ian McCluskey, "Legacy of a View: The Secret Story of the Shire," Oregon Public Broadcasting, Portland, https://www.opb.org/television/programs/oregon-field-guide/article/columbia-river-gorge-shire-history-john-yeon-nancy-russell/ (accessed April 24, 2020).

67 Warren interview.

68 John Yeon, "Statement: Columbia River Gorge Commission," Bonneville, OR, January 15, 1980, 2.

69 Yeon to Giambardine (c. 1980); John Yeon, "Columbia Gorge National Recreation Area," proposal, n.d. (1970), 3–5.

70 John Yeon, letter to Janet McLennan, August 4, 1977, in the author's possession.

71 Editorial, *Oregonian*, October 13, 1970; Gertrude Glutsch Jensen, letter to the editor (c. 1970), in author's possession; Yeon to Giambardine, 4.

72 John Yeon, letter to Governor Robert W. Straub, August 3, 1977, in the author's possession; John Yeon, letter to Janet McLennan, August 4, 1977, in the author's possession.

73 Shirley A. Woodrow, letter to John Yeon, April 4, 1979, in the author's possession; Phil Keisling, "Getting on Board with Vic," *Willamette Week*, January 5, 1981; Oregon Revised Statutes 182.010; Earl Warzynski (secretary treasurer to Governor Vic Atiyeh), May 20, 1980, in the author's possession; Vic Atiyeh (Oregon governor), memorandum to Whom It May Concern, April 25, 1980. While Warzynski's letter to the governor came after Atiyeh's memorandum, the letter's information was likely known beforehand.

74 John Yeon, letter to Janet McLennan, August 1977; John Yeon, written statement, February 22, 1982, in the author's possession.
75 Russell, Steno 33.

CHAPTER 3

1 Yeon to Select Committee, 1981, 2; "Experts Say Real Estate Boom Will Span I-205 Bridge Delay," *Columbian* (Vancouver, WA), April 1981; Chuck Williams and Craig Collins (Friends of the Earth), letter to John E. Hansel (National Park Service), February 28, 1979, in the author's possession.
2 Chuck Williams, *Bridge of the Gods, Mountains of Fire: A Return to the Columbia Gorge* (Portland, OR: Graphic Arts Center, 1980), 26; Spencer Heinz, "Building Pressure Mars Scenic Horizon, Official Says," *Sunday Oregonian*, August 26, 1984.
3 Chuck Williams (Friends of the Earth), letter to William Whalen (director, National Park Service), May 1, 1978, in the author's possession; Williams, letter to Robert Herbst (assistant secretary, National Park Service), May 2, 1979, in the author's possession. The other two areas proposed by Williams for NSA designation were Lake Tahoe and Jackson Hole. The "earlier Interior Urban Parks Study" was a 1975 Interior Urban Parks Study.
4 National Park Service, *Study of Alternatives for the Columbia River Gorge*, (Denver, CO: National Park Service, April 1980), 14, 15, 25, 73.
5 *Study of Alternatives for the Columbia River Gorge*, 26, 74, 181. The NPS wanted to "test the waters" and get its report out quickly and did not make a recommendation. See Lorna Stickel, memorandum to Don Clark (Multnomah County), July 31, 1980.
6 Oral Bullard, "Should they Build in Our Gorge?" *Sunday Oregonian*, February 1, 1976; Vera Dafoe and Craig Collins, "Early History of the Columbia Gorge Preservation Effort," memorandum, September 22, 2011–January 2012, in author's possession.
7 John Yeon, letter to Richard Giambardine, n.d. (1980), in the author's possession; Columbia Gorge Coalition, "Statement Presented to the Columbia River Gorge Commissions Regarding the National Park Service Study of the Columbia Gorge," news release, January 16, 1980, in the author's possession; John Yeon, letter to Rich Giambardine (National Park Service), August 4, 1980, in the author's possession. See also Columbia Gorge Coalition, "The Columbia Gorge," brochure, c. 1980, in the author's possession.
8 Tom Stimmel, "Gorge Policy Goals Mired in Feuding," *Oregon Journal*, January 17, 1980; "Draft Position of the Oregon Columbia River Gorge Commission," December 6, 1979. See also Vera Dafoe and Kate McCarthy, "Statement of Reasons," Oregon Columbia River Gorge Commission, January 14, 1980.
9 Barbara Bailey, meeting notes, March 13, 1980, in the author's possession; Don Bundy, "Gorge Feels Sting of Political Winds," *Oregonian*, March 17, 1980; Raymond Mungo, "Dixy Lee Ray: How Madame Nuke Took over Washington," *Mother Jones* 2, no. 4 (May 1977); Vic Atiyeh (Oregon governor), Dixy Lee Ray (Washington governor), and Clarence Irwin (chair, Washington Columbia River Gorge Commission), letter to Cecil Andrus (secretary of the Interior), January 18, 1980, in the author's possession; John Yeon, memorandum to Nancy Russell, memorandum re Gorge politics and agencies, n.d. (c. 1981), in the author's possession.
10 Nancy Russell, testimony to Oregon Columbia River Gorge Commission, Bonneville, OR, January 15, 1980, in the author's possession; Tom Stimmel, "Gorge Policy Goals Mired in Feuding," *Oregon Journal*, January 17, 1980; John Yeon, "Statement: Columbia River Gorge Commission," Bonneville, OR, January 15, 1980. See also Jeanie Senior, "Parks' Study Letter Divides Gorge Panel," *Oregonian*, January 17, 1980.
11 Dafoe and Collins, "Early History," 4–5; Tom Stimmel, "Gorge Policy Goals Mired in Feuding," *Oregon Journal*, January 17, 1980; Jeanie Senior, "Columbia Gorge Stand Finds Conflicting Views," *Oregonian*, January 22, 1980. See also Senior, "Letter Divides Gorge Panel."
12 Bailey, meeting notes, March 1980. See also Russell, Steno 3 (March 27–September 3, 1980); Barbara Bailey, interview by the author, October 18, 2016. See also John Yeon, memorandum to Nancy Russell, n.d. (c. 1981), in the author's possession.

13 Russell, Steno 75, September 19–December 10, 1992; letter to Michael Leonard. See also Barbara Robinson, telephone call with the author, January 31, 2014; Nancy Russell interview (Larson, January 2007); Russell, Steno 33.

14 Phil Keisling, "Getting on Board with Vic," *Willamette Week*, January 5, 1981; Samuel S. Johnson, letter to Vic Atiyeh (Oregon governor), March 18, 1980, in the author's possession.

15 Nancy N. Russell, letter to Samuel S. Johnson, March 24, 1980, in the author's possession; John Yeon, letter to Nancy Russell, n.d. (c. 1981). See Wallace K. Huntington, letter to Tom Vaughn (executive director, Oregon Historical Society), March 25, 1980, in the author's possession. See also Tom Alkire, "Twilight for the Gorge," *Willamette Week*, April 21, 1980; Samuel S. Johnson to Vic Atiyeh (Oregon governor), April 14, 1980, in the author's possession.

16 Samuel S. Johnson to Vic Atiyeh (Oregon governor), April 14, 1980, in the author's possession; Don Bundy, "Gorge Feels Sting of Political Winds," *Oregonian*, March 17, 1980; Editorial, KGW-TV, May 28, 1980. See also Editorial, *Willamette Week*, June 9, 1980; "Gorge Post Filled," *Oregonian*, January 29, 1981; "Aftermath of Appointment," *Hood River News*, June 5, 1980; John Yeon to Vic Atiyeh (Oregon governor), March 20, 1980, in the author's possession; "Ambitious Undertaking Traces Gorge History," *Columbian*, October 7, 1980. See also Craig Collins, interview by Bob Peirce, June 2, 2005. Friends of the Earth published *Bridge of the Gods, Mountains of Fire, A Return to the Columbia Gorge*, by Chuck Williams, in 1980, but it failed to generate the public attention or revenue its author had hoped for.

17 Nancy Russell, "Involvement in Gorge Effort," handwritten, 1980, in the author's possession; John Yeon, letter to Diane [last name unknown], n.d., in the author's possession; *Oregonian*, July 27, 1980; Samuel S. Johnson, letter to Nancy N. Russell, July 11, 1980; John Yeon, letter to Jennifer Dorn, August 6, 1980, 2.

18 Nancy Russell, memorandum re Nani Warren, n.d. See also Helene Biddle Dick, letter to Gretchen Hull, November 18, 1980.

19 Nancy N. Russell, "The Columbia River Gorge," *The Gardeners*, newsletter, Portland Garden Club (October 1980); Nancy Russell, memorandum re Nani Warren; John Yeon, letter to Nancy Russell, n.d. (c. 1981); Dick to Hull, November 1980; Russell, Steno 59, October 22, 1987–February 2, 1988. Oregon, Washington, California, and Hawaii were the four states in Garden Club of America's Zone XII.

20 Nancy Russell to Gretchen Hull, September 3, 1980; Helene Biddle Dick, letter to Gretchen Hull, November 18, 1980.

21 Russell, Steno 4; Nancy Russell, memorandum re Nani Warren, n.d.

22 "Complaint for Declaratory Judgment and Injunction," *Montchalin et al. vs. Skamania County et al.*, October 14, 1981; Jeanie Senior, "Housing Project Target of Gorge Commission," *Oregonian*, November 13, 1980.

23 Donald E. Clark (sheriff) to Mark O. Hatfield (Oregon governor), September 29, 1964, in the author's possession. See also Don Clark, interview by Bob Peirce, August 2004; Don Clark, interview by Ernie Bonner (College of Urban and Public Affairs, Portland State University), February 2000, https://www.pdx.edu/usp/planpdxorg-interview-don-clark.

24 Don Clark, interview by the author, May 30, 2013. See also Clark interview, August 2004; Donald E. Clark (county executive), letter to Cecil Andrus (secretary of the Interior), November 14, 1980; Clark interview, May 30, 2013.

25 Clark interview, August 2004; Tom Stimmel, "The Embattled Gorge: Substantial Threat Seen to Resource Value," *Oregon Journal*, September 12, 1981; Mary Marvin, "Personality: Nancy Neighbor Russell '53," *Scripps College Bulletin* (Spring 1988). See also Clark interview, June 2, 2015; Don Bundy, "Unit Named to Battle for Gorge," *Oregonian*, November 19, 1980.

26 Don Bundy, "Unit Named to Battle for Gorge," *Oregonian*, November 19, 1980; Multnomah County, news release, November 18, 1980, in the author's possession; Russell, "Statement, PGC Monthly Meeting, November 20, 1980." The two businessmen were David Cannard and Mitch Bower. The proposal for protection of only the western Gorge

was an initial position taken by the PGC in 1979. See Mrs. Donald G. Drake (president, Portland Garden Club) to Vic Atiyeh (Oregon governor), November 10, 1980, in the author's possession; Nancy N. Russell, "Statement, Portland Garden Club, November 18, 1980," in the author's possession. The groups included Columbia Gorge Coalition, The Nature Conservancy, Audubon Society, Columbia–Willamette Rock Garden Society, Portland chapter of the Native Plant Society of Oregon, Columbia River Citizens Compact, National Affairs and Legislative Committee of the Garden Club of America, Friends of the Earth, Oregon Environmental Council, Oregon Rare and Endangered Plant Studies Center, and the Sierra Club. See Multnomah County, news release, November 18, 1980. As conservation chair for the Portland Garden Club, Nancy Russell mentions in her November 20, 1980 report on the monthly meeting (in the author's possession) "the American Institute of Architects, the American Institute of Landscape Architects, The Native Plant Society, The Nature Conservancy, The Audubon Society, The Columbia Gorge Coalition, Jean Siddall Chairman of the Oregon Rare and Endangered Plant Project, The Dalles Planning Commission, The Port of The Dalles, and Helen Thompson telling of the interest of the Garden Club of America and the wonderful response she has already had from individual G.C.A. members from all over the country." See also Don Bundy, "Unit Named to Battle for Gorge," *Oregonian*, November 19, 1980.

27 Editorial, *Oregonian*, November 19, 1980; Editorial, *Oregon Journal*, December 15, 1980; Editorial, *Columbian*, November 20, 1980, December 28, 1980; Tom McCall, "Commentary, Tuesday, November 18, 1980," KATU-TV, Portland, OR; Editorial, *Skamania County Pioneer* (Stevenson, WA), March 21, 1981; Yeon interview, 30.

28 John Hayes, "Watt Visit Sparks Protest, Raises Funds," *Oregonian*, December 19, 1981. Ken Lewis, a political insider and shipping businessman, had assured Russell that passage of legislation would only take two years. See Russell, Steno 6, January 13–November 25, 1980. Even Don Clark thought this was likely. See Jack Pement, "Gorge Group Foresees Scenic Status by '82," *Oregon Journal*.

29 "Gorge Preservation," *The Dalles Chronicle* (The Dalles, OR), January 10, 1981; "Clark County Hedges Gorge Backing," *Oregon Journal*, January 30, 1981.

30 Friends of the Columbia Gorge, discussion paper, February 1981, 9.

31 Don Bundy, "Unit Named to Battle for Gorge," *Oregonian*, November 19, 1980; Mrs. Donald G. Drake, letter to Vic Atiyeh (Oregon governor), drafted by Nancy Russell, November 10, 1980, in the author's possession.

32 Pat Moser, "Efforts Renewed to Have Feds Control Gorge," *Columbian*, November 18, 1980; Bill Hemingway, letter to the editor, *Hood River News*, November 27, 1980; Nancy Russell, "About Don Clark," speech, April 23, 1991, Portland, OR, in the author's possession; Clark interview, May 30, 2013.

33 Clark interview, June 2, 2015.

34 Russell, Steno 7; Clark interview, May 30, 2013; Don Clark, letter to Skamania County Commission, November 14, 1980, in the author's possession; Don Clark, letters to Robert Lee (planning director, Skamania County), November 28, 1980, January 9, 1981, in the author's possession.

35 Friends of the Columbia Gorge, list of associate sponsors, September 1982; Russell, Steno 13. The former governors were Robert Straub, Tom McCall, Dan Evans, and Cecil Andrus; future governors were Neil Goldschmidt and Barbara Roberts.

36 Brot Bishop, Don Frisbee, John Gray, Charles Luce, Bob Noyes, Louis Perry, Jordan Schnitzer, and Bob Wilson, letter to Howard Vollum, November 30, 1982, in the author's possession.

37 Mills interview.

38 Russell, Steno 7; Eric Pryne, "The Gorge: It Hasn't Been the Same Since 24 Homesites Were Requested," *Seattle Times, Pacific Magazine*, May 24, 1981; Russell, Steno 19. Jewett was also Washington's Republican nominee for Senate in 1982 and would run against Senator Scoop Jackson in 1982.

39 Ellen Emry Heltzel, "Friends Pack Food, Issues into Columbia Gorge Picnic," *Oregonian*, August 4, 1981; Russell, Steno 26. When Russell started her effort, and for years afterward,

all of the senators and representatives in the two states' congressional delegations were men.

40 "Columbia Gorge Slide Program Script," June 27, 1981, 6–8, in the author's possession. There are questions about whether "She Who Watches" is a petroglyph, a pictograph, or both. See Jane Gargas, "Columbia River Petroglyphs Show Beauty of Ancient Art," *Yakima Herald Republic*, November 4, 2012, https://www.heraldnet.com/news/columbia-river-petroglyphs-show-beauty-of-ancient-art/.

41 Russell, Steno 26, Steno 27, Steno 14, Steno 29.

42 Russell, Steno 5.

43 Friends of the Columbia Gorge, testimony, Hearing on Proposed City Council Resolution Endorsing the National Scenic Area Designation, before the Vancouver City Council, October 18, 1982.

44 Russell, Steno 6.

45 Editorial, "Gorgeous Gorge," *Tri-City Herald* (Kennewick, WA), November 19, 1981; Editorial, "Preserve the Gorge," *Walla Walla Union Bulletin*, July 17, 1981; Editorial, "Who Can Better Protect the Gorge?" *Tribune* (Lewiston, ID), April 5, 1982; Russell, Steno 13.

46 Steve Meredith, "Soaring County Population Muddies Gov. Plans," *Tribune* (Vancouver, WA), February 24, 1981; Steve Jenning, "Big Electronics Manufacturers Plug into Clark County," *Oregonian*, February 15, 1982; Editorial, "Check Project's Regional Effects," *Oregonian*, September 22, 1980; Gail L. Achterman, speech to Portland Chamber of Commerce, January 18, 1982, 2, in author's possession. See also Eric Pryne, "The Gorge: It Hasn't Been the Same Since 24 Homesites Were Requested," *Seattle Times, Pacific Magazine*, May 24, 1981.

47 John Yeon, open letter to Governor Spellman's Select Committee on the Columbia Gorge, October 26, 1981, in the author's possession.

48 By straight line, Klickitat County's western boundary starts approximately forty-three miles east of the Gorge's western entrance; by car, the distance is closer to fifty miles.

49 "Commissioners Torn on Comp Plan," *Goldendale (WA) Sentinel*, February 26, 1981; Brian Rust, "Officials Work on Gorge Zone," *White Salmon (WA) Enterprise*, May 7, 1981.

50 Skamania and Klickitat Counties Boards of Commissioners, "Statement of Policy of Columbia Gorge," April 1, 1981, in author's possession; Eric Pryne, "The Gorge: It Hasn't Been the Same Since 24 Homesites Were Requested," *Seattle Times, Pacific Magazine*, May 24, 1981; Brad Remington and Kent Lauer, "Western Zirconium to Cooperate on Industrial Emission," *Standard-Examiner* (Ogden, UT), March 23, 1980. See also Jeanie Senior, "The Dalles Opposed to Proposed Metals Plant," *Sunday Oregonian*, December 26, 1976; Andrew Mershon, "Zirconium Firm Unfazed by Partner's Pullout," *Oregonian*, January 20, 1977; Jeanie Senior, "Other Sites Sought for Planned Zirconium Plant," *Oregonian*, February 10, 1978; Robert Olmos, "Metals Plant Lured to Utah," *Oregonian*, June 22, 1978; "Speculators! Columbia River Gorge Island," *Wall Street Journal*, July 23, 1982; Jeanie Senior, "Hood River Port Seals Purchase of Wells Island," *Oregonian*, August 23, 1983.

51 *Study of Alternatives for the Columbia River Gorge*, 35.

52 National Park Service, *Columbia River Highway: Options for Conservation and Reuse*, prepared by Diane Ochi (Cascade Locks, OR: National Park Service, 1981), 63–64, 66; Allen Houston, "Oregon Leads in Preservation: Fund Cuts Pose Problem," *Oregonian*, September 27, 1982; *Study of Alternatives for the Columbia River Gorge*, 39; John Hayes, "Plan to Stabilize Sand Dune along I-84 Fought," *Oregonian*, January 28, 1982; William F. Willingham, *Water Power in the "Wilderness": The History of Bonneville Lock and Dam* (Portland, OR: US Army Corps of Engineers, Army Engineer District, 1984), 58. Larry Upson, letter to the editor, *Bend (OR) Bulletin*, August 13, 1982. The removal of artifacts was completed by a $1.2 million contract let by the Army Corps of Engineers. See generally, endnote 6 (Willingham at 68): Rick Minor et al., *An Overview of Investigation at 45SA11: Archeology in the Columbia River Gorge* (Eugene, OR, 1986). See also Nancy N.

Russell, chairperson, Friends of the Columbia Gorge, letter to Harley Brown, July 20, 1983. See Chapter 4 for further discussion.

53 John Yeon, letter to Vic Atiyeh (Oregon governor), December 10, 1979.

54 Except for Reed Island, a Washington State park that was offshore and not in this segment (which includes the north bank only). Brookside Enterprises, "Final Environmental Impact Statement: Columbia Gorge Riverfront Estates" (August 1983), 25.

55 "I-205 Bridge ready," *Clark History*, a publication of the *Columbian*, http://history.columbian.com/i-205-bridge/ (accessed April 30, 2020); Rick Bella, "Plaque Honors Jackson at Span Dedication," *Oregonian*, December 15, 1982.

56 *Clark History*; Vancouver City, WA, city council hearing, 9; Eric Pryne, "The Gorge: It Hasn't Been the Same Since 24 Homesites Were Requested," *Seattle Times, Pacific Magazine*, May 24, 1981.

57 Military Grave Search, http://findgrave.org/george-rizor-oregon-5817300/ (accessed October 16, 2017); George A. Rizor Jr., letter to Harriet Burgess (vice president, Trust for Public Land), November 10, 1983; Rick Bella, "Contractor Denied Help on Gorge Plan," *Oregon Journal* (Portland), April 15, 1982; Minutes, Skamania County Planning Commission, Stevenson, WA, July 12, 1983, 5. Rizor was a "dedicated and committed Christian" according to his pastor. See Pat Moser, "Ex-Soldier in the Thick of Gorge War," *Columbian*, July 13, 1981.

58 David Kern, "In the Gorge: Road Building Starts on Private Land," *Columbian*, September 18, 1981; Pat Moser, "Ex-Soldier in the Thick of Gorge War," *Columbian*, July 13, 1981.

59 R-J Land Development, Inc., Corporate Reinstatement License: Renewal/Annual Report, State of Washington, April 4, 1985. Rim View Estates was recorded on May 14, 1981.

60 Don S. Willner, letter to Yvonne Montchalin, Larry Upson, John Yeon, and Susan Cady, October 19, 1981.

61 Editorial, "Gorge Threatened," *Columbian*, October 30, 1980.

62 John Yeon, letter to David Arnold, November 27, 1981. To understand Yeon's comparison, it is helpful to know that Vancouver was the largest city in southwest Washington (population 43,000 in 1980). It is the seat of Clark County and is located on the Columbia River about eighteen miles west of the Gorge entrance. The new city referenced by Yeon was Cascade Villages, a proposed $1.3 billion city of forty-five thousand people just west of the entrance to the Gorge. See Editorial, "Check Project's Regional Effects," *Oregonian*, September 22, 1980. Rumors of new short-plat subdivisions in Klickitat County would soon prove true. See Sverre Bakke, "Board Nixes Moratorium," *White Salmon Enterprise*, August 23, 1984.

63 George Cameron Coggins and Doris K. Nagel, "'Nothing Beside Remains': The Legal Legacy of James G. Watt's Tenure as a Secretary of the Interior on Federal Land and Law Policy," *Boston College Environmental Affairs Law Review* 473 (1990), 27, 491–2, 497–8.

64 Lawrence Rakestraw, "A History of Forest Conservation in the Pacific Northwest, 1891–1913" (thesis, University of Washington, 1955), chap. 2, https://foresthistory.org/wp-content/uploads/2017/01/A-HISTORY-OF-FOREST-CONSERVATION-IN-THE-PACIFIC-NORTHWEST.pdf (accessed April 30, 2020). The Gifford Pinchot National Forest, which now extends over almost 1.4 million acres in southwest Washington, consists largely of rugged, heavily forested, mountainous land through which several major rivers flow.

65 Denny Ceizyk, "Historical Mortgage Rates: Averages and Trends from the 1970s to 2020," https://www.valuepenguin.com/mortgages/historical-mortgage-rates#nogo; Pat Moser, "Timber Woes," *Columbian*, January 24, 1982; Lila Fujimoto and Jay McIntosh, "Skamania: County's Joblessness One of Highest; Lifestyles Suffering," *Daily News* (Longview, WA), May 10, 1982; Kathie Durbin, *Tree Huggers: Victory, Defeat and Renewal in the Northwest Ancient Forest Campaign* (Seattle: The Mountaineers, 1996), 47–48. See also Craig Welch, "A Brief History of the Spotted-Owl Controversy," *Seattle Times*, August 6, 2000, https://archive.seattletimes.com/archive/?date=20000806&slug=4035697 (accessed April 30, 2020). The local chamber of commerce estimated the unemployment rate to be at 60 percent. See Editorial, "Little Trust in Gorge," *Columbian*, April 10, 1981;

Elisabeth L. Lyon, "Enhancement of Tourism in the Columbia River Gorge" (August,1982), 5; David Cannard letter, October 30, 1981, in the author's possession.

66 Eric Pryne, "The Gorge: It Hasn't Been the Same Since 24 Homesites Were Requested," *Seattle Times, Pacific Magazine*, May 24, 1981; Editorial, *Skamania County Pioneer*, July 16, 1982, April 10, 1981.

67 Michael Sean Cowan, letter to the editor, *Skamania County Pioneer*, February 10, 1981; John Leonard, letter to the editor, *Skamania County Pioneer*, February 10, 1981; Spencer Heinz, "Building Pressure Mars Scenic Horizon, Official Says," *Sunday Oregonian*, August 26, 1984.

68 Statement of Louise Weidlich, Land Management in the Columbia River Gorge: Hearing before the Subcommittee on Public Lands and Reserved Water of the Committee on Energy and Natural Resources United States Senate, 98th Cong., November 8, 1984, 606; "Friends of the Gorge Co-Chairman Tells Need for Federal Control Measures," *Skamania County Pioneer*, March 27, 1981. See also Editorial, "Future History?" unknown Gorge newspaper, n.d., in author's possession.

69 Russell, Steno 25.

70 Envelopes, October 1981, in the author's possession; Russell, Steno 20; Linda Keene, "Gorge Lobbyist's Pay Object of Controversy," *Oregon Journal*, July 10, 1981; Nancy N. Russell, letter to Greg Nokes, January 24, 1994, in the author's possession. See also Jeanie Senior, "Odell Sawmill to Close, Idle 65 Workers," *Oregonian*, September 9, 1982.

71 American Land Rights Association, "Chuck Cushman: Founder and Executive Director," http://www.landrights.org/Staff.htm (accessed July 1, 2019); Steve Forrester, "Watt Era Affects Gorge Protection Fight," *Register Guard* (Eugene, OR), June 2, 1982; Chuck Williams, "The Park Rebellion: Charles Cushman, James Watt, and the Attack on the National Parks," *Not Man Apart* (June 1982), 7, 9, 19. Cushman even took credit for Watt's moratorium on parkland purchases. See Williams, "The Park Rebellion," 23. It is unclear who donated the $22,000 to the Gorge Defense League to hire Cushman. Skamania County commissioners told both Russell and Williams — but later denied — that Cushman was paid with county funds, and the *Pioneer* reported that Skamania County commissioners had hired Cushman. See Katy Tichenor, "Local Control of Columbia River Gorge to Require Tactical Planning," *Skamania County Pioneer*, February 20, 1981. Leick said that the month-old League raised the money through "bake sales, donations, and local charities," which seems implausible unless the donors included the county or timber companies and their families. See Keene, "Gorge Lobbyist's Pay," *Oregon Journal*, 1981.

72 Nancy N. Russell, letter to Robert L. Bartley, editor, *Wall Street Journal*, June 11, 1982; "Gorge Meeting," *Sentinel*, February 26, 1981; Solveig Torvik, "States at Odds on Columbia Gorge's Fate," *Seattle Post-Intelligencer*, July 20, 1981; Linda Keene, "Battle Looms over Columbia Gorge Future," *Oregon Journal*, June 27, 1981; "Chuck Cushman Advocates Local Populace Conduct their Own Gorge Field Hearings," *Skamania County Pioneer*, March 26 1986; Williams, "The Park Rebellion," 12; Cushman, PCC speech, 1982. Cushman disputed this charge, but Williams offered to provide witnesses. The average size of a family in 1980 was 2.76 people, so 15,000 families would equal 41,400 people. See Robert Pear, "Average Size of Household in US Declines to Lowest Ever Recorded," *New York Times*, April 15, 1987.

73 "Critic of Federal Control Documents Reasons Why," *Hood River News*, January 22, 1981; David Kern, "Gorge-Control Debate Getting Warmer," *Columbian*, April 8, 1981; "Bill Would Protect Cypress Island, Columbia Gorge from Developers," *Seattle Times*, February 13, 1981; "Commissioners Oppose Gorge Control Proposals," *Skamania County Pioneer*, April 17, 1981; David Kern, "State Senate Votes for Bistate Gorge Council," *Columbian*, April 2, 1981. A conservation easement typically involves a landowner's permanent conveyance to a government agency or nonprofit organization certain rights to develop his or her property. The CE bill died when the state's bond rating was lowered, increasing interest costs on bonds, but Russell also accurately attributed its failure to the Washington legislature's general lack of interest in the Gorge. See Marcia Wolf, "Zimmerman Loses Vote; Bauer Wins," *Columbian*, January 26, 1982.

74 David Kern, "Panel to Eye Gorge Control," *Columbian*, April 23, 1981; Linda Keene, "10 Named to Produce Gorge Plan," *Oregon Journal*, July 15, 1981; Editorial, *Columbian*, July 15, 1981; Editorial, *Oregonian*, July 30, 1981; Pat Moser, "States Are Apart on Gorge Control," *Columbian*, October 7, 1981; Select Committee on the Columbia Gorge, "Findings, Recommendations and Elements of a Management Alternative for the Columbia River Gorge," 4, 14, in author's possession; Linda Keene, "Panel Gives OK to Gorge Plan," *Oregon Journal* December 3, 1981. This plan was approved as an amendment to an earlier failed bill, and the committee was formed in April 1981. See Russell, Steno 40.

75 Editorial, *Columbian*, December 10, 1981; Editorial, *Skamania County Pioneer*, November 27, 1981; David Kern, "Gorge-Control Debate," *Columbian*, 1981.

76 Stickel memorandum, 1980; John Yeon, "Comments on Gorge Plan," February 16, 1981, in the author's possession.

77 John Yeon, comments regarding tributaries, n.d., in the author's possession; *Study of Alternatives for the Columbia River Gorge*, 28–29.

78 Yeon, comments regarding tributaries; Russell, Steno 9.

79 Friends of the Columbia Gorge, "Legislative Concepts for a National Scenic Area in the Columbia Gorge," May 18, 1981, 16, in the author's possession; Friends of the Columbia Gorge, Discussion Paper, February 1981, 8. See also Douglas H. Strong, *Tahoe: An Environmental History* (Lincoln: University of Nebraska Press, 1984). This would include joint approval, with the lead agency, of the Gorge management plan, and an early suggestion by the Friends had the Commission taking over the lead agency's powers after five years. See "Legislative Concepts," 17.

80 *Study of Alternatives for the Columbia River Gorge*, 185; John Yeon, letter to Dennis Buchanan (commissioner, Multnomah County), October 17, 1980, in the author's possession; Russell, Steno 9.

81 John Yeon, letter to Janet McLennan, September 1, 1976; Yeon, NRA proposal, n.d.; John Yeon, letter to Nancy Russell re Gorge politics and agencies, n.d. (c. 1981).

82 John Yeon, letter to Nancy Russell re Gorge politics and agencies, n.d. (c. 1981); National Park Service, "Options for Conservation and Reuse." The Department of the Interior also had issued a report in 1977 on the Oregon Trail. See Department of the Interior, Bureau of Outdoor Recreation, *The Oregon Trail: A Potential Addition to the National Trails System* (April 1977), in the author's possession; National Park Service Organic Act, 16 U.S.C. §1 (1916); John Yeon, letter to Robert W. Straub (Oregon governor), August 3, 1977; John Yeon, letter to Nancy Russell re Gorge politics and agencies, n.d. (c. 1981).

83 Cushman, speech, Portland Community College, 1982; Friends of the Columbia Gorge, "Columbia Gorge Legislative Proposal: Public Comment Synopsis," February, 1981; Russell, Steno 7; Jerry Routson (commissioner, Hood River); Editorial, *Hood River News*, June 4, 1981; Mark O. Hatfield (US senator, chairman, Appropriations Committee), letter to Governor John Spellman, February 23, 1981; Vic Atiyeh (Oregon governor) to Mark Hatfield, October 28, 1981; Connie Y. Chiang, with Michael Reese, "Evergreen State: Exploring the History of Washington's Forests; A Curriculum Project for Washington Schools," Center for the Study of the Pacific Northwest, http://www.washington.edu/ uwired/outreach/cspn/Website/Classroom%20Materials/Curriculum%20Packets/ Evergreen%20State/Section%20II.html (accessed April 30, 2020). This calculation was completed in 1985 by Chuck Williams. See Columbia Gorge Coalition, letter to Mark Hatfield (US senator), February 15, 1985. Oregon also had two national monuments and a national memorial, and Washington had a national historic park and two national historic sites. Only 0.3 percent of Oregon lands (174,992 acres) were part of the National Park system, while 4.4 percent of Washington lands were included in the system (1,930,485 acres). See also Russell Sadler, "Old Notions Ignore Tourism's Value," *Oregonian*, January 28, 1985.

84 Pat Moser. "Parks Official Doubts," *Columbian*, March 5, 1981; Yeon oral history, 31. See also Pat Moser, "Gorge Protection 'Complex,' Says Next Park Service Boss," *Columbian*, May 4, 1980.

85 R. E. Worthington (regional forester, US Forest Service), letter to Russell E. Dickenson (regional director, National Park Service), December 28, 1979, in the author's possession; John Yeon, meeting notes, December 17, 1980, in the author's possession; R. E. Worthington (regional forester, US Forest Service), letter to Donald E. Clark (executive, Multnomah County), October 24, 1981.

86 Friends of the Columbia Gorge, discussion paper, February 1981, 9; Nancy N. Russell, letter to Randall Revelle, January 28, 1980; Russell, Steno 7.

87 Friends of the Columbia Gorge, "Summary of Legislative Concept Proposal," May 12, 1981; Sally Anderson, memorandum to Gail Achterman, June 29, 1981; John Yeon, "Comments on Gorge Plan," 1981; John Yeon, letter to Dan Evans (US senator), September 18, 1984; Chuck Williams (Columbia Gorge Coalition), letter to Ron Wyden (US representative), December 21, 1982.

88 Friends of the Columbia Gorge, news release, September 15, 1981, in the author's possession.

89 128 Cong. Rec. S 3174-85 (daily ed. March 31, 1982), S3176.

90 Russell, Steno 59, Steno 17. Russell had been appointed by the Portland Garden Club to serve as its official conservation delegate, and at the meeting Russell was presented with GCA's XII Conservation Award.

91 Pat Moser, "Atiyeh Ready to Change Stance on Gorge Control," *Columbian*, March 12, 1981; John Yeon, letter to Vic Atiyeh (Oregon governor), June 9, 1981; Randy Gragg, "The Long View," *Portland Monthly*, June 2012, 67; Nancy Russell, letter to John Yeon, n.d., in the author's possession. Atiyeh also worried about a gubernatorial challenge from Don Clark. See Tom Fluharty, "Governor: Economy Better by the Fall," *Gresham Outlook*, April 27, 1982.

92 Robert K. Leick, letter to the editor, *Columbian*, September 25, 1982; Leick, "Testimony Presented to Governor's Select Committee," September 1, 1981; Chuck Williams, letter to the editor, *Skamania County Pioneer*, March 15, 1981; editorial, *Skamania County Pioneer*, December 10, 1982; Bill Dietrich, "And, Now, the Bottom 18 Local News Stories," *Columbian*, January 1982; advertisement, *Skamania County Pioneer*, August 13, 1982.

93 Nancy N. Russell (chair, Friends of the Columbia Gorge), to Neil Goldschmidt (Oregon governor) May 5, 1987.

94 Aubrey Russell interview, October 26, 2016.

95 Marie Hall, interview by the author, April 4, 2013.

96 Yeon statement, 1982.

97 John Yeon, letter to Richard Allison, April 22, 1982, in the author's possession.

98 Vancouver City Council hearing, 10.

CHAPTER 4

1 Columbia River Gorge Commission, "Skamania County West End Land Use and Parcelization Patterns," Staff Report, February 2, 1983, 1, 4. The Commission's study area encompassed approximately thirteen miles along the Columbia River in Skamania County, from its border with Clark County (three miles east of the Gorge entrance at Gibbons Creek) upriver to Beacon Rock. The first three miles along the river in Clark County, from Gibbons Creek east to the Clark-Skamania border, were omitted from the study.

2 Author's conversation with Nancy Russell, n.d. See also Sam Johnson (director, The Nature Conservancy Oregon), letter to Nancy Russell. July 2, 1982.

3 See Obituary, Huey Johnson, Resource Renewal Institute, http://www.rri.org/about_huey.php (accessed January 25, 2019).

4 Trust for Public Land Executive Committee, "OR, Hood River County, Yoerger Property," Resolution Fact Sheet, July 26, 1979.

5 For instance, TPL might pay $5,000 to option a property for eighteen months. After TPL had the property independently appraised, the purchase price might be set at 1 million dollars and the landowner gift at $150,000. TPL would use the eighteen-month option

term to lobby Congress to appropriate 1 million dollars for a federal agency—perhaps the Forest Service, Park Service, or Fish and Wildlife Service—to buy the optioned property. TPL would buy the property at the end of the option period and immediately sell it to the Forest Service for 1 million dollars. The agency would have purchased property it could not have otherwise for the same price it would have paid without TPL (federal law generally requires federal agencies to offer fair market value for properties and not negotiate below-FMV deals as private organizations could). The landowner would receive $850,000 cash plus a significant tax deduction and capital gains offsets; and TPL would have placed important private lands into public conservation ownership while funding operations with a $150,000 gift. Federal funding became particularly problematic during the Reagan administration, and TPL started to partner more with state agencies.

6	Nancy Russell, speech to Bainbridge Island Land Trust, Bainbridge Island, Washington, November 21, 1989, in the author's possession. The Gifford Pinchot National Forest's boundaries started several miles upriver from Beacon Rock. Note that Harriet Burgess was Harriet Hunt when Russell first met her but would soon marry Joe Burgess.

7	Nancy Russell, letter to Dave Cannard, January 4, 2003, in the author's possession; Nancy Russell, letter to Harriet Hunt, August 12, 1980; Russell, Steno 4, Steno 34, Steno 14.

8	Vic Atiyeh (Oregon governor), "State of the State," speech, January 10, 1983; David L. Cannard, letter to Richard Allison (administrative assistant to Governor John Spellman) and Karen Rahm (director, Planning and Community Affairs), January 18, 1983, in the author's possession. See also Editorial, "Etch Atiyeh Legacy in Basalt," *Oregonian*, January 15, 1983.

9	Russell, Steno 45.

10	Statements of Nancy N. Russell, Bill Benson (commissioner, Skamania County), Robert Packwood (US senator), Hearing on the Columbia River Gorge before the Committee on Commerce, Science, and Transportation, US Senate, 98th Cong., 1st sess. (February 10, 1983), 48–51, 68, 71.

11	Editorial, "Inaction in the Gorge: Another Retreat," *Columbian*, March 1, 1983.

12	129 Cong. Rec. S1850-57 (daily ed. March 1, 1983), S1850, S1857.

13	Vic Atiyeh and John Spellman, "Joint Statement on the Columbia River Gorge," March 15, 1983, in the author's possession; A Bill to Authorize the Establishment of a National Scenic Area, Statement of Nancy Russell, Hearing on S. 627 Before the Subcommittee on Public Lands and Reserved Water of the Committee on Energy and Natural Resources United States Senate, 98th Cong., 1st sess. (March 25, 1983), 114.

14	Russell, Steno 27, Steno 40. The record was held open after the hearing.

15	Hearing, Public Lands Subcommittee, 83, 417, 498–99; Scotta Callister, "Gorge Hearing Airs Opposing Views," *Oregonian*, March 26, 1983

16	Mark O. Hatfield (US senator), Hearing, Public Lands Subcommittee, 418–19.

17	Mark O. Hatfield, Hearing, 418–19.

18	Nancy N. Russell, letter to Mark Hatfield (US senator), March 26, 1983.

19	Regional Planning Council, "Port of Camas/Washougal Master Plan," April 1983, 6, 8–9; Jeffrey P. Breckel (director, Oregon and Washington Columbia River Gorge Commissions), letter to Mark Turpel (Regional Planning Council), January 26, 1984; John Yeon, letter to Harriet Burgess, June 14, 1984.

20	Hidden Harbor FEIS, 2, 26, 33; "Information Bulletin: Hidden Harbor," landowner bulletin, n.d. Note that some earlier articles incorrectly referenced a seventy-eight-lot development. Hidden Harbor was to be located approximately three miles upriver from Rizor's proposed subdivision and two miles below Beacon Rock.

21	Landowner bulletin, 3, 5.

22	Skamania County Planning Commission, minutes, July 12, 1983.

23	Skamania County Planning Commission, motion for approval of Columbia Gorge Riverfront Estates, August 9, 1983; Jeanie Senior, "Gorge Panels Urge Moratorium on Development," *Oregonian*, October 17, 1983. See also newsletter, Friends of the Columbia Gorge (Autumn 1983).

24 Editorial, *Columbian*, August 5, August 19, 1983; Editorial, *Oregonian*, August 10, 1983; Editorial, *Walla Walla Union Bulletin*, August 10, 1983; Editorial, *Daily Astorian*, August 11, 1983; Steve Neal, "Home Sites Threaten Columbia River Falls," *Chicago Tribune*, September 21, 1983; Senior, "Gorge Panels Urge Moratorium," *Oregonian* 1983.

25 "Lake Tahoe Plan Holds Lessons for Columbia Gorge," *Columbian*, April 10, 1983; Russell, Steno 31; Eric Pryne, "Bill to Preserve Columbia Gorge May Cross an Old Chasm of Split Opinions," *Seattle Post-Intelligencer*, October 2, 1985. The Tahoe Regional Planning Agency (TRPA) was enjoined from approving any development proposal until the states adopted a management plan that did not violate the compact. See order granting preliminary injunction, *California v. Tahoe Regional Planning Agency*, US Dist. Ct. Case No. Civ. S-84-0561 EJG and S-84-0565 EJG (E.D. Cal., filed June 5, 1984). The most thorough analysis of the history of the Lake Tahoe Area, which includes a comprehensive examination of TRPA, is Strong, *Tahoe: An Environmental History*.

26 Carol Kirchner, memorandum to Nancy Russell, Dave Cannard, Susan Cady, Kristine Simenstad, February 2, 1982, in the author's possession; Dave Fielder, "Jackson Gives Grange Crowd Image of his Youthful Vigor," *Columbian*, June 27, 1983; Henry M. Jackson (US senator), statement, 129 Cong. Rec. S11,829 (daily ed., August 4, 1983); Nancy Russell, letter to Charles Luce, November 25, 1982. Jackson chaired the Senate Interior and Insular Affairs Committee from 1963 to 1980. The laws he guided through Congress included the National Environmental Policy Act, the Wilderness Act, the Land and Water Conservation Fund, the National Wild and Scenic Rivers Act, and the National Trails Systems Act. When introducing the governors' bill, Jackson stated: "I want to make it abundantly clear . . . that I have taken no position relative to the merits of the Governor's proposal. . . . I would not want my introduction of this measure today to be construed by anyone as an endorsement." See also Russell, Steno 25.

27 "'A Fitting Tribute': Olympic Wilderness Renamed for Longtime Outdoors Advocate, Former Gov. Dan Evans," *Seattle Times*, August 18, 2017; Nancy Russell, memorandum to Charles Luce, November 25, 1982, in the author's possession.

28 "Changing Bonneville's Role as Power Provider to the Northwest," *Northwest Power and Power Planning Council, Council Quarterly* (Summer 2006), 6, 8.

29 John Harrison, "Colonel of Columbia Gorge Stuns Foes," *Columbian*, November 6, 1983.

30 John Harrison, "Colonel of Columbia Gorge Stuns Foes."

31 "Columbia's Gorge Is Focus of Battle," *New York Times*, December 20, 1983; Editorial, *Oregonian*, October 28, 1983; Harrison, "Colonel of Columbia Gorge Stuns Foes"; Editorial, *Skamania County Pioneer*, October 28, 1983.

32 Russell, Steno 34, Steno 37. Russell subsequently crossed out these lines, probably not wanting to complain to her friend. See also Russell, Steno 13, Steno 34, Steno 47.

33 Nancy Russell, letter to Don Frisbee, May 27, 1984, in the author's possession; Russell, Steno 33, Steno 34, Steno 35, Steno 37, Steno 40, Steno 53.

34 Russell, Steno 34; Nancy N. Russell, letter to board members, Friends of the Columbia Gorge, August 22, 1984; "Bargain Sale Option Agreement," Seller D. M. Stevenson Ranch and Buyer Trust for Public Land, April 20, 1984; Trust for Public Land, "Steigerwald Lake Project," Fact Sheet, May 29, 1984.

35 Nancy Russell, notes on conversation with Joe Mentor, n.d., in the author's possession.

36 Russell, Steno 41, Steno 37; Wally Stevenson, interview by the author, September 4, 2013. See also Russell, Steno 34 and Steno 41.

37 Jeremy Gillick, "Boom with a View: Economics vs. Environment in the Gorge," *Willamette Week*, https://www.wweek.com/portland/article-8392-boom-with-a-view.html (accessed May 10, 2020). The federal agencies were the Army Corps of Engineers and the US Fish & Wildlife Service.

38 Joel Connelly, "A 'Straight Arrow' Politician Honored for What he Did Outdoors," *Seattle Post-Intelligencer*, June 13, 2016, https://www.seattlepi.com/local/politics/article/A-Straight-Arrow-honored-for-preserving-wild-8110910.php (accessed May 1, 2020); "Senate Panel Approves Gorge Land Purchase," *Columbian*, August 3, 1984; Nancy N. Russell, letter to Mr. and Mrs. Robert B. Wilson, June 11, 1984.

39 Russell, Steno 37; Editorial, *Sunday Oregonian*, June 10, 1984; Editorial, *Columbian*, June 11, 1984.

40 John Yeon, letter to Harriet Burgess, June 14, 1984, in the author's possession; Russell, Steno 38; John C. Ramig (Special Groups Coordinator), letter to Nancy Russell, September 26, 1984, in the author's possession; Russell, letter to board members, Friends of the Columbia Gorge, August 22, 1984; Nancy Russell, Welcoming Remarks, Hatfield event, August 29, 1984, in the author's possession.

41 The $10 million included almost $6 million to buy the property and additional funds to restore Gibbons Creek, build trails, and so forth.

42 Stevenson interview.

43 Nancy Russell, letters to Charles Luce, November 25, 1982, April 2, 1983, in the author's possession; Nancy N. Russell, letter to Governor Tom McCall, December 5, 1982; Russell, Steno 34; Steve Forrester, "Congress Awaits New NW Senator," *Columbian*, September 27, 1983; Trust for Public Land, "Schaefer–St. Cloud Ranch," Fact Sheet, June 12, 1984. See also Trust for Public Land, "Columbia Gorge Preservation Program," proposal, May 1987, 12, in the author's possession; Nancy Russell, letter to Charles Luce, March 22, 1983, in the author's possession.

44 Russell, Steno 37.

45 Nancy Russell, memorandum re loans to Trust for Public Land, October 27, 2004; "Prime Rate History," 2019, http://www.fedprimerate.com/wall_street_journal_prime_rate_history.htm (accessed October 15, 2019); Robert W. McIntyre (senior vice president and chief financial officer, Trust for Public Land), letter to Bruce Russell, November 25, 1987, in the author's possession; Ralph W. Benson (vice president and general counsel, Trust for Public Land), letter to Bruce Russell, July 5, 1984. This was an installment sale, where TPL paid $155,000 in cash with the balance to be paid over time secured by a promissory note.

46 Nancy Russell, letter to Harriet Hunt, September 4, 1981. Montchalin had also sold The Shire to John Yeon and, at Russell's request, had been a plaintiff against George Rizor. Even Skamania County's Park and Recreation plan called for public access to the river there. See Hidden Harbor, FEIS, 83.

47 Industrial Forestry Association, "New Drive for Federal Control of the Columbia Gorge," December 1, 1980. The Mount St. Helens National Volcanic Monument Act was enacted in August 1982. The Washington wilderness bill was introduced in the Senate in March 1983, passed in May 1984, and became law in July.

48 Nancy N. Russell, letter to Mrs. Tom McCall (Audrey), September 29, 1983; Russell, letter to Mrs. McCall for Dan Evans (US senator), n.d.; Jeanie Senior, "Rowena Dell Dedication Spurs Warning," *Sunday Oregonian*, April 4, 1982; Russell, Steno 32.

49 Bob Packwood and Mark Hatfield, letter to Senate colleagues, January 27, 1984.

50 Newsletter, Friends of the Columbia Gorge (Summer/Fall 1984).

51 Russell, Steno 15, Steno 15, Steno 15, Steno 36. See also Nancy Russell, notes from telephone call from Ron Wyden (US representative), December 9, 1995, in the author's possession; Friend of the Columbia Gorge, press conference, 1984; Editorial, March 27, 1983. See also Friends of the Columbia Gorge, statement at press conference, March 20, 1984, in the author's possession.

52 Russell, Steno 27; *Winds in the Gorge* (Summer 1983); Editorial and cartoon, *Seattle Post-Intelligencer*, February 22, 1983; Editorial, *Seattle Post-Intelligencer*, March 26, 1984.

53 Kristine Simenstad, weekly staff reports, October 3–14, October 31–November 4, 1983), in the author's possession; *Winds in the Gorge* (Fall 1983, Summer/Fall 1984); Russell, Steno 39 (August 21–September 28, 1984).

54 Friends of the Columbia Gorge, statement at press conference, March 20, 1984; Russell, Steno 39.

55 John Harrison, "Jung Pushes ahead with Gorge Subdivision Plan," *Columbian*, February 21, 1984; Jeanie Senior, "Gorge Commission Cites Lack of Need," *Oregonian*, March 23, 1984; idem, "Board OKs Housing in Gorge," *Oregonian*, September 26, 1984.

56 Sverre Bakke, "Commissioners Conditionally Approve Burdoin Plats," *Goldendale (WA) Sentinel*, August 23, 1984; Sverre Bakke, "Board Nixes Moratorium," *White Salmon (WA) Enterprise*, August 23, 1984; Jeanie Senior, "Ruthton Park up for Sale," *Oregonian*, January 3, 1983; Columbia River Gorge Commissions, "Ruthton Park Traded to County," *Gorge Notes* (July 1984); Russell, Steno 39; "Executive Director's Report," *Winds in the Gorge* (Spring 1984).

57 Nancy N. Russell, letter to Harley Brown, July 20, 1983, in the author's possession.

58 Nancy N. Russell, letter to Tom Throop (speaker, House of Representatives), December 15, 1984; Russell Steno 41. See also "Executive Director's Report," *Winds in the Gorge* (Spring 1985); Russell, Steno 48; "Decry 'Bill Stuffing,'" *Oregonian*, May 1985; Tom Braman, "Skamania Hydro Ban Loses," *Columbian*, March 1, 1985; Holly Gilbert, "Arlo Guthrie Sings Praises of 'Roll on Columbia,'" *Oregonian*, April 23, 1985; RCW 1.20.073 (1987) http://www.netstate.com/states/symb/song/wa_roll_on_columbia.htm (accessed May 2, 2020).

59 See Friends of the Columbia Gorge, executive director's report, in *Winds in the Gorge* (Summer/Fall 1984); Jim Running, "Friends of Gorge Oppose Location of Port of Entry," *Oregonian*, January 20, 1984; John Enders, "Decision Due on Site of Truck Port of Entry in Gorge," *Oregonian*, September 13, 1984; Russell, Steno 35.

60 Running, "Friends Oppose Port of Entry," *Oregonian*, 1984; Alan Hayakawa, "Voter-dictated Home Rule Amendment Throws County Officials into Turmoil," *Oregonian*, November 14, 1976; John Enders, "Decision Due on Site of Truck Port of Entry in Gorge," *Oregonian*, September 13, 1984. See "No Truck Port in Gorge," *Oregonian*, August 4, 1984.

61 Nancy Russell, "In My Opinion," *Oregonian*, January 31, 1984; "No Truck Port in Gorge," *Oregonian*, August 4, 1984; Russell, Steno 35; John Enders, "Decision Due on Site of Truck Port of Entry in Gorge," *Oregonian*, September 13, 1984. See also "Troutdale Officials Rap Port-of-Entry Choice," *Oregonian*, October 11, 1984.

62 David Hoffman, "Watt Submits Resignation as Interior Secretary," *Washington Post*, October 10, 1983; Jeanie Senior, "Gardner Signals State Policy Shift on Gorge Control," *Oregonian*, November 9, 1984.

63 Advertisement, *Skamania County Pioneer* and *White Salmon Enterprise*, November 1, 1984.

64 Dan Evans (US senator), statement, US Senate hearing, November 1984, 2, 3. A bill can be introduced at any point during a two-year Congress. It will remain eligible for consideration throughout the duration of that Congress until it ends or adjourns sine die. A new Congress begins at noon on January 3 of each odd-numbered year following a general election, unless it designates a different day by law. A Congress lasts for two years, with each year constituting a separate session; 1985 was the first year of the two-year legislative session. US House of Representatives, Office of the Clerk, http://clerk.house.gov/legislative/legfaq.aspx (accessed June 15, 2018).

65 Esson H. Smith (Columbia Gorge United) and Chuck Williams, statements, US Senate Hearing, November 1984, 406, 294.

66 Yeon to Dunn, November 1984.

67 John Harrison, "Gardner Backs Strong Federal Gorge Control," *Columbian*, November 8, 1984; US Senate Hearing, November 1984, 32–33; Senior, "Gardner Signals Shift," *Oregonian*, November 1984. Gardner's testimony was read by his representative, Dave Michener.

CHAPTER FIVE

1 Russell, Steno 29; "The Columbia River Gorge: Management by Whom?" Outdoor Unlimited, Inc., April 1982, in the author's possession; Bill Dietrich, "And, Now, the Bottom 18 Local News Stories," *Columbian*, January 1982; Joe Wrabek, *A Columbia Gorge Primer*, PARK-MAN publication, 1983, in author's possession.

2 Vera Dafoe, interview by the author, March 12, 2011. See also Tom Vaughan (executive director, Oregon Historical Society), interview by the author, October 31, 2012.

3 Russell, Steno 50; Nancy Russell, letter to Paul C. Pritchard, March 3, 1986; Russell to Paul Pritchard, "Suggestions for Remarks to Portland Garden Club, 4/17/86," February 3, 1986.

4 P.E.O. website, https://www.peointernational.org/about-peo (accessed May 16, 2018); Russell, Steno 6.

5 Russell, Steno 37; Hearing, Public Lands Subcommittee, 506; Packwood and Hatfield to Senate colleagues, 1984; Russell to Pritchard, "Suggestions for Remarks," 1986. Packwood was named chair of the Senate Finance Committee in 1985.

6 Russell, Steno 9.

7 Susan Black, interview by the author, July 23, 2013; Mary Bishop, interview by the author, December 13, 2006. Mary Bishop was Brot Bishop's wife.

8 Russell to Pritchard, "Suggestions for Remarks," 1986.

9 Sally Russell, interview by the author, February 16, 2017; Peyton Chapman, conversation with the author, February 3, 2013.

10 Bob Neighbor, interview by the author, May 22, May 28, 2014. See also Aubrey Russell interview, November 14, 2016.

11 Newsletter, Friends of the Columbia Gorge (Summer 1983); Russell, Steno 30.

12 Hammond interview, February 1, 2017.

13 Hammond interview, February 1, 2017; Kristine Simenstad-Mackin, interview by the author, July 10, 2014.

14 Harriet Burgess, letter to Robert Schaefer, February 28, 1985; order granting preliminary injunction, *California v. Tahoe Regional Planning Agency*, US Dist. Ct. Case No. Civ. S-84-0561 (E.D. Cal., filed June 5, 1984); Russell, Steno 45; Harriet Hunt, "Land Acquisition by the Forest Service in Columbia Gorge," April 18, 1979, in the author's possession.

15 Yeon to Giambardine, 1980; Russell, Steno 44.

16 Martin Broussard, letter to Don Vaughan, January 21, 1985, in the author's possession; Bob McIntyre "The Typical Project As Seen By," n.d.

17 Russell, Steno 45; Trust for Public Land, "Kerr, Clark County, Washington," Fact Sheet, February 14, 1986.

18 NCED, "Conservation Easements and the National Conservation Easement Database, https://www.conservationeasement.us/storymap/index.html (accessed May 3, 2020); Don Vaughan, memorandum to Harriet Burgess, November 18, 1984, in the author's possession; Wendy Reif, "Washougal Family Sells their Farm to Save It," *Columbian*, September 23, 1985; Carolyn Ritter, "The Jemtegaard Family: 1871–1985," October 6, 1985, http://www.columbiagorge.org/wp-content/uploads/docs/Jemtegaard,_Bendikt_and_Gertrude.pdf (accessed May 3, 2020); Vaughan, letter to Harriet Burgess, "Jemtegaard Property," 1984. A simpler plan would have been to buy (and convey to the USFS) an easement from the existing farmer, allowing him or her to retain the underlying farm, but for a variety of reasons—mostly relating to the age of the current farmers, as seen in the Jemtegaard transaction—this was not possible.

19 Trust for Public Land, "Rolf Jemtegaard: Skamania County, Washington," Fact Sheet, June 28, 1985, 7; Reif, "Washougal Family Sells," 1985. Note that the Jemtegaards owned another 150 acres that TPL would negotiate to purchase.

20 Don Vaughan, memorandum to Harriet Burgess, October 8, 1985; "Columbia Falls Natural Area in Skamania County," *Ear to the Ground*, March 29, 2011, https://washingtondnr.wordpress.com/2011/03/29/6675/ (accessed May 5, 2020). See also Trust for Public Land, "A Request for Funding: Land and Water Conservation Fund; FY 1987" (1987), 10. This amount was 80 percent of the property's appraised fair market value, so the donation to TPL would be 20 percent of FMV, assuming that the eventual "take-out" agency bought the land for the amount that TPL's appraiser considered its fair market value.

21 Russell, Steno 47.

22 "Agency Buys Gorge Acreage," *Columbian*, September 26, 1985; Lois M. Kemp, "Plant List—Coyote Wall to Major Creek," November 1980, in the author's possession; Warren W. Caldwell and Roy L. Carlson, "Further Documentation of 'Stone Piling' During the

Plateau Vision Quest," *American Anthropologist*, no. 56 (1954): 441–42; Emory Strong, letter to Dr. Richard D. Daugherty (Washington State College), June 14, 1976. It is believed that these rock formations served many purposes: hunting, food storage, burials, lookouts, and fighting positions as well as spirit quest sites. See Chuck Sams, telephone conversation with the author, April 24, 2019, and Boyd, *People of The Dalles*, 118. There were lands held by the Department of the Interior in trust for Native people in the eastern Gorge, but these are not traditional "public lands" with public access. See also Don Vaughan, memorandum to Harriet Burgess, February 13, 1986, in the author's possession.

23 Trust for Public Land, "Lauterbach (Catherine Creek), Klickitat Co., WA: Authorization to Acquire and Convey," March 15, 1985, in the author's possession; Russell, memorandum re loans, 2004; Harriet Burgess, memorandum to Marty Rosen, May 23, 1985, in the author's possession. The Reagan administration's antipathy to buying private lands for conservation purposes had forced TPL, nationally as well as in the Northwest, to open up new markets, exploring the use of state agencies as "take-outs."

24 In 1985, TPL's administrative budget was $3.5 million. See Touche Ross, "Trust for Public Land and Related Organizations: Combined Statements of Functional Expenses; Years ended March 31, 1986 and 1985."

25 Nancy Russell, letter to Mike Salsgiver, October 4, 1985. See also Russell, Steno 48. This was in the process of changing, as TPL witnessed — first hand — the dangers of being tied to a single, federal market headed by President Reagan; by 1985, however, TPL had not been able to sufficiently diversify into state and local markets or build an extensive donor base.

26 Russell, Steno 43. See also Nancy N. Russell, letter to Mark Hatfield (US senator), March 21, 1985, in the author's possession; Russell, Steno 46, Steno 48; Bowen Blair, contemporary notes. See also Russell, Steno 50.

27 Russell, Steno 43; National Park Service, "Past Directors of the National Park Service," https://www.nps.gov/aboutus/nps-directors.htm (accessed June 12, 2017); Iver Peterson, "New Director of National Park Service Outlines His Goals and Policies," *New York Times*, June 7, 1985. See also Bowen Blair, contemporaneous notes, Department of Interior staff meeting, Washington, DC, March 13, 1985, in author's possession.

28 Marie Pampush, memorandum to Bowen Blair, in the author's possession; Chuck Williams, letter to Mike McCloskey (executive director, Sierra Club), March 13, 1985, in the author's possession; Kristine Simenstad, weekly staff reports (April 21–May 3, 1985).

29 Mark O. Hatfield, Bob Packwood, Slade Gorton, and Dan Evans, letter to Nancy N. Russell, March 29, 1985, in the author's possession; David Whitney, "Study Favors Slightly Smaller Columbia Gorge Scenic Area," *Oregonian*, April 26, 1985.

30 Russell, Steno 53; Friends of the Columbia Gorge, "Gorge Group Opts for Park Service," news release, May 22, 1985.

31 Nancy Russell, letter to Allan Comp, May 29, 1985.

32 Nancy N. Russell, letter to Charles H. Odegaard (Midwest regional director, National Park Service), May 20, 1985; "Testimony of Friends of the Columbia Gorge, Columbia Gorge Scenic Area Senate Workshop," June 12, 1985, in author's possession; David Whitney, "Gorge Bill Leaves Hard Feelings Within Oregon Delegation," *Oregonian*, October 26, 1986; Russell, Steno 46. Experts included Russ Jolley and Lois Kemp (botany), Don and Roberta Lowe (hiking trails), Stephen Dow Beckham (history), Ivan Donaldson (history), Cliff Crawford (history), and John E. Allen (geology).

33 Friends of the Columbia Gorge, "Management Alternatives for the Columbia River Gorge," June 28, 1985, in the author's possession; Friends of the Columbia Gorge, Management Alternatives, 1985, 5–6; Jeanie Senior, "County Board Asks End to Gorge Group," *Oregonian*, June 15, 1985; Don Jepsen, "Washington Committee Rejects Gorge Budget," *Oregonian*, April 23, 1985; Russell, Steno 46. Funding was restored to the commission but late in the process, and barely. The FOCG report also noted that the Power Planning Council's constitutionality was still being litigated.

34 See also Ed Malbin, letter to Laurie Aunan, July 9, 1996, in the author's possession; Russell, Steno 46, Steno 47.

35 Meeting report, staff meeting, Oregon and Washington senators and governors, Lacey, WA, August 14–15, 1985. Wyden's and Bonker's staff were invited to observe.

36 Jeanie Senior, "Gorge Commissions Voice Concerns Over Evans' Proposals," *Oregonian*, May 24, 1985; David Whitney, "NW Solons Near Accord on Gorge Protection," *Oregonian*, September 13, 1985.

37 Russell, Steno 46.

38 Bowen Blair, memorandum to Nancy Russell, August 30, 1985. Before the year was out, Hatfield gave three reasons for his support of the Forest Service to Portland City Commissioner Mike Lindberg, who had written him to support National Park Service management: (1) the Forest Service was a major Gorge landowner; (2) "on balance," its track record in the Gorge was good; and (3) the Forest Service had shown "needed sensitivity" to private landowners in the Gorge. "Nothing I have heard or seen," Hatfield emphasized "has convinced me that the Forest Service should not be designated as the lead federal agency." See Mark O. Hatfield, letter to Mike Lindberg, December 20, 1985; "Interior Secretary Hodel Airs Views on Gorge Scenic Area Proposals," *Skamania County Pioneer*, September 25, 1985.

39 Friends of the Columbia Gorge, memorandum, August 9, 1985; Russell, Steno 48, Steno 49, Steno 47. See also Rolla J. Crick, "Japan-America Parley to Begin Wednesday," *Oregonian*, September 2, 1985

40 Eric Pryne, "Bill to Preserve Columbia Gorge May Cross an Old Chasm of Split Opinions," *Seattle Post-Intelligencer*, October 2, 1985; Phil Cogswell, "Gorge Bill: Devil Is in the Details," *Oregonian*, September 20, 1985; Editorial, *Seattle Post-Intelligencer*, September 7, 1985; Editorial, *Columbian*, September 13, 1985; Shelby Scates, "Now or Never for Columbia Gorge," *Seattle Post-Intelligencer*, October 27, 1985.

41 Chuck Williams, letter to Ron Wyden, December 21, 1982; Chuck Williams, letter to Bowen Blair, November 15, 1985.

42 Brock Evans, memorandum to Oregon and Washington State Columbia Gorge Leaders, December 18, 1985.

43 99th Cong., 2d Sess., February 6 (legislative day, January 27), 1986, August 14 (legislative day, August 11), 1986. See also John Harrison, "NW Senators Introduce Gorge Bill," *Columbian*, February 6, 1986; 132 Cong. Rec. S1147-56 (daily ed., February 6, 1986). Weaver was also campaigning as the Democratic nominee against Packwood for his Senate seat but later withdrew from the race. The Wyden/Morrison bill was supposed to be identical to the senators' bill, but to everyone's surprise—including its sponsors—it was different. For a detailed analysis of the various bills, see Bowen Blair, "The Columbia River Gorge National Scenic Area: The Act, its Genesis and Legislative History," 17 Envtl. L. 863 1986–1987, 898.

44 Editorial, *Oregonian*, February 9, 1986; Editorial, *Columbian*, February 6, 1986; Editorial, *Seattle Post-Intelligencer*, February 10, 1986; Editorial, "Saving Columbia Gorge," *Bremerton (WA) Sun*, March 3, 1986; Friends of the Columbia Gorge, National Audubon Society, Portland Audubon Society, Sierra Club, Wilderness Society, Oregon Environmental Council, "Columbia Gorge Action Alert," n.d. (1986), in the author's possession.

45 Douglas N. Jewett (city attorney, Seattle), letter to Nancy Russell, April 3, 1986.

46 Committee to Save the Columbia Gorge, door hanger, KATU-TV, KOIN-TV, KGW-TV, April 12, 1986, in author's possession; executive director's report, newsletter, Friends of the Columbia Gorge (Spring 1986).

47 Daniel J. Evans, letter to Doug Jewett, April 23, 1986; Debbie F. Craig, letter to Bowen Blair and Friends of Columbia Gorge executive committee, May 7, 1986; Nancy Russell, Dave Cannard, and Mitch Bower, letter to Dan Evans, May 13, 1986. See also Bowen Blair, memorandum to Friends of the Columbia Gorge board of directors, May 29, 1986.

48 Millard McClung, interview by the author, October 13, 2012.

49 "A Bill to Establish the Columbia Gorge National Scenic Area, and for Other Purposes," June 17, 1986: Statement of Malcolm Wallop, Hearing on S.2055 Before the Subcommittee

on Public Lands, Reserved Water and Resource Conservation of the Committee on Energy and Natural Resources United States Senate," 99th Cong., 2d sess., 187.

50 Statement of Bob Packwood and statement of Peter Myers, Hearing on S.2055, 68–69, 127, 134.

51 Statement of Dan Evans, Hearing on S.2055, 971.

52 Statement of Commissioner Bill Benson, statement of Commissioner Ed Callahan, Hearing on S.2055, 365, 394.

53 Statement of Lois Jemtegaard, statement of Edgar Cleveland, Hearing on S.2055, 642–43, 645.

54 Statement of Dan Evans, Hearing on S.2055, 692, 702, 780. The July recess was upcoming, after which Congress would be in session for five-week and four-week periods.

55 Hearing before the Subcommittee on National Parks and Recreation of the Committee on Interior and Insular Affairs House of Representatives, 99th Cong., 2d sess., on H.R. 4114, 4134, 4161, 4221; statement of Larry Craig, Hearing before the Subcommittee on National Parks and Recreation, 464.

56 Statement of Representative Denny Smith, statement of Jim Weaver, Hearing before the Subcommittee on National Parks and Recreation, 583, 584, 585.

57 Statement of John Yeon, September 9, 1985, in the author's possession; Yeon, letter to Carol and Jim Gardner, June 18, 1986, in the author's possession.

58 Yeon, letter to Carol and Jim Gardner, June 18, 1986.

59 Senate Hearing before the Subcommittee on Public Lands, June 1986, 137; Editorial, *Oregonian*, July 14, 1986. The Gorge Commissions had been leasing office space from Skamania County in the former county jail. See "2 Panels on Gorge Evicted," *Oregonian*, July 9, 1986.

60 Jeanie Senior, "Broughton Lumber to Close," *Oregonian*, July 17, 1986; Broughton Lumber Co. to Suspend Operations," *Skamania County Pioneer*, July 1986; Russell, Steno 39; North American Wholesale Lumber Association Inc., "Bulletin 21–84," November 12, 1984. See also Ed Callahan, letter to the editor, *Oregonian*, July 21, 1986; Russell Steno 53; Columbia Gorge Commissions, "Timber Production on Lands in the Columbia Gorge," November 1984, in the author's possession. One Crown Zellerbach official was forced to apologize to Senator Packwood for distributing false information about Packwood's legislation. See Russell Steno 10, Steno 39.

61 Columbia River Gorge Act of 1986; and Columbia Gorge National Scenic Area Act, August 1, 1986: Hearing before the Subcommittee on Forests, Family Farms, and Energy of the Committee on Agriculture House of Representatives, 99th CONG., 2d sess., on H.R. 4114, H.R. 4134, H.R. 4161, and H.R. 4221; statement of Charles Whitley, Hearing before the Subcommittee on Forests, Family Farms, and Energy, 52; Subcommittee on Forests Hearing, 1986, 11–13; Jeanie Senior, "Gorge Bill Hearing Plays Familiar Themes," *Oregonian*, August 2, 1986.

62 David Whitney, "NW Senators to Strengthen Gorge Bill," *Oregonian*, August 5, 1986; Blair, "The Act, its Genesis," 912; S 2055, 99th Cong., 2d Sess. (Feb. 6 [legislative day, Jan. 27], 1986, August 14 [legislative day, August 11], 1986), 56, 78.

63 Russell, Steno 48, Steno 50, Steno 52. For instance, knowing that the director of the Vancouver-based M. J. Murdock Charitable Trust was a history buff, Russell sent him copies of Lewis and Clark's journals, with maps outlining their Gorge encampments. She then put together a tour of the sites, which included a TPL project, and pointed out where the trust's benefactor, M.J. Murdock, had died in a plane crash. She organized a separate tour for more than a dozen potential major donors of Miller Island, a one-thousand-acre island in the eastern Gorge that has cultural significance for the Yakama Nation, Nez Perce Tribe, Confederated Tribes of the Warm Springs Reservation, and the Confederated Tribes of the Umatilla Indian Reservation. See Russell, Steno 46, Steno 48; Harriet Burgess, letter to Robert M. Schaefer, February 25, 1986.

64 Boyd, *People of The Dalles*, 36–37.

65 Leverett Richards, "US Purchase of Game Area Celebrated," *Oregonian*, April 2, 1986.

66 Jeanie Senior, "Shorelines Development Permit Reversed," *Oregonian*, March 12, 1986; Hidden Harbor FEIS, 26, 33.

67 Martin J. Rosen, letter to Nancy Russell, July 30, 1986. The unsold lots at Rim View Estates were placed under a sixty-day option on July 22, 1986; the Russells entered into their loan agreement with TPL on July 23; TPL opened escrow to complete the purchase, for $297,500, on September 26, 1986.

68 Much of TPL's additional $700,000 in debt carried interest rates that exceeded 10 percent. TPL had also spent more than $100,000 for appraisals, property taxes, insurance, and other costs, some of which were reoccurring. Bob McIntyre, memorandum to Harriet Burgess, September 17, 1986, in the author's possession. See also "The Trust for Public Land Schedule of Notes Payable," November 30, 1987.

69 Congressional Research Service, "Congressional Proposals to Establish Land Use Controls for the Columbia River Gorge: Issues of Constitutional Authority," August 30, 1984; CRS memorandum, August 30, 1984, 15, 18. See also Congressional Research Service, "Constituent Question as to the Constitutional Authority of the United States to Condemn Land for Purposes of Scenic Preservation," October 1, 1982; Congressional Research Service, "A Legal Analysis of House Bills in the 99th Congress on the Columbia River Gorge," May 15, 1986; CRS memorandum, August 30, 1984, 5, 8. The Cape Cod National Seashore, for instance, was 15 percent the size of the Gorge and only 4 percent of its lands were privately held. See "Nonfederal Lands Within the National Seashore," https://www. nps.gov/caco/learn/management/upload/nonfederallands.pdf (accessed June 13, 2019). See also National Park Service, Land Resources Division, Listing of Acreage (Summary), December 31, 2014, https://irma.nps.gov/Stats/FileDownload/1198.

70 Statement of Denny Smith, Hearing before the Subcommittee on National Parks, June 19, 1986, 583.

71 David Whitney, "Panel OKs Columbia Gorge Bill," *Oregonian*, August 15, 1986.

72 David Whitney, "Gorge Legislation Faces Obstacle Course," *Oregonian*, September 30, 1986. See Blair, "The Act, its Genesis," 915. The key delegation members who cosponsored the bill were Representatives Weaver (D-OR), AuCoin (D-OR), Bonker (D-WA), Wyden (D-OR), Lowry (D-WA), Miller (R-WA), and Dicks (D-WA). See House Committee on Agriculture, Calendar, HR 5625, October 1, 1986.

73 David Whitney, "House Panel Due to Take Up Gorge Bill," *Oregonian*, October 2, 1986; Steve Forrester, "October Is a Month of Surprises," *Daily Astorian*, October 11, 1986; Joseph T. Wrabek, "Stop Congress's National Adjournment Park," *Wall Street Journal*, September 26, 1986.

74 David Whitney, "Gorge Bill Delayed by Stalling," *Oregonian*, October 3, 1986; Martha A. Miles and Caroline Rand Herron, "Congress Misses Another Target for Adjournment," *New York Times*, October 5, 1986; Whitney, "Gorge Legislation Faces Obstacle Course," *Oregonian*, September 30, 1986.

75 Eric Pryne, "Committee Tricks Help Advance Bill on Columbia Gorge," *Seattle Times*, October 8, 1986.

76 132 Cong. Rec. S15628-50 (daily ed. Oct. 8, 1986), S15628–S15650; James C. Flanagan, "Committee Sends Stripped-down Gorge Bill to House," *Oregonian*, October 8, 1986. For details on the changes, see Blair, "The Act, its Genesis," 923–24. See also Eric Pryne, "Columbia Gorge Measure Advances," *Seattle Times*, October 9, 1986.

77 Blair, "The Act, its Genesis," 918–19. The subcommittee had fewer Republican firebrands than the Interior Committee did.

78 Steve Forrester, "October Is a Month of Surprises," *Daily Astorian*, October 11, 1986; Mark O. Hatfield, letter to Bob Smith (US representative), October 9, 1986; David Whitney, "Gorge Bill Passed by Senate," *Oregonian*, October 18, 1986. See also "Congress OK's Huge Money Bill," *Seattle Times*, October 18, 1986.

79 Sine die was on Saturday, October 18, but Congress's last legislative day was October 17. "History, Art and Archives: United States House of Representatives," https://history.house. gov/Institution/Session-Dates/All/ (accessed June 12, 2019).

80 Steve Forrester, "October Is a Month of Surprises," *Daily Astorian*, October 11, 1986; Ken Bergquist (acting assistant attorney general), letter to Representative Morris Udall (US representative), October 14, 1986; 132 Cong. Rec. H10462-70, 132 Cong. Rec. H10485-90, 132 Cong. Rec. H11121-48 (daily ed. October 16, 1986), H10487. See also Blair, "The Act, its Genesis," 926-27; David Whitney, "Hope Fading Fast for Legislation on Gorge," *Oregonian*, October 15, 1986.

81 David Whitney, "NW Demos Fail to Get Gorge Bill Released," *Oregonian*, October 16, 1986; "Columbia Gorge: House Votes 290-91 for Bill Despite Smiths' Opposition," *Walla Walla Union Bulletin*, October 17, 1986.

82 Steve Forrester, "Northwest Senators Push Revised Gorge Measure," *Columbian*, August 13, 1986. The House could not take up the Gorge bill on the same day that the Rules Committee acted, so if the committee did not meet before midnight, then the House could not consider the Gorge bill until Friday. See Evan Roth, "Foley's Strategy Revives 'Dead' Gorge Bill," *Columbian*, October 20, 1986; Steve Forrester, "Gorge Foes Fail to Halt NW Coalition," *Journal-American* (Bellevue, WA), October 20, 1986; David Whitney, "Gorge Bill Leaves Hard Feelings within Oregon Delegation," *Sunday Oregonian*, October 26, 1986.

83 Forrester, "Gorge Foes Fail," 1986. "Columbia Gorge: House Votes 290-91 for Bill Despite Smiths' Opposition," *Union Bulletin*, 1986; Whitney, "Gorge Bill Leaves Hard Feelings," 1986; Roth, "Foley's Strategy," 1986; *Tacoma News Tribune*, December 14, 1986. Congressman Morrison also believed that this bill was the best bill his constituents could get, that a future bill might include the National Park Service or have greater restrictions on Gorge residents.

84 132 Cong. Rec. H10462-70, 132 Cong. Rec. H10485-90, Cong. Rec. H11121-48 (daily ed. Oct. 16, 1986), H10462, H10464; H11124, H10462-70, H11147, H10468. Congressman Weaver—who had managed much of the debate for Democrats—supported this amendment, as he worried that members were growing tired and believed the governors would make these appointments anyway. See Blair, "The Act, its Genesis," 929–930.

85 David Whitney, "Hope Fading Fast for Legislation on Gorge," *Oregonian*, October 15, 1986; David Whitney, "House-Passed Gorge Bill Fate Still 'Perilous'," *Oregonian*, October 17, 1986; David Whitney, "Gorge Bill Sent to Reagan," *Oregonian*, October 18, 1986.

86 Whitney, "Gorge Bill Passed by Senate," 1986; Dorothy Collin, "Congress Ends Logjam to Pass Flurry of Bills," *Chicago Tribune*, October 19, 1986.

87 Executive Director's Report, newsletter, Friends of the Columbia Gorge (Spring 1987); Bruce Russell, letter to Aubrey Russell, October 16, 1986, in the author's possession; Russell, Steno 54. In 1989, the Western Forestry Center changed its name to the World Forestry Center.

88 Bruce Russell, letter to Aubrey Russell, October 18, 1986.

89 Bruce Russell, letter to Aubrey Russell; Nancy Russell, letter to Aubrey Russell, October 23, 1986, in the author's possession; David Whitney, "Gorge Bill Sent to Reagan," *Oregonian*, October 18, 1986.

90 James C. Flanagan, "Hatfield Led Late Lobbying to Get Reagan to Sign Gorge Bill," *Oregonian*, November 24, 1986.

91 "Declares Mourning Period for Skamania County," Skamania County Resolution No. 1986-44, October 20, 1986. See also Joe Wrabek, "President Reagan Is Key to Saving Columbia Gorge People from Bill," *Skamania County Pioneer*, October 22, 1986; *Skamania County Pioneer*, October 22, 1986; Jeanie Senior, "County Officially Mourns Gorge Action," *Oregonian*, October 22, 1986.

92 David Whitney, "Gorge Bill Awaits Fate with Reagan," *Oregonian*, November 7, 1986; Linda Keene, "Meese Urges Veto of River Gorge Bill," *Spokesman-Review* (Spokane, WA), November 7, 1986.

93 Linda Keene, "Meese Urges Veto of River Gorge Bill," *Spokesman-Review*, November 7, 1986.

94 Russell, Steno 54; "Timber Companies Reverse Stance on Gorge Bill," *Sunday Oregonian*, November 16, 1986; Flanagan, "Hatfield Led Late Lobbying," 1986.

95 James C. Flanagan, "Hatfield Led Late Lobbying to Get Reagan to Sign Gorge Bill,"
    Oregonian, November 24, 1986; "Timber Companies Reverse Stance on Gorge Bill,"
    Sunday Oregonian, November 16, 1986; Don Bonker, "The Columbia River Gorge
    Management in Peril from Lack of Two-State Funding," *Seattle Times*, November 11,
    2011; Don Bonker, letter to the author, May 20, 2013.

96 Antoinette Hatfield, interview by Kevin Gorman, August 2, 2018.

97 Statement on Signing H.R. 5705 Into Law, 22 Weekly Comp. Pres. Doc. 1573 (November
    17, 1986); "Reagan Signs Gorge Bill Before Expiration," *Tri-City Herald* (Pasco, WA),
    November 19, 1986.

CHAPTER 6

1   Russell, Steno 47, Steno 77, Steno 55, Steno 68.

2   Russell, Steno 71; *Columbia Gorge United v. Clayton K. Yuetter*, the Columbia Gorge
    Commission and Friends of the Columbia Gorge, US District Court for the District of
    Oregon, CV No. 88-1319-PA, May 23, 1990, 9; Russell, Steno 64, Steno 77; Editorial,
    Oregonian, November 19, 1986.

3   Andy Dignan, "He's Arbitrator and Umpire; Gritty and Gray-Haired," newsletter, Friends
    of the Columbia Gorge (Spring 1987); Editorial, *Skamania County Pioneer*, April 1, 1987;
    Joanna Grammon, "Draft Guidelines Undergo DC Scrutiny," *Skamania County Pioneer*,
    April 1, 1987; Russell, Steno 53. See also Kathleen Glanville, "Draft Interim Guidelines
    for Gorge Area Win Favor," *Oregonian*, April 15, 1987.

4   "Columbia Gorge Draft Criticized," *Oregonian*, June 9, 1987. See also Editorial, *Sunday
    Oregonian*, April 26, 1987.

5   Editorial, *Sunday Oregonian*, April 26, 1987; "Columbia Gorge Draft Criticized,"
    Oregonian, June 9, 1987. Democrat Brock Adams had replaced Slade Gorton in the
    November 1986 election.

6   Bowen Blair (executive director, Friends of the Columbia Gorge), to Dale Robertson
    (chief, United States Forest Service), May 8, 1987.

7   A thirteenth member, appointed by the Secretary of Agriculture, was able to deliberate
    with the commission but could not vote.

8   Russell, Steno 60. See also Russell, Steno 59.

9   Kathleen Glanville, "Corbett Petition Opposes Appointment of Russel," *Oregonian*, June
    9, 1987; Nancy Russell, letter to Aubrey Russell, April 16, 1987, in the author's possession.
    Almost 10 percent of Corbett residents (a population of 2,942 in 1990) signed the petition.
    See "People in Zip 97019 (Corbett, OR)," https://www.bestplaces.net/people/zip-code/
    oregon/corbett/97019 (accessed June 10, 2019).

10 Bruce Westfall, "Benner to Direct Agency," *Columbian*, September 15, 1987; Editorial,
    Skamania County Pioneer, September 23, 1987. The initial vote to hire Benner was actu-
    ally 11 to 1, with Skamania County's representative voting for a local candidate. Don Clark
    then successfully moved that the vote be made unanimous. See Joanna Grammon, "1,000
    Friends' Dick Benner is New Gorge Director," *Skamania County Pioneer*, September 16,
    1987.

11 Douglas P. Ferguson, letter to Nancy Russell, December 9, 1986, in the author's posses-
    sion. For instance, if TPL bought a property for $1 million and negotiated a $200,000 gift
    from the landowner, its gross cost would be $800,000. If TPL held the property for three
    years and incurred $175,000 in costs, its net gain would be $25,000, which would be
    covered *if* the Forest Service, through its independent appraisal review process, determined
    the land's fair market value (and its purchase price) was $1 million.

12 Russ Pinto, memorandum to Harriet Burgess, Nelson Lee, and Holly Haugh, June 9, 1987,
    in the author's possession; Harriet Burgess, letter to Nancy Russell, March 24, 1987, in the
    author's possession.

13 Editorial, "Willing Sellers in Gorge Will Have to Wait," *Skamania County Pioneer*,
    February 18, 1987; Editorial, *Skamania County Pioneer*, February 3, 1988. The federal
    government is exempt from paying local property taxes. Nonprofit organizations are
    allowed to generate revenue through sales of land and other commodities. Although critics

called the margin between TPL's purchase and sale prices—when landowner donations were considered—a "profit," this was incorrect.

14 Harriet Burgess, note to Russ Pinto, n.d., attached to Arthur W. Default, letter to Russ Pinto, December 3, 1987, in the author's possession. The author's calculations are summarized in "AAA–BB LIST–All projects, most info, by date conveyed – BB 021116," in the author's possession.

15 Russ Pinto, memorandum to Harriet Burgess and Nelson Lee, June 19, 1987, in the author's possession.

16 Glenda J. Kimmel, letter to Trust for Public Land, November 18, 1987, personal collection; Curtis A. Skaar, letter to Russ Pinto, December 10, 1987, in the author's possession; Glenda J. Kimmel, letter to Trust for Public Land, April 28, 1988, personal collection. See also Russ Pinto, memorandum to Ralph W. Benson, May 10, 1988, personal collection.

17 Ivan Donaldson, "History of Skamania County" (unpublished manuscript, 1959–1960), 14–16. Sheridan was slightly wounded in the battle. See also David Lewis, "Philip Henry Sheridan (1831-1888)," *The Oregon Encyclopedia*, https://oregonencyclopedia.org/articles/philip_sheridan_1831_1888_/ (accessed June 8, 2019).

18 Harriet Burges, letter to Dale Robertson (chief, US Forest Service), September 28, 1987, in the author's possession; David O'Brien, letter to Russ Pinto, July 25, 1988, in the author's possession. TPL's policies generally prohibited revealing gross and net returns on transactions because that information—especially if used for individual transactions—could be misleading. For instance, TPL might have a net loss of $200,000 on each of five projects (especially in the Gorge) and then break even on the sixth project, which netted $1 million. Opponents to TPL's work would promote the $1 million net gain and not mention the combined $1 million net losses on the other five transactions.

19 This was Washington State's only park on the north bank; Reed Island is also a state park but is located in the river and is accessible by boat only.

20 Russell, Steno 55.

21 Bowen Blair, memorandum to Steve Crew, August 9, 1989, in author's possession; Jeanie Senior, "Gorge Groups Trade Less-Than-Friendly Words Over Expulsion," *Oregonian*, March 20, 1989.

22 Minutes, Board of Directors Meeting, Friends of the Columbia Gorge, December 8, 1988, in the author's possession.

23 Testimony of Brad Jones, Columbia River Gorge Commission, January 24, 1989; Bruce Westfall, "Governor Declines Action on Cannard Loan," *Columbian*, February 10, 1989; Sharon Nesbit, "Ex-Director Accuses Gorge Lobby Group of Illegal Actions," *Outlook* (Gresham, OR), December 17, 1988; Brad Jones, letter to the editor, *Columbian*, December 27, 1988; "Jones' Memo Looks at Friends," *Hood River News*, January 4, 1989.

24 Friends of the Friends, brochure, n.d., in the author's possession; Friends of the Friends, letter to Friends of the Columbia Gorge membership, March 10, 1989; Minutes, Special Membership Meeting of Friends of the Columbia Gorge, March 19, 1989; Editorial, *Columbian*, February 5, 1989; Editorial, *Columbian*, February 26, 1989. See also Blair to Crew.

25 Friends of the Friends, letter to Friends of the Columbia Gorge membership, March 10, 1989.

26 Bruce Westfall, "Friends of Gorge Expel Adversary," *Columbian*, March 20, 1989; Jeanie Senior, "Gorge Groups Trade Less-Than-Friendly Words Over Expulsion," *Oregonian*, March 20, 1989; Nancy Russell, "Membership Meeting" speech, March 19, 1989, in the author's possession; Westfall, "Friends Expel Adversary," 1989; Minutes, Special Membership Meeting of Friends of the Columbia Gorge, March 19, 1989. The four hundred votes in favor are an approximation, based on attendance estimated by the *Oregonian* and the *Columbian*, as it would have taken too long to count actual votes in favor.

27 Bruce Russell, letter to Aubrey and Wendy Russell, March 19, 1989, in the author's possession; Nancy Russell, letter to Mr. and Mrs. Ivan Donaldson, April 8, 1989, in the author's possession.

28 Brock Evans with George Venn, *Endless Pressure, Endlessly Applied: The Autobiography of an Eco-Warrior* (La Grande, OR: Wake-Robin Press, 2020). Evans used this phrase with the author several times.

29 While Russell ultimately failed to keep the garbage trucks from using Gorge highways, she stopped public funding from underwriting the trucking company and kept it from using the National Scenic Area for staging and storage. Most importantly, Seattle, which had been watching the controversy, decided to send its garbage to Arlington by rail. Mark Kirchmeier, "Truckers, Critics Clash at Hearing on Hauling," *Oregonian*, August 4, 1989; Michael Rollins, "Garbage Trucking Opponents Talk Referendum," *Oregonian*, March 25, 1989.

30 "Broughton Lumber Co. Unveils Resort Plans," *Enterprise* (White Salmon, WA), June 22, 1989; newsletter, Friends of the Columbia Gorge (Summer 2007).

31 Editorial, *Oregonian*, December 12, 1998, August 6, 1998; Lauren Dodge, "House in Columbia River Gorge Sparks Property Rights Battle," *Los Angeles Times*, January 17, 1999; Sam Howe Verhovek, "Dream House with Scenic View Is Environmentalists' Nightmare," *New York Times*, April 24, 1999; Erik Meers, "Cliff Hanger," *People Magazine*, July 19, 1999; Randy Fitzgerald, "Mugged by the Law," *Reader's Digest*, September 2000; *BEA House–Skamania County v. Columbia River Gorge Commission et al.*, 4, 11.

32 Cordell, "Scenic Drive," *Portland Monthly* (2006), 26; Todd Murphy, "Wallets Open up for Campaigns," *Portland Tribune*, October 29, 2004. This was during the 2004 election cycle.

33 Chuck Williams, letter to Nancy Russell, November 8, 2000, in the author's possession; Vera Dafoe, letter to Nancy Russell, January 17, 2004, in the author's possession; Aubrey Russell interview, October 26, 2016; Nancy Russell, letter to Gary Kahn, April 1, 1994, in the author's possession.

34 Julie Wilson, "You Own the Columbia River Gorge," *Town & Country* (September 1992), 95.

35 Russell, Steno 59; Columbia River Gorge Commission, meeting, July 24, 1990 (transcribed August 26, 1996).

36 Oversight Hearing on the Columbia River Gorge National Scenic Area Act: Hearing before the Committee on Appropriations, United States Senate, 104th Cong., 2d sess., September 13, 1996, 180; Bill Hulse, "My Involvement in the Discovery Center and Wasco County Historical Museum," WamPinRock News (Wamic, OR), n.d. https://www.gorgediscovery.org/wp-content/uploads/2014/10/Hulse_article.pdf (accessed May 5, 2020); *Morning Call* (Allentown, PA), July 5, 1998.

37 Russell, Steno 80.

38 Dan Harkenrider, speech, Cape Horn dedication, August 13, 2011, video, author's possession.

39 Daniel J. Evans, "Why I'm Quitting the Senate," *New York Times*, April 17, 1988.

40 Nancy Russell, memorandum to Paulette Carter-Bartee, March 3, 1994, in the author's possession; Nancy N. Russell, letter to Mark O. Hatfield, July 28, 1995, in the author's possession; Hatfield to Russell, August 3, 1995, in the author's possession; Mark O. Hatfield, as told to Diane N. Solomon, *Against the Grain: Reflections of a Rebel Republican* (Ashland, OR: White Cloud Press, 2000); Brian T. Meehan, "Sheer Preservation," *Oregonian*, February 15, 1998.

41 Kevin Gorman, interview by the author, August 30, 2019.

42 Kim Brater, "Volunteers and Hikers Turn Out for Gorge Appreciation Week," 10th Anniversary Special Edition, Friends of the Columbia Gorge, October 1996; newsletter, Friends of the Columbia Gorge, November 1998; Russell, Steno 104.

43 Gorman interview; newsletter, Friends of the Columbia Gorge (Fall 1999, Summer 2000); Lisa M. Cameli, Eric T. Mogren, and Craig W. Shinn. *The Columbia River Gorge Commission: An Assessment of Organizational Capacity* (Portland, OR: Portland State University, 2014) 26.

44 Russell, Steno 106.

45 Charles Wilkinson, *Blood Struggle: The Rise of Modern Indian Nations* (New York, London: W.W. Norton & Company, 2005) 272; Veronica E. Velarde Tiller, *Tiller's Guide to Indian Country* (Albuquerque: BowArrow Publishing Company, 2005), 908; Tiller, *Tiller's Guide*, 907 and https://warmsprings-nsn.gov/history/ (accessed October 12, 2021); Cynthia D. Stowell, *Faces of a Reservation: A Portrait of the Warm Springs Indian Reservation* (Portland: Oregon Historical Society Press, 1987), xii; Wilkinson, *Blood Struggle* (New York, London: W.W. Norton & Company, 2005) 275–277.

46 The vision of restoring the Mosier Twin Tunnels is largely credited to Craig Collins, the former president of the Columbia Gorge Coalition.

47 Gronowski and Kloos, "Historic Study," 108, 2.

48 Tiller, *Tiller's Guide*, 908.

49 Russell, Steno 100.

CHAPTER 7

1   Russell, Steno 9.

2   Nancy N. Russell "Vision for the Future, Columbia River Gorge," September 16, 1987.

3   Trust for Public Land, "Toward a Columbia Gorge Protection Fund: A Proposal Submitted to the Ralph L. Smith Foundation," September 1989, in the author's possession.

4   William Clark, November 2, 1805, in Moulton, ed. *The Journals of the Lewis & Clark Expedition*, https://lewisandclarkjournals.unl.edu/item/lc.jrn.1805-11-05#lc.jrn.1805-11-05.01; Kristine M. Kaeding, "Monument or Folly? Maya Lin's Bird Blind at The Sandy River Delta, Oregon" (thesis, University of Oregon, Eugene, 2010), 37. https://scholarsbank.uoregon.edu/xmlui/bitstream/handle/1794/10824/Kaeding_Kristine_M_ma2010su.pdf?sequence=3&isAllowed=y.

5   Timothy Egan, "Bridal Veil Journal—Town's 9 People Told: Make Way for Nature," *New York Times*, May 11, 1991; Editorial, *Oregonian*, November 9, 1992.

6   Russell, Steno 4. Three years later, Russell reminded Burgess that "those who know and love the gorge the best agree that Franz Lake is at the top of the list." See Russell, Steno 34.

7   Russ Jolley, *Wildflowers of the Columbia Gorge* (Portland: Oregon Historical Society Press, 1988), xiii–xiv.

8   Russell, Steno 78.

9   W. Duncan Strong, W. Egbert Schenck, and Julian H. Steward, "Archaeology of the Dalles–Deschutes Region," *University of California Publications in American Archaeology and Ethnology*, vol. 29 (1930–1932): 22. Technically, only 75 percent of Miller Island was in private ownership, and that was the portion that TPL bought and sold to the Forest Service. The remainder of the island had been owned by another federal agency and was transferred to the Forest Service by the National Scenic Area Act.

10 Russell, Steno 73.

11 Trust for Public Land, "Columbia River Gorge Protection Fund: Final Report to Meyer Memorial Trust," November 30, 1992, 14.

12 Barbara Robinson, interview by the author, November 18, 2013.

13 Robinson interview, November 18, 2013.

14 Robinson interview, November 18, 2013.

15 Bruce Russell, letter to Aubrey Russell, April 18, 1988, in the author's possession; Nancy Russell, interview by Kevin Gorman, n.d.

16 Aubrey Russell interview, October 26, 2016.

17 Bruce Russell, letter to Aubrey Russell, April 18, 1988.

18 Robinson interview, November 20, 2013. Professional guides Don and Roberta Lowe, for instance, called the trail a "perpetually enchanting outing." See "Feature Hike of the Quarter with Don and Roberta Lowe: The Cherry Orchard," newsletter, Friends of the Columbia Gorge, n.d. See generally "Glories of Gorge Persist Despite Winter's Wreckage," *Oregonian*, April 23, 1997.

19 Kathie Durbin, "Forest Service Buys Gorge Land Where Lewis and Clark Expedition Likely Camped," *Columbian*, September 25, 2003; Nancy N. Russell, letter to Jim Luce,

March 29, 2001; Bruce Russell, letter to Aubrey Russell, March 2, August 26, 1992. It is difficult to know on which property at the mouth of Major Creek the Corps of Discovery camped, as Bonneville Dam has considerably altered the Columbia's shoreline in that area.

20 Petition to the Klickitat County Board of Adjustment Regarding Conditional Use Application No. CU-93-06, March 22, 1993, in the author's possession; Kevin Gorman, interview by the author, August 30, 2019; Russell, letter to Columbia River Gorge Commission, 2000. See also Nancy N. Russell, letter (with attachments) to Columbia River Gorge Commission executive director and four commissioners, October 16, 2000.

21 Russell, Steno 83. The official name of the park would be the Historic Columbia River Highway State Trail and the Mark O. Hatfield Trailhead just east of Hood River.

22 Alert, Friends of the Columbia Gorge, August 29, 1994, in the author's possession; Russell, Steno 92; Jeanette B. Kloos, *Historic Columbia River Highway Master Plan* (Portland: Oregon Department of Transportation, June 2001), 84.

23 Russell, Steno 88.

24 Kathy Durbin, *Bridging a Great Divide: The Battle for the Columbia River Gorge* (Corvallis: Oregon State University Press, 2013), 216–21. See also map, "Proposed Special Management Area," n.d., in the author's possession.

25 Bullard, *Lancaster's Road*, 7.

26 Northwest Regional Planning Commission (June 1935), 31; Russell, Steno 80.

27 Randy Gragg, "The Long View," *Portland Monthly*, May 24, 2012; Richard Brown, interview with the author, July 11, 2013; Nancy Russell, "Remarks at The Shire re: John Yeon," June 19, 2003.

28 Dan Huntington, interview by the author, August 29, 2019.

29 National Park Service, *Study of Alternatives for the Columbia River Gorge*, (Denver, CO: National Park Service, April 1980), 214; Bruce Westfall, "Protecting the Panorama," *Columbian*, October 13, 1989.

30 Arthur J. Carroll, "Draft Acquisition Decision and GMA Designation Determination," July 25, 1997, in the author's possession; Nancy N. Russell, letter to Area Manager (Carroll), August 25, 1997, in the author's possession.

31 Nancy N. Russell, letter to Arthur J. Carroll (area manager), March 7, 1995, in the author's possession; Nancy Russell to Harriet Burgess (American Land Conservancy), March 1, 1995, in the author's possession. Dan Evans was no longer a senator, but he maintained influence with some former colleagues.

32 Dan Huntington, letter to the editor, *Skamania County Pioneer*, April 30, 1997.

33 RaeLynn Gill, "West-End Resident Points Way to New State Park, Trail System," *Skamania County Pioneer*, January 22, 1997; Editorial, *Columbian*, January 29, 1997.

34 Slade Gorton (US senator for Washington), "Gorton Will Support Appropriation for Cape Horn," news release, April 17, 1997; Bruce Westfall, "Gorge Property Plans Criticized," *Columbian*, April 18, 1997.

35 William Sullivan, "Hikers: Gorge Yourselves," *Register-Guard* (Eugene, OR), March 28, 2006; Nancy Russell, notes for speech, Three Rivers Land Trust, n.d., in the author's possession; Arthur J. Carroll (area manager), letter to Dan Huntington, April 17, 2000, in the author's possession.

36 Kevin Gorman, email to the author, January 28, 2000.

37 Nancy Russell, letter to Dave Cannard, January 4, 2003, in the author's possession.

38 While the Rim View Estates subdivision was not halted by the Friends, its push for legislation and its willingness to litigate limited the sale and development of the lots.

39 Lynn Burditt (area manager), Presentation to Columbia River Gorge Commission, June 9, 2015; Land Exchange Summary Table, US Forest Service, National Scenic Area, September 29, 2014, in the author's possession. Many of these lands were acquired from TPL. Eight thousand acres is a low number as it does not include the direct purchase — without the assistance of the Trust for Public Land — of lands by non-US Forest Service agencies.

40 Gragg, "The Long View," 2012; Brown, interview with the author; Russell, Steno 85. Richard Brown ensured that the sale of Chapman Point was subject to tight development restrictions.

41 Russell, Steno 100.

42 Kevin Gorman, eulogy for Nancy Russell, October 5, 2008.

43 Laurie Rahr, interview by the author, January 28, 2013.

CHAPTER 8

1 Aubrey Russell, letter to author, April 1, 2020, in author's possession.

2 Hunty Wall, interview by the author, September 17, 2013, 7; "What is ALS?": ALS Association, http://www.alsa.org/; Jonathan Eig, *Luckiest Man: The Life and Death of Lou Gehrig* (New York: Simon and Schuster, 2005), 233–34.

3 Barbara Robinson, interview by the author, November 18, 2013.

4 Russell, Steno 31; Cordell, "Scenic Drive," *Portland Monthly*, 2006, 4; Bowen Blair, memorandum to executive committee and staff, December 31, 1986, in the author's possession.

5 Russell, Steno 90.

6 Dan Huntington, interview by the author, August 29, 2019; "Columbia Gorge Gateway Project," Columbia Land Trust, n.d., in the author's possession. The Stevensons wanted to keep the house, which was on a separate parcel from the field. See Huntington interview.

7 Raymond Hickey, letter to Columbia Land Trust, board of directors, May 19, 1998, in the author's possession; Dan Huntington, email to the author, January 27, 2020; Kevin Gorman, interview by the author, August 30, 2019; Huntington interview; Minutes, Friends of the Columbia Gorge, July 8, 2004; Kevin Gorman, telephone call with the author, March 16, 2020.

8 Michael Milstein, "Columbia Gorge's Vista Changed by Conservation Gift," *Oregonian*, March 14, 2005; newsletter, Friends of the Columbia Gorge (Spring 2005). The other half of Yeon's estate went to Reed College in Portland.

9 Kevin Gorman, telephone call with the author, March 16, 2020.

10 Dan Huntington, letter to Nancy Russell, July 28, 2004; David Cannard, promissory note to Bruce and Nancy Russell, February 13, 2004, in the author's possession. Cannard bought the land for $474,000 in August 1996. He spent $150,000 on surveys and clearing brush, incurred other costs, and sold most of the land eight years later to the US Forest Service for $740,000. See also Dan Huntington, list of Forest Service purchases in Cape Horn area, August 29, 2019.

11 Dan Huntington, letter to Nancy Russell, July 28, 2004, in the author's possession.

12 Dan Huntington, email to the author, January 27, 2020, 6. See also Huntington interview; Huntington to Russell, July 28, 2004.

13 Dan Huntington, email to Nancy Russell and Kevin Gorman, October 12, 2004, in the author's possession; Huntington interview; Nancy Russell, interview by Kevin Gorman, n.d.

14 Bruce H. Russell, "Suggestions for 'Funeral,'" September 2004, in the author's possession; Hammond interview by the author, February 8, 2017; Bruce Russell, "40 Love!" cartoon, January 11, 1972, in the author's possession.

15 Marie Hall, letter to the author, December 8, 2013; Aubrey Russell interview, October 26, 2016.

16 "Executive Director's Letter," newsletter, Friends of the Columbia Gorge (Summer 2005); Barbara Robinson interview, November 20, 2013.

17 Aubrey Russell interview, October 26, 2016.

18 Hammond interview, February 8, 2017.

19 Nancy Russell, speech, Friends of the Columbia Gorge 25th Anniversary Dinner, November 12, 2005, in the author's possession.

20 Purchase Option Agreement, Grantor Irma Collins and Marie Collins-LeDoux, Grantee Nancy Russell, August 17, 2005, in the author's possession. The $20,000 annual payments and property tax payments were not creditable to the purchase price.

21 Hahn and Associates, Inc., Phase I Environmental Site Assessment, 281 Rim Drive, March 14, 2006, 16, in the author's possession; Geoff Roach, meeting notes, March 6, 1996, in the author's possession; statement of Edgar Cleveland, Hearing before the Public Lands Subcommittee, 645.

22 Melissa M. Ryan, email to Aubrey Russell, December 29, 2005, in the author's possession; Geoff Roach, notes, telephone call with Edgar Cleveland, March 12, 1996, in the author's possession.

23 Geoff Roach, email to Bowen Blair, January 7, 2005, in author's possession; Geoff Roach, memorandum to Tom Tyner, June 3, 2005, in the author's possession.

24 Kevin Gorman interview; Melissa M. Ryan, email to Kevin Gorman, December 14, 2005, in the author's possession.

25 "Budget–Cleveland Cape Horn Project," Friends of the Columbia Gorge Land Trust, n.d., in the author's possession; Harriet Burgess, letter to Don Frisbee, March 24, 1987, in the author's possession; Kevin Gorman, telephone call to the author, March 16, 2020.

26 Barbara Robinson, letter to the author, November 18, 2013, author's possession.

27 Aubrey Russell interview, October 26, 2016.

28 Marie Hall, interview by the author, April 4, 2013.

29 Richard Lang, fax to Dan Huntington, March 7, 2006, in the author's possession; Nancy Russell, letter to Richard Lang, March 7, 2006, in the author's possession.

30 Tony Hovey, letter to Nancy Russell, November 15, 2005, in the author's possession; "Director's letter," newsletter, Friends of the Columbia Gorge (Summer 2007); Kevin Gorman interview.

31 Polly Morrow, interview by the author, March 18, 2020. See also Katy Muldoon, "Gorge and Hikers Lose a Fearless Friend," Oregonian, September 21, 2008.

32 US Forest Service, "Summary of Land Acquisition: Columbia River Gorge National Scenic Area through October 1, 2019," December 16, 2019, in the author's possession; Trust for Public Land, non-US Forest Service land acquisitions in National Scenic Area, created by the author, January 17, 2020. Data excludes land exchanges.

33 Morrow interview; Aubrey Russell, video of ambulance trip, September 3, 2008.

34 Dietrich, "Bottom 18," Columbian, January 1982.

35 Matt Villano, "Return to Cape Horn," Land & People (Spring/Summer 2009).

36 Barbara Robinson, email to the author, January 23, 2020.

37 Trust for Public Land, "Lyle Point, Klickitat County, Washington," project profile, n.d., in the author's possession.

38 Kloos, "Historic Columbia River Highway Master Plan," 15, 16.

39 D. K. Row, "Review: 'Wild Beauty' at the Portland Art Museum," Oregonian, October 5, 2008. See also Timothy Egan, Short Nights of the Shadow Catcher: The Epic Life and Immortal Photographs of Edward Curtis (New York City: Houghton Mifflin Harcourt, 2012); Aubrey Russell, eulogy for Nancy Russell, October 5, 2008, in the author's possession.

Bibliography

Note: The author relied on several private collections, including the Nancy Russell collection managed by her son, Aubrey Russell, in Portland, Oregon. The uncurated collection is composed of research material, correspondence, articles, litigation, legislation, and internal documents from Friends of the Columbia Gorge, Portland Garden Club, Garden Club of America, and Trust for Public Land collected by Nancy Russell over three decades. Of special note is a collection of steno books. The 109 lined stenographer pads are each fifty to one hundred pages long and date from 1980 to 2006, with two periods—from February 7 to June 18, 1990, and from April 23 to August 18, 1999—missing.

The uncurated John Yeon collection includes documents relating to the Columbia River Gorge and The Shire, assembled by Yeon over his lifetime. These papers are located in the Aubrey Watzek house, managed by the University of Oregon's John Yeon Center for Architecture and the Landscape in Portland, Oregon.

The Trust for Public Land recycles most of its documents as a matter of policy after several years. Some material relating to administration, land acquisition in the Columbia Gorge, and correspondence can still be found at TPL's offices in Oregon, Washington, and California, as well as in the Russell collection and in the author's possession.

The author has copies in his possession of many of the original documents in the Russell and Yeon papers and found in TPL's various offices.

The author has approximately ninety-six combined minutes of video footage from Portland Metropolitan area news stations—primarily KATU, KOIN, KGW, and KOAP—from 1980 through 1986, in his possession. These news clips primarily cover efforts to enact National Scenic Area legislation and to prevent development in the Gorge. Highlights include coverage of Colonel Rizor's subdivision, the Governors' bill, placing action alerts on door handles in Clark County, congressional passage of the National Scenic Area Act, and the act's signing by President Reagan.

MANUSCRIPT COLLECTIONS

Henry J. Biddle Papers. Ax 645, Special Collections and University Archives, University of Oregon Libraries, Eugene.

Bowen Blair Papers. Friends of the Columbia Gorge, 1982–1988, and Oregon Field Office, Trust for Public Land, 1989–2010. In author's possession, Portland, OR.

Friends of the Columbia Gorge. Documents relating to Friends of the Columbia Gorge, Portland, OR. Online archive, 1981–2020, https://gorgefriends.org/who-we-are/annual-reports-newsletters-list.html.

Nancy N. Russell Papers. Portland, OR.

Trust for Public Land Papers. Offices in Oregon, Washington, and California.

John Yeon Papers. Aubrey Watzek house, University of Oregon, Portland.

INTERVIEWS

Note: Between October 2012 and July 2020, the author interviewed fifty-four people, several of them multiple times. All interviews were recorded except for six that were conducted by mail or email. All recordings and transcripts are in author's possession. Interviewees: Steven Andersen (email), Sally Anderson, Hon. Victor Atiyeh, Eve Bachman, Roger Bachman, Barbara Bailey, Chris Beck (email), Mary Bishop, Susan Black, Hon. Don Bonker, Elizabeth Brooke, Richard

Brown, Dave Cannard, Don Clark, Craig Collins (email), Vera Dafoe, Maggie Drake, Gerry Frank, Michael Frome, Joan Gamble, Kevin Gorman, Marie Hall, Betsy Neighbor Hammond, Sis Hayes, Gretchen Hull, Dan Huntington (including email), Jeanette Kloos (email), Michael Lang, Charlie Mansfield (email), Kate McCarthy, Millard McClung, Nancie McGraw, Mike Metz, Kate Mills, Antone Minthorn, Polly Morrow, Bob Neighbor, Laurie Rahr, Geoff Roach, Barbara Robinson, Bill Rosenfeld, Aubrey Russell, Sally Russell, Chuck Sams, Dottie Schoonmaker, Kristine Simenstad-Mackin, Wally Stevenson, Tom Tyner, Tom Vaughan, Hunty Wall, Patricia Wall, Nani Warren, Lyn White, Susi Wilson (unrecorded phone call and letter).

Clark, Don. Interview by Ernie Bonner (College of Urban and Public Affairs, Portland State University), Portland, OR, February 2000, transcript. https://www.pdx.edu/usp/planpdxorg-interview-don-clark (accessed in July 2018).

Gorman, Kevin. Interviews with Antoinette Hatfield, August 2, 2018, transcript; Nancy Russell, c. 2005, transcript; Don Clark, c. 2005, transcript; and Nancy Russell, c. 2005, video. Copies of transcripts and video in the author's possession.

Gamwell, Jim (caretaker, The Shire), and Adam Yapo (assistant to Gamwell). Interview by Robert Melnick and Karen Johnson (University of Oregon), n.d. Transcript in the author's possession.

Jensen, Gertrude Glutsch. Interview by Roberta Watts (Oregon Historical Society), December 7, 1977–January 17, 1978. https://digitalcollections.ohs.org/oral-history-interview-with-gertrude-glutsch-jensen-transcript (accessed June 2018).

Larson, Hillary. Oral history of Nancy Russell, Portland, OR, November 2006 to January 2007. Copies of eight taped interviews in the author's possession.

Peirce, Bob. Interviews of fourteen people, in conjunction with research on Nancy Russell, 2004–2005. Copies of transcripts in the author's possession. Interviewees: Gail Achterman, Barbara Bailey, Bowen Blair, Don Clark, Phyllis Clausen, Victor Clausen, Craig Collins, Kevin Gorman, Russ Jolley, Phillip Jones, Kate Mills, Bob Shoemaker, Barbara Walker, Don Willner.

Williams, Chuck. Interview by Clark Hansen, January 22, 1999, The Dalles, OR, for the Center for Columbia River History, Vancouver, WA, transcript. http://www.ccrh.org/oral/ohsoh/williamsc.php (accessed in May 2019).

Yeon, John. Interview by Marian W. Kolisch, December 14, 1982, January 10, 1983, American Art's Northwest Oral History Project, Archives of American Art, Smithsonian Institution, Washington, DC. Transcript. https://www.aaa.si.edu/collections/interviews/oral-history-interview-john-yeon-12428 (accessed February 10, 2017).

LEGISLATION AND HEARINGS

Note: From 1982 to 1986, more than a dozen bills were introduced in Congress to protect the Columbia River Gorge. For a detailed accounting of these bills, see Bowen Blair Jr., "The Columbia River Gorge National Scenic Area: The Act, its Genesis and Legislative History." *Environmental Law* 17 (1986–1987): 863-969.

Columbia River Gorge National Scenic Area Act, US Code 16 (1986), §§544 et seq.

National Park Service. Organic Act, US Code 16 (1916) §1.

Oregon Legislature, Senate. "For an Act Relating to the Establishment of the Columbia River Gorge Commission." SB357, introduced February 24, 1953.

Skamania County. Resolution. "Declares Mourning Period for Skamania County, No. 1986-44." October 20, 1986.

US Congress, House of Representatives, Committee on Agriculture. "Columbia River Gorge Act of 1986," "Columbia Gorge National Scenic Area Act." Hearing before the Subcommittee on Forests, Family Farms, and Energy, 99th Cong., 2d sess., August 1, 1986.

US Congress, House of Representatives, Committee on Interior and Insular Affairs. "To Establish a Columbia Gorge National Scenic Area." Hearing before the Subcommittee on National Parks and Recreation, 99th Cong., 2d sess., June 19, 1986.

US Congress, Senate, Committee on Commerce, Science, and Transportation. "The Columbia River Gorge." Hearing before the Committee on Commerce, Science, and Transportation, 98th Cong., 1st sess., February 10, 1983.

US Congress, Senate, Committee on Energy and Natural Resources. "A Bill to Authorize the Establishment of a National Scenic Area to Assure the Protection, Development, Conservation, and Enhancement of the Scenic, Natural, Cultural, and Other Resource Values of the Columbia River Gorge in the States of Oregon and Washington, to Establish National Policies to Assist in the Furtherance of this Objective, and for Other Purposes." Hearing before the Subcommittee on Public Lands and Reserved Water, 98th Cong., 1st Sess., March 25, 1983.

US Congress, Senate, Committee on Energy and Natural Resources. "A Bill to Establish the Columbia Gorge National Scenic Area, and for Other Purposes." Hearing before the Subcommittee on Public Lands, Reserved Water and Resource Conservation, 99th Cong., 2d sess., June 17, 1986.

US Congress, Senate, Committee on Energy and Natural Resources. "Land Management in the Columbia River Gorge." Hearing before the Committee on Commerce, Science, and Transportation, 98th Cong., 2d sess., November 8, 1984.

US Congress, Senate, Committee on Appropriations. "Oversight Hearing on the Columbia River Gorge National Scenic Area Act." Special Hearing before the Committee on Appropriations, 104th Cong., 2d sess., September 13, 1996.

US Congress, Senate, Committee on Appropriations. "A Bill to Establish the Mount Hood National Parks in the State of Oregon." S. 6397. 64th Cong., 1st sess., introduced in Senate on June 20, 1916.

LITIGATION

California v. Tahoe Regional Planning Agency. US Dist. Ct. Case No. Civ. S-84-0561 EJG and S-84-0565 EJG (E.D. Cal., filed June 5, 1984).

Columbia Gorge United v. Clayton K. Yuetter. Columbia Gorge Commission and Friends of the Columbia Gorge, US District Court for the District of Oregon, CV No. 88-1319-PA, May 23, 1990.

"Complaint for Declaratory Judgment and Injunction." *Montchalin et al. vs. Skamania County et al.*, October 14, 1981.

Martin v. Reynolds Metals Company. 224 F. Supp. 321, 224 F. Supp. 978.

Skamania County v. Columbia River Gorge Commission et al. 26 P.3d 241 (2001).

REPORTS

Baldwin, Pamela. *A Legal Analysis of House Bills in the 99th Congress on the Columbia River Gorge*. Washington, DC: Congressional Research Service, May 15, 1986.

Boardman, Sam H. *Recorded Events of How a State Park Was Acquired by Washington and Missed by Oregon*, n.d. In the author's possession.

Brookside Enterprises. "Final Environmental Impact Statement: Columbia Gorge Riverfront Estates." Vancouver, WA, August 1983. In the author's possession.

Bureau of Planning and Sustainability. *East Portland Historical Overview and Historic Preservation Study*. Portland, OR, March 2009. In the author's possession.

Carroll, Arthur J. "Acquisition Decision and GMA Designation Determination." Draft. Hood River, OR: US Forest Service, July 25, 1997. In the author's possession.

Cameli, Lisa M., Eric T. Mogren, and Craig W. Shinn. *The Columbia River Gorge Commission: An Assessment of Organizational Capacity*. Portland, OR: Portland State University, 2014.

Columbia Gorge Committee, Pacific Northwest Regional Planning Commission. *Land Program Recreation Project, Columbia Gorge, Oregon–Washington*. Portland, OR, June 1935. In the author's possession.

Columbia Gorge Committee, Pacific Northwest Regional Planning Commission. *Columbia Gorge Conservation and Development*. Portland, OR, January 1937. In the author's possession.

Columbia River Gorge Commission. *Management Plan: Columbia River Gorge National Scenic Area* (amended). White Salmon, WA, August 2016. http://www.gorgecommission. org/management-plan/plan/ (accessed May 12, 2019).

Columbia River Gorge Commissions. "Skamania County West End Land Use and Parcelization Patterns." Stevenson, WA, February 2, 1983. In the author's possession.

Columbia River Gorge Commissions. "Timber Production on Lands in the Columbia Gorge." Stevenson, WA, November 1984. In the author's possession.

Columbia River Inter-Tribal Fish Commission. *Salmon Range*. Portland, OR. http://www. critfc.org/fish-and-watersheds/columbia-river-fish-species/columbia-river-salmon/ (accessed April 21, 2020).

Corn, M. Lynne. *A Comparison of Provisions of Bills Introduced in the 99th Congress to Create a Columbia Gorge National Scenic Area*. Washington, DC: Congressional Research Service, June 11, 1986.

Friends of the Columbia Gorge. "Columbia Gorge Legislative Proposal: Public Comment Synopsis." Portland, OR, February 1981.

Friends of the Columbia Gorge. *Legislative Concepts for a National Scenic Area in the Columbia Gorge*. Portland, OR, May 18, 1981. In the author's possession.

Friends of the Columbia Gorge. "Summary of Legislative Concept Proposal." Friends of the Columbia River Gorge, Portland, OR, May 12, 1981.

Gronowski, Nancy H., and Jeanette Kloos. *A Study of the Historic Columbia River Highway*. Salem: Oregon Department of Transportation, November 1987.

Hahn and Associates, Inc. "Phase I Environmental Site Assessment, 281 Rim Drive." Portland, OR, March 14, 2006.

Jolly, Donald G. "Final Environmental Impact Statement: Hidden Harbor." Vancouver, WA, July 1984. In the author's possession.

Lyon, Elisabeth L. "Enhancement of Tourism in the Columbia River Gorge." Portland, OR, August 1982. In the author's possession.

"Maintenance and Management of The Shire." John Yeon Papers, n.d., School of Architecture and Allied Arts, University of Oregon, Eugene.

Meltz, Robert. *Constituent Question as to the Constitutional Authority of the United States to Condemn Land for Purposes of Scenic Preservation*. Washington, DC: Congressional Research Service, October 1, 1982.

Meltz, Robert. *Congressional Proposals to Establish Land Use Controls for the Columbia River Gorge: Issues of Constitutional Authority*. Washington, DC: Congressional Research Service, August 30, 1984.

Minor, Rick et al. *An Overview of Investigation at 45SA11: Archeology in the Columbia River Gorge*. Eugene, OR: Heritage Research Associates, 1986.

Northwest Power and Conservation Council. *Salmon and Steelhead*. Portland, OR. http://www. nwcouncil.org:81/history/SalmonAndSteelhead.asp (accessed April 21, 2020).

Regional Planning Council of Clark County. *Port of Camas/Washougal Master Plan*. Vancouver, WA, April 1983.

Select Committee on the Columbia Gorge. *Findings, Recommendations and Elements of a Management Alternative for the Columbia River Gorge*. Olympia, WA, 1981. In the author's possession.

State of Oregon, Department of Transportation. *A Study of the Historic Columbia River Highway*. Salem: ODOT, 1987.

Trust for Public Land. "A Request for Funding: Land and Water Conservation Fund; FY 1987." Trust for Public Land, San Francisco, 1987.

Trust for Public Land. "Prior Judgments Involving Reynolds Metal Land." Trust for Public Land, San Francisco, September 4, 1990.

Trust for Public Land. "Columbia River Gorge Protection Fund: Final Report to Meyer Memorial Trust." Trust for Public Land, San Francisco, November 30, 1992.

Tweed, William C. *Recreation Site Planning and Improvement in National Forests: 1891–1942.* Washington, DC: US Forest Service, November 1980.

US Congress, House of Representatives, Committee on Interior and Insular Affairs, Subcommittee on Public Lands and National Parks. *Land Acquisition Policy and Program of the National Park Service.* 98th Cong., 2nd sess. June 1984.

US Department of Agriculture. *Reservation for Recreation Purposes of Lands within the Oregon National Forest Adjacent to the Columbia River Highway.* Land Classification Order. Washington, DC, December 24, 1915.

US Department of Agriculture, Forest Service. *Summary of Land Acquisition: Columbia River Gorge National Scenic Area through October 1, 2019.* Hood River, OR: US Forest Service, December 16, 2019.

US Department of Agriculture, National Park Service. *Columbia River Highway: Options for Conservation and Reuse.* Cascade Locks, OR: National Park Service, 1981.

US Department of the Interior, Bureau of Outdoor Recreation. *The Oregon Trail: A Potential Addition to the National Trails System.* Washington, DC, April 1977.

US Department of the Interior, National Park Service. *Study of Alternatives for the Columbia River Gorge.* Denver, CO: National Park Service, April 1980.

US Department of the Interior, National Historic Landmarks. "Aubrey Watzek House" (draft). Washington, DC: National Park Service, n.d.

US Forest Service, National Scenic Area. "Land Exchange Summary Table." Hood River, OR, September 29, 2014.

Washington State Parks and Recreation Commission. *Beacon Rock State Park: Land Classification and Long-Term Boundary Plan, Skamania County, Requested Action.* Olympia, WA, September 4, 1998.

NEWSPAPERS

Bend Bulletin (Bend, OR)
Bremerton Sun (Bremerton, WA)
Chicago Tribune
Clark County Tribune (Vancouver, WA)
Columbian (Vancouver, WA)
Daily Astorian (Astoria, OR)
Daily News (Longview, WA)
Goldendale Sentinel (Goldendale, WA)
Hood River News (Hood River, OR)
Journal–American (Bellevue, WA)
Los Angeles Times
Morning Call (Allentown, PA)
New York Times
Oregon Journal (Portland)
Oregonian (Portland)
Outlook (Gresham, OR)
Portland Tribune (Portland, OR)
Register Guard (Eugene, OR)
Seattle Post-Intelligencer
Seattle Times
Seattle Times, Pacific Magazine
Skamania County Pioneer (Stevenson, WA)

Spokesman–Review (Spokane, WA)
Standard–Examiner (Ogden, UT)
Tacoma News Tribune (Tacoma, WA)
The Dalles Chronicle (The Dalles, OR)
The Dalles Times Mountaineer (The Dalles, OR)
Tribune (Lewiston, ID)
Tribune (Vancouver, WA)
Tri-City Herald (Kennewick, WA)
Wall Street Journal
Walla Walla Union Bulletin (Walla Walla, WA)
Washington Post (Washington, DC)
White Salmon Enterprise (White Salmon, WA)
Willamette Week (Portland, OR)
Yakima Herald Republic (Yakima, WA)

BOOKS AND PUBLISHED ARTICLES

Abbott, Carl, Sy Adler, and Margery Post Abbott. *Planning a New West: The Columbia River Gorge National Scenic Area.* Corvallis: Oregon State University Press, 1997.

Aguilar Sr., George W. *When the River Ran Wild! Indian Traditions on the Mid-Columbia and the Warm Springs Reservation.* Portland: Oregon Historical Society Press, 2005.

Allen, John Eliot, Marjorie Burns, and Scott Burns. *Cataclysms on the Columbia: The Great Missoula Floods.* 2d ed. Portland, OR: Ooligan Press, 2009.

Arnold, Ron, and Alan Gottlieb. *Trashing the Economy.* Bellevue, WA: Free Enterprise Press, 1994.

Barber, Katrine. *Death of Celilo Falls.* Seattle: University of Washington Press, 2005.

Barber, Katrine and Andrew H. Fisher, eds. *Remembering Celilo Falls.* Special issue, *Oregon Historical Quarterly* 108, no. 4 (Winter 2007).

"Beacon Rock in the Gorge of the Columbia." *Skamania County Heritage* 3, no. 1 (June 1976).

Berlow, Lawrence H. *Reference Guide to Famous Engineering Landmarks of the World: Bridges, Tunnels, Dams, Roads and Other Structures.* Phoenix: Oryx Press, 1998.

Biddle, Henry J. "Beacon Rock on the Columbia: Legends of Traditions of a Famous Landmark." *WPO Publication,* no. 3 (1925; reprinted in July 1978).

Blair, Bowen Jr. "The Columbia River Gorge National Scenic Area: The Act, its Genesis and Legislative History." *Environmental Law* 17 (1986–1987): 863-969.

Boyd, Robert. *People of The Dalles: The Indians of Wascopam Mission.* Lincoln: University of Nebraska Press, 1996.

Boyd, Robert. *The Coming of the Spirit of Pestilence: Introduced Infectious Diseases and Population Decline among Northwest Coast Indians, 1774–1874.* Seattle: University of Washington Press, 1999.

Braasch, Gary. "The Rise and Fall of the Columbia River Gorge." *Oregon Rainbow* 1, no. 2 (Summer 1976).

Bullard, Oral. *Crisis on the Columbia.* Beaverton, OR: Touchstone Press, 1968.

Bullard, Oral. *Konapee's Eden: Historic and Scenic Handbook, The Columbia River Gorge.* Beaverton OR: TMS Book Service, 1985.

Bullard, Oral. *Lancaster's Road: The Historic Columbia River Scenic Highway.* Beaverton, OR: TMS Book Service, 1982.

Burns, Jess. "A War, the Chainsaw and the 2nd Great Cutting of the Northwest." Oregon Public Broadcasting, Portland. http://www.opb.org/news/series/battleready/chainsaw-history-world-war-2-forests-lumber/ (accessed April 23, 2020).

Cabell, Mrs. Henry F., and Mrs. Benjamin M. Reed, comp. *The Portland Garden Club: The First Fifty Years; 1924–1974.* Portland, OR: Portland Garden Club, 1974.

Caldwell, Warren W., and Roy L. Carlson. "Further Documentation of 'Stone Piling' During the Plateau Vision Quest." *American Anthropologist*, no. 56 (1954): 441–42.

Caro, Robert. "The Power Broker, I: The Best Bill-Drafter in Albany." *New Yorker* (July 15, 1974).

Christensen, Mark. "Beauty and the Battle over the Columbia River Gorge." *Western's World* (November 1984).

Clark, Ella Elizabeth. *Indian Legends of the Pacific Northwest*. Berkeley: University of California Press, 1953.

Coggins, George Cameron, and Doris K. Nagel. "'Nothing Beside Remains': The Legal Legacy of James G. Watt's Tenure as a Secretary of the Interior on Federal Land and Law Policy." *Boston College Environmental Affairs Law Review* 17, no. 3 (1990): 473–550.

"Columbia River Canneries." *On the Water*. Washington, DC: Smithsonian National Museum of American History. http://americanhistory.si.edu/onthewater/exhibition/3_6.html (accessed April 21, 2020).

Cordell, Kasey. "Scenic Drive." *Portland Monthly* (August 2006).

Cook, Scott. *Curious Gorge*. Bend, OR: Maverick Publications, 2010.

Coues, Elliott, ed. *The History of the Lewis and Clark Expedition*, 3 vols. New York: Francis P. Harper, 1893.

"Dixy Lee Ray: How Madame Nuke Took over Washington," *Mother Jones* 2, no. 4 (May 1977).

Dohnal, Cheri. *Columbia River Gorge: Natural Treasure on the Old Oregon Trail*. Mount Pleasant, SC: Arcadia Publishing, 2003.

Donaldson, Ivan J., and Frederick K. Cramer. *Fishwheels of the Columbia*. Portland: Binford and Mort, 1971.

Dupris, Joseph C., Kathleen S. Hill, and William H. Rodgers Jr. *The Si'lailo Way: Indians, Salmon and Law on the Columbia River*. Durham, NC: Carolina Academic Press 2006.

Durbin, Kathie. *Tree Huggers: Victory, Defeat and Renewal in the Northwest Ancient Forest Campaign*. Seattle: The Mountaineers, 1996.

Durbin, Kathie. *Bridging a Great Divide: The Battle for the Columbia River Gorge*. Corvallis: Oregon State University Press, 2013.

Edwards, G. Thomas. "The Final Ordeal: The Oregon Trail in the Columbia Gorge, 1843–1855." *Oregon Historical Quarterly* 97, no. 2 (Summer 1996).

Egan, Timothy. *Short Nights of the Shadow Catcher: The Epic Life and Immortal Photographs of Edward Curtis*. New York: Houghton Mifflin Harcourt, 2012.

Eig, Jonathan. *Luckiest Man: The Life and Death of Lou Gehrig*. New York: Simon & Schuster, 2005.

Fahl, Ronald J. "S. C. Lancaster and the Columbia River Highway: Engineer as Conservationist." *Oregon Historical Quarterly* 74, no. 2 (1973).

Fisher, Andrew H. *Shadow Tribe: The Making of Columbia River Indian Identity*. Seattle: University of Washington Press, 2010.

Foster, Charles H. W. *Experiments in Bioregionalism*. Needham, MA: Cape Cod National Seashore Advisory Commission, June 1984.

Gragg, Randy. "The Long View." *Portland Monthly* (June 2012).

Gragg, Randy, Bowen Blair, and Kenneth I. Helphand. *John Yeon Landscape: Design Conservation Activism*. New York: Andrea Monfried Editions, 2017.

Harmon, Rick, ed. *The Columbia River in History*. Special issue, *Oregon Historical Quarterly* 93, no. 3 (Fall 1992): 228–335.

Harvey, Athelstan George. *Douglas of the Fir*. Cambridge, MA: Harvard University Press, 1947.

Hausel, W. Dan. *Guide to Prospecting and Rock Hunting in Wyoming*. Information Pamphlet 11, Laramie, WY, 2004. http://wsgs.wyo.gov/products/wsgs-2004-ip-11.pdf.

Hays, Samuel P. *Conservation and the Gospel of Efficiency: The Progressive Conservation Movement, 1890–1920*. Cambridge, MA: Harvard University Press, 1959.

Holohan, Thomas V. "Referral by Default: The Medical Community and Unorthodox Therapy." *Journal of the American Medical Association* (March 27, 1987). http://jama.jamanetwork.com/article.aspx?articleid=365219 (accessed March 8, 2018).

Hulse, Bill. "My Involvement in the Discovery Center and Wasco County Historical Museum." *WamPinRock News*. Wamic, OR, n.d.. https://www.gorgediscovery.org/wp-content/uploads/2014/10/Hulse_article.pdf (accessed May 5, 2020).

Industrial Forestry Association. "New Drive for Federal Control of the Columbia Gorge." *Circular* no. 826 (December 1, 1980).

"Inter-Tribal Free Trade Zone Re-Establishment." National Congress of American Indians. *Resolution ABQ-10-055* (November 14-19, 2010). https://www.ncai.org/attachments/Resolution_SwPyEaTycKClhXwhEjKfOohuvcOPCSzrmthuYRISgeuOFeExHus_ABQ-10-055_rev.pdf

Jolley, Russ. *Wildflowers of the Columbia Gorge*. Portland: Oregon Historical Society Press, 1988.

Josephy, Alvin M., ed. *Lewis and Clark Through Indian Eyes*. New York: Alfred A. Knopf, 2006.

Kaeding, Kristine M. "Monument or Folly? Maya Lin's Bird Blind at The Sandy River Delta, Oregon (2006, Confluence Project)." Thesis, University of Oregon, 2010. https://scholarsbank.uoregon.edu/xmlui/bitstream/handle/1794/10824/Kaeding_Kristine_M_ma2010su.pdf?sequence=3&isAllowed=y.

Karson, Jennifer, ed. *As Days Go By: Our History, Our Land, and Our People; The Cayuse, Umatilla, and Walla Walla*. Portland: Oregon Historical Society Press, 2006.

Kessler, Lauren. *Stubborn Twig: Three Generations in the Life of a Japanese American Family*. New York: Penguin Books, 1993.

Kloos, Jeanette B. *Historic Columbia River Highway Master Plan*. Portland: Oregon Department of Transportation, June 2001.

Lancaster, Samuel. *The Columbia: America's Great Highway through the Cascade Mountains to the Sea*. Atglen, PA: Schiffer Publishing, 1915.

Lansing, Jewel. *Portland: People, Politics, and Power, 1851–2001*. Corvallis: Oregon State University Press, 2003.

Lodewick, Robin. "Almeta Barrett: A Pioneer Woman Botanist in Oregon." *Oregon Flora*. Corvallis: Oregon State University Herbarium, October 2003. https://archive.org/stream/oregonfloranewsl9132oreg/oregonfloranewsl9132oreg_djvu.txt (accessed March 18, 2019).

Loy, William G., Stuart Allan, Aileen R. Buckley, and James E. Meacham. *Atlas of Oregon* 2d ed. Eugene: University of Oregon Press, 2001.

MacColl, E. Kimbark. *Growth of a City: Power and Politics in Portland, Oregon, 1915 to 1950*. Portland, OR: The Georgian Press, 1979.

Marshall, Jim. "Dam of Doubt." *Collier's* 99 (June 19, 1937).

Marvin, Mary. "Personality: Nancy Neighbor Russell '53." *Scripps College Bulletin* (Spring 1988).

McArthur, Lewis A. *Oregon Geographic Names*. Hillsboro, OR: Binfords and Mort, 1952.

McDonald, Steve. "Historic Logging and Milling Photos." *The Forestry Forum*. www.forestryforum.com/board/index.php?topic=18781.280 (accessed May 25, 2019).

Meers, Erik. "Cliff Hanger." *People Magazine*, July 19, 1999.

Meinig, D. W. *The Great Columbia Plain: A Historical Geography, 1805–1910*. Seattle: University of Washington Press, 1968.

Michigan Family History Network. "Bay County's Lumber, Salt and Coal Industries and Transportation Facilities." *Hardwood Record* 41 (January 10, 1916). http://www.mifamilyhistory.org/bay/gansser_IX.htm.

Moulton, Gary, ed. *The Journals of the Lewis and Clark Expedition*, vol. 6. Lincoln: University of Nebraska Press, 1990. https://lewisandclarkjournals.unl.edu.

"Mugged by the Law." *Reader's Digest*, September 2000.

Mullins, William H. *The Depression and the Urban West Coast, 1929–1933*. Bloomington: Indiana University Press, 1991.

Mylot, Elizabeth. "The Landscape: Camas." *Metroscape* (Summer 2008). https://pdxscholar.library.pdx.edu/cgi/viewcontent.cgi?article=1067&context=metroscape (accessed March 18, 2018).

Neighbor, Nancy. "The Good American Family." *Garrulous Pine*. Portland, OR: Catlin Gabel School, 1949.

Nisbet, Jack. *The Collector: David Douglas and the Natural History of the Northwest*. Seattle: Sasquatch Books, 2009.

North American Wholesale Lumber Association. *Bulletin 21-84* (November 12, 1984).

Northwest Power and Power Planning Council. "Changing Bonneville's Role as Power Provider to the Northwest." *Council Quarterly* (Summer 2006).

Ochi, Diane. *Columbia River Highway: Options for Conservation and Reuse*. Cascade Locks, OR: National Park Service, 1981.

O'Donnell, Terence. *That Balance So Rare: The Story of Oregon*. Rev. ed. Portland: Oregon Historical Society Press, 1997.

Rakestraw, Lawrence. "A History of Forest Conservation in the Pacific Northwest, 1891–1913." Thesis, University of Washington, 1955. https://foresthistory.org/wp-content/uploads/2017/01/A-HISTORY-OF-FOREST-CONSERVATION-IN-THE-PACIFIC-NORTHWEST.pdf (accessed April 30, 2020).

"Rejuvenated Pioneer Oregon Home." *The Spectator* 61, no. 22 (July 3, 1937).

Reynolds, Phyllis Cantrell, comp. *The Portland Garden Club: The Years 1975–2000*. Portland, OR: Portland Garden Club, 2000.

Ritz, Richard Ellison. *Architects of Oregon*. Portland, OR: Lair Hill Publishing, 2002.

Roberts, Wilma, and Carolyn Z. Shelton. *Celilo Falls: Remembering Thunder, Photos from the Collection of Wilma Roberts*. The Dalles, OR: Wasco County Historical Museum Press, 1997.

Ronda, James P. *Lewis and Clark among the Indians*. Lincoln: University of Nebraska Press, 1984.

Russell, Nancy. "Why We Must Protect the Columbia Gorge." *Historic Preservation* 36, no. 3 (June 1984).

Russell, Nancy. "Taking on the Gorge." *The Gardeners* (Portland Garden Club), December 1983.

Russell, Sally. "Distinguished Alumni Award Recipient Nancy Neighbor Russell '49." *Catlin Gabel School Summer Magazine* 40 (1998–1999).

Schick, Jordis, ed. *Oregon Blue Book 1983–1984*. Salem: State of Oregon, February 1983.

Schoonmaker, Peter K., Bettina von Hagen, and Edward C. Wolf, eds. *The Rain Forests of Home: Profile of a North American Bioregion*. Washington, DC: Island Press, 1997.

Seale, William. *The Garden Club of America: 100 Years of a Growing Legacy*. Washington, DC: Smithsonian Books, 2012.

Seufert, Francis. *Wheels of Fortune*. Portland: Oregon Historical Society Press, 1980.

Simpson, J. P., and L. C. Swan. "Improvements in the Lumber Industry." *Annals of the American Academy of Political and Social Science* 193, no. 1 (September 1, 1937).

Smith, Dean S. "Columbia Gorge: Great Gateway to the Pacific." *National Parks* 56, no. 1–2 (January–February 1982).

Solomon, Diane N. *Against the Grain: Reflections of a Rebel Republican*. Ashland, OR: White Cloud Press, 2000.

Spamer, Earle E. *Grand Canyon: Colossal Mirror*. Philadelphia: Raven's Perch Media, 2022.

Spranger, Michael S. *Columbia Gorge: A Unique American Treasure*. Collingdale, PA: Diane Publishing, 1997.

Stowell, Cynthia D. *Faces of a Reservation: A Portrait of the Warm Springs Indian Reservation*. Portland: Oregon Historical Society Press, 1987.

Strong, Douglas H. *Tahoe: An Environmental History*. Lincoln: University of Nebraska Press, 1984.

Strong, Emory. *Stone Age on the Columbia River*. Hillsboro, OR: Binfords and Mort Publishers, 1960.

Strong, W. Duncan, W. Egbert Schenck, and Julian H. Steward. "Archaeology of the Dalles–Deschutes Region." *University of California Publications in American Archaeology and Ethnology* 29 (1930–1932; reprint 1965).

Tiller, Veronica E. Velarde. *Tiller's Guide to Indian Country*. Albuquerque, New Mexico: BowArrow Publishing Company, 2005.

Tuhy, John E. *Sam Hill: The Prince of Castle Nowhere*. Portland, OR: Timber Press, 1983.

Ulrich, Roberta. *Empty Nets: Indians, Dams and the Columbia River*. Corvallis: Oregon State University Press, 1999.

Villano, Matt. "Return to Cape Horn." *Land and People* (Spring–Summer 2009).

Wilkinson, Charles. *Blood Struggle: The Rise of Modern Indian Nations*. New York, London: W. W. Norton and Company, 2005.

Williams, Chuck. *Bridge of the Gods, Mountains of Fire: A Return to the Columbia Gorge*. Portland, OR: Graphic Arts Center, 1980.

Williams, Chuck. "The Park Rebellion: Charles Cushman, James Watt, and the Attack on the National Parks." *Not Man Apart: A Friends of the Earth Reprint* (June 1982).

Willingham, William F. *Water Power in the "Wilderness": The History of Bonneville Lock and Dam*. Portland, OR: US Army Corps of Engineers, 1984.

Willis, Peg. *Building the Columbia River Highway: They Said It Couldn't Be Done*. Charleston, SC: The History Press, 2014.

Wilson, Fred W. "The Lure of the River." *Oregon Historical Quarterly* 34, no. 1 (1969).

Wilson, Fred W. "Steamboat Days on the Rivers." *Oregon Historical Society* (March, June 1933; March 1950; reprint 1969).

Wilson, Julie. "You Own the Columbia River Gorge." *Town & Country* 146, no. 5148 (September 1992).

"Wood Use in US Housing." *Forest Research Notes* 13, no. 1 (2016). http://www.forestresearch-group.com/Newsletters/Vol13No1.pdf (accessed May 13, 2020).

Wrabek, Joe. *A Columbia Gorge Primer*. Cascade Locks, OR: PARK-MAN, 1983.

Yeon, John B. "The Issue of the Olympics." *American Forests* 42 (June 1936).

Index

Maps and photographs are indicated by italicized page numbers. Note entries are indicated by an "n" after the page number and followed by the note number. Photographs in the color plates (following page 132) are indicated by *plates*, followed by plate number(s).